IRVING
TO
IRVING

Books By Charles A. Madison

Irving to Irving: Author–Publisher Relations, 1800–1974
Eminent American Jews
Yiddish Literature
Book Publishing in America
The Owl Among Colophons
Leaders and Liberals in 20th-Century America
American Labor Leaders
Critics and Crusaders

CHARLES A. MADISON

IRVING TO IRVING

AUTHOR~PUBLISHER RELATIONS 1800~1974

R. R. Bowker Company
New York & London, 1974
A Xerox Education Company

XEROX

808.02
M26i
91506
Jan. 1975

Published by R. R. Bowker Co. (A Xerox Education Company)
1180 Avenue of the Americas, New York, N.Y. 10036
Copyright © 1974 by Charles A. Madison

Printed and bound in the United States of America

Library of Congress Cataloging in Publication Data
Madison, Charles Allan.
  Irving to Irving: author-publisher relations, 1800–1974.
Bibliography: p.
  1. Authors and publishers—United States. I. Title. PN155.M27 808'.02 74-10528
ISBN 0-8352-0772-2

To

S.S.S. and J.M.Y.

CONTENTS

Preface

Byron's telling phrase, "Now Barabbas was a publisher," has long stigmatized book publishers as crass exploiters of hapless authors. In my half century with the publishing industry, and in my research of its history when writing *Book Publishing in America* (1966), I found this accusation without merit. On the contrary, I was again and again impressed by the depth of intimacy between publishers and certain of their authors. Although I indicated some of these friendships in my history of publishing, my interest in the human aspect of publishing was such that I was moved to make a more detailed study of the subject—hence this book.

To state a truism, the writer works in isolation. The novelist weaves out of his own inner emotions and experience; the poet expresses his inmost thoughts and perceptions in heightened imagery; both, for all their surging egos, tend to be assailed by self-doubt which they feel must be stilled before they can present their writing to the world. Friends and relatives, no matter how devoted and helpful, cannot still these doubts; only their publishers and editors, who have to be objective and are financially concerned, can persuasively assure them of the acceptability of their work or offer certain guidance toward that end. In the process a relationship develops consisting of mutual trust and, often, intimate friendship. This congeniality was approximated more often in years gone by and only rarely today. Nevertheless, the need for this author-editor relationship is an essential element in book publishing, and many editors continue to serve their authors as critics, friends, and even creditors.

As for the "Barabbas" element, I have come upon only one publisher in this century who was remiss in paying royalties to his authors; yet even he, Mitchell Kennerley, has to his credit the encouragement of new writing at a time when most publishers refused to consider anything unconventional. In general, however, I have found that publishers deal honestly with their writers; and if at times they stick to the letter of their contractual arrangements, they seldom press their legal advantages. To the best of my awareness, most complaints of disgruntled authors have been based more on fancied grievances than on actual abuses.

When authors severed relations with publishers on an unhappy note, it was as often as not the author who was at fault. Thus, William James impulsively accused Henry Holt of sharp practice—only to learn the truth and apologize, but their relationship was impaired. Likewise, Anthony Hope and Paul Leicester Ford left Holt after he had promoted them to popularity to accept the lures of a rival publisher. Again, Edith Wharton, having been nursed into prominence by the Scribner firm, decided to accept Appleton's tempting offer while continuing to profess her loyalty to the Scribner people. Sherwood Anderson acted similarly after B. W. Huebsch had done his modest best to promote his books.

On the whole, however, earlier authors cherished the friendship of their editors. Of almost thirty prominent authors throughout a century and a half, discussed in this book, only Theodore Dreiser had no reason to think well of his several publishers. Most of the others have had unusually happy relations with their publishers and editors. Some, men like Hawthorne, Fitzgerald, Wolfe, and Steinbeck, had become extremely dependent on their editors for personal friendship and financial support. And so deep had become the friendship of editors with Louisa May Alcott, Edna St. Vincent Millay, and Margaret Mitchell, that they became more concerned for the interests of their authors than for the profit to their firms.

Throughout the book my sympathy was frankly with publishers who strove to maintain high literary standards and to give publishing the aura of a profession. After 1900, however, commercialization began largely to dominate the industry. As the literary agent and corporate control of major firms tended to lessen the literary quality of book publishing, the relationship between author and editor lost some of the personal closeness. It was one thing, for instance, for a Santayana to publish his books with the Scribner firm without having met his editors, for if the relationship seemed impersonal, it was cemented by mutual admiration and understanding. It is quite another thing at present when certain popular writers are indifferent to the friendship of their editors and prefer to transact their business through their agents.

In calling my book, *Irving to Irving: Author-Publisher Relations, 1800–1974*, I wished not only to indicate its wide scope but to intimate the deterioration of author-publisher relations during this century. Thus, Washington Irving went to Putnam's rescue in 1857 when the financial panic was forcing him to bankruptcy; Clifford Irving, on the other hand, sought to deceive his publisher to his own gain by brazen fraudulence. Although the scheming Irving is an extreme instance of an author's attitude toward his publisher, his behavior suggests the current deterioration of the closeness formerly quite common between author and publisher.

❦

This book, and especially the latter half, could not have been written without the use of unpublished letters between authors and publishers as well as copyright materials from published sources. Publishers, librarians, and literary executors have generously given me permission to quote passages which help to give authenticity to these relationships. To all of them I am extremely grateful—especially to the Princeton Library, the Library of Congress, the New York Library and its Berg Collection, to Mr. Charles Scribner, to Doubleday & Company, and to The Viking Press. I should add that much of the Holt material came from my little book, *The Owl Among the Colophons* (1966). Only Alfred A. Knopf, the distinguished publisher, now retired, refused to cooperate with me in the inclusion of any of his authors—maintaining that he was writing his own book on the subject. The unpublished letters continue, of course, to be the property of their owners and may not be used without permission; the same holds true of all copyrighted quotations.

Mr. Edward E. Booher of McGraw-Hill, a warm friend, was good enough to read the entire manuscript and offer me welcome encouragement; John Hall Wheelock, the noted poet formerly with the House of Scribner, read the five chapters on the Scribner authors; Mark Schorer read the chapter on Sinclair Lewis; Cass Canfield read the chapter on Edna St. Vincent Millay; Marshall Best and Edwin Kennebeck read the chapters on Viking authors; to each of them I am deeply grateful. I am especially obligated to Mrs. Sylvia S. Smith who has read the entire manuscript with scrupulous care and whose stylistic improvements are to be found on nearly every page. The editors of Bowker have made numerous helpful suggestions, for which I am of course grateful.

The Source Materials section lists books, articles, and correspondences which I have read in preparation for the book.

C. A. M.

February 15, 1974

1.

Early Book Publishing

Colonial Americans, on the whole, did more reading than their peers in Europe. They imported most of their books from England, but throughout the eighteenth century more and more of their reading was gradually printed locally—largely works of pietistic or practical content. An Englishman visiting the colonies about the middle of the century observed: "The common people are on a footing, in point of literature, with the middle ranks of Europe. It is scarce possible to conceive the number of readers with which even every little town abounds." Most of the books read were those current in England, with only a slight lag in time.

Since few colonists were able to buy all the books they desired to read, and since no public libraries were yet in existence, lending libraries came into being. Thus Benjamin Franklin established a circulating library in Philadelphia before one was started in London. And in ordering books from England, he wrote: "Your authors know but little of the fame they have on this side of the ocean. We read their works with perfect impartiality, being at too great a distance to be biased by the factions, parties, and prejudices that prevail among you."

Enterprising booksellers began early to reprint locally the more popular books by British authors, both to supply the demand for them more readily and to sell them at a lower price. Neither booksellers nor readers expected native writers, very few in number and with little popular appeal, to compete with established European authors. Those colonists who did write, mostly ministers and compilers of almanacs, paid a printer to produce a small edition—usually limited to 500 copies. The exceptions were a few popular almanacs, some of which had large sales. Nathaniel Ames's *Almanack*, for instance, sold as many as 60,000 copies a year; Franklin's *Poor Richard's Almanac*, being much more sophisticated, sold 9,771 copies in 1776.

Isaiah Thomas, one of the most enterprising printers of the time, became the first publisher in colonial America. He set up a number of printing partnerships with his more able employees, at one time the number extending to sixteen. In his desire to keep the presses busy he began to bring out editions of books in current demand. Among the most successful of his publications were Perry's *Dictionary*, which in time sold 54,000 copies; Perry's *Spelling Book*, which had a sale of about 300,000 during the years 1775–1804; *Laus Deo*, a music book; and several editions of the Bible. He also published Daniel Defoe's *Robinson Crusoe*, John Bunyan's *Pilgrim's Progress*, as well as almanacs and books of maxims.

The increasing restiveness of the colonists under British rule after 1750 caused a number of them to write pamphlets and books on the subject of American independence. These they had printed at their own expense and arranged with booksellers to market them. Most notable of these works was John Dickinson's *Letters from a Farmer in Pennsylvania to the Inhabitants of the British Colonies*. In 1774 *Votes and Proceedings of the American Congress* was reprinted thirty-two times. The most popular tract was Thomas Paine's *Common Sense*, which sold around 100,000 copies in ten weeks. All of these books appeared without benefit of a publisher. Each author did the best he could to bring his writings to the attention of the reading public.

As the demand for books increased with the establishment of peace, the more enterprising printers and booksellers were encouraged to assume the functions of the publisher, proceeding conservatively, yet pragmatically, to engage in modern publishing practices. For some years they merely marketed books, printed at the author's expense, on the customary commission basis—a usage certain authors preferred. David Kaser, in his history of Carey and Lea, a leading publishing firm in the early decades of the nineteenth century, stated:

> The United States, in 1820, had seen no publisher in the modern sense of the word; i.e., a person who, in addition to his responsibilities as a financial middleman, labors with an author to improve his works, to mold his reputation, and to develop a mutual feeling of trust and obligation, to their mutual profit. In 1822 neither author nor publisher wholly trusted the other.

In time, however, more and more publishers began to bring out books at their own risk, often lessening it by paying neither royalty nor a share of the profit until the recovery of the original investment; on occasion they paid the author an agreed-upon sum for the book's copyright. As contact with authors increased, the relationship with them—or at least some of them—became warm and occasionally intimate. The more astute publishers were fully aware of the sensitivity and insecurity of the artistic temperament and did what they could to bolster egos and to offer guidance and practical assistance.

Mathew Carey, an Irish journalist who migrated to Philadelphia in 1782, became the first professional publisher in the new republic. Imbued with the ideals of democracy, for which he had suffered imprisonment in Ireland, he in 1790 established himself as a publisher, issuing the first American edition of the Douay Bible. Three years later he opened a bookstore in order to further the sale of his books. Genuinely interested in literature—in 1825 he retired from publishing to devote himself to writing—he early became faithful to his authors and served them both as friend and as businessman. Over the years he brought out books by the leading British authors—these being in great demand—but at the same time he manifested an even greater interest in American writers.

An instance of his successful promotion of books as well as of his encouragement of authors may be seen in his relations with Susanna H. Rowson, the English novelist. In 1791 her novel, *Charlotte Temple: A Tale of Truth*, was published in London. Three years later Carey brought out an American edition. There being no international copyright law until 1890, Rowson's book could not be copyrighted in the United States and Carey was not obliged to pay her a royalty. Yet he refused to take advantage of this inequity. He actively promoted this romance and reprinted it more than 200 times before its popularity waned. To indicate his success with it and to express both his delight and encouragement, he wrote to Rowson:

> It may afford you great gratification to know that the sales of *Charlotte Temple* exceed those of any of the most celebrated novels that ever appeared in England. I think the number disposed of must far exceed 50,000 copies, and the sale still continues.

It should be noted that in the 1790's such a sale was truly phenomenal.

Carey had a most interesting relationship with Parson Mason Locke Weems, his best-selling author and hawker of books extraordinary. Weems, a Virginian, was for a time a minister and later claimed to have had Washington as a parishioner. He was hardly a typical clergyman, and in 1792 he became one of Carey's salesmen. A highly colorful personality, jolly and mundane despite his parson's garb, which he wore long after he had left the church, he early exercised remarkable suasiveness as a hawker of books. He was able to gauge the likely market of them with astonishing accuracy—although his estimates continued to seem too optimistic to the realistic Carey. Thus, given the marketing of Oliver Goldsmith's *History of the Earth and Animated Nature* in his Virginia area, he wrote Carey: "For my sake—for your sake and for God's sake send me *instantly* 200 copies." In the end his sales reached a thousand copies.

Weems, lazy, apparently irresponsible, self-indulgent, and easygoing, was even more successful as an author. Able to assess popular taste with uncanny accuracy and wielding a ready pen, he wrote a number of widely read books, among them *Lover's Almanac* and biographies of Revolutionary heroes, all of them published by Carey. His most popular work was his biography of George Washington, which sold in edition after edition—each enhanced by yarns he had tested while hawking books. It was in the sixth edition that the story of the cherry tree first appeared; not chopped down, as in later editions, but "barked so terribly that I don't believe the tree ever got the better of it." By 1829 the book was in its eighty-fourth edition and by far the most popular of the books about Washington.

All through their years of association Carey and Weems carried on a correspondence bristling with accusations, complaints, censure, and defense; but underlying all of it was an intimacy and an understanding which kept publisher and hawker–author firmly united. Weems seemed to Carey extravagant and disorganized, dilatory and slipshod; Weems accused his employer–publisher of being stodgy and penny-pinching, without insight or imagination. Both being free-spoken, their clashing was unavoidable. And proud of his success as a salesman and an author, Weems countered Carey's caustic criticism by reminding him that he was making much money for the firm and receiving much too little for himself.

As early as 1797 Weems pleaded "a poor peccavi" to Carey's accusation of dilatory reporting but insisted he was too busy selling books to write: "However to tell you the truth I had much rather be selling books than writing letters even to *yourself.* I wish you to send fewer letters, but I wd with all my soul, that you would send books." This bickering persisted through the years. In 1807 Carey wrote:

> I believe you incapable of being made, by any experience or any admonition, a man of business. After seducing me into the folly of consigning so large a property as I have forwarded to you, you write me letters in so indecent [and shocking a?] style, is treatment my soul revolts at. My connection with you has been from its earliest contact, a source of chagrin, vexation and loss.

Yet an underlying sense of humor in both men and an awareness of mutual interests kept their recurring explosiveness from ending in a definite breach. This relationship was well summarized by Van Wyck Brooks:

> Weems admonished Mathew Carey, who replied with violent diatribes against his unbusinesslike ways. The publisher and his hawker upbraided each other: they quarrelled, they chaffed, they hobnobbed, they consulted, they agreed. The parson was too loose and his chief was too stingy, but they laughed at themselves as much as they laughed at each other; and Carey had good reason to stick to the irresponsible Weems, who was one of his most profitable authors.

2

Washington Irving and James Fenimore Cooper

Washington Irving was the first American writer to attain major literary status outside the United States. From 1807, when the appearance of *Salmagundi* established his reputation as a man of letters, until the end of his life in 1859 he remained highly esteemed both in this country and abroad. Following custom and what he considered his own best interest, he had his books printed at his own expense and then arranged with booksellers/publishers to market them on a commission basis. As he lived in England for many years, he had either his brother or his friend Henry Brevoort represent him in this country—obtaining the copyright and making arrangements with publishers. Thus, in connection with the American edition of *The Sketch Book* he wrote to Brevoort:

> I wish the copyright secured for me, and the work printed and then sold to one or more booksellers, who will take the whole impression at a fair discount, and give cash or good notes for it. This makes short work of it, and is more profitable to the author than selling the copyright.

In 1828 Brevoort arranged with Carey and Lea, then the most active publishing house in the country, for a seven-year lease on Irving's four books in return for annual payments of $600 plus the assumption of unsold copies of previous editions. In explaining the transaction, he wrote to Irving:

> First you will be a gainer in money—second your writings, in their hands and under their management will be pushed into a much wider circulation among a new class of readers to whom they have hitherto been nearly inaccessible. It is thus that Cooper's Works have been made productive; had they been published in the shape that yours have been, they would neither have brought him bread nor reputation.

For several years Carey and Lea promoted Irving's books with considerable success; then interest in them slackened and the firm let them go out of print.

Irving returned to the United States in the 1840s. While still in England he had made the acquaintance of George Palmer Putnam, who was in charge of

Wiley and Putnam's London office. In their friendly talks Putnam spoke enthusiastically about his interest in bringing out a collected edition of Irving's works. Having excellent literary taste and being an eager promoter of worthy books, he felt confident in the marketability of such an edition. John Wiley, the senior partner, considered the project too risky, however, and Putnam dropped it.

When the partnership was dissolved in 1848, shortly after Putnam's return to New York, Putnam obtained as his share the literary books of the company. With this as a nucleus he started his own firm. One of his first acts was to approach Irving with his previous proposal. Irving was by then reconciled to his declined popularity, but Putnam's optimism encouraged him to accept an arrangement stipulating that a uniform edition of his books was to be published in five years, and that for the exclusive right to them he was to receive a royalty of 12½ percent of the published price.

Putnam immediately publicized the projected edition and stated that *The Sketch Book*, the first volume, was to be issued that September. "The whole series," his circular read, "revised and enlarged by the author, will be comprised in twelve duodecimo volumes . . . beautifully printed with new type, and on superior paper, made expressly for the purpose." So confident was Putnam of the fresh appeal of these books, mostly long out of print, that he guaranteed Irving a royalty of $1,000 the first year, $2,000 the second, and $3,000 the third. His energetic promotion kindled interest in Irving's writings among a new generation of readers, so that enough copies were sold to pay Irving considerably more than the annual guarantee.

This business association developed into a warm friendship. When Putnam sent Irving a package of books with his Christmas greetings in 1852, Irving's New Year's wishes made clear his personal cordiality:

> I take pleasure in expressing the great satisfaction I have derived, throughout all our intercourse, from your amiable, obliging and honorable conduct. Indeed I never had dealings with any man, whether in the way of business or friendship more perfectly free from any alloy.

> That these dealings have been profitable is merely owing to your own sagacity and enterprise. . . . You had confidence in the continued vitality of my writings when my former publishers had almost persuaded me they were defunct. You called them again into active existence and gave them a circulation that I believe has surprised yourself. In rejoicing at their success my satisfaction is doubly enhanced by the idea that you share in the benefits derived from it.

Five years later Putnam was in financial distress. Continued loss from the highly regarded *Putnam's Monthly Magazine*, which Thackeray considered "much the best magazine in the world," embezzlement by a young partner, and the economic panic of 1857, causing booksellers owing the firm considerable sums of money to default, brought Putnam to the brink of bankruptcy. When Irving learned of his friend's plight, he evidenced his concern by buying the stereotype plates of his books for cash but letting Putnam continue their use. Two years later Putnam had sufficiently recovered from his losses to repurchase the plates, for in the interim Irving had refused offers from other publishers who were eager to make him their author.

Putnam was of course deeply grateful for this act of devoted friendship and subsequently intensified his promotion of the uniform edition, so that by 1880 the firm had paid Irving and his heirs around $175,000 in royalties.

On the whole there was little mutual trust between authors and publishers during the early decades of the nineteenth century; writers, failing to attract an adequate readership, blamed their publishers; the latter, lacking both experience and capital, functioned mainly as booksellers. A conspicuous exception was the friendship between James Fenimore Cooper and Charles Wiley, which had preceded by a quarter century Irving's relationship with Putnam. Wiley was twenty-five years old when he opened his bookstore in 1807. A lover of books, eager for congenial companionship, with an engaging personality, he gradually attracted men of wit and intellect to his store and began to publish some of their books. The back room of his store became a meeting place for these frequent visitors and soon became known as The Den.

In 1820, traveling on business in upstate New York, Wiley met Cooper, and their acquaintance soon ripened into friendship. Wiley did not then know that Cooper was the author of the anonymously published novel, *Precaution*. When Cooper moved nearer to New York City he became the chief attraction of The Den. When he offered Wiley the manuscript of *The Spy*, Walter Scott's fiction was at its height of popularity. Although Wiley thought well of the story, he was aware of the risk of bringing out an anonymous American novel and limited the edition to a thousand copies. To his pleasant surprise the edition was quickly exhausted. A second printing of 3,000 copies sold within two months, and a third edition of 5,000 copies soon followed. It was the first American novel to attract such wide circulation. Wiley early expressed his gratification in a letter to Cooper:

> *The Spy* has succeeded over and beyond my expectations, and they were not easily to be exceeded. We have sold 100 to M. Carey and Lea, 100 to Lockwood, each at six months, 50 to Gilley at three months, besides 24 copies to several others. We have also retailed a very considerable number ourselves. A number of copies have been sold or sent on commission to the principal towns in different states. We have sold or sent off on commission about 600 copies, and think it probable the whole edition will be sold in three months.

Although Cooper received nearly $5,000 in royalties on the book, he thought he could do better still by following Irving's procedure—having his subsequent books printed at his own expense and then selling the editions to booksellers at a discount. Being neither of a generous nor genial nature, he refused to give them the discount they requested. Consequently they would not handle more than the first printing of *The Pioneers* despite the continuing demand for it by interested readers. In 1824 he arranged with Wiley to publish *The Pilot*, which Wiley did with much success but with little profit to himself. The following year he paid Cooper $5,000 for the right to print 10,000 copies of *Lionel Lincoln*, which amounted to a royalty of 25 percent. This novel failed, however, to attain the expected popularity. Meantime Wiley had become seriously ill and was unable to attend to his business.

Cooper thereupon contracted with Carey and Lea to take over his published books as well as his new novel, *The Prairie*, for the payment of $7,500. His new publisher, a leader in the field, was able to promote Cooper's books in areas hitherto unreached, thereby expanding their popularity. Thereupon he received $5,000 for the four-year lease on the copyright of *The Last of the Mohicans*; indeed, the novel sold so well that the firm decided to make plates for it to economize on the reprintings, and Henry Carey informed Cooper that "this has not happened to any living author of works of fancy."

After 1829 Cooper became tendentious in his writing—*The Deerslayer* excepted—and his books ceased to appeal widely to readers of fiction. Moreover, his political conservatism during the rise of Jacksonian liberalism and his contentious character tended to alienate his erstwhile admirers. His books ceased to be profitable, and Carey and Lea lost interest in them.

3.

Ticknor & Fields
& Hawthorne

Nathaniel Hawthorne's relations with his publishers, William D. Ticknor and James T. Fields, were perhaps the most intimate friendships on record. In his early years as a writer Hawthorne was a moody, pessimistic, and highly insecure person. With an irresistible urge to write in the face of cold discouragement, he completed and published his first novel, *Fenshawe* (1828), which failed to attract attention. Nor did his shorter pieces of fiction; all appeared in print and seemed forgotten.

Yet a few readers found his stories of unusual merit. Samuel G. Goodrich, a publisher with keen critical judgment, found in Hawthorne's anonymous writings evidence of "extraordinary powers." On inquiry he learned that the name of the author was N. Hawthorne, which he assumed was "a disguise." An exchange of letters enabled him to meet this anonymous writer and he was impressed by his "very substantial personage." Yet he found him "unsettled as to his views; he had tried his hand in literature, and considered himself to have met with a fatal rebuff from the reading world." Hawthorne told him that he needed to earn a living and was leaning "toward a mercantile profession."

Goodrich sought to dispel his despondence and to assure him of his success as a writer "if he would persevere in a literary career." Thereafter Hawthorne was pleased to write pieces for Goodrich's annual, *The Token*. "Occasionally," Goodrich reminisced, "an astute critic seemed to see through them, and to discover the soul that was in them, but in general they passed without notice." Goodrich deplored this neglect and wrote several articles "directing attention to these productions," but found no response. He then asked John Pickering, a man of literary discernment, for his opinion of Hawthorne's writings and was told "that they displayed a wonderful beauty of style, with a kind of double vision, a sort of second sight, which revealed beyond the outward forms of life and being, a sort of Spirit World, somewhat as a lake reflects the earth around it and the sky above it."

Thus encouraged, Goodrich urged Hawthorne to prepare a volume of his published writings. Hawthorne was agreeable, but Goodrich, having temporarily given up book publishing, was unable to find a publisher willing to take the risk. He finally interested an agent of the Stationers' Company, provided the firm was idemnified in case of loss. H. Budge, a lifelong friend of Hawthorne, learned of this need of a guarantee and readily joined Goodrich in giving it. With the cost of printing a thousand copies of *Twice Told Tales* amounting to $450, the publisher requested a guarantee of $250.

Hawthorne, completely unaware of this arrangement, agreed to a royalty of 10 percent. The volume appeared in 1837 and sold very slowly. Goodrich, with the benefit of hindsight, was later to write extravagantly, "It was deemed a failure for more than a year, when a breeze seemed to rise and fill its sails, and with it the author was carried to fame and fortune." Five years later a second series of stories was published, containing some of Hawthorne's most notable short fiction, but this book also failed to attract many readers.

Meanwhile Hawthorne worked for a time in the Boston Custom House. He also spent a year in Brook Farm, much to his disappointment. In 1842 he married Sophia Peabody and settled in the Old Manse in Salem. From 1846 to 1849 he held a post in the Salem Custom House. In the latter year George Palmer Putnam, eager to promote books by Americans, started the publication of The Library of American Books. Familiar with Hawthorne's early writings, he arranged to bring out *Mosses from an Old Manse* in two volumes. Genuinely eager to promote the book along with the other volumes in the series, Putnam nevertheless failed to arouse much interest in it, so that the total royalties on it came to $144.09. In his effort to explain his failure to gain a readership for him—and implying that the fault lay more with the book than with his promotional ability—he wrote to Hawthorne about the success of some of his publications and stated that the sale of Susan Warner's *The Wide, Wide World* had netted her $4,500 in six months.

This information only discouraged Hawthorne the more. Having just then "been ejected from the Custom House," and galled by the thought that most readers were interested in the sentimental fiction of women writers, he was ready to forego the effort of further publication. Nor did even so sympathetic a publisher as Putnam offer him any further encouragement, being then preoccupied with more remunerative authors.

Brooding over his failure as a writer, Hawthorne came to resent the shallowness of popular taste, which embittered him for years thereafter. This he later expressed in a letter to Ticknor:

> America is now wholly given to a d——d mob of scribbling women, and I should have no chance of success while the public taste is occupied with their trash—and should be ashamed of myself if I did succeed. What is the mystery of these innumerable editions of [Maria Susanna Cummings's] *Lamplighter* and other books neither better nor worse?—worse they could not be, when they sell by the 100,000.

Hawthorne was in this depressed state when James Fields came from Boston to inquire if he had a book ready for publication. He had made Hawthorne's acquaintance about ten years earlier, after seeing Longfellow's review of *Twice*

Told Tales in *The North American Review*. As junior partner of Ticknor & Fields, he had made it his business to know what was being written and by whom, and to attract the better writers to the firm by his genuine admiration and encouragement. Having heard that Hawthorne had lost his job with the Custom House and assuming that he must have been writing while there, he had come to inquire what he might have for publication. Hawthorne, however, denied he had anything to show him.

"Nonsense," he continued, "what heart had I to write anything when my publishers have been so many years trying to sell a small edition of *Twice Told Tales?*"

Fields was not daunted, however, and began to encourage him to write. To this Hawthorne responded, "Who would risk publishing a book for *me*, the most unpopular writer in America?" Thereupon Fields assured him that Ticknor & Fields would gladly publish him, and offered to print an edition of 2,000 copies of anything he would care to write. Still Hawthorne appeared negative, asserting he had "no money to idemnify a publisher's losses on my account." Still Fields persisted, telling him he would guarantee him against such possible loss and continued to insist there must be some manuscript written over the past few years. Later he wrote:

> I remember that I pressed him to reveal to me what he had been writing. He shook his head and gave me to understand he had produced nothing. At that moment I caught sight of a bureau or set of drawers near where we were sitting; and immediately it occurred to me that hidden away somewhere in that article of furniture was a story or stories by the author of *Twice Told Tales*, and I became so positive of it that I charged him vehemently with the fact. He seemed surprised, I thought, but shook his head again.

By then it became time for Fields to catch his train back to Boston and he prepared to leave. He was already going down the stairs when Hawthorne called him back. He handed him a manuscript and said, "How in heaven's name did you know this thing was there? As you have found me out, take what I have written and tell me after you get home and time to read it if it is good for anything. It is either very good or very bad—I don't know which."

Fields read some of the manuscript on the train and that evening he wrote Hawthorne a letter of glowing praise. On his return to Salem to discuss publication he urged Hawthorne to omit the short stories and to extend the long one, named "The Custom House," into a novel. For in addition to the novella, the material contained a number of short stories, the whole entitled *Old-Time Legends*. Hawthorne, at first incredulous that so important a house as Ticknor & Fields should offer him a contract on the basis of first-draft fiction, greatly appreciated Fields' sage advice and agreed to expand the longer story and to reserve the shorter ones for later. In their subsequent correspondence he wrote:

> As regards the size of the book, I have been thinking a good deal about it. Considered merely as a matter of taste and beauty, the form of publication which you recommend seems to me much preferable to that of the *Mosses*.

In the present case, however, I have some doubts of the expediency, because, if the book is made up entirely of *The Scarlet Letter*, it will be too sombre. I found it impossible to relieve the shadows of the story with so much light as I would gladly have thrown in. Keeping so close to its point as the tale does, and diversified no otherwise than by turning different sides of the same dark idea to the reader's eye, it will weary very many people and disgust some. Is it safe, then, to stake the fate of the book entirely on this one chance? A hunter loads his gun with a bullet and several buckshot; and, following his sagacious example, it was my purpose to conjoin the one long story with a half dozen shorter ones, so that failing to kill the public outright with my biggest and heaviest lump of lead, I might have other chances with the smaller bits, individually and in the aggregate. However, I am willing to leave these considerations to your judgment, and should not be sorry to have you decide for the separate publication.

Here was an ideal collaboration between author and publisher. Fields, possessed of keen critical insight and deeply appreciative of the artistic temperament, came to Hawthorne when he was at his lowest ebb of literary discouragement. Perceiving the essence of a fine novel within the mass of written material submitted to him, he cheered Hawthorne with warm praise, persuaded him to omit the shorter pieces and to complete and polish the longer narrative. Imbued with fresh encouragement, Hawthorne was stimulated to do his best writing. The result was fame for Hawthorne and financial benefit to both him and the firm.

The Scarlet Letter was printed in an edition of 5,000 copies—a large number in 1850 for a book by an author of hitherto small appeal. As was then the practice, the type was immediately distributed for further use. To their delighted surprise, Ticknor and Fields saw the edition exhausted within ten days. The novel was at once reset and stereotyped to meet the continued demand. In the course of their relationship—with the other of Hawthorne's subsequent books, published upon completion as a matter of course—a friendship between him and the partners was formed and cemented which remained exceptionally close to the end of their lives.

The firm of Ticknor & Fields was in 1849 rapidly becoming the most prestigious house in publishing. It brought out books by nearly all the prominent American authors as well as a number of European ones. Like Putnam, the partners were as much interested in the quality of their books and the reputation of their authors as in their own financial enrichment. Like Charles Wiley, Ticknor made the back room of his Old Corner Bookstore a congenial meeting place for his authors and friends, superior both in numbers and distinction to those of Wiley's Den. In the firm's years of greatest activity it catered to a galaxy of authors. A contemporary critic stated:

> The sterling worth, the mercantile dignity and sound judgment of Ticknor, and the swift perception, the brilliancy and social charm of Fields, gave in their union, power, reliability, and geniality to the establishment and the Old Corner became the constant resort of wits, poets, scientists, philosophers, and the distinguished of all professions.

Nearly all of these men at one time or another sought Ticknor's advice and assistance, and he gave it with a full heart. In *Hawthorne and His Publisher*, Caroline Ticknor wrote:

> Mr. Ticknor possessed great personal charm; he was a singularly handsome man, with graceful manners and a cordial and sympathetic personality; he instantly inspired confidence and won in a brief space of time warm and true friendships which he never failed to retain. Many young authors, who later won places of great distinction, came to him for counsel and guidance, while their elders relied upon his judgment and advice in regard to the writing as well as to the printing of their works.

If authors dealt with Ticknor as the senior partner who arranged for the publication of their books and the terms of their contracts, they turned to Fields for editorial assistance and encouragement, which he gave enthusiastically and often with critical insight. A poet of modest merit, he approached authors as a fellow writer, but with admiration, even flattery, in order to gain their confidence and friendship. Having no children and being socially inclined, Fields and his wife made their home a gathering place for writers and wits. Oliver Wendell Holmes's dedication in *The Guardian Angel* (1867) well expresses the regard most authors had for Fields:

> To James T. Fields, a token of kind regard, from one of the many writers, who have found him a wise, faithful, and generous friend.

Tryon and Charvat, having carefully examined the cost books of the firm, stated with undoubted reliability:

> The firm took the lead in establishing a new phase of author-publisher relations. It had been Fields's ambition not only to draw toward his house the great works of literature but to hold the loyalty of his writers in permanent bonds of affectionate attachment. Tactful and reverent appreciation was showered by the partners on authors' hungry spirits; and royalties in each filled their purses. . . . In the field of belles-lettres it offered the best terms that could be expected, and its vigorous promotion of poetry and other "non-commercial" literature won for Fields the designation of the "American Moxon" [the generous British publisher].

Once Hawthorne became their author, the friendship between him and the partners became exceptionally close. Fields, as his editor, encouraged, prodded, and criticized his writing, providing him with the helpful attention he needed. In 1850, working on the manuscript of *The House of Seven Gables*, Hawthorne wrote to him:

> I write diligently, but not so rapidly as I had hoped. I find the book requires more care and thought than *The Scarlet Letter*; also I have to wait oftener for a mood. *The Scarlet Letter* being all in one tone, I had only to get my pitch, and could then go on interminably. Many passages of this book ought to be finished with the minuteness of a Dutch picture, in order to give them their proper effect. Sometimes, when tired of it, it strikes me that the whole is an absurdity, from beginning to end; but the fact is, in writing a romance, a man is always, or always ought to be, careening on the utmost verge of a precipitous absurdity, and the skill lies in coming as close as possible without actually tumbling over.

He further stated that both he and Mrs. Hawthorne liked this work better than *The Scarlet Letter*, yet added modestly, "But an author's opinion of his book just after completing it is worth little or nothing, he being then in the hot or cold fit of fever, and certain to rate it too high or too low." When published, the romance met with wide favor both in the United States and England.

Hawthorne's next book, *The Blithedale Romance*, was equally well received. Fields, being then in London, arranged for the simultaneous publication in both countries and obtained an advance of £200 from the English firm. He also arranged for the British publication of Hawthorne's later books, thereby adding considerably to his income.

During Hawthorne's seven years in Europe he kept an intimate correspondence with both partners. When he began thinking of returning to the United States, he pleaded with Fields to help him get re-established on his arrival:

> Pray have some plan for me before I get back, not that I think you can possibly hit on anything that will suit me. . . . It would be an exceeding delight to me to meet you or Ticknor in England, or anywhere else. At any rate, it will cheer my heart to see you all and the old Corner itself, when I touch my native soil again.

In the interim *The Marble Faun* was published in both countries and favorably reviewed. Referring to its reception in a letter to Fields, he wrote, "When I get home I will try to write a more genial work; but the Devil himself always seems to get into my inkstand, and I can only exorcise him by penful at a time."

Fields was in Europe during Hawthorne's preparation to return to the United States and helped him with the various arrangements for the journey; he also accompanied him on the steamship to Boston.

Some time later, when including Lockhart's life of Walter Scott in the firm's Household Edition series, Fields, knowing it was Hawthorne's favorite book, dedicated it to him. Hawthorne was deeply moved by this honor:

> I am exceedingly gratified by the dedication. I do not deserve so high an honor; but if you think me worthy, it is enough to make the compliment in the highest degree acceptable, no matter who may dispute my title to it. I care more for your good opinion than for those of a host of critics, and have an excellent reason for so doing; inasmuch as my literary success, whatever it has been or may be, is the result of my connection with you. Somehow or other you smote the rock of public sympathy on my behalf, and a stream gushed forth in sufficient quantity to quench my thirst though not to drown me. I think no author can ever have had publishers that he valued so much as I do mine.

If Fields was Hawthorne's editor and close friend, Ticknor became his intimate personal companion and generous publisher. He quickly gained Hawthorne's complete trust, so that the latter increasingly came to depend upon him in all things affecting his life and daily affairs. He let Ticknor attend to all his financial dealings as well as his personal predilections. Moreover, loath to travel alone or to attend to necessary details, he had little difficulty in persuading Ticknor to join him on his trips and to look after his needs. As the latter stated in this connection, "He has no care. He leaves the entire business part with me. If he wants a pair of gloves I pay for them, as I do all bills for joint accounts. He says this is the only way he can travel with comfort, and it is no trouble to me."

He did even more for his favorite author. Again to quote Caroline Ticknor:

> Ticknor supplied just that which Hawthorne felt he lacked and understood precisely what was needed before the other asked for it. . . . Hawthorne, who was from the first singularly dependent upon the office of his devoted friend, called upon him for a thousand and one small errands and commissions which would fill the modern publisher with wonder. And Ticknor took pleasure in performing a great variety of thoughtful services which his friend would not have dreamed of suggesting.

Thus Ticknor bought cigars for Hawthorne, kept his accounts, and paid his bills. When President Franklin Pierce, Hawthorne's classmate and close friend, invited him to Washington, Ticknor bought Hawthorne the suit he was to wear on the trip and agreed to accompany him to the capital; and when President Pierce persuaded Hawthorne to remain a few days longer, Ticknor did so also because he knew his friend would be disappointed if he had left without him. In 1853, when Hawthorne was appointed American counsul at Liverpool, Ticknor went with him to help him get there and get settled. Later, when Ticknor was in London on business, Hawthorne urged him to visit him in Liverpool before leaving for Boston: "Do try to spend two or three days here before sailing. I shall feel as if my last friend was leaving me when you do go abroad."

Hawthorne was of course fully appreciative of his friend's kindnesses. When he received a supply of cider, he responded: "I know that nobody but yourself could have sent me the cider, and it tastes all the more deliciously for the knowledge." In acknowledging a shipment of cigars he wrote: "I thank you for the excellent lot of cigars, and expect to have as much enjoyment as a man can reasonably hope for in this troublesome world while smoking them after breakfast and dinner. Their fragrance would be much improved if you would come and smoke in company."

In 1862, being in poor health, Hawthorne yielded to the then common assumption that a trip south would prove beneficial. Again he asked Ticknor to join him, and once more his devoted publisher complied. They journeyed as far as Washington, and on his return Hawthorne did feel much better. Asked by Fields, then editor of *The Atlantic Monthly*, which the firm had taken over, to write an article on his reactions to the war spirit in the capital, Hawthorne was pleased to oblige. Having met President Lincoln and been unfavorably impressed by his physical homeliness and seeming uncouthness, he described him critically yet with acute insight. With the war then going badly for the North, Fields was distressed by this disparaging attitude and urged Hawthorne to delete the passage—although he later apologized for having been "squeamish" about it. Complying with the request with some reluctance, Hawthorne added sarcastically, "What a terrible thing it is to try to let off a little bit of truth into this miserable humbug of a world."

His health continued to deteriorate. We learn from Longfellow's diary, January 1863: "At Fields's saw Hawthorne; whom I have not seen for months. He looks gray and grand, with something very pathetic about him." Yet Hawthorne continued working on his new book, *Our Old Home*, which consisted mostly of notes he had made while American consul at Liverpool. Wishing to express his appreciation to his friend Franklin Pierce, who had given him the appointment, he dedicated the book to him. Pierce, however, was not considered a Northern supporter and was disdained by many Bostonians. When the dedication became known, a number of Hawthorne's friends urged Fields to effect the elimination of the damaging inscription. Hawthorne resisted the deletion as an act of "poltrooney" on his part.

> I cannot, merely on account of pecuniary profit or literary reputation, go back from what I have deliberately felt and thought it right to do; and if I were to tear out the dedication, I would never look at the volume again without remorse and shame. As for the literary public, it must accept my work precisely as I think fit to give it, or let it alone.

Yet not wishing to appear the martyr, he modified the wording to minimize the objection.

In 1864, hoping to benefit from another trip south, he asked Ticknor to accompany him. At the time Ticknor suffered from a head cold, but Dr. Oliver Wendell Holmes assured him he "was good for twenty years." Hawthorne came to Boston and stayed with Fields for the night. The latter was distressed at Hawthorne's apparent debility: "I was greatly shocked by his invalid appearance. The light in his eye was as beautiful as ever, but his limbs seemed shrunken and his usual stalwart vigor gone."

The two travelers reached New York by easy stages. The weather being foul, they remained there several days, during which Ticknor wrote to his wife that he was in fine shape. In fact, however, he was getting worse, and by the time the two reached Philadelphia Ticknor had become fatally ill with pneumonia. Hawthorne, always the one cared for and looked after, now did what he could to nurse his friend and watched over him during the final hours. The ordeal took its inevitable toll. Fields wrote subsequently:

> Hawthorne returned at once to Boston, and stayed here over night. He was in a very excited and nervous state, and talked incessantly of the sad scenes he had just been passing through. We sat late together, conversing of the friend we had just lost, and I am sure he hardly closed his eyes that night. In the morning he went back to his home in Concord.

Hawthorne remained in a state of restless misery. It was as if he felt responsible for Ticknor's death, and the thought of his guilt preyed on his mind. His health deteriorated still further, and his friend Franklin Pierce persuaded him to go on a visit to New Hampshire on the assumption that a change of scene was helpful to one's health. Dr. Holmes had examined Hawthorne beforehand and had approved of the trip. But the strain of the journey proved too severe for his debilitated condition and he died. "His passing," Fields commented, "was like losing a portion of our own household, so closely interwoven had become the interest and affection of the two families."

This extraordinary relationship between an author and his publisher was made possible by the peculiar character of the first and the special qualifications of the second. Hawthorne was in certain respects neurotic, egotistical, cantankerous, yet also lovable and idealistic; Ticknor was solid, sensible, an admirer of talent, glad to guide and assist those he liked. The two men complemented each other so delicately and delightfully that their friendship blossomed into an intimacy rarely encountered. Howard T. Ticknor, a son, well described Hawthorne's dependence on his father:

> What he needed, sought, and kept was a friend stronger and more expert in practicality even than himself, to whom also he could confide upon occasion his personal thoughts, his professional hopes, and his fancies and criticisms in regard to literature and aesthetics. Nowhere else, not even in his journals, was Hawthorne so frank as in the many intimate letters which he sent to his confidante from abroad. . . . He liked best to be taken to such plain, miscellaneous hotels as the Astor, or Bixby's, to be entered anonymously as "a friend" of his companion, to carry no money, to know nothing of the details of the journey, to make only chance acquaintances whom he could anatomize, but who could have no clue to him, and to be brought back home as mutely as he had been taken away.

After Ticknor's death the firm was reorganized with Fields as the senior partner. The latter, lacking Ticknor's generous scrupulosity, paid Hawthorne's heirs less than was their due. Although the price of books had almost doubled during the war years to cover higher costs, the royalty was not increased. When Mrs. Hawthorne threatened to sue, Fields sought to satisfy her by offering to arbitrate their differences; explaining that Ticknor had "obliged the firm to pay the highest rate of copyright it ever paid"; that no written contracts existed; and that the increase in price covered only the higher costs of production. After further dickering, Mrs. Hawthorne agreed to a compromise, preferring "peace to pence."

4.

Ticknor & Fields
& Longfellow

Of the celebrated list of authors published by Ticknor & Fields, Henry Wadsworth Longfellow was the most popular as well as the most profitable. And the relations between him and the partners were, if not as close as those between Ticknor and Hawthorne, increasingly cordial and mutually gratifying throughout the many years of their association.

Longfellow always acted like the proverbial Yankee in his eagerness to reap profit from his writings. Unlike Hawthorne, he had great confidence in the appeal of his poetry and was determined to obtain the highest fees from magazine editors and the best terms from book publishers. When Ticknor, in 1833 still an inexperienced publisher, brought out Longfellow's first volume, *Coplas de Manrique*, the young poet was disappointed to find him, like other Boston publishers, confining his marketing activity to New England. Eager for a nation-wide readership, and having learned that New York and Philadelphia publishers catered to this wider market, he brought his new writings to them. Thus, during the ensuing decade his work was issued by Harper & Brothers, Samuel Coleman, and Carey and Hart.

Coleman was most generous to him. Having brought out *Voices in the Night* in 1839, he agreed to pay $375 in notes for *Hyperion*—"said notes payable in three and six months." These terms being the best he was then able to obtain, Longfellow wrote to his father:

> At all events, I get the book very handsomely printed, and widely circulated; and this is a great point. As to success, I am very sanguine. I look upon the work of my hands with a very complacent smile; and it will take a great deal of persuasion to convince me that the book is not good. This is my candid opinion.

Unfortunately, Coleman went bankrupt soon after; nor was Longfellow fully satisfied with the other publishers he dealt with.

Living in Cambridge in the early 1840s, he decided to publish with John Owen, the local bookseller. He soon found that while Owen paid well and put out attractive books, he was not aggressive in his promotion and did not sell as many copies of his books as he had expected. In time Owen's poor health made him even less active. In April 1846 Longfellow recorded in his diary: "He has no head for business. Everything seems going to ruin." A month later he noted: "His affairs in a sad plight and he no head to extricate himself. Meanwhile my books going out of print and no proper prospect of setting matters right for a long while. Lucky for me I have the Philadelphia and New York editions to rely on."

In the meantime he was being courted by the affable James Fields. Although Longfellow was no longer a Ticknor author, he joined many of his Bostonian friends in frequenting the Old Corner Bookstore. There Fields came to know him and to praise his poetry. Responding to this laudation, Longfellow in 1839 sent him a copy of *Voices in the Night*. Fields expressed warm enthusiasm and invited him to address the members of the Mechanics Apprentice Library.

Increasingly frequent contact with Fields gave the poet a favorable impression of the witty and cordial young publisher, of whom his biographer W. S. Tryon wrote: "A story sprang to life on Fields' lips for every occasion. At a dinner table he could blunt the acerbity of Carlyle or silence the volubility of Charles Sumner; at home or behind the green curtain of the Old Corner office he evoked shouts of laughter."

When Fields learned of Longfellow's dissatisfaction with Owen, he had little difficulty in persuading the increasingly popular poet to return to the Ticknor firm—now free of its parochial limitations and already the prestigious publisher of many prominent authors. Thus in June 1846, Longfellow noted: "Passed an hour talking to Ticknor about publishing my books." The following day, being a shrewd bargainer, he wrote to Ticknor:

> I have been reflecting upon your offer for the Poems, yesterday, and I confess that with all the good-will in the world, I cannot bring myself to be satisfied with it. I really do not think you offer enough. My own offer I think much nearer to the mark. I proposed that you should give me 22½ c. per volume, you say 15. If you will make it 20c. I will be satisfied. This is the utmost I'm willing to do: and I must say that I think you will have a very good bargain of it at that. Please let me hear from you as soon as possible.
>
> P.S. Both Bryant and Halleck receive from Harpers twenty-five cents per copy on their poems, which is twenty-five percent of the retail price.

Ticknor acquiesced without further bargaining and noted at the end of the letter: "Agreed to July 14, 1846, W. D. T."

Two weeks later, now ready to leave Owen, Longfellow noted in his diary: "Determined to take my books from Owen, though with great regret."

The first book to appear under the Ticknor imprint was a new edition of *Outre-Mer*, Longfellow's travel notes of the 1830s. By October he had transferred all his books to the Ticknor firm and also gave it his new anthology, *The Estray*. As was then a common practice, he had paid for and owned the plates and copyrights for the published volumes, with the exception of *Poets and Poetry in Europe* and the Philadelphia illustrated edition, and was therefore able to demand and obtain a relatively high royalty, first from his previous publishers and subsequently from Ticknor.

One day Hawthorne and a Salem friend came to dine with Longfellow. At dinner the friend told his host that he had been trying to persuade Hawthorne to write a story based on the Acadian legend about a girl who, in the forced dispersion of the Acadians, was separated from her lover and passed her life waiting for and seeking him—only to find him dying in a hospital when both were old. When Hawthorne again refused to make use of the legend, Longfellow said to him: "If you have really made up your mind not to use it for a story, will you give it to me for a poem?" Hawthorne readily agreed, and Longfellow was soon at work on *Evangeline: A Tale of Acadie.*

Shortly thereafter Fields learned that the poet was discussing the publication of the poem with the Harpers. Anxious lest he go to them, Ticknor immediately bid for it and yielded to Longfellow's sharp bargaining. He first proposed a fifty-cent edition, with a royalty of 12½ cents per copy. When Longfellow proposed a more expensive edition, Ticknor suggested an increase in price to seventy-five cents with a twenty-cent royalty, or $400 cash on the day of publication for the right to print 2,000 copies from Longfellow's plates. When the latter still demured, Ticknor wrote him:

> We regret we cannot meet your views in relation to Evangeline as we should like to publish the volume. It does seem to us that we have made you a liberal offer,—certainly much more so than the Harpers, for they simply offer to receive the Vol. on Sale, at your price. Now on these terms, we sh'd be glad to make you a better offer,—i.e. to pay you for all sold *40 cents* each, and this we consider quite as favorable for ourselves as the previous offer we have made you.

They finally agreed to bring out the poem in several editions, variously priced. Meanwhile Bogue of London arranged to issue an illustrated edition, and Ticknor bought a hundred sheets for the American market. If Ticknor made the best offer hitherto given to an American poet, no previous American poem was so well received and sold so widely, thus making Ticknor pleased to have taken the risk. Longfellow was equally satisfied, stating: "I have received greater and warmer commendations than on any other previous volume." Thereafter he was no longer tempted by the possibility of going to another publisher.

In 1848 he was at work on a novel, *Kavanaugh: A Tale.* Already established as the most popular American poet and storyteller—80 percent of his verse was in the form of a story of a historical nature—he was less secure about his fiction, and in March 1849 he confided to his diary:

> My mind perplexed about Kavanaugh. The title is better than the book, and suggests a different kind of book. One more long, spiritual chapter must be written for it. The thought struck me last night. It must go into the book as the key-stone into the arch. An idea so very obvious, yet coming so late!

The novel was successfully launched and 4,000 copies were sold during the first week. In the same year *The Sea-Side and The Fire-Side* appeared with equal success. Any volume with Longfellow's name as author was now certain of a wide and enthusiastic reception. Ticknor & Fields, taking full advantage of his popularity, brought out the first edition of his collected poems in two volumes. Aggressively promoted, enlarged in later editions, the book became the standard collection of Longfellow's poetry and sold in large numbers year after year.

Author and publishers worked in tandem to extend the popular appeal of his work to its utmost limits. Longfellow, indeed, sought systematically and patiently to attract American readers to the delights of poetry. The inherent worth and high moral tone of his poems helped to gain this end, especially because they contained favorable references to poets and literature. Fields, on his part, extended himself in his effort to advance Longfellow's reputation. He curried favor with prominent reviewers to assure favorable notices. To Bayard Taylor, an influential critic, he wrote: "I send you the first copy of *Kavanaugh* that goes to New York. I hope you will notice it yourself in the *Tribune.*" This tactic he used with many others. To some he even intimated what should be stressed in the review, and occasionally he sent editors notices written by himself. To back up these reviews he advertised the books freely. When the Boston *Traveller* printed an unfavorable review of one of Longfellow's books, he sent the editor an indignant letter of protest and canceled the firm's advertising—which created an awkward situation for him but which stimulated sales. In his enthusiastic loyalty to Longfellow Fields declined the opportunity to publish Edgar Allen Poe for fear of the effect on the popularity of his friend's work. To this same end, when editing his manuscripts, he did not hesitate at one point to suggest that a poem "needs a closing line less like a sermon and more like a song."

In November 1841 Longfellow noted in his diary: "This evening it has come into my mind to undertake a long and elaborate poem by the holy name of *Christ*; the theme of which would be the various aspects of Christendom in the Apostolic, Middle, and Modern Ages." He completed the second part first. Entitled *The Golden Legend*, it was published in 1851 and "had a great sale." Bogue of London gave one hundred pounds "by way of copyright" for the English edition.

Reading proof of his new book, *The Song of Hiawatha*, Longfellow noted, "I am going idiotic about this song, and no longer know whether it is good or bad." Widely publicized on its appearance, the poem sold in large numbers, around 20,000 the first year. In 1858 his next work, *The Courtship of Miles Standish*, achieved equal popularity. Fields ordered a first printing of 10,000 copies; faced with an extraordinary advance—5,000 copies in Boston alone—he immediately ordered a second printing of the same size. Longfellow was of course elated. To Charles Sumner he wrote that the English publisher had paid £150 for the advance sheets. And somewhat later he stated gloatingly: "An army of twenty-five thousand—in one week Fields tells me that in London ten thousand were sold the first day." In celebration of this event he noted in his diary: "I gave a dinner to Ticknor and Fields, the publishers, in honor of the success of Miles Standish."

By this time he and Fields had become intimate friends. From his summer home in Nahant, he wrote in August 1859 to Fields, then in London:

> Next time, tell me about Hawthorne and his new book; and about your walks and
> talks with the publishers. I have not seen any English papers this summer, and am
> therefore rather in the dark. Occasionally, one of Ticknor & Co.'s advertisements
> in the Transcript glares at one like a lantern; and I am dazzled with the names of
> new books gathered by your hand in London.

The following year he complained to Fields that all kinds of people send him their poems and take up his time. "What shall I do? These poems weaken me very much. It is like so much water added to the spirit of poetry." Fields responded sympathetically. All the while the two kept seeing each other frequently, either in the Old Corner or in Fields's home, where friends and authors often met for a meal and convivial talk.

Hitherto Longfellow's life, on the whole, had been serene and satisfying, making it easy for him to imbue his verse with the affirmative optimism which characterized much of it. More than twenty years earlier, while in Europe with his first wife, he had experienced the grief of her sudden death in Rotterdam. The trauma left him desolate; in time, however, he recovered from the shock and reverted to his bright outlook on life. His marriage several years later to Frances Appleton, whose father bought them Craigie House as a wedding present, proved blissfully congenial. The death of a young daughter caused him a keen but brief period of grief.

Suddenly his tranquil world seemed to collapse. In 1861 Mrs. Longfellow was sealing packages of curls cut from her little girl's hair, when an ignited match fell on her light summer dress. Severely burned, she died the following day. This time the tragedy so affected the bereaved poet that his natural serenity turned to anguished sorrow. For several years he suffered an emotional numbness that silenced his muse and kept him socially secluded. To occupy his mind and to avoid the constant dwelling on his tragedy, he began to translate Dante's *Divine Comedy*, an undertaking that took five years to complete.

Fields was of course very close to him during this melancholy period. Shortly after his bereavement Longfellow noted: "Fields came out and passed an hour with me. He is very sympathetic." In every way he was able, Fields sought to comfort him, to soften his grief with consoling talk, to bring him little presents. When the translation of the first cantos were ready, he asked to have them printed in *The Atlantic Monthly*. Longfellow appreciated this attention. In his diary he noted: "He gives me a picture of Stradivarius in his workshop among his violins." He also thanked Fields for a packet of books, intimating his continued deep loneliness. When Fields, however, sought to revive the poet's interest in his previous social activities and suggested membership in the Union Club, Longfellow begged off by stating that he would most likely not go there more than once a year.

> I do not feel at all up to it. Strange as you may think it, I find no longer any pleasure in such things, nor find any interest in going about among men. Whenever I try it I fail utterly. I had rather be here at my work as long as the day continues; for the night cometh wherein no man can work.

His depression gradually lifted, and he was in time again able to write verse and prose as in the past. On the completion of the manuscript which he originally had called *Sudbury Tales*, he wrote to Fields to ask that the title be changed to *Tales of a Wayside Inn*. On its publication he again celebrated the occasion by having Ticknor and Fields as his dinner guests. To promote the volume, Fields published an article on Longfellow by G. W. Curtis in *The Atlantic Monthly*. This kind of publicity was of course not unnoticed by others, and James C. Austin commented: "As the book was a Ticknor & Fields publication, the release of Curtis's article was designed to promote sales. This was typical of Fields's promotional tactics, which he employed to the full in publicizing Longfellow." Aided by this kind of promotion, the book attracted many readers, selling over 15,000 in a relatively short time.

Longfellow was, of course, shocked and grieved when he learned of Ticknor's sudden death, and noted in his diary:

> Ticknor published my first volume, the *Coplas de Manrique*, in 1833—more than thirty years ago. I saw him the day before he went away, merry and rejoicing in the prospect of a pleasant journey—he knew not whither; but hoping to go from New York to Havana, and by New Orleans homeward.

With Ticknor's passing, the firm lost its economic anchorage. Fields, now the senior partner, was unable to add to his editorial astuteness the financial solidity of the counting room. The innovations he introduced expanded the firm's overhead without resulting in additional income. Giving up the Old Corner and the retail book business served only to lessen the anticipated profits. Moreover, Fields was becoming more of a literary man than a publisher, and in 1871 he decided to retire and leave the firm in the control of his junior partner, James R. Osgood. Now a relatively free man, Fields deepened his attachment to Longfellow, exerting himself in behalf of his literary interests and visiting him socially at every opportunity. His biographer Tryon stressed this increasingly close relationship:

> In these later years Fields drew closer to Longfellow and of all his American writers the Cambridge poet was his most intimate friend. Little of the affection found its way into words; the action spoke for itself. They were constantly in each other's company. Together they attended an art exhibit. They celebrated each other's birthdays every year with appropriate festivities. Evening after evening, once a week, Fields was one of the inner group to hear the progress of the poet's translation of the *Divine Comedy* and on its completion Fields gave a great dinner at the Parker House in the translator's honor.

The ending of this long and devoted friendship Longfellow recorded in April 1881 in this brief statement: "A sorrowful and distracted week. Fields died on Sunday, the 24th. Dr. Palfrey died on Tuesday. Two intimate friends in one week!"

In the interim he had completed part 3 of *Christus* in 1868, part 1 in 1871, the whole, united by introduction, interludes, and a finale in 1873. The long poem was received with respect and admiration, but not too many read it through. The following year his friend Sam Ward arranged with Robert Bonner of the New York *Ledger* to pay Longfellow $3,000 for *The Hanging of the Crane*—with $1,000 to himself for "lyrical brokerage." Osgood, told about it by Longfellow, was reluctant to have the poem appear first in a newspaper, but acquiesced in the arrangement when assured the work would be printed without illustrations and under Longfellow's copyright. A month later Osgood published an attractively illustrated edition of the poem.

In 1875, eager to bind the popular poet to the firm, Osgood offered Longfellow an annuity of $4,000 in lieu of royalties, with an additional 10 percent royalty for eight months on new books. The poet demurred. Harper & Brothers, having learned of the offer, made their own bid—with Fields secretly helping them—and agreed to pay $1,000 for "Mouturi Salutaris," the amount suggested by the poet. Informed of this, Osgood immediately went to Longfellow's home to negotiate a binding settlement. An entry in Longfellow's diary for August stated: "Signed agreement with Osgood & Co. for ten years' right of publishing my books for $4000 annually, in equal quarter payments. My new book, on old arrangement at ten percent for nine months; then, on payment of $500, to be added to the others." This bargaining netted him an extra month's royalties and an additional $500. Even so, remembering his relationship with both Ticknor and Fields, he thought that Osgood had treated him "cavalierly," especially after the latter had mismanaged the *Complete Poetical Works*, which was issued incomplete and poorly organized.

To make amends, the head of the newly reorganized firm, now named Houghton, Osgood & Company, brought out a deluxe subscription edition surpassing in elegance of dress and princely adornment any previous book by an American writer. The plates and illustrations cost $60,000 for the three-volume edition, containing 600 illustrations, 30 in full pages, by leading artists. The price for the set ranged from thirty to eighty dollars, depending on the sumptuousness of the binding. Issued in 1883, a year after Longfellow's death, 50,000 subscriptions were obtained within a year—a fitting memorial to a poet who was long enshrined in school books.

5.

Incidental Relationships

Not all publishers, then or later, were as cordial and devoted as Wiley and Putnam and Ticknor, nor were all authors as trusting and intimate as Irving and Hawthorne and Longfellow. After 1830 Harper & Brothers rose to leadership in American publishing; but the four brothers, able and hardworking, built their success on a purely business basis. Most of their books were British importations because they sold more widely and because they could not be copyrighted in the United States and could therefore be republished without obligation to authors or original publishers; later, as competition increased, they made token payments to British publishers for the privilege of obtaining sheets of the books they wanted before their competitors could acquire published copies, but that hardly lessened their profitability. H. W. Boynton thus referred to the Harpers: "Their prosperity was largely founded on the lack of an international copyright law, and they were from the first to last opposed to the enactment of such a law."

An instance of their within-the-law attitude was evidenced in their relation with Fredericka Bremmer, a prominent Swedish author in the 1840s. Putnam, an early and ardent advocate of an international copyright law, became interested in one of her new novels and arranged to pay her a royalty. Following the practice of the then "courtesy of the trade" principle—that the publisher who first made public announcement of his interest in a foreign book gained the sole right to publish it—he advertised his intention to issue Bremmer's new book. To his dismay he soon learned that the Harpers, their adherence to the "courtesy" principle notwithstanding, were bringing out the same book.

In 1849, when the American edition of her new book was to appear, Bremmer visited the United States. Putnam welcomed her and became her host while she was in New York. Apprised that she was in need of funds and knowing that he would not be able to give her much royalty if he had to compete with the Harper unauthorized edition, he went with her to the Harper office in the hope of persuading the brothers to abide by the "courtesy" practice. He told Fletcher Harper, the brother in control, that since Bremmer was a guest of this country and in need of money, he hoped that the firm would refrain from bringing out the unauthorized edition. Harper listened politely and replied, "Mr. Putnam, courtesy is courtesy and business is business," and bowed them out of his office. Soon the Harper cheaper edition appeared and thereby greatly lessened the sale of the Putnam edition. Years later Putnam's son declared: "The four Harpers who constituted the original Harper & Brothers were staunch Methodists and keen men of business. They appear to have had little respect for any 'right' that could not be enforced by law."

This attitude was also illustrated in the publication of Richard H. Dana, Jr.'s *Two Years Before the Mast*. The Harpers had published the elder Dana's work, and when he asked them to publish his son's book they agreed to do so, offering a royalty of 10 percent *after* the sale of the first thousand copies. Since in those days not many books sold as many as a thousand copies, the father, unfamiliar with the bad publishing conditions at the time, thought his son could do better elsewhere. When several publishers declined to take the book, he returned to the Harpers the next time he was in New York. Now, however, they refused the manuscript, and it was only after several prominent writers had urged them to publish it did they agree to take the work and offered a payment of $250 for the copyright. In writing to his son about the transaction, the elder Dana stated: "They are sharp and vulgar men to all appearance, but you could do nothing with anyone else." To everyone's surprise the book achieved quick and wide popularity, attaining a sale of 10,000 copies during the first year. Thereupon friends suggested that the firm share with Dana its profits on the book, but the Harpers firmly insisted that a bargain was a bargain.

Yet when they thought they could make a profit on an American author they did not hesitate to compete with other publishers to get him. In 1838 Little, Brown and Company had published William H. Prescott's *Ferdinand and Isabella*. The book established Prescott's reputation and sold widely. Five years later the Harpers lured him away by paying him $7,500 for the right to sell an edition of 5,000 copies of *The Conquest of Mexico*—Prescott to provide them with the plates. "It was an enormous price," Prescott admitted at the time, "which I should not have had the courage to ask of any publisher. I hope they may not be disappointed, for their sakes as well as mine." Indeed, these terms, according to Ticknor, "were more liberal than had ever been offered for a work of grave history on this side of the Atlantic."

Prescott's relations with the Harpers were outwardly cordial, and they later published his *History of the Reign of Ferdinand and Isabella the Catholic* and *The Conquest of Peru*. Yet he was not wholly happy with them, since their high prices for his books kept them from competing with their lower-priced British histories. In protest he once wrote to Fletcher Harper, "Who will give two dollars a volume for Prescott, when they can buy Macaulay for seventy-five cents?" Fletcher Harper was verbally sympathetic but remained unmoved, continuing to make this price differential because Macaulay's *History of England* cost the firm only $650 as against $7,500 for the Prescott book. It was no surprise therefore that when Phillips, Sampson and Company of Boston made him a better offer in 1854 he readily agreed, transferring all his books to that firm. Being a New England gentleman, however, he glossed over his discontent, stating: "I have left the Harpers not from any dissatisfaction with them for they have dealt well by me from first to the last, but because they were not prepared to come up to the liberal offer made by the other party." And to the Harpers he wrote:

> I am entering on a new enterprise in my arrangement with the Boston house. How it will turn out time will show. But whether well or ill, I cannot forget the long and pleasant relations I have had with you, in which the good understanding which should subsist between author and publisher has not been interrupted for a moment.

Ironically, the payments to Prescott had become so high that the books ceased to be profitable despite their popularity. Moreover, the financial panic of 1857 brought Phillips, Sampson and Company into bankruptcy and Prescott's books were bought at auction by J. B. Lippincott, the highest bidder.

The vagaries of publishing and author-publisher relations may be observed in connection with the publication of *Uncle Tom's Cabin*. Dr. Bailey, editor of *National Era*, a small abolitionist weekly in Washington, arranged with Harriet Beecher Stowe to write a serial story. She sent him weekly installments, each read to her family before it was mailed. Catherine Beecher, a sister, submitted the projected story to Phillips, Sampson and Company, but the firm refused it for fear that its antislavery sympathy would antagonize its numerous customers in the South—assuming that the novel would hardly sell a thousand copies.

The manuscript was then submitted to John P. Jewett, who had moved to Boston six years earlier and had since operated a small marginal publishing house. Jewett accepted the story and offered Stowe a choice between a 10 percent royalty and half of the profits. On the advice of knowledgeable friends she preferred the royalty arrangement—thereby forfeiting a small fortune.

Jewett urged Mrs. Stowe to reduce the length of the narrative to one volume, but she insisted that the story had written itself and must remain uncut. Jewett optimistically issued a printing of 5,000 copies. The edition sold within two days. Eager to supply the phenomenal demand, Jewett began printing the book day and night and increased his office space as well as his staff to handle the sales, which came to 300,000 during the first year. Before the demand slackened several years later, sales in the United States reached around 5 million copies, in various cheap editions, and an even larger number in the rest of the world. In 1882, thirty years after publication and at Stowe's seventieth birthday celebration, H. O. Houghton, the publisher, stated at the party:

> You have all doubtless heard the apocryphal stories of the difficulties encountered by the author of *Uncle Tom's Cabin* in getting a publisher, and of the marvelous sales of the first editions; but few here probably realize how great is its circulation today. This book began by being a prophecy, and is now history, and it is the rare felicity of its author to realize this fact in her own life time.

Jewett's part in connection with this book was less felicitous. He had greatly expanded his overhead to take care of its large sales, and when the demand lessened he had no other books of wide appeal to provide the needed income. When the panic of 1857, which "was disastrous to many fortunes invested in the bookmaking business," struck him he had no choice but to submit to bankruptcy.

The foregoing discussion concerned the nature and diversity of author-publisher relations, mostly prior to the Civil War. It was a period when the relatively new book publishing industry was undergoing the growing pains of trial and error, when young men of intellectual and literary inclinations entered bookselling and publishing not merely to earn their livelihood but also to establish cultural careers; and ultimately failing or flourishing according to their abilities and the influence of fickle fortune. It was also a time when the young nation began to bring forth writers who strove to be heard, with Philadelphia, Boston, and primarily New York becoming cynosures of culture and attracting men of literary ambition. Authors and publishers sought one another and bargained for advantage; but on the whole their relations were friendly and equitable—with some friendships unusually close. Some years later William Dean Howells, who was both author and editor all his adult years, well summarized this relationship:

> I for one wish to bear witness to the constant good faith and uprightness of publishers. . . . It is true that publishers will drive a hard bargain when they can, or when they must, but there is nothing to hinder an author from driving a hard bargain, too, when he can, or when he must; and it is to be said of the publisher that he is always more willing to abide by the bargain when it is made than the author is, perhaps because he has the best of it. But he has not always the best of it; I have known publishers too generous to take advantage of the innocence of authors; and I fancy that if publishers had to do with any race less difficult than authors, they would have won a repute for unselfishness that they do not now enjoy.

6.

The Gilded Age

In what has become known as the Gilded Age—the period from the end of the Civil War to the end of the century—men of great energy and unbridled ambition made the most of their extraordinary opportunities: the availability of an unexploited continent of fabulous resources; technical inventions accelerating the ongoing industrial revolution; millions of immigrants ready to give their brawn for bread. These exploiters were for the most part without formal education or interest in the intellectual pursuits of New England's earlier genteel generation. Both irresponsible and ostentatious, they had the economic power to set the prevailing cultural and ethical standards of their fellow Americans.

If the Gilded Age was characterized by crass materialism in the counting room and by pseudogentility in the parlor, its leading book publishers stood out by their encouragement of literary standards and sound ethics. Not that the publishing industry was free of the taint of guile and sharp practice; the "pirates" and certain others were on a lesser scale as greedy and unscrupulous as the "robber barons" of finance and industry. Yet in a real sense they were only the dregs of an expanding industry. The established publishers, conscious of their cultural responsibilities, strove to turn publishing into a gentleman's profession. Most of them were of commendable families, well-educated, early attracted to the arts and sciences, and sensitively insistent on fair dealing with both authors and competitors.

Despite their generally conservative tendencies and limited enterprise, these publishers sought earnestly to enhance the standards of American literature in an age of philistine pretension. Amongst themselves they adhered more or less firmly to the "courtesy" principle, and all but one of them urged the Congress to enact an international copyright law. Despite the unfair competition of the "pirates," they voluntarily paid European authors for the books that they published, although this lofty attitude was at times observed more in the breach than otherwise. Many years later, Henry Holt, the most idealistic of these publishers, had this to say:

All these old publishers—Putnam, Appleton, Harper and Scribner—were incapable of petty or ostentatious things, and were much more inclined to friendly cooperation and mutual concession than to barbarous competition. The spectacle of a crowd of other men making fools of themselves exercised upon them no temptation to do as the herd did. No one of them, or of a few more, would go for another's author any more than for his watch; or, if he had got entangled with another's author through some periodical or other outside right, would no more hold on to him than to the watch if the guard had got caught on a button.

At the end of the Civil War the firm of Harper & Brothers was at the apex of its power and prestige. The four brothers, now elderly and considerably mellowed, were still shrewd men of business, but the sharpness of their dealings frequently yielded to their concern for the public esteem of their house. More and more also, they were relinquishing their control to their sons and nephews; and the younger Harpers were eager to gain the respect of their fellow publishers. "Brooklyn Joe" Harper, who headed the firm during the later years of this period, was ethically a cut above his father and uncles, although he too tended to make the most of opportune advantages. He was aggressive yet affable, at once subtle and simple, and widely considered a "business genius." Like his elders he favored the "courtesy" principle when it was to his advantage or of no material importance. Thus, when James A. Froude edited Thomas Carlyle's *Reminiscences*, he claimed the right to issue the book by virtue of trade "courtesy" and an arrangement with the late Carlyle himself. Charles Scribner, however, asserted that Froude was his author and that he had arranged with him to publish the edited manuscript. Neither publisher yielded. Harper brought out a cheap edition at fifty cents; Scribner issued two editions—one cloth at $2.50 and a paperback at sixty cents.

In 1881 Joe Harper contracted with William Dean Howells to receive an annual stipend for his writings and for editing "The Easy Chair" in *Harper's Magazine*—a task he relinquished six years later because it interfered with his writing of fiction. Their relationship was amicable, and Howells remained loyal and cooperative to the end. Harper gave him complete freedom as a columnist for the magazine; the one exception being the censorship of his piece protesting the hanging of the Chicago anarchists.

Another satisfied Harper author was George du Maurier. He had for years been illustrating fiction for the firm. In 1894 the company paid him $10,000 for the copyright of his novel, *Trilby*. When the book spurted into bestsellerdom, the Harper management—Joe had retired that year—voluntarily began paying du Maurier a royalty of 15 percent, which gave him an additional $25,000, plus $22,000 for the play based on the novel. This act of generosity was a long step upward from the firm's behavior toward Charles A. Dana, Jr.

Joe Harper's relation with Rudyard Kipling, however, was a reversion to the firm's old stand. In 1889 it rejected Kipling's *Plain Tales from the Hills*. When his work gained popularity both in England and in this country, Harper brought out a volume of his short stories—those which had appeared in *Harper's Maga-*

zine plus several others. The material being uncopyrighted, the firm sent Kipling a draft for ten pounds in lieu of royalties. Still smarting from the rejection, and incited by Walcott Balestier, his future brother-in-law who was arranging to have his writings published by the "pirate" J. W. Lovell in the United States, Kipling returned the draft with a stinging letter of denunciation. The editor of *The Athenaeum*, a friend of his and a critic of American "pirates," wrote in condemnation of Harper's treatment of British authors, stating: "When an author is unknown to fame, they, it would seem, content themselves with insulting him; when he is celebrated, they insult and rob him."

Harper protested the slander in a modest reply. Yet a few English writers, relatively content with their treatment by the Harpers, felt outraged by this splenetic outburst. Protesting the slur on their American publisher in a letter to *The Athenaeum*, Walter Besant, William Black, and Thomas Hardy declared:

> It seems a clear duty to us, who have experienced honourable treatment from this firm, to enter a protest against the sweeping condemnation. . . . We wish to record the fact that, in the course of many years' friendly business relations with Messrs. Harper & Brothers, such has not been our experience. Whether it is a question of acquiring for any of their periodicals the foreign author's rights, they are just as liberal in their dealings as any English house. In the matter of book publication we have always found them willing and desirous to do what is possible for the foreign author, whose interests the American law not only fails to protect, but entirely ignores.

Joe Harper, highly gratified, wrote to thank them. "We are very proud indeed of such a tribute, and from such a source. It is an honor that any publisher might covet, and there are no three living authors whose joint expression of confidence we could more highly value."

Unabashed and with the cockiness of youthful arrogance, Kipling publicly entered the fray with a sarcastic poem entitled "The Rhyme of the Three Captains," which duly appeared in *The Athenaeum*. He obviously enjoyed poking fun at these august defenders of a firm he considered an American "pirate." In time, however, this animosity gradually became dissipated, largely as a result of his unsavory experience with Lovell, for when a Harper editor some years later suggested a series of articles on the Western cowboy, Kipling declined with regret because of previous commitments.

W. H. Appleton, who headed the firm of D. Appleton and Company during this period, was truly representative of the gentlemen publishers. He combined caution with enterprise in his business dealings and treated his authors with respect and liberality. It was largely in their behalf that he became one of the most aggressive advocates of an international copyright law. In one of his many trips to Washington he told the Congress: "You give a patent to a man who invented a mouse-trap, but you don't give a copyright to Herbert Spencer, the greatest philosopher since Socrates."

Neither a scholar nor a writer himself, he in time became the leading publisher of books in science and philosophy. In this achievement he was the beneficiary of E. L. Youmans's dedication to science. In 1847 Youmans, then a poor and nearly blind youth, was browsing in the firm's bookstore, unable to buy the books he wanted to read. Appleton noticed the youth's curiosity and approached him. Learning that he had not the means to buy the book in his hands, the sympathetic publisher lent it to him. Deeply appreciative of this kindness, Youmans reciprocated by offering helpful suggestions about books by scientists. Before long Appleton employed him as science editor. In this capacity Youmans began to take an active part in the heated controversy between the advocates of science and religion raging during the 1850s. Championing the right of science to free inquiry, he corresponded with scholars at home and abroad and persuaded Appleton to publish many of their books.

When the firm brought out Charles Darwin's *On the Origin of Species by Means of Natural Selection*, leading churchmen and traditional scholars attacked Appleton for undermining religion. Although conventionally pious and the publisher of numerous books on religion, he believed in the freedom to publish and backed Youmans with unequivocal firmness: "The duty of a publisher involves reasonable watchfulness that nothing immoral, indecent or sacreligious should be printed and there the responsibility ends." And at Youmans's recommendation he in time brought out the writings of Thomas Huxley, John Tyndell, and numerous other scholars—some of them in the famous International Science Series, edited by Youmans.

Youmans expounded the Darwinian theory of evolution in his own writings, which Appleton published, and over the years he became known as the most forceful Darwinian in the United States. John Fiske praised him as the "interpreter of science for the people." One of Youmans's great achievements was the discovery of Herbert Spencer in 1860. Spencer was then still unknown even in England, but the perceptive editor was highly impressed with his early essays and persuaded Appleton to publish his *Education*. The book was highly successful, and the firm subsequently brought out Spencer's later work, the sale of which came to about a half million copies. The relations between the author and editor-publisher were exemplary, and in 1872 Spencer wrote to Appleton in acknowledging a royalty statement: "The amount you were good enough to enclose both surprised and gratified me. I did not look for anything like so large a total." It must be stressed that these payments were in a sense voluntary, as the books could not be copyrighted in this country.

The firm also brought out a strong list in history. One of its leading items was John Bach McMaster's *History of the People of the United States from the Revolution to the Civil War*. The manuscript of the first volume came to the office unsolicited. Written in a scrawly script, it did not seem promising to the editorial readers and they did not think that a teacher of engineering at Princeton, McMaster's position at that time, could write authoritative history. W. H. Appleton did not like to let a manuscript go without at least looking it through, and he took the McMaster work home with him. The engaging style and appealing content impressed him favorably and he read some passages to his family. The response was enthusiastic. On returning to the office the following morning he wrote McMaster a highly laudatory letter of acceptance. At the time he had no idea of the number of volumes the history was to contain, but that did not concern him once he was satisfied with the merit of the book. The first volume appeared in 1883 and was highly praised by reviewers. The correspondence between author and publisher quickly ripened into a warm friendship, which continued with Appelton's successors after his death. As each volume was completed it was published and promoted aggressively. The eighth volume was brought out in 1913, thirty years after the appearance of the first.

The firm engaged in another interesting author-publisher relationship in connection with Edward N. Wescott's *David Harum*. Six publishers had rejected the manuscript before it was submitted to Appleton, one asserting that it was "vulgar and smells of the stables." Ripley Hitchcock, an editor, read it and found it poorly organized, but he perceived its potential popularity if properly revised. In discussing it with Wescott he advised him to begin the narrative with chapter 11, which dealt with the horse trade, rewrite the novel by omitting certain tedious passages, and emphasize the natural interest of the story. Wescott was then in the terminal stage of tuberculosis, but he followed Hitchcock's advice, cooperating with him throughout the revision, and completed the final version shortly before he died. When the posthumous novel appeared six months later, it gained wide popularity and sold a total of two million copies, including cheap reprints.

7.

Thomas Niles
&
Louisa May Alcott

After 1865, New York became the center of American book publishing. The firms in Philadelphia and Boston, so active and even distinguished during the previous decades, either lacked the energy to maintain their positions of prominence or completely disappeared. Thus, the original Mathew Carey firm in Philadelphia, having undergone several changes of management, ultimately limited its activity to medical texts; similarly, after Ticknor's death in 1864 the house of Ticknor & Fields in Boston experienced some spasmodic spurts, only to be absorbed by the firm headed by Oscar Houghton.

In a small way, however, the Boston firm of Roberts Brothers, which began the publishing of books in 1864 under the direction of Thomas Niles, achieved for a time a distinction rivaling the major New York houses. Born in 1825, Niles worked as a clerk for Ticknor & Fields from 1839 to 1855. When he was not given the recognition he felt he deserved, he left to publish books on his own, only to fail in the panic of 1857. Engaged by Roberts Brothers, successful printers of photograph albums, to take charge of their expansion into book publishing, Niles began to function with a critical perspicuity and imaginative enterprise that soon gave his publishing list of books exceptional qualitative distinction. A bachelor, lacking in the social graces, completely absorbed in his work, he remained practically unknown outside of the publishing industry. Yet he attracted to his list such authors as Louisa May Alcott, George Sand, Helen Hunt Jackson, William Morris, Jean Ingelow, Edwin Arnold, Emily Dickinson, and dozens of others, each of whom he promoted with conspicuous ingenuity and success. Toward the end of his career the New York *Times* stated: "Mr. Niles has been the boldest publisher in Boston. . . . His skillful handling of books has made the reputation of several American authors."

The author who most profited from his prodding and guidance, and to whom he felt closest, was Louisa May Alcott. From earliest childhood she had been keenly conscious of the grim presence of poverty. Her father, the eminent utopian idealist and a lovable human being, lacked the abilty to earn a living, so that his family was ever on the verge of penury. But if his daughters were at times without food, they enjoyed in abundance the love and devotion of intelligent parental care. And in one way or another, friends and relatives made up for the material improvidence of the visionary Bronson Alcott.

Louisa early began to seek ways of earning money. Because of her intellectual upbringing and environment, she turned to writing as a likely means of remunerative work. From the age of fifteen she had written stories which she or her father submitted to periodical editors, and frequently obtained a few dollars for those that were accepted. When her writing did not bring in enough, she taught school and sewed clothes to augment her income; but writing romantic tales, mostly for young readers, remained her determined effort to achieve success. "Some day," she stated in her diary, when fees for her stories did not exceed ten dollars, "I'll do my best, and get well paid for it."

In 1854, at the age of 22, she had George Briggs publish her first book, *Flower Fables*, a collection of tales with which she amused Emerson's daughter Ellen. The juvenile was considered "very sweet," and for an edition of 1,600 copies she was paid thirty-two dollars. Inscribing a copy to her mother, she wrote: "You will accept it with all its faults and look upon it merely as an earnest of what I may yet do; for with so much to cheer me on, I hope to pass in time from fairies and fables to men and realities."

In order to concentrate on her writing and to live her own life, she moved into a furnished room in Boston, where at first she earned most of her income from sewing. "Sewing won't make my fortune," she wrote, "but I can plan stories while I work, and then scribble 'em down on Sundays." In 1859 James Russell Lowell, then editor of the newly established *Atlantic Monthly*, accepted one of her stories and paid her fifty dollars. Thus encouraged, she stated: "I've not been pegging away all these years in vain, and may yet have books and publishers and a fortune of my own."

At this time she began to write an adult novel, *Moods*, a somewhat stilted and sentimental story which her father submitted to several publishers. James Redpath considered it too long and told Alcott that a new author should not begin with a two-volume novel. Ticknor felt it was not up to his standard. Aaron K. Loring finally agreed to take it if it were shortened considerably. Eager to have the novel published, Louisa eliminated ten chapters in the revision. The first reviewers were mildly favorable and it began to sell fairly well; then an influential reviewer expressed doubt as to its morals, and Loring, fearing public criticism, stopped promoting it. "Some fear it isn't moral," Louisa commented ruefully, "because it speaks freely of marriage."

Meanwhile she taught a kindergarten class to earn money. When she resigned to give all her time to writing, James Fields, who was interested in the school, told her, "Stick to your teaching; you can't write." Willful and irritated, she asserted: "I won't teach; and I can write, and I'll prove it."

With the Civil War at a critical pass in 1862, Louisa enlisted as a nurse and went to an army hospital in Washington. Some months later she contracted typhoid pneumonia and had to resign. Having in the interim written long letters about her experiences to members of the family, she was persuaded to revise them into publishable sketches. These appeared serially in Frank B. Stanton's *Commonwealth* and attracted considerable attention. Niles, who was about to start publishing books for Roberts Brothers, was impressed by their originality and realism and offered to publish them in book form. Redpath also liked the sketches and made a similar offer; because he was then better known than Niles, Louisa favored him and he paid her $40 for *Hospital Sketches*. Pleased with its modest success, she wrote to him: "I'll try not to be 'spoilt,' and think ten or fifteen years of snubbing rather good training for an ambitious body... The inspiration of necessity is all I've had, and it is a safer help than any other." Fourteen years later, reflecting on her subsequent success and recalling that she had preferred Redpath to Niles, she admitted meekly: "Shortsighted Louisa! Little did you dream that this same Roberts Brothers were to help you make your fortune a few years later."

At the time *Hospital Sketches* was published her income was indeed meager, amounting to $380 in 1864, $600 in 1865, and rising to $1,000 in 1867. In 1865 she was able to take her first trip to Europe by serving as companion to an ailing young woman. Despite her inability to move about freely, she greatly enjoyed visiting cities and museums. On her return she continued to write stories for various magazines.

In September 1867 Bronson Alcott went to see Niles about one of his own books which he wished published. Their talk soon turned to Louisa, and Niles suggested that a book by her about girls would have wide appeal. He had observed the popularity of such books for boys as Mary Mapes Dodge's *Hans Brinker* and the stories of "Oliver Optic," and believed that a similar juvenile about girls would do equally well. In his search for an author, it occurred to him that Louisa, whose realistic simplicity in *Hospital Sketches* had impressed him favorably, and whose current experience as editor of a juvenile periodical should help her to gauge the proper level of interest, would prepare the kind of book he wanted. Alcott, knowing the direction of his daughter's mind, countered it with the suggestion of a fairy book, but Niles insisted that he wanted a simple story for girls.

Alcott reported Niles's suggestion to Louisa, but she was not interested. Instead she proposed to Niles that he publish a collection of her stories. Without actually rejecting the idea, he urged her to do the girls' book first. Although she was earning $500 a year as editor of *Merry's Museum*, the need of additional money was ever present in her thoughts. With that in mind she yielded to Niles's persistent urging. In May 1868 her diary stated: "Niles, partner of Roberts, asked me to write a girl's book. I said I'd try." Knowing few girls outside of her sisters and having earlier thought of writing about their mutual experiences, she consulted with them and their mother. All agreed it might be fun to see themselves as characters in a book. She also remembered Henry James's intimation, in a review of *Moods*, that she might some day write a fine novel if she wrote about things and people she really knew. Now was her opportunity, she felt, with a book which would "have no *ideas* in it, only facts, and the people shall be as ordinary as possible."

The writing did not come easy. She chose to describe the family's happier moments, with enough sorrowful incidents to give the story an impression of truthfulness. Yet her pen was impeded by the lack of freedom for her imagination to roam on the wings of fancy. "So I plod away," she noted in her diary, "although I don't enjoy this sort of thing. Never liked girls or knew many, except my sisters, but our queer plays and experiences may prove interesting though I doubt it." Because her father was in the habit of calling his daughters "little women," she made it her final title instead of *The Pathetic Family.*

Writing fast once she had begun, as was her habit, she sent the first twelve chapters to Niles for his evaluation. He found them rather dull and told her so. She was inclined to agree, but thought that "simple books are very much needed for girls, and perhaps I can supply the need." Neither was Niles discouraged, and he urged her to complete the story without delay. This she did in six weeks and brought him a manuscript of 402 pages. Being a bachelor and knowing little about girls' interests, he had a young niece and several of his little acquaintances read the story. All were enthusiastic, which cheered him greatly. The completed story also pleased Louisa: "Not a bit sensational, but simple and true, for we really lived most of it; and if it succeeds that will be the reason for it. Mr. N. likes it better now and says some girls who have read the manuscript say it is 'splendid.' As it is for them, they are the best critics, so I should be satisfied."

In arranging for publication of the book, Niles told Louisa that he was ready to pay her $1,000 for the copyright but advised her to keep the copyright and accept a royalty arrangement instead. This she did, and seventeen years later she confided to her diary: "An honest publisher and lucky author, for the copyright made her fortune, and the 'dull book' was the first golden egg of the ugly duckling."

By the time the book was published Niles's confidence in its popularity had strengthened. On the day of its appearance he noted, "This delightful book is destined to have a great run this fall." The first printing of 2,000 copies sold out quickly. And he ordered more and more printings as the sale accelerated. He also realized that the book needed a sequel, as some of its readers became eager to learn the later fate of the sisters. Louisa readily complied, and again completed the new manuscript in six weeks. It was published early in 1869, sold widely, and was subsequently made a part of the first volume. Meanwhile so great was the demand for the first book that Roberts Brothers had to announce: "The great literary hit of the season is undoubtedly Miss Alcott's *Little Women,* the orders for which continue to flow in upon us to such an extent as to make it impossible to answer them with promptness. We are now printing the twenty-third thousand." This popularity was duplicated in England. Niles, greatly pleased, decided to bring out a new printing of *Hospital Sketches,* which was denied him originally and which he felt certain would benefit from the success of *Little Women.* At the end of that year, fully appreciative of her altered status as an author, Louisa wrote:

> After toiling so many years along the uphill road,—and always a hard one to
> women writers,—it is peculiarly grateful to me to find the way growing easier at
> last, with pleasant little surprises blossoming on either side, and the rough places

made smooth by courtesy and kindness of those who have proved themselves friends as well as publishers.

In time *Little Women* achieved worldwide popularity, and the royalties were making Louisa and her family well-to-do. It should be added that Niles, giving cash bonuses to his successful authors in addition to royalties in his eagerness to retain their good will, was especially generous to Louisa, whom he considered his most profitable author. On her part, after years of struggle and insecurity, Louisa at last felt ideally situated as a writer. As her biographer Ednah D. Cheney stated "Miss Alcott had now secured publishers in whom she placed perfect confidence, and who henceforth relieved her of her worry of business matters, dealing directly and fairly with her, and consulting her interests as well as their own."

Affluence did not lessen Miss Alcott's urge to write; nor did Niles slacken his prodding to keep her at it. In 1870 she wrote *An Old-Fashioned Girl*, in which the heroine experienced many of her own bitter days when she was working hard to earn money and suffered slights and disappointments in the process. Niles promoted the book energetically, fully confident of its wide appeal. To booksellers he announced: "As the demand for the book will be immense, the Trade will oblige us with their orders immediately." And so it was: 5,000 copies were sold during the first week of publication, and 44,000 within nine months. That year Niles informed Louisa that no other American author had received as much as she in royalties—$12,292.50.

Now having enough money to indulge herself as she wished, she went to Europe at her own expense and enjoyed the attention paid to her. While in London Niles's brother William entertained her lavishly. On her return Niles met her at the boat and informed her of the large advance sale of *Little Men*, a book based upon the lives of her two nephews whose father had died unexpectedly. Indeed, too shy to pay court to her openly, Niles sent her roses anonymously and looked after her affairs with the devotion of a close friend. Katherine Anthony well described this relationship:

> Louisa May Alcott and her publisher, Thomas Niles, stood in their relations a good deal like Queen Elizabeth and Sir Francis Walsingham. Regal though Louisa was, Niles kept a strict rein on her policies. . . . After Niles had become acquainted with Louisa, the relationship between them developed into a personal friendship. . . . He kept strict watch on Louisa's style, often telling her specifically how to write, what to avoid, and what to strive for, and he was full of appreciation of her hard-won successes. A quiet, unaggressive man, he was a real influence on her work and a partner in her achievements.

> He watched over her health—until he gave up in despair—her finances, her practical affairs, with the devotion of a brother. Louisa trusted him. . . . Could it have been Mr. Niles who sent her the anonymous bouquets every day for a while after her return from abroad? He long kept a firm place in her personal life, retired and solitary though it was in the main.

As always in the past, Louisa continued to devote herself to the welfare of her family. Herself suffering from various pains and aches, she worried about her mother's poor health, about the sudden death of her brother-in-law and the care of her widowed sister and her children, about the career of her younger sister. All the while she stoically endured pain and physical fatigue. Yielding to Niles's prodding and advice, she wrote *Aunt Jo's Scrap Book* in 1871 and *Shawl's Straps* the following year.

Now a popular celebrity, she found herself in great demand as a contributor to magazines, with fees many times as large as in previous years. More out of habit than ambition, she worked strenuously, with breaks owing to illness, not knowing how to relax. Niles persisted in cautioning her about her deteriorating health, but she simply could not slow down—being tempted by lucrative offers and enjoying the limelight of her popularity. Thus in 1874, she wrote in her *Journal* in connection with one of her stories:

> Funny time with the publishers about the tale; for all wanted it at once, and each tried to outbid the other for an unwritten story. I rather enjoyed it, and felt important with Roberts, Low, and Scribner all clamoring for my " 'umble" works. No peddling poor little manuscripts now, and feeling rich with $10. The golden goose can lay her eggs for a good price, if she isn't killed by too much driving.

These temptations notwithstanding, she still wanted to write something "serious," something of an adult nature that would enhance her reputation as a writer. With this in mind she began to write *Work*. Completing the manuscript in 1873, she sold the serial rights for $3,000. Niles, sympathizing with her desire for literary distinction, engaged a leading artist to prepare twenty-seven illustrations for the book and promoted it vigorously. It was not, however, the kind of book her admirers wanted, and although the firm obtained ten thousand subscriptions for it, the volume did not have the continued sale of her earlier fiction. To keep her income from shrinking, Niles brought out three of her earlier volumes in a cheap edition called *Alcott for the Million*.

By this time in chronic poor health, Louisa found herself lacking the energy to concentrate on a long work. As often as she could, she wrote short stories, which editors eagerly accepted. Some were later collected for book publication. Much of her writing appeared in *St. Nicholas*, the juvenile magazine edited by the astute Mary Mapes Dodge. When the latter prevailed upon her to write the serial *Jack and Jill*, Miss Alcott commented: "After two years of rest, I am going to try again; it is so easy to make money now, and so pleasant to have it to give. A chapter a day is my task, and not that if I feel tired. No more fourteen hours a day; make haste slowly now." When the story was published in book form it had a wide sale.

Niles continued to bring out various editions of her books to take advantage of their continued popularity. In 1880 he issued a luxuriously illustrated edition of *Little Women* for the Christmas gift market. The volume contained 200 pictures, was finely printed and bound in green and gold, with gilt edges, and priced at five dollars. A firm advertisement, no doubt composed by Niles himself, stated: "It is safe to say that there are not many homes which have not been made happier through the healthy influence of this celebrated book, which has now become a classic and which is, in its present dress, a charming volume for the centre table of the domestic fireside."

Although *Work* did not satisfy her longing for eminence as a writer of adult fiction, the yearning to achieve it persisted in her consciousness. No longer able to write a new work, she turned to *Moods*, her first adult novel, which she continued to cherish—"for into it went the love, labor, and enthusiasm that no later book can possess." She revised it with all the affection and effort she was capable of. Niles, always eager to cooperate with his favorite author, brought out the new edition in 1882 and promoted it extensively; yet relatively few of her admirers were interested in the revised version.

During the 1880s Louisa's energy was gradually failing, so that in 1886 her doctor forbade her from undertaking any lengthy writing. Somewhat earlier, acknowledging Niles's holiday greeting and aware of her current debility, she wrote:

> Thanks for the good wishes and news. Now that I cannot work it is very agreeable to hear that the books go so well, and that the lazy woman need not worry about things.

> I appreciate my blessings I assure you. Heartily I wish I could "swamp the book room with Jo's boys," as Fred says, and I hope to do it by and by when head and hand can safely obey the desire of the heart which will never be too tired or too old to remember and be grateful.

And well she might. For her royalties, exclusive of fees from magazines, totaled by this time around $200,000. Niles, moreover, was bringing out a collected edition of her writings in twenty-five volumes, thus giving her the prominence of other major writers.

Early in 1888 her father died, and shortly thereafter she too breathed her last at the age of fifty-five. Her death affected Niles deeply. For twenty years he had served her with exceptional loyalty and devotion having cared for her more as an intimate friend than merely as a successful author. In the words of Prof. R. F. Kilgour, Niles's association with Miss Alcott "had been one of the most perfect relationships in the history of American publishing."

With Louisa gone, Niles, the highly successful publisher but a shy and reserved person, lost interest in his lifework. For the next several years he functioned without his accustomed energy and astuteness. In 1894 he decided to take his first vacation and went to Italy. There he became ill and died. *Publishers' Weekly* expressed a common judgment of those who knew Niles well:

> He magnified his office by making it a truly literary function, and he had no stronger desire than to add good names to his very choice catalogue, to publish the best books, and to see that the authors of them receive their due reward. His warmest friends were among his authors, and in their mutual relations all traditions of distrust were set aside.

With Niles gone, Roberts Brothers began to drift more or less aimlessly, losing authors to other publishers, undertaking projects which Niles had planned but which his successors failed to bring to fruition—so that in 1898 the older firm of Little, Brown and Company readily acquired its assets and gave its imprint to a famous list of books.

8.

Henry Holt
vs.
Popular Authors

Of the gentlemen publishers after the Civil War, Henry Holt best exemplified their solid conservatism, their ethical soundness, and their sincere devotion to literature and scholarship. Unlike his peers, however, he failed to develop enduring relationships with a number of his prominent authors. Himself a writer of note as well as an outstanding editor and literary critic, he lacked flexibility and ingratiation in his dealings with authors. His editorial criticisms and his refusal to curry favor or compete for manuscripts tended to alienate both writers and agents; not a few of his authors, however, were grateful for his helpful criticisms and admired his ethical integrity.

A Yale graduate, a religious and intellectual rebel while a student, uninterested in his legal studies, he at the age of twenty-five decided to make publishing his life's work. As a student he was impressed with a remark made by Daniel C. Gilman, then Yale librarian and later the distinguished president of Johns Hopkins University: "If you find on a book the imprint of Ticknor & Fields it is probably a good book." In becoming a publisher he aimed to bring out books that would earn his imprint a similar reputation. Having early made textbooks a highly profitable part of his business, he was able to indulge his wish to publish only those works of general interest which he considered of "intrinsic worth." This attitude is best illustrated late in his career in connection with Stuart Sherman's *On Contemporary Criticism*, submitted to him in 1917. After reading it himself, he asked Alfred Harcourt, his trade manager, for his reaction. When the latter advised rejection because of its limited appeal, Holt's response was in keeping with his lifelong philosophy of publishing:

> When I sent you Stuart Sherman's Ms. I was entirely ready to lose whatever it will cost to publish it, unless you should find in it something loudly calling for modification and he would be unwilling to make the modification. There being nothing of that kind, I want you to go ahead with it. He is by common consent the finest literary critic in America, and it is worth our while to lose some time, tissue and money on him, for the sake of the luster he'll cast on our list.

Holt was at his best as an editor. Himself a literary practitioner, keenly perceptive of superior writing, adhering to high artistic standards, he approached every manuscript with the idea of giving its author the full benefit of his critical acuity. Most authors accepted his suggestions more or less gratefully, but now and then one was only irritated or even angered by his proferred advice.

His relation with Prof. A. S. Packard, a scholarly zoologist, exemplified his reaction to academic writing. Some time after Professor Packard had contracted to prepare a text in zoology, he gave no evidence of working on it. Holt prodded him several times without getting an affirmative response. About 2 1/2 years after the contract had been signed Holt received a sample chapter. He read it with his usual care and responded with a long letter of critical comment. First he chastised him for sending him a messy manuscript and pointed out that writing of this untidiness prejudiced a reader and was therefore unfair to the author. He then told him of the folly of sending material out of context. "A chapter out of the middle of an organically constructed book is, at best, a hard one to take as a sample. Its relations with what goes before are too essential a part of it." His chief criticism, however, pertained to the unsuitability of the material for the student for whom it was intended.

> I find what I probably told you I expected to find: that you need assiduously cultivate ignorance in order to do this work well. I presume you selected this chapter to send on the conviction that if I passed it without criticism, I would pass anything else in the book. If I were to judge from it, you have started to make your book contain about four times as many facts as the mind for which it is intended can assimilate, and not over one-fourth of the exposition and little sentences by way of guidelines and reminders that such minds need. . . . For the sake of crowding in your facts—many of which have no significance to the student using his first book, you use a condensed and technical style of expression that presupposes a considerable familiarity with the subject. You prefer a technical word where a common one will answer the common student's purpose. . . .

Needless to say, after both had agonized over the manuscript, with feelings at times rubbed raw, the final result was a book that remained a standard work for many years.

Although Holt's tough criticism of Packard's text ended to their mutual benefit, his dealings with certain prominent trade authors culminated in frustration. As in earlier instances, his difficulties arose from an insistence on literary excellence as well as on a high ethical standard in the face of unscrupulous competition, aggravated by the emergence of the mercenary literary agent—to him a serpent in Eden.

Aiming from the outset to make publishing a gentleman's profession, he aspired to deal with authors in a spirit of mutual confidence and loyalty. He was confronted early, however, by competition from piratical publishers; and even the normally ethical ones again and again breached the "courtesy" principle when it suited them. The enactment of the international copyright law and the growing prominence of the literary agent quickly put an end to the "courtesy" practice, and the scramble for established authors put publishers like Holt at a great disadvantage. His ethical stance and his high editorial standards caused him to lose one popular author after another.

His refusal to compete for books he had not seen and found worthy made him chary of the literary agent, whom he had come to consider an interloper and mercenary meddler between author and publisher. In 1890 he wrote to A. P. Watt, one of the first and most successful of English agents, concerning a book which interested him. "If the matter is to be in any sense one of competition among publishers, pray spare yourself the trouble of communicating with us any further as we do not enter into competition." Watt never forgot nor forgave the caustic implication of Holt's attitude.

The year before, Holt had published *Three Men in a Boat*, which he had acquired from an English publisher on the basis of merit and without any knowledge of the author. Soon after the humorous novel achieved wide popularity in the United States, its author, Jerome K. Jerome, informed Holt that he had received a tempting offer for his next book from the American publisher J. W. Lovell. Holt replied that "Mr. Lovell is one of our most eminent pirates," that he had brought out a pirated edition of Jerome's *Stage Land* at ten cents a copy, and that Lovell was in financial difficulties. He then urged him to "be careful how you are misled by brilliant offers." Somewhat later Holt told him he was paying him half of the profits on his book, which is greater than the 10 percent royalty of the contract, which he would resume "when the sale of the book gets slow."

When the new copyright law was about to be passed by the Congress in 1890, Holt advised Jerome to hold up the English publication of his new book until it could also be copyrighted in the United States and thus avoid piracy. In due time Hold received the manuscript and brought it out in an illustrated edition, as was then the practice, but the novel found little popular appeal. Watt, having in the interim become Jerome's agent, soon asked Holt for an advance of one hundred pounds and a royalty of 15 percent on Jerome's forthcoming book. Holt yielded most reluctantly—after Watt had threatened to give the book to another publisher.

Several years later Watt demanded the same terms for Jerome's latest work without giving Holt the opportunity to examine it. With the previous novel having failed to earn the advance, Holt balked. To Arthur Waugh, his new representative in England, he declared: "I for one have got through yielding to ridiculous terms for the sake of pleasing Watt and British authors." Watt thereupon sold the novel to Dodd, Mead and Company, who agreed to the advance and a royalty of 20 percent. This turn of events deeply perturbed the principled and prudent Holt, who felt that "there was no place for literary agents in my impractically ideal relations between established authors and their established publishers." Yet loath to lose Jerome, he wrote to Waugh:

> Can't you make Jerome see through Watt's jumping at the chance to sell that book of his away from me? Of course he wanted to break up any publisher's monopoly of anybody. If you can get me a fair chance at Jerome's novel, if it is worth having, I probably can make some sort of arrangement with Dodd for keeping up some sort

of uniform edition; and Dodd can't make any arrangement with me: for he has done a questionable thing.

Yet he did not want Jerome to come back to him "reluctantly." And when Jerome later asked him to stop the sale of one of his books, Holt informed Waugh: "To you I say freely (hoping you will say it emphatically to him) that it is rather cheeky of him to ask us to suppress a book of which we have a quantity on hand, for the sake of his other books, when most recent, and therefore the most valuable (commercially) of his other books are in the hands of other publishers." And when Jerome did offer him a book in 1901, Holt's response was unfeignedly negative.

Anthony Hope (Anthony Hope Hawkins) was another author whose cordial relations with Holt ended in frustration. In 1894 Holt published Hope's novel, *The Prisoner of Zenda*. A highly charged romance in tune with the popular fiction of the time, it became a best seller, with twenty-six printings the first year, and continued to sell widely for many years. Holt and Hope were soon close friends, and five of the author's earlier novels, which had failed to attract readers, were republished by Holt in 1895.

Tempted by Watt, however, Hope permitted himself to be courted by other publishers. Learning that both Appleton and Stokes had made him attractive offers, Holt realized that Watt's greed was at the bottom of it. To an earlier of his London representatives he expressed his perturbation in April 1895:

> The influence of Watt and some other influences have tended of late to prevent authors sticking to one publisher, and have led to a general scramble. It is a state of affairs I am sorry for. . . . Anthony Hope, although I published the first book that made his reputation here, and although he has had the decency to say that he proposes to offer me the sequel to it, seems to throw himself open to the general scramble.

Two years later Holt agreed to pay Hope £150 on the publication of *Rupert of Hentzau*, 15 percent on the sale of the first 5,000 copies, 17 1/2 on the next 2,500, and 20 percent thereafter. When Hope visited the United States about that time, Holt entertained him warmly. He told him of his plan to bring out an illustrated edition of *The Prisoner of Zenda* uniform with the forthcoming *Rupert of Hentzau*; he also suggested doing the same for *Dolly Dialogues* if Hope would "prepare two or three new Dialogues which we can copyright and pronounce the pirated editions incomplete." Holt's friendship and overtures notwithstanding, he received none of Hope's other books—Watt retaliating for his refusal to deal with him as Hope's agent.

When the manuscript of *Rupert* reached Holt, he read it attentively and offered his keen editorial recommendations:

> Be patient with a suggestion that may strike you as inartistic. I have an idea that *Rupert* would probably sell two or three times as many if, somehow, "they lived happily ever after," or that it would sell between its present chances and those

brilliant ones if "in death they were not parted." . . . I shan't be surprised if that notion of having the same monument cover both of them right royally, double action epitaph and all, will satisfy your artistic sense as well, or even better (oh my cheek!) than the unsociable death of poor Rassendyl alone.

Hope accepted the first suggestion but not the second. Holt still felt that the latter emendation "could be arranged in a couple of paragraphs; and I am too stupid to see that it would be inartistic. But you are not as stupid as I am." Published in 1898, *Rupert* had an advance sale of 20,000 copies, and although its popularity did not reach that of *Zenda*, it by far outsold Hope's other novels.

Mrs. Ethel L. Voynich was an even greater disappointment to the scrupulous publisher. The daughter of William Boole, the eminent mathematician, she had married a Lithuanian exile whose ill health made residence in southern Italy highly desirable. In need of earning money, she wrote *The Gadfly*, a novel about revolution in Italy. Published in England, it failed to gain favorable attention. Nor did American publishers show any interest in it. As Holt wrote later, it "was offered to every other respectable publisher in New York, and possibly some not so respectable, before it was offered to me." He read it without prejudice, accepted it for publication, and paid Voynich thirty pounds advance and a 10-percent royalty.

Brought out in 1896, *The Gadfly*'s reception was critically auspicious, and its sale increased from month to month. With this book in mind, Holt wrote to Waugh: "The impression grows stronger in me that more people want a good thing in America than in England, and that there are not so many here as with you, who will take a poor thing or merely average thing at any price."

Competition among publishers was at its keenest in the 1890s. The notable success of *The Gadfly* caused nine of them to go after Voynich's next book. Since her need for money remained great, she was inclined to accept the highest offer. Holt was naturally chagrined at this scramble for his author, and at the advice of his English agent he not only increased the royalty on *The Gadfly* but agreed to an advance of £150 on the new novel, with a royalty of 15 percent on the first 5,000 copies, 17 1/2 on the next 2,500, and 20 percent thereafter.

Complications connected with the dramatization of *The Gadfly* brought Voynich to New York. Holt had her as his house guest and did what he could to protect her stage rights in the play. He also arranged for the serialization of the new novel in *Century Magazine*.

When the manuscript reached him, he found it artistically deficient in certain places and advised revision in the light of his critical suggestions. For all her respect for Holt as a publisher, Voynich refused to make the changes. Waugh informed Holt:

> She declines to alter a word, and feels therefore, that the book must go elsewhere for America. She said she was very sorry for this since she had the greatest regard for you personally and had hoped to have all her books with you. She still intends to offer you her next book, when, in the course of years, it is ready. The present book is now offered to Doubleday & Page.

Some time later F. N. Doubleday, in a casual conversation with Holt, told him that Voynich had agreed to make some changes for him. In righteous indignation he wrote her: "Of course your refusing to revise for me, and then sending the book revised to another publisher, is something that my imagination cannot explain. I will have to await explanation from you." On inquiry Waugh learned that she had made only a few minor stylistic emendations and was deeply hurt by Holt's letter.

True to her promise, however, she sent Holt the manuscript of her third novel late in 1903. He readily accepted it, but lowered the royalty offer to 10 percent on the first 2,500 copies, with an increase to 15 percent on the next 2,500 copies, and 20 percent thereafter. When she requested a larger advance and better terms, he advised her that if she could get them from another publisher she was free to do so. Moreover, having by then read the manuscript critically, he again suggested certain changes. Once more Voynich refused, telling him: "What made me feel that our points of view are utterly incompatible was your asking me to 'let you cut out,' as 'pretty but unnecessary' the final scene, which I regard as the keystone to the whole book, and which has cost me more to write than I can tell you."

Holt's response was in character:

> My suggestion to you to cut out put in or change, was simply a suggestion for your consideration, and in no sense a requirement; and I cannot realize my having made the suggestions as legitimately bearing at all on the question of your withdrawing the Ms.

> I have reason to believe that I offer more suggestions regarding Mss. than publishers generally do, and perhaps I have also reason to believe that a larger percentage of my suggestions is taken, than that of publishers in general; whether to the benefit of authors or not, of course there is not means of determining.

The relations between the two remained broken. The books Voynich published elsewhere did poorly; but *The Gadfly* continued to sell well over many years, and over a half century later flared into popularity in both Soviet Russia and China owing to its revolutionary content.

Holt had no better luck with some of his popular American authors, conspicuously with Paul Leicester Ford. This writer, badly crippled from childhood, had made his father's extensive library his university and became highly erudite. Devoting himself to the writing and compiling of books, he edited the writings of a number of eminent Americans and wrote considerable fiction. In 1894 he submitted the manuscript of *The Honorable Peter Stirling* to Henry Holt. The latter liked it well enough to agree to publish it, but was uncertain of its salability and required of Ford a deposit of money in case the novel sold fewer than a thousand copies within three years. The book, to some extent anticipating the muckraking fiction of the 1900s, sold better than Holt had anticipated, totaling 1,500 copies during the first eighteen months.

In June 1895, having struck up a friendship with Holt, Ford asked him to familiarize him with the way books were normally accepted and published. The elderly publisher was glad to oblige, explained the process in detail, and added:

> In fact, in this shop no book is taken on any one verdict but my own, and mighty seldom at that; I generally preferring in the very rare instances where for some personal reason I attack a Ms. at first hand, to see how it will strike somebody else, though I did send *Called Back, Three Men in a Boat*, and *The Prisoner of Zenda* to press of my own independent notion.

> When a book has been published six months, and you see an advertisement of it from this shop, as you may today in the *Times, Tribune*, and *Post*, you can know that the book has some life in it. *Stirling* is now selling an average of about 30 a week.

> When you get your other book done, don't you be going off to other publishers with it after you have found some fame under my wing—unless of course you are making on an order from Harper.

As chance would have it, that summer A. M. Robinson, a San Francisco bookseller, found in the novel definite resemblance between Peter Stirling and President Grover Cleveland. He ordered a hundred copies and began to recommend the novel to his customers in the light of his presumed discovery. His enthusiasm for the story proved contagious. Before long this telltale revelation interested readers in Denver, then Chicago, Cleveland, and finally New York. Everywhere the novel sold in quantity, keeping it on the best-seller list for the next four years. Thereafter it continued to sell in cheaper editions.

Their friendly relations notwithstanding, Holt learned in 1896 that Ford had given his new novel to Dodd, Mead and Company. Beginning his letter to him by stating how well *Stirling* was going, Holt continued in quiet anger:

> Perhaps even your modesty will not prevent your realizing that I find the fact of your having placed the Ms. of your new book (which you had already spoken of to me) in the hands of another firm, a disagreeable surprise. I hope that your doing so has not arisen from any dissatisfaction with our handling of your old one. If it has not, the result of your publishing elsewhere (if you do so), would do us an injustice, as the literary public will inevitably assume the dissatisfaction, whether it exists or not.

> The fact that Dodd, Mead & Co. would endeavor to get serial rights for you hardly seems to cover the situation. We could make that endeavor just as easily as they; and talk of anybody having a pull on a magazine that it's worth while to have a pull on, is nonsense: for if anybody had, the magazine would not be worth the pull.

Ford's explanation did not satisfy Holt, and his acknowledgment, while outwardly cordial, also included caustic barbs. Their subsequent correspondence lacked the previous geniality. Holt reported some favorable comments on *Stirling*, offered an advance on royalty if needed, and urged the completion of *The Federalist*, which Ford had previously agreed to edit for him.

Late in October 1898 Ford wrote to the firm in abusive anger in response to a bill for excessive alterations. The reply, signed by a member of the firm, was a peculiar climax to what had begun as a cordial author-publisher relationship:

Your letter of October 26 being such as we are not accustomed to receiving from gentlemen, or from anybody, we have delayed answering it until we could refer it to the head of the firm who is absent.

Though you say that you have published seventy books without receiving a bill for alterations, *Peter Stirling* was, we believe, your first novel, and *The Federalist* you did not see through the press yourself. Be all that as it may, however, we have published more than seven times seventy books, have rendered a bill for alterations every time they were excessive (which has not been seldom), and have never before received a letter deciding the case against us without investigation. Nor have we ever before, under any circumstances that we can remember, even from some writer vastly less able to express himself than you are, [received] a letter containing a passage which could justifiably, whether correctly or not, be interpreted as an attempt at blackmail.

Such a letter, while permitted to stand, of course renders discussion or even explanation impossible.

Though not signed by Holt, the letter bears the imprint of his gentlemanly indignation and caustic style. Ford tried to retract his curtness in his next letter, asserting only that some of the charges should have been borne by the firm. The Holt office did not deign to reply.

It should be stressed, however, that not a few authors were deeply appreciative of his personal interest and candid editorial suggestions. One of these was Dorothy Canfield Fisher. Thus in 1911, when a rival publisher made her an attractive offer for her new novel, she used the "formula" employed by her on previous similar occasions: "No thank you sir. I'm engaged to Mr. Holt." Four years later, when Holt was already semiretired, his sage advice after a reading of the manuscript of *The Bent Twig*, brought from her the following response:

I pity you with all my heart if you have never known the exciting pleasure you have just given me, if you have never had the electrifying experience which has just ended for me with the last page of the proofs! It's been one of the dreams of my life, to have just such criticism as that, illuminating, full, precise, and accurate as a surgeon's scalpel. . . . Blessings on your keen eye.

Yet when Alfred Harcourt left Holt in 1919 to start his own firm, Fisher forgot her "engagement" to the old publisher and joined the exodus of Holt authors who favored Harcourt as their publisher. (Holt's dealings with three major authors manifest aspects of relationship that require detailed treatment and are treated in separate chapters.)

9.

Henry Holt

& Henry Adams

More than his fellow publishers, Henry Holt belonged to the nation's social and intellectual elite. He associated with civic leaders, prominent writers and artists, and eminent scholars—men who belonged to the "best families" and who had achieved nation-wide prestige. This exclusiveness was of course a snobishness common to many leading Americans of the period. That conventional propriety was also important to Holt was evidenced as late as 1912, when he was uncertain whether or not to associate personally with Henri Bergson, whose *Creative Evolution* he had published that year—Bergson having come to Columbia University to deliver a series of lectures. His dubiety was caused by his prejudice against Jews, yet Bergson's eminence as a philosopher made Holt desirous of breaking bread with him. He therefore sent Alfred Harcourt, his editor and a Columbia graduate, to the university to ascertain "if he is a gentleman." On receiving an affirmative report he invited Bergson to his home for dinner and enjoyed his guest's incisive thinking.

One of Holt's close friends was Henry Adams. Social companions and intellectual peers, they shunned talk of money or business. Thus, much as Adams admired Holt personally, he preferred to keep their friendship on a high level and gave his historical writings to other publishers, which was perfectly agreeable to Holt.

It was only when Adams wrote a novel and wanted it published anonymously, that he turned to Holt. In 1879 he sent him the manuscript of *Democracy, an American Novel* "under a pledge of dead secrecy," and insisted on paying the cost of publication. Holt of course complied with his friend's request, and the identity of the novel's author indeed remained unknown until it was revealed in 1915 by the biographer of John Hay, a mutual friend of both Holt and Adams.

When the novel was about to be published, a "Literary Note" in the New York *Tribune* announced:

> The Leisure Hour Series [a successful list of good fiction] is to have added to it the first novel by an American author. The scene is laid in New York and Washington, and its author would appear to be a resident of one place or the other. It is estimated that many readers will imagine they see portraits in the book.

The reception was mildly favorable, and a second printing was ordered a month after publication. The English edition, having been publicly praised by William Gladstone, did much better.

Several months later Adams wrote Holt: "Dear Pirate: The time has come when I want to make a twenty-five cent edition of the scandalous libel. If there is no profit in it for you, there ought to be glory." He added that the accumulated royalties should cover the possible loss. And in a subsequent letter he urged: "Announce as much as you please that a twenty-five cent edition is coming out or is out; but don't spend your money on advertising opinions of the press."

On the receipt of a copy of the cheap edition Adams thanked Holt for the trouble and added: "The truth is, I was afraid the little bastard was fairly becoming British, and my parental heart could not stand such a perversion of nature." He also offered to pay the cost of unsold copies of the cloth edition.

Unaware of Adams's distress on account of his wife's mental depression and suicide, Holt in November 1885 suggested that *Democracy* receive fresh promotion. The response was: "By-gones are pretty well by-gones, and I am not so particular as I was; but, all the same, I am peculiarly anxious not to wake up the critics just now. . . . I never had so many reasons for wishing to be left in peace, as now." Nevertheless, over the ensuing years the novel retained a relatively active life, being reprinted twenty times in all. Adams, pleased with its unexpected appeal, wrote gloatingly to his brother Brooks, "The wholesale piracy of *Democracy* was the single real triumph of my life."

In 1884 Adams had sent Holt the manuscript of his second novel, *Esther*. It was published under Adams's proposed pseudonym of Frances Snow Compton. Eager to see what would happen if no review copies were sent out and no announcement of its availability were made in an advertisement, Adams instructed Holt accordingly. When the latter remonstrated, he was told to wait two years before they would consider "whooping up" the novel. In a later letter Adams noted: "The experiment I wished to try was whether authorship without advertisement was possible. I understand you agree with me that the result, as far as a single experiment can go, proves that advertisement is necessary to authorship." As it was, the novel sold a total of 514 copies, and Adams bought the remainder of the printing and destroyed it.

In line with this experiment Adams asked Holt to place the novel with an English publisher and permit him to send out review copies. "I want to test English criticism and see whether it amounts to more than our own. I care little for readers and dread notoriety more than dyspepsia, but I like the amusement of a literary conundrum." The result was no more successful than the American experiment, British readers finding the story of little appeal.

Having at last recuperated from the long depression caused by his wife's suicide, Adams wrote to Holt in March 1890 shortly before sailing to the South Seas:

> With the year 1890 I shall retire from authorship. As an occupation I can recommend it to the rich. It has cost me about a hundred thousand dollars, I calculate, in

twenty years, and has given me that amount of amusement. In July I sail from San Francisco for new scenes and adventures, leaving to younger and better men whatever promotion my vacancy may cause in the service. I hope they will enjoy it as much as I have done.

Nine years later, responding to Holt's inquiry about a new book from his pen, Adams wrote in a similar vein—some years before he had completed his two most famous books:

> The only novel I care to write or to read is the story of how good people get completely out of this world into something else. You may wipe the sponge over all I ever did, in other words, burn or otherwise destroy all record of it. I doubt seriously whether God Almighty, in case he exists, will ever ask to see it, and I think I'm tolerably certain not to put it in evidence on the trial. As for literary work, I have handed my ink-pot over to my brother Brooks, who has ten times my intelligence, and who will say at least ten times in excess of what I could do.
>
> Oh, yes! I've wanted to say lots of things. But what is the use! "What do they understand?" Not even their blossoming interest tables. Let me be born a Jew!

The friendship between the two men continued unabated, if at a distance much of the time. When Holt learned that his friend was writing again, he was too much the gentleman to act the aggressive publisher, and made no effort to show his interest in possible publication; as in the past, he felt that it was up to Adams to make the first move in that direction. When he learned in 1913 that Adams had completed and privately printed what was presumably his autobiography, he wrote to ask for a copy.

> My Dear Historian:
> Can you remember as far back as when you were that to me, and I was your dear philosopher to you? I remember the time so vividly that I find no difficulty in telling you that Pumpelly spoke to me the other day about your book *The Education of Henry Adams* in such a way that I want you to send me a copy.

Adams was at the time in Paris, sufficiently recovered from a stroke to be on his feet again but feeling more mordant than ever, as is evident from his reply:

> I was moved to a laugh when I read your letter yesterday. That three old men like Pompelly, you and me, should go muddling about each other's forgetfulness still, after we were dead and forgotten these thousand years, seems a merry jest, but Shakespeare said something about comparing him with the bettering of the time as an excuse for such behavior in his own case, and although no one has yet found the betterment he kindly promised, no doubt everyone revels now in plenty of Shakespeare and such to encourage you to read me. Unluckily, I don't carry my immortal works in my pocket. I must wait for winter, but if I survive till December I will try to find a copy of my immortal thoughts. But pray remind me of it, for I remember nothing over night;—least of all, about myself, which is a subject fit only for the ghosts. Oh, yes, I like it! but I think even the ghosts are rather bored. Well they may be!
>
> It is no great use wishing you all the blessings of youth and loveliness but whatever fall in your way I trust will do you good. For my own part I want only personal beauty. It has a good influence on my contemporaries.

After Adams died in 1918, Holt wrote to Sen. Henry Cabot Lodge, Adams's literary executor, to suggest that *Esther* might now be brought out in reverse— over Adams's name and given active promotion. Lodge replied: "*Esther* is new to me. I have never heard of it and as I have been an intimate friend of Mr. Adams for nearly half a century I am a little surprised that I never saw it or heard a word from him in regard to it." Two months later, however, Lodge wrote again: "I know that Mr. Adams wrote *Esther* and I know the facts as to his experiment to be as you describe them." The family, he continued, felt never-theless that "it would neither be agreeable to Henry, nor would it be for his rep-utation, for either *Democracy* or *Esther*, whatever that may be, to be repub-lished." That ended the matter as far as Holt was concerned, although no objection was raised to his new edition of *Democracy* six years later.

Although Holt received a copy of *Education* and no doubt would have liked to bring out an edition under his own imprint—he must have by then learned that Houghton Mifflin had published *Mont-Saint-Michel and Chartres*—he contin-ued to act the gentleman, waiting for Adams to approach him rather than take the initiative, which he considered unprofessional. But Adams, too, was a gentle-man, and preferred not to mix friendship with business, although he did not ever expect to publish the book himself.

When after years of urging and entreatment by Ralph Adams Cram, Adams let him arrange for the publication of *Mont-Saint-Michel and Chartres*, he did so on the condition that the royalties "be set aside to provide copies for impe-cunious architects." Ferris Greenslet of Houghton Mifflin published the book for Cram; it was readily acclaimed by artists and critics and sold in relatively large numbers.

As early as 1907, when Greenslet first learned about the existence of *Educa-tion*, he had borrowed from a friend of Adams one of the available hundred cop-ies of the privately printed edition and read it with growing excitement, aware of its literary merit and potential popularity. He at once began to urge Adams to let him publish the book for the general public, but was brusquely refused. Other publishers had of course also heard of the work and made Adams attractive of-fers; but he rejected all overtures, insisting that the material needed completion and he was then unable to do it. Greenslet alone persisted in repeated entreaties, abetted by several of Adams's close friends.

In 1915, taking stock on his seventy-seventh birthday, he decided to prepare the book for posthumous publication. Taking into his confidence Henry Cabot Lodge, who had recently been elected to the presidency of the Massachusetts Historical Society, he wrote to Lodge: "I send you herewith a sealed packet con-taining a copy of my *Education* corrected and prepared for publication." He in-cluded an "Editor's Preface," signed with Lodge's initials, to complete the de-ception that he had no part in the editing and publication of the book. In the same spirit he replied to the latest of Greenslet's appeals—twisting the truth to suit his sardonic humor:

The Education was written ten years ago and put into type, tentatively, to be circulated, for correction and suggestion, among persons interested. Not one—except Charles Eliot—ever returned the volume or offered me a word of advice, and I was still waiting in 1912, quite unable to cope with my difficulties, when I was suddenly struck down by an illness which put an end to all thought of further literary work.

Nothing could be done. I would not let the thing go, in its incomplete, uncorrected, tentative form; I could not destroy or suppress it; I could not let anyone else touch it. I could only sit still and trust to time to forget it.

Greenslet was sympathetic but refused to be put off, having heard a rumor about the arrangement with Lodge. At his first opportunity he visited Adams in Washington, and once more insisted that even in its presumably unpolished state the *Education* was a work of great merit and that he would be honored to publish it. Adams, he recorded, received him "in a singularly amiable and obliging, if slightly fantastic mood," and said to him:

You have been a great nuisance to me for nearly ten years. I have decided to punish you, and make the punishment fit the crime. I am arranging to leave the *Education* to the Massachusetts Historical Society. When I am dead, you can publish it for them. You will lose money on it. That will be your punishment. You won't have long to wait. My doctor told me yesterday that I can't live over a month.

He lived three years longer, to the age of eighty. And Greenslet, who had striven so long and so persistently to get the book, lost no time in arranging for its publication. As it turned out, the "loss" which Adams had predicted facetiously turned out to be a highly profitable undertaking. *The Education of Henry Adams* sold 12,000 copies in three months, became a leading best seller on the 1918 nonfiction list, and was awarded a Pulitzer Prize the following May.

10.

Henry Holt
& William James

As might have been surmised from Henry Holt's letter to Prof. A. S. Packard, his relations with authors were not always tactful and tolerant. He was of too forthright and sincere a nature not to irritate the sensitive writer whom he had to prod or guide editorially. This attitude at times became painfully acute in his relations with William James.

In the 1870s, influenced by the high quality of Appleton's International Scientific Series, Holt conceived the idea of bringing out a high-level series of books by American scientists. Scholars on both sides of the Atlantic were seething with the excitement of scientific experimentation and religious controversy. The theory of evolution was fought over with almost fanatical rancor. Holt, a disciple of Herbert Spencer, proceeded to launch the American Science Series, in which he included books by the most eminent American scholars on subjects dealing with the latest scientific theories and developments.

One of the books he wished to include in the series was a study of psychology, in 1878 still a new and nebulous discipline. His first choice was John Fiske, a close friend and the leading Spencerian in the United States. Fiske, however, was at the time too committed to assume a new project and suggested William James as the likeliest scholar to write such a book. Holt lost no time in approaching him. The response was prompt and favorable: "Nothing would please me better than to do the Psychology for your series of American Science books. Your proposal merely gives definiteness to an intention which I have long harbored in my mind but should probably have still longer postponed without this spur." He made clear, however, that his other engagements and his uncertain health would keep him from completing the manuscript before the fall of 1880.

Holt replied he was "a little staggered by the length of time which you think it would take to write the Psychology . . . but because I know to my cost that what is generally taught at our higher institutions as 'Mental Science' or 'Metaphysics' is a good deal worse than nothing at all," he would acquiesce in the delay and was sending him a contract on the same terms as those for the other books in the series.

Five months later James, now married and all the more concerned about his commitments, informed Holt that he doubted he could complete the manuscript at the stipulated time. Holt expressed his disappointment but added, "my *impulse* is to draw on faith and hope, and wait for yours."

James persisted in what he soon perceived to be a Herculian undertaking despite the most painful agonies of authorship. Neurasthenic, subject to psychosomatic illness, exceptionally conscientious, eager to produce a work of high merit in a discipline that was still inchoate and sciolistic, he struggled with the very expression of new ideas and concepts until they emerged from his pen with crystal clarity. But the effort was tremendous and time-consuming.

Shortly after he began to work on the book he still felt relatively optimistic. In 1879 he wrote to his Harvard colleague Josiah Royce: "I am writing (very slowly) what may become a textbook in psychology." Four years later, having made little progress, he complained to his French friend, M. Renouvier, that he now understood "why no really good classic manual in psychology exists. . . . It is impossible to write one at present, so infinitely more numerous are the difficulties of the task than the means of their solution. Every chapter bristles with obstructions that refer one to the next ten years of work for their investigation." To his brother Henry he wrote about the same time: "I have made a start with my psychology which I shall work at, temperately, through the vacation and hope to get finished a year from next fall, *sans faute.*" After another three years, in 1887, he still hoped to "have the book finished a year from now. . . . The truth is, that the 'science' is in such a confused and imperfect state that every paragraph presents some unforeseen snag, and I often spend many weeks on a point that I didn't foresee the difficulty at all." Even when he saw the end in plain view, he still grumbled to Henry: "I have to forge every sentence in the teeth of irreducible and stubborn facts. It is like walking through the densest brushwood."

All through the 1880s sporadic letters from Holt and responses from James concerned the latter's throes of authorship and the publisher's sympathetic patience. In the process, dealing with other matters of mutual interest as well, their friendship quickly ripened. In April 1887 Holt gladly accepted James's offer of intimacy: "Certainly: 'Drop the Mister' and I'll drop the Prof. We've made one or two spasmodic attempts in the direction before, I believe, but, much to my regret, circumstances made our intercourse too spasmodic throughout." Two years later Holt reminded him that the contract made him the negotiator for the English edition but that he would be glad to let him choose his own publisher if he were so minded, but James assured him he would rely on him to select the publisher. That November Holt inquired about James's health, his new house, and then added facetiously, "All these things call up a vague, though possibly mistaken, impression that you once had some idea of sending me the manuscript of a *Psychology* to publish. If you remember anything of the kind, please let me know how the matter stands."

With the end of his twelve-year task at hand, James became anxious to get the book to press. In January 1890 he informed Holt that he would soon bring 350 pages for the printer—that he was eager to see them in type. Holt's discouraging response was that he would be pleased to see the material, "but don't bring me anything to start making the book before you bring me the Ms. complete. When you do that latter, we'll try to dispose all the orbs in the system to make the world roll smoothly." James's reaction to this forthright, practical statement was a characteristic explosion:

> Publishers are demons, there is no doubt about it. How silly it is to fly in the face of the accumulated wisdom of mankind, and think just because one of them appears genial socially that the great natural law is broken and that he is also a human being in his professional capacity. Fie upon such weakness.

Holt, realizing that he had been too brusque in his refusal to set type on only part of the manuscript, now tried to explain:

> If you were gradually being converted into a demon, however, by the disappoint-ments occasioned by authors, you would know all about it. I *never* began printing an installment of a Ms., so far as I can remember, without having to stop work be-fore the book was finished, thus forcing the printer to put away the apparatus in place for it, and giving him excuses (which they always avail themselves of to the full) for dilly-dallying with the rest of the work when it came, and eventually get-ting the work out later and after vastly more friction than would have been the case if it had not been begun till the Ms. was all ready.

James responded to this unvarnished explanation with caustic irony:

> Poor publisher, poor fellow, poor human being, ex-demon! How those vermin of authors must have caused you to suffer in your time to wring from you such a ti-rade! Well, it has been very instructive to me to grasp the publisher's point of view. Your fatal error however has been in not perceiving that I am an entirely *different kind* of author from any of those you had been in the habit of meeting, and that *celerity*, celerity incarnate, is the motive and result of all my plans and deeds.

With the manuscript ten years overdue and not yet ready, James's use of "celerity" aroused Holt's sarcasm and he stressed the irony of the word in this instance. His fondness for James, however, caused him to add: "but your sins, which are many, are forgiven, as you know. . . . And now you have the blessings necessary to keep you up to your standard of 'celerity,' and a few marginal ones simply as illustration of the affectionate nature of my prayers for you."

James, however, refused to believe that typesetting on his book could not start with a part of the manuscript. Ignoring Holt's reason for not doing so, he again wrote him:

> I don't see why you shouldn't be beginning already to decide on the page. The Ms., to my great regret, is panning out bigger than I thought it would. I fear there will be no less than about 460,000 words, which would require 575 words on a page to make a book of 800 pp. I can't possibly cut this thing down, as it all belongs to-gether; and I trust this bulk will not unfit it for the "Series."

Since Holt could not decide on the size of the page and the length of the book until he knew definitely the number of words it had—he subsequently had to extend the work to two volumes—he remained unmoved by James's exhortations.

What has destroyed your confidence in me? I've told you twice and given you long strings of reasons based on an experience hundreds of times as large as you can possibly have in such matters, that I am not going to set any of that book until I have it all. You may think that if I were to turn tail and do it, you would still have some faith in me, but you wouldn't, and I wouldn't have any in myself.

Inwardly annoyed by Holt's presumed stubbornness, James nevertheless exerted himself to complete the manuscript and delivered it early in May 1890. Two weeks later he wrote that he felt "no further responsibility whatever about having the thing published in October," and asked that the proofs be sent to him during the summer months. Some weeks later, overcome by a feeling of self-abnegation as he examined the proofs, he acknowledged to Holt:

No one could be more disgusted than I at the sight of the book. *No* subject is worth being treated of in 1000 pages! Had I ten years more, I could rewrite in 500; but as it stands it is this or nothing—a loathsome, distended, tumified, bloated dropsical mass, testifying to nothing but two facts: 1st, that there is not such a thing as a science of psychology, and 2nd that W J is an incapable.

Holt had ordered the printer to set type with all possible speed. About the time the proofs began to reach James he wrote to his brother: "I take little pride or pleasure in the accursed book, which has clung to me so long, but I shall be glad to have it out, just to show that I *can* write a book." All summer he sweated over the proofs, but all went well and the two-volume work was ready in October as he had wished.

The book was universally acclaimed as a stellar American contribution to the new science of psychology. It was, however, too long and too costly for wide class use. At Holt's urging James prepared a briefer edition, with nearly half of it new material, and it soon became known as "Jimmy" to "James" for the larger work. In his usual self-deprecatory manner he belittled its worth—terming it a work bereft of "all humor and pathos, all interest." Then he added ironically, "The larger work seems a decided success—especially from a literary point of view. I begin to look down on Mark Twain!"

At James's request Holt sent him an accounting of sales. He also informed him that although the contract stipulated a payment of $14^3/_{10}$ cents per set of sheets sold to England, he considered this amount inadequate and was increasing it to $33^1/_3$ cents, "which I trust will be satisfactory to your temporal and spiritual welfare."

The two were, despite their recent troubled and caustic correspondence, close personal friends. They shared a common interest in psychic research and frequently exchanged views on life and philosophy. Although Holt was more the publisher with James than he was with Henry Adams and other men of national distinction, he preferred to be a friend bound by mutual intellectual and social interests.

When he asked James for a photograph to be used in the promotion material on his books, the latter balked with characteristic playfulness: "I stand on my rights as a free man. You may kill me, but you shan't publish my photograph. Put a blank 'thumbnail' in its place. Very very sorry to displease a man I love so much."

This profession of love notwithstanding, he could not quite forget Holt's forthright sharpness in their correspondence. It is not at all unlikely that Mrs. James, under the impression that Holt was not paying her husband a high enough royalty, had fanned this passing irritation into active resentment. This emerged passively in September 1895, when Holt asked if he had another manuscript ready. "Haven't you got another book to put to press or can't you make one ready? I'm not the only person in the country that thinks that anything you have to say is sure to be worth saying." James made no response to this inquiry until the following June. He then told him he had a volume of essays ready for publication and added coyly that a Scribner representative had also asked him for a book. "I don't suppose there is any money in such a volume," he continued, "but I told him I would send him the Ms. and then get a bid from you, and give it to the highest! Isn't that good business? . . . Wealth is now my only ideal."

Very sensitive about author loyalty and hurt by James's seeming dereliction, yet wishing to appear nonchalant about it, Holt wrote him at length—he later regretted not to have gone to Cambridge for a personal talk—first assuring him he was writing in "an amiable and friendly spirit."

> You ask me, after laying down your auction scheme, "isn't that good business?" No, my dear boy, it is not. It's very bad business. The "good business" point of view for both author and publisher, is this: When an author is identified with a house, every new book of his gives the publisher a new chance to boom his old ones. If his books are scattered all over creation, he loses this benefit, and it is too important a one to lose. . . . Most publishers, like other men, are fools; and you authors, if you escape the fools, may be but lambs before the wolf. So your only safety is to find as nearly a regenerate and merciful wolf as you can, and then stick to him and let him take care of you.

He further stated that Scribner and Longmans, who had also asked for the manuscript, were upright publishers and would do well by him—"assuming of course that they have had as much of a chance to learn how to love you as I have"—but they were not likely to go into auctions "to get authors away from their colleagues." As far as he was concerned, he would like to say: "There's occasionally a publisher with an ambition (a perfectly vain one perhaps) to conduct his business like a gentleman, and to receive—even perhaps by deserving—the confidence of his clients that he will do by them as well as a reasonable and honest conduct of business permits." This was his position, he added, although he was no longer as quixotic as he was in 1879 when he refused to take on James's brother Henry as an author because he "didn't want to take away Osgood's client." As for James's new writings, he could only say: "If you want to know what I would naturally do with you on these new books you speak of, I will tell you with pleasure after I have seen the copy; but I shall not on account of your auction scheme, do anything different from what I would do anyhow."

James, unaware of the "courtesy" practice among respectable publishers, could not help resenting Holt's patronizing "ideal of father and son relationship." He saw no merit in being bound to one publisher and failed to appreciate this practice of monopoly. As a matter of fact, he pointed out to Holt,

> Appleton, Scribner, and Longmans have all spontaneously solicited me for "copy" with no reference made to you. . . . Your veto of the auction business has aroused in me all the freeman-blood of my ancestors, and makes it now quite impossible to publish the book with you, when before it was not only possible, but probable.

Yet he ended the letter with the avowal that "as *men*, we shall love each other far more after this exchange of letters than we ever did before."

When, soon after, he learned that Holt had communicated with Scribner about the matter, he became very upset and accused Holt of, in effect, forbidding "the Scribners to continue negotiating with me, and in principle confined me to the alternative of either ignoring your existence as a publisher and immediately resorting to some third house, or of passively giving you the book to deal with as you pleased." Would it not be fair, he asked, "to notify Scribners that the boycott had been lifted?"

Holt's sensitiveness was making him edgy: he became impatient with James for questioning his ethics. "I happen to know," he replied with forced restraint, "that my effect on Scribner was precisely as imaginary as you have thought it possible to be; and that his course of conduct, as carried out, was clearly decided before he had exchanged a word with me on the subject." He reiterated his position regarding the manuscript, and ended by assuring him placatingly: "well, even if you quarrel with me on such grounds as I've quoted, you do it in such a lovely way that you still keep me, affectionately yours."

Five months later James informed him that he decided to give the book, *The Will to Believe*, to neither him nor Scribner; and having failed with Houghton Mifflin, he gave it to Longmans. "As I have said before," he continued blandly, "I don't harbor a particle of resentment, and when I have got ready a manuscript on *Talks to Teachers on Psychology* which I expect to do next summer, I will offer the same to you."

Despite the distrust and resentment impairing their friendship, their relations remained outwardly cordial. They corresponded about the promotion of "James" and "Jimmy"; Holt consulted James on John Dewey's ability to write an original work on ethics, and was assured that Dewey could; James also veered him away from Havelock Ellis's *Sexual Inversion*.

In November 1898 James sent Holt the manuscript of *Talks to Teachers on Psychology and to Students on Some of Life's Ideals*. "What I wish," he wrote, "is that you would kindly look over the manuscript to gain some idea of its value, and then if you wish it, name the most favorable contract with me which you are willing to accord." Two weeks later, having heard favorably from Holt, he wrote again:

> I have decided that I had better manufacture the book myself and publish it on commission. Will you take it thus, full advertising it in your routine ways, and taking 10% of the list price for handling? If you will, you may have the work, as I had rather you should publish it than another.

Although this procedure was common nearly a century ago and still practiced in isolated cases, it was no longer acceptable to established publishers. The proud Holt was at first nonplussed by the proposal: he felt that James questioned his integrity as a publisher—apart from the fact that the likely result would be a poorly made book. On reflection, however, he decided to acquiesce in the proposal out of friendship for James: "Have it all your way; but for God's sake, don't get stuck; for if you do, all sorts of devils—incarnate and excarnate—will whisper to you that it was because your publishers ran no risk of failure, and had small temptations to success, and therefore neglected the book." Yet he assured him that he would "treat the book as our own" and promote it vigorously. "You may be edified to know," he added, "that your book will be the only one (so far as I can recall) that we have on commission."

Holt, on several occasions, did his best to clarify the details of marketing *Talks*, an educational book not suited for use as a class text; he also explained the necessary discounts to booksellers and the difference between net and retail prices. Unaccustomed to these details of the business, James was only confused by them, which made him uneasy and caused him to complain:

> Your epistolar manners are so rough that unless I had had already some acquaintance with them, I would have supposed that your effusion of the first was meant as a notification that you didn't care for the book. . . . This last letter of yours reminds me of certain other letters I got during the *Psychology* time—well and humorously meant no doubt, but *rough!*—and I tremble at the prospect of their continuance.

Holt hastened to assure him he had never meant to be rough with him. "I never intended to say anything sarcastic in a letter unless I want to quarrel with a man, and I never wanted to quarrel with you. Hence if you saw anything sarcastic in any of mine, it was not there." James, quick to feel hurt and resentful, yet generous of spirit, was readily assuaged:

> Since you are now so sweet again let me say that the roughness in the past of which the memory haunts me was solely in the *Psychology* days, when you playfully danced clog dances on my sensibilities. . . . Dear Holt let us both be old enough to practice in accordance with the experience of mankind, and not conduct business correspondence in sarcastic terms.

> Whereupon let us be friends again—until the next encounter.

As Holt had feared, the appearance of *Talks* displeased both him and James, since the printer had no designer to plan the attractiveness of the page and binding. Moreover, the printer had made an inferior set of plates, handicapping the book for possible adoption by reading circles in several middle western states. James admitted to Holt that it was "the worst printed book" he had seen at the printer's and ordered a new set of plates; he added that he was now ready to "leave the whole matter of size and price absolutely in your hands. You know more about it than I do." Yet he soon complained he was not receiving his full share of the income from state adoptions. Holt, sensing suspicion on James's part and feeling hurt by it, explained the customary procedure in these adoptions and assured him he was getting his full share. Then he added wistfully concerning his position as publisher:

I have come to the conclusion that when I declined to bid on that book of yours, my head was swelled—I entertained an optimistic view of the publishing business which the more sober judgment of my declining years does not justify. I had come to regard it as a "profession," in which it was undignified to bid for work or seek to get it away from a competitor; and I had myself lived up to this standard—with the result (among others) I verily believe, of losing a great deal of business to concerns whose views were not as top-lofty as mine. I have come to realize, largely through the help of such concerns, that the "profession" idea does not hold water.

An explosive incident in 1901 again played havoc with their friendly relationship. The Holt firm had ordered a shipment of *Talks* sent to its Chicago office. The printer complied and received a signed acknowledgment. But a clerk in the New York office neglected to enter the shipment in the receiving book, and the letter-invoice went in error to the correspondence file, so that the James account was not credited with the order. When James received the bill from the printer without later getting his share of the income from the order, he impulsively suspected fraud and wrote to Holt accordingly. The latter being in his summer home in Vermont, his associate in the office expressed shock at the oversight and offered the firm's humble apologies:

> Such errors could not occur with books we manufacture, as we have a long-tried system of treble checks against them. In the case of *Talks* we have been without such checks, you having the only means of comparing your printer's and binder's bills with your reports of books received and accounted for.

A revised account was enclosed together with a check which included interest on the unpaid amount. A copy of the interchange was forwarded to Holt, who wrote immediately to express his "surprise and disgust" that anything of the kind should have happened in his firm. Also explaining how the oversight occurred, he added with assurance: "Fortunately the blunder is too absurd to make it possible that any thought of intention should have crossed a reasonable mind." But at that time he was not dealing with a reasonable mind: far from allaying James's suspicion, his letter only excited James's fertile and frenetic imagination. His impulsive reply was an outburst of sheer choler:

> You make the whole business a more perfect abyss of unintelligibility than before, by repeating what I can only call the utterly *silly* explanation of the letter which accompanied the check.

> The plain and flagrant fact is that in your last two ½ yearly accounts the *sales were falsified* to correspond to a false number of copies received. The error was systematic. You may in explanation "change the receipt signing clerk" (*all* the receipts are by the same hand) and "no counter-check whatever," as if your own orders to printer, his letters of invoice, and your own sales-books didn't exist. When you add that such an "experience was probably bound to come sooner or later," to what sort of bookkeeping methods do you confess!!

> Am I a baby six years old that you should write me such rubbish? The only impression such irrelevant explanations can *possibly* arouse is that the firm is nervously

concerned to conceal something, and thinks that for a man of my lack of business experience that kind of thing will do as a sop.

Now, my dear Holt, stand up and tell the whole truth. What, until this last correspondence was only a puzzle, has been converted *by your letters* in a grave suspicion of dealings which will not bear the light. It is up to you to dispel the suspicions by something more than what you write.

Confident that you can do so if you will, I remain faithfully yours.

The damning accusation wounded Holt's ego to its utmost depth: that a man of James's stature, long his close friend, should accuse him of fraud and sharp practice! Yet his extensive reply was masterful in its restraint. After giving James a simple detailed account of his method of bookkeeping, he offered to have him come to New York at the firm's expense and examine the books for himself. As for his accusation, his letter was "the most inconsistent human document I ever saw. It seemed to say, 'My dear Holt, I have confidence enough in your honor to believe that you will confess yourself a damned rascal'.... I think it does you and me a grave injustice."

James's response was mildly apologetic:

My last letter to you at Burlington was based on a misconception by which you have rightly explained to yourself its excessively "strenuous" tone. My own unaided genius enabled me to escape from the misconception a couple of hours after I had mailed my letter, but I thought I would await your reply before I sent a postscript. . . .

Well! the atmosphere is cleared, and I am glad of it!. . . .

Believe me, yours, as ever, W. J.

The nonchalant tone of the letter, in view of the damning accusation in the previous one, again "nonplussed" Holt and left him in a bitter mood. Referring again to the inadvertent error, he proceeded to analyze James's outburst with the acid of repressed reproach:

If, before sending you a semi-annual settlement, we had sent you or Ellis [the printer] for a semi-annual statement, the errors would have been found, and the settlement would have been correct, you would not have imagined sales doctored to conceal stealages, and would have entertained no suspicions that I was trying to take advantage of your inexperience in business to cover up something that would not bear the light, and would not have exhorted me to "stand up and tell the whole truth." Your thinking any of these things when you had our receipts in your hands, is a failure of your intelligence that perplexes me, but what perplexes me even more is that, having acknowledged your suspicions to a man with whom you have exchanged salt, and whose reputation, so far as I know, has stood without blemish during a business career of nearly forty years you should, in yours of the 3rd, content yourself, after finding yourself mistaken, with merely calling your remarks "strenuous," expressing satisfaction that "the atmosphere is cleared," and signing the assurance that you are his "as ever."

James's reply was a rueful reflection on his impulsive condemnation of a circumstance unwarranted by the facts as he now saw them:

The whole thing is simple to me now, but so long as I conceived of the return of sales being based only on positive entries of all sales made, it threw me into a greater perplexity than I ever remember being thrown into before. If I had only waited a couple of hours before writing that letter on which you animadvert so gracefully in your last, or if you and the firm had only been at the outset as explicit as you afterward became about your usual method of bookkeeping, that letter would certainly never have been written, nor would I now have to apologize for it, as I hereby do. I always explode too abruptly, and I certainly did so in this case. Your tone with me on the contrary has been exemplary, and I only pray you to forgive and forget, yours repentantly.

Holt accepted the apology gracefully. "It's all right and you make it right so manfully that one can hardly regret the occasion. 'Yours as ever' and, I suspect, a little more so."

That Christmas James sent him this greeting: "Let us all thank Heaven that the nightmare episode is over. I am only sorry that it doesn't appear that I have to disgorge anything." Holt's response several days later: "Wishing you a Happy New Year, where publishers shall not vex nor moths break in and steal." James again, by return mail: " 'Rest perturbed spirit!' and pardon a mind 'perplexed in the extreme' for stirring up so much trouble for you. I feel ashamed of the inordinate extension of my business enterprise!"

Thus ended the close yet agitated relationship. The friendship persisted, at least formally; yet James did not offer Holt another book, nor is there any indication that the latter had asked for one.

A coda to this extraordinary relationship came about a year after James's death. A Holt representative having called on Professor Leigh R. Gregor, James's brother-in-law, to tell him about the firm's new books, reported that Mrs. James continued to believe that the company had treated her late husband unfairly. Still acutely sensitive on this point, Holt sent Professor Gregor copies of the entire correspondence between himself and James. In the accompanying letter he asserted that Mrs. James, "who is said never to change her mind, made up her mind that I had treated Professor James unfairly, from a set of circumstances which I am now also under the necessity of explaining to you, and has never changed it." He asserted that, contrary to Mrs. James's assumption, the contractual terms for *Psychology* were "substantially the same as with all the eminent men who contributed to the same Series"; that the royalty on the book had in fact been voluntarily increased. And he concluded: "If the misconceptions of all this miserable business under which you have labored, has been conveyed by you to anybody else, is it too much to ask that you now convey the explanation?"

Still later, when James's son Henry was preparing his father's *Collected Letters*, Holt sent him the originals of those in the firm's files and told him the dispute regarding *Talks* was "the unhappiest episode in my business career (not to consider my personal relations)." Henry acknowledged the receipt of the letters with thanks and added:

May I therefore seize the occasion to tell you how pleased my own relations with your firm have been since father's death, and to say that in going over the accounts and sales figures as I have had to do during the last few years I have been very sensible of the interest and skill that have been devoted to the circulation of my father's books. Long before his death he had dismissed the matter that you refer to as the unfortunate result of unintentional error and misunderstanding.

For quite understandable reasons none of the letters referring to the *Talks* episode were included in the *Collected Letters*. Nor did Professor Ralph Barton Perry make mention of them in his comprehensive two-volume biography of William James.

11.

Holt Co.

& Robert Frost

Robert Frost's dealings with Henry Holt & Company exemplify an author–publisher relationship quite different from any treated in this book. Although he remained with the firm for nearly a half century, he was on several occasions eager to leave it—and did not do so only because he wanted all his writings under one imprint and Holt executives would not release the volumes on their list. Also, despite his low opinion of the firm, and the frequent changes of personnel, he liked the men who dealt with him and recognized that he benefited greatly from their devotion and generosity.

Frost was a complex personality, at once high-minded and vindictive, outwardly modest yet deeply jealous of potential rivals; and, avid for recognition and adulation, he was both generous and selfish, philosophical and gossipy.

He was born in San Francisco of New England parents. Only ten when his father died, he was never able to forget the harsh beatings of his early years. His mother returned to Lawrence, Massachusetts, and Frost went to school there until graduation from high school. In his senior year he fell in love with Elinor White; although at first cool to him, causing him much grief, she later agreed to marry him.

Restless and uncertain of what he wished to do, he entered Dartmouth College, and later Harvard University, but left each not long after. He then worked at odd jobs; later he taught school and farmed. He had early begun to write verse, some of which was published in local newspapers. But for years he submitted poems to established magazines only to feel humiliated by rejections.

In 1912, in his late thirties and father of four children, he decided to sell his farm, bought with money given to him by his grandfather, and went to England in the belief that he could live there cheaply and devote himself to writing. Later that year he submitted the manuscript of *A Boy's Will* to the small publishing firm of David Nutt & Company. It was accepted and published in 1913. The following year the firm published his *North of Boston*. Both books were favorably reviewed in English periodicals, and Ezra Pound praised his work in *Poetry*, published in Chicago. Edward Thomas, the English poet who later became Frost's close friend, wrote of *A Boy's Will*: "These poems are revolutionary because they lack the exaggeration of rhetoric. Many, if not most, of the separate lines and separate sentences are plain and in themselves nothing. But they are bound together and made elements of beauty by a calm eagerness of emotion."

Mrs. Henry Holt, who wrote verses herself and who followed current trends in poetry, came upon a copy of *North of Boston* in the summer of 1914 and was so impressed with its authentic freshness that she highly recommended it to her husband. She also wrote to Frost in England to express her enthusiasm for his work. Simultaneously Amy Lowell, who had also read and liked the volume, urged Houghton Mifflin and Macmillan to bring out an American edition. While these two firms were not interested, Henry Holt, respecting his wife's judgment, recommended the volume to his office staff. His son Roland thereupon wrote Mrs. Nutt in England:

> Mrs. Henry Holt, who is very enthusiastic over Robert Frost's *North of Boston*, has very kindly loaned us her copy. The two readers we had look at these poems found them uncommonly interesting and, while we cannot see a paying market here for this particular volume, still we are so interested in this author's work that if you have some later book of his for which you would care to offer us the American rights, we would be most happy to consider it.

Ten days later Alfred Harcourt, head of the Holt trade department, also wrote to Mrs. Nutt:

> Following our letter of Sept. 2 and in regard to Frost's *North of Boston* we are inclined on further consideration to take a small edition of this book, say 150 copies in sheets, if it has not already been placed in the American market, and if you can supply them at a reasonable price. Of course, while we admire this book, it would not, we fear, be worth our while to take it up unless you could assure us that we can have the refusal of the American market on the author's next book.

Nutt replied to the first letter on September 12: "We could not offer you rights on his new book if you do not push the present volume to some extent." Feeling that Americans should in some manner assist England in the war recently started by Germany, she added: "We consider that under present political circumstances American publishers ought to show some willingness to help English publishers who have had sufficient daring and intelligence to recognize the talent of one of their own countrymen."

Apprised of Holt's interest in his book, Frost wrote to his young friend Sidney Cox on January 1, 1915: "This is only to say that Henry Holt will supply the book in America."

With the war making conditions for Frost more difficult, he was planning to return to the United States and was naturally concerned about the safety of the Atlantic crossing. In the same letter to Cox he stated: "If you never hear from me again, write Henry Holt & Co. Publishers, New York."

Nutt sent 150 sets of sheets as requested, and Holt published the book on February 20, 1915. Two days later Frost and his family reached New York. By chance he bought a copy of the recently founded *New Republic* and found in it not only one of his major poems but a very favorable review of *North of Boston* by Amy Lowell. He also visited the Holt office and was told by Harcourt that the Boston booksellers had bought most of the 150 copies and that he had ordered 200 additional sheets. He also handed him the sizable check from the *New Republic*—which was to him a godsend, as he was almost penniless. A few days later, pleased with Harcourt's friendliness, he wrote to Cox: "You know that Holt's have my book out. Pretty cover. But the best of Holt's is that they are going to be a father to me."

When Nutt was slow in replying to Harcourt's request for more sheets, he informed Frost that if the sheets did not show up soon he planned to print the book in this country and take his chances on straightening things out with Nutt, the book having lost its American copyright. Frost was entirely agreeable, and wrote on March 15 that it "might be better to bring out a small American edition than run the risk of losing a market by wasting time over such a haggler as Mrs. Nutt."

By this time Harcourt perceived Frost's potential popularity and was eager to make the most of it. Unaware that Amy Lowell had submitted *North of Boston* to two American publishers, he told Frost that he wanted to publicize the fact that the book was first published in England simply because Frost happened to be living there at the time and that the poems had not previously been submitted to an American publisher. On hearing from Frost ten days later, Harcourt informed Henry Holt, then in Vermont: "I enclose a letter from Robert Frost which Mrs. Holt will like to see. From the attention Frost was receiving it looks as if we should thank her for the most distinctive addition to our list this year." Two months later he told Holt's secretary that Frost had visited him at home. "He has more quality and a more lovable personality than anybody I've come at all close to for some time, and his character and brains have deepened my faith in his poetry. He's a 'real feller'—no mere poet!"

Harcourt had arranged for two prominent literary Bostonians to see Frost when he reached that city on his way to New Hampshire. The poet was on his best behavior in his talks with these and others in Boston who he thought would help his reputation. He telephoned Amy Lowell to thank her for the favorable review, and accepted her invitation to dine with her. He also visited Ellery Sedgwick, editor of *The Atlantic Monthly*, and enjoyed the irony of his warm reception and the eager acceptance of poems—this prestigious monthly having previously rejected his offerings. He continued to be polite to his new admirers, and controlled his vengefulness toward those who were critical of him or who had previously ignored him. To John Bartlett, a former student who had become his friend, he wrote: "Christ forgive me the sin of vengefulness: from this hour forth I will have no more of it. Perhaps I only say so because for the moment I am sated."

Meanwhile Harcourt was finding Nutt unreasonable in her insistence on keeping Frost's adherence to the terms of his contract with her—asserting that he submit his next book to her alone. When she refused any arrangement with the Holt firm for the American rights to Frost's work, Harcourt consulted with the company lawyers to see if the contract could be declared invalid. Frost on his part wrote Harcourt: "You may believe I am anxious to hear of any hope of being wrested from Mrs. Nutt. It seems to me that if I am to remain the lady's for life there will be no more poetry. What would be the use of writing just to be cheated out of royalties by her?" For he had at no time received any royalties or an accounting of sales.

The Holt lawyers informed Harcourt that since Frost had carried out the provisions of the contract but Nutt had not, he could either demand an accounting and royalties or declare the contract void. At their suggestion Frost wrote her to this effect. Not hearing from her for several months, he stated to her in April 1916: "You are hereby notified that all my obligations under my contract with you dated December 16, 1912, and also all your rights thereunder are at an end"—the wording having been supplied by the lawyers. In a postscript he added: "I don't like writing this sort of letter. Won't you return my contract and I'll waive my claims for royalties on copies you've sold? Perhaps I'd even let you sell, free of royalty, the stock you now have on hand if you will tell me what it is namely the sheets and bound [copies] separately." When Nutt refused to release him, her letter, at the advice of the Holt lawyers, went unanswered. She threatened suit, and matters dragged until her firm went bankrupt.

During these months of uncertainty Frost was in financial distress, having no income except from the occasional acceptance of a poem. When Harcourt telegraphed him in August 1915 to come to New York for consultation, Frost told him frankly that he had not "the money in hand to pay my fare to New York." Then, after a reference to Nutt, he continued:

> I mustn't go into harrowing details, but I really have reached a pass where I must earn a little or perish. I trust you see no reasons legal; moral or ethical why I should not accept that part in the success of the book that you wanted me to have. Let me speak frankly. At the moment when I have so much to be glad of in the general approval of my book, I am actually nearer worrying about money than I have had to be for a number of years.

Harcourt sent him a check for $200 by return mail and stated:

> We are going to take our chances on Mrs. Nutt, and pay you what would amount to a royalty of 10% on our sales of *North of Boston* and *A Boy's Will* in our own reprint. We expect to continue this honorarium unless we should be stopped. . . . Don't worry. You're going to be able to publish poetry and get your just dues. We'll go into all that when you come down. Of your troubles that I've heard, hay fever is the worst.

After visiting Harcourt as his houseguest, he wrote Louis Untermeyer, with whom he was establishing what was to be a lifelong friendship, that "Harcourt is the best ever," and that he was delighted to learn that he too was becoming a Holt author.

Frost's reputation during this period was becoming firmly established. Quality magazines were requesting his poems, and many persons were telling him how much they admired his books. *The Atlantic Monthly* published an enthusiastic essay on his first two books by Edward Garnett, the prominent English critic. In February 1916 Dorothy Canfield Fisher, having met the Frosts, wrote Harcourt: "I heaved a long, satisfied sigh of pleasure to know that Mrs. Frost is as fine as her husband . . . though I'd known it ever since I saw him. He looks like a man whose wife is as fine as he . . . that's one of the ways he looks. . . . And isn't it simply glorious about 6000 copies of *North of Boston* and still going!" The following year another Holt author, Carl Sandburg, wrote Harcourt: "Met Frost; about the strongest, loneliest, friendliest personality among the poets today; I'm going to write him once a year; and feel the love of him every day."

Early in 1916, when Harcourt urged him to prepare another volume for publication, Frost hesitated—"with Mrs. Nutt hanging over me the way she undeniably is." Fearing that it would cost him a good deal of money before he was free of her, he added: "I confess I rather hate the prospect of having to divide all I am ever likely to earn by writing between her and the lawyers. It would put me all out of sorts—quite fundamentally out of sorts." Yet he urged Harcourt to visit him about it; knowing he had the book to publish and eager to do it under the best obtainable terms: "I would like it if our differences touching the next book would resolve into a sort of pow-wow or battle of wits like a horse trade in which time is no object and in which the decision goes to the best talker." At the end of the pow-wow Frost agreed to let the firm publish *Mountain Interval* that November.

The volume was well received. Overly sensitive to unfavorable criticism, however, Frost resented the least intimation of a flaw in his poems. When some unflattering literary gossip reached him, he wrote Harcourt that E. J. H. O'Brien, the anthologist, "turned up again with the base insinuation that people like what I write because of the reputation you have made for me. I don't like the business but I don't want to antagonize anyone whose friendship won't hurt us. Am I too hard on O'Brien?" And he admitted: "I get to railing and I can rail myself into damning my best friends to Hell."

Frost's financial condition remained precarious. The sale of his books was relatively small, and he was earning little from individual poems. In December 1916 President Meiklejohn of Amherst College sent Stark Young to Frost's home in Franconia to offer him a teaching position for the second semester with a full professor's salary of $2,000. Although he was not eager to give his time to teaching, and although he had earlier taken a strong dislike to Young, he decided to accept the offer. Harcourt had also come to his assistance by arranging for a monthly retainer of one hundred dollars as an occasional adviser on manuscripts—a gratuity which stopped only after Frost went to the University of Michigan in 1921 as a Fellow in the Creative Arts at a salary of $5,000 a year.

Frost never quite forgot his wife Elinor's early coolness toward him. Although he truly loved her and greatly depended on her in his writing, he reacted to Amy Lowell's praise of her with an impulsive expression of his unwarranted resentment in a letter to Untermeyer on November 7, 1917:

> I really like least her mistake about Elinor. That's an unpardonable attempt to do her as the conventional helpmeet of genius. Elinor has never been of any earthly use

to me. She hasn't cared whether I went to school or worked or earned anything. She has resisted every inch of the way my efforts to get money. She is not too sure that she cares about my reputation. She wouldn't lift a hand or have me lift a hand to increase my reputation or even to save it.

In 1919 Robert Frost made his first effort to leave Holt. In that year Alfred Harcourt and Donald Brace, major executives of the firm, formed their own publishing company. As head of the trade department, Harcourt had close contacts with Holt's trade authors and little difficulty in taking the best of them with him, among them Carl Sandburg, Walter Lippmann, Joel Spingarn, Louis Untermeyer, and Dorothy Canfield Fisher. He had also invited Frost, and the response was unequivocal.

> There is only one answer possible to your question. I am under obligation to Henry Holt & Co. for endless favors. But so far as I am concerned you are Henry Holt & Co. You are all the Henry Holt & Co. I have known and dealt with. Where you go I naturally go. I am with you with all my heart.
>
> I promise to do all I can to make you a great publisher even as I expect you to do all you can to make me a great author. Always yours.

On July 4 Frost again wrote a letter of encouragement and wished he himself were part of the new company. "I shall hope to have a book on one of the earliest lists of the new firm. But we *will* try to have my affairs straightened out so that I won't have Mrs. Nutt hanging over me, however shadowly when I next publish, won't we?"

In the light of these letters it might seem strange that Frost did not become a Harcourt author. Years later he made clear why he had changed his mind. From the first it was his fixed wish to have all his volumes with one publisher, mainly to assure a complete edition of his poems when that became desirable. On inviting Frost to join the new firm, Harcourt assured him that he would arrange to take over the volumes under the Holt imprint. When Frost visited him in the fall and asked if his books were already released, Harcourt told him the transfer had been made. On being asked to see the correspondence, Harcourt pretended to look for the letters; unable to produce them, he invited Frost to lunch with the statement that his secretary would look for them in the meantime. When no such letters appeared on their return, Frost became suspicious and decided to remain with Holt. In January 1920 he explained his position facetiously to Sidney Cox:

> At the time you wrote me about your proposed book I was hanging as it were between two publishers and not in a position to do anything for you with either. Harcourt my friend had quarreled with my friend Henry Holt. . . . It looks now as if I would belong to Henry Holt because he refuses to surrender me to Alfred Harcourt, on demand and representation. I'm like the lady who didn't care much either way so long as it was settled one way or the other.

What sweetened the situation for Frost was that Harcourt's place at Holt was taken by Lincoln MacVeagh, a young man of classical interests and pleasing personality. He soon made evident his admiration for Frost's poetry and reassured him of his retainment as consultant at one hundred dollars monthly. Frost readily acknowledged his friendly regard for MacVeagh to Prof. G. R. Elliott of Amherst: "The latest interposition in my favor when I had ceased to deserve further clemency is an appointment as *Consulting Editor of Henry Holt & Co.* I owe this under Heaven to Lincoln MacVeagh." On the same day he also wrote Mac-Veagh: "Not so much what you did as the way you did it convinces me that I have been right all along in looking for a business relationship into which friendship could enter. I like to see the opposite of cynicism in me rewarded. Of course thanks no end."

MacVeagh had Frost read a number of poetry manuscripts and received sound advice. To Ridgely Torrence, Frost wrote: "It is true I am a scout for Henry Holt. How did you penetrate my disguise? Now what I am particularly out for is left handers with something besides speed on the ball." Thus, concerning Glenn Dresbach's poems he suggested that Holt "go slow on him"; much as he disliked to see a good book lost, he thought it had "too much of it to be good," and urged cutting. "That's what we should be here for," he added. "A lot of young writers only come to something by a reduction they make themselves or others make for them." His reaction to Babette Deutsch's *Portraits and Pageants* was more favorable. "She can write. She has more poetic ideas than all the poets in manuscript I have read this year put together. She's a perceptible person."

As much as he liked MacVeagh personally, he became annoyed with him for what he thought a mishandling of his books in England. On April 28, 1920, he complained to Untermeyer:

> I'll tell you what puts me off the game a whole lot. It's the state of my affairs with publishers. MacVeagh spoiled all with Heinemann by making overtures to Mrs. Nutt without consulting him. Heinemann is put out and I am disappointed. My troubles over there aren't ended and my troubles here are pretty well begun. What's the use of writing stuff that I don't know who is to own in England and America. I am going to write a drama after this and let poetry go to hell.

In the early fall of 1921 Frost took up his fellowship at the University of Michigan and resided in Ann Arbor until the following June; he did so again in February 1923 until June; and finally in February 1926. His income from the fellowship, from royalties, from permission fees, which Holt paid him in full, from lectures, and later from his academic connection with Amherst kept him adequately provided for in the years ahead despite his considerable family expenditures.

In 1922 Holt brought out a new and more attractive edition of *North of Boston* and, despite Frost's fears to the contrary, arranged with Heinemann for British editions of Frost's three books. The following spring the firm published *Selected Poems*. MacVeagh's warm tribute to the poems on the jacket elicited the following comment from Elinor Frost—belying Frost's earlier statement about her: "Robert was greatly pleased, and I myself felt it deeply that you should realize how much there is to the poetry that those who have written about it either don't see at all, or touch on very lightly."

Frost's hypersensitivity to criticism caused him to react to less favorable reviews with sharp vengefulness. When Burton Rascoe, a daily reviewer, wrote adversely about his poetry, Frost composed a vituperative response—which he later had the good sense not to mail. Aware of this streak in him, he wrote Bartlett subsequently about his "Indian vindictiveness," adding: "Really I'm awful there. I am worse than you know. I can never seem to forgive people that scare me within an inch of my life."

MacVeagh had for some time been urging him to prepare the manuscript of a new volume of poems. On June 2, 1923, after several postponements, he finally agreed: "I've decided to be good and stop writing any more into the New Hampshire poem. You shall have the manuscript in a week or so now." *New Hampshire* was published in November—with a royalty of 15 percent of list—and became the volume for which Frost was awarded his first Pulitzer Prize.

During this period his friendship with MacVeagh had deepened. After Elinor and he were his house guests in New York during January 1923, Frost wrote him: "Thanks for your kindness. You are the only hold (or should I say holt?) the Holts have on me I sometimes think." When MacVeagh intimated the following November, after *New Hampshire* had been launched successfully, that he was about to leave the firm, Frost replied at once, for the first time addressing him as "Dear Lincoln":

> (If it isn't too late to change my name for you) The only move you would have to seek my approval of before you made it would be getting out and leaving me alone with the heirs of Henry Holt. I'll bet that is what you're contemplating, but if I thought at all seriously, I would come right down to New York to talk you out of it.

When MacVeagh did leave Holt at the end of the year to form The Dial Press, Frost felt homeless within the firm. He had no cause for complaint—the Holt staff favored him in every way possible—but he missed the warm friendship and devotion Harcourt and MacVeagh had extended to him. He did not find the sons of Henry Holt, who were now in charge of the trade department, congenial. In June 1925 he intimated to Untermeyer that he was undecided about remaining with Holt. Referring to his next book of poems, he said, "I can't make up my mind about, whether to throw it to Holt, Harcourt, MacVeagh, or Knopf." When the poems of *West-running Brook* were nearly ready in 1927, he received overtures from several publishers. His friend Fred Melcher told him that Holt was in poor shape and advised him to move to Scribner. Frost then confided his problem to J. R. Wells, a private publisher. After telling him how he had "failed dismally" when he tried to go with Harcourt in 1919, he continued: "I made a bad business of it. The wonder was that I had anybody the least friendly in the firm. The weakness of my position was that I couldn't bear to go to a new publisher and not take my four old books with me. I've got to keep my books together."

The Holt firm was in 1928 undergoing financial reorganization—"going public" to enable the major executives to buy the assets of the Holt estate. In the interim the management agreed that it could not afford to lose Frost. R. H. Thornton, head of the college department, was sent in May to Frost's home in New Hampshire to assure him that the firm would do as well with his new book as any other publisher. Although he was not in the trade division, he was a former college teacher of English and a Southerner, gentle of manner and appreciative of good writing. Frost liked his approach and deferential behavior, yet he believed that he would nevertheless refuse to release his books if he went to another publisher. Aware, however, of his advantageous position, he drove a hard bargain: his royalty was to begin at 15 percent and rise to 20 percent after the sale of 5,000 copies; the book was to be illustrated by J. J. Lankes's woodcuts; there was to be a limited as well as a trade edition; an advance to $2,000 was to be paid on demand; there was to be a collected edition within one or two years; finally, Frost was to receive a monthly stipend of $250 and whatever annual royalties in excess of $3,000 might accrue. The deal was closed when Mrs. Frost, who looked after business matters, decided in Holt's favor. On his return to New York Thornton wrote him: "I am enclosing to you copies of the contract for your new book of lyrics. I need not tell you how happy I am that you are going to publish the volume with us; my visit to you must already have made that evident."

After the Holt firm was reorganized, Thornton informed Frost that he was being given the first stock certificate for ten shares with the compliments of the management. Herschel Brickell, a book reviewer, was engaged as head of the trade department at the end of 1928. Frost liked him well enough, but preferred to deal with Thornton. With *West-running Brook* published successfully, both Frost and the firm began to arrange for the appearance of the *Collected Poems*. The volume was designed with special care, and every effort was made to give the limited edition the most beautiful format of any book published in 1930. As before when he was about to publish a book, Frost was again assailed by doubts and anxiety. To Untermeyer he wrote: "The book of all I ever wrote, when it comes out this fall, ought to do something toward accounting to me for these false years. But I've seen it in proof and it looked like no child of mine. I stared at it unloving. And I wonder what next." Yet when the volume was actually ready, he wrote Thornton:

> I want to tell you how perfect a book I think you have made for me. I wouldn't have a thing different in the make-up, whatever I might want to blot or alter in the content. . . . I tremble and am never too happy at being exposed to the public with another book. I hope this one won't be badly received. I should like to know in general, though it is better for me to shut my eyes and ears to details.

In 1931 the *Collected Poems* gained him his second Pulitzer Prize. The National Institute of Arts and Letters awarded him the equally important Russell Loines Poetry Prize and hailed him as "the poet of the period whom it would most like to crown." Eager to capitalize on these honors, he urged Brickell to make use of them in promoting the book. "Harrison Morris gave me the enclosed [clipping]," he wrote "to help you in telling the world. . . . He says you can advertise the Award as much as you like."

Brickell's departure from the firm in 1932, owing mainly to the severe depression, had no effect on Frost, since he had become close with Thornton. Despite the drastic reduction in book sales, Frost's royalties in 1932 came to $4,532.45, and even in 1933, the worst year of the depression, total royalties almost covered the $3,000 annual advance. When the renewal of the monthly advance was formalized, E. N. Bristol, president of the firm, acknowledged Frost's acceptance: "May I add that I am happy you consented to continuing the arrangement through 1934. We do ourselves a good turn by assuming all the risk, and I shall be delighted if your royalties for the year add something—a good deal—to your income, as well as to ours." This agreement was renewed annually until 1938.

Frost was always cautious about doing anything which might impair his popular appeal. When The New School for Social Research invited him in 1930 to deliver several lectures on poetry, he feared that the alleged reputation of the school as a center of liberalism might hurt the sale of his books; he accepted the invitation only after Melcher had assured him the lectures would add to his popularity. This eagerness to expand his renown and consequently the sale of his books caused Mrs. Frost in 1933 to advise Thornton to discuss with Frost the brochure on his poetry which the firm was planning to prepare. "We really ought to try to stir up the public libraries in small places." This brochure, incidentally, was later metamorphosed into the volume of essays by various critics entitled *Recognition of Robert Frost*, edited by Thornton, in honor of Frost's twenty-five years as a published poet.

Family illness, some of it very serious, caused Frost much anguish and took up a good part of his time during the 1930s. Yet he persisted to the best of his ability to write, lecture, and teach. By 1935 he felt he had written enough for a new volume and was again concerned about its reception. When Thornton consulted him about Henry S. Canby's request for permission to print one of the poems in *The Saturday Review of Literature*, he was advised to grant it. "I'm sure it will be good advance advertising for the new book to let Henry Canby have Two Tramps."

A Further Range was ready for publication in 1936. On March 16 Thornton wrote him:

> I have just sent you a telegram announcing that the Book-of-the-Month Club has chosen *A Further Range* as a dual choice along with André Maurois's new book. The choice means delaying publication of the book a bit, as they are unable to take the book for May. . . . The minimum guarantee is for 50,000 copies, for which they will pay us $7000, to be divided according to the contract between yourself and us.

The volume also brought him his third Pulitzer Prize, and sold unusually well. Another honor that year was his appointment by Harvard University as the Charles Eliot Norton Lecturer on Poetry. The Holt firm further manifested its appreciation of having so eminent an author by issuing *From Snow to Snow*, a handsome brief collection of Frost's seasonal poems for his admirers and collectors. In addition Thornton edited the volume of essays on his poetry as a gesture of the firm's good will.

This devotion of the firm notwithstanding, Frost in 1937 threatened to leave it because it was publishing a textbook of critical essays in which he was not included. The volume had been prepared by Prof. Morton D. Zabel, an established academic critic, at the urging of Charles Madison, managing editor of the Holt college department. The book had reached the plating stage and was soon to be published when Frost happened to visit the office and was shown the proofs by Thornton on the assumption that the volume might interest him. When Frost saw that the table of contents had no essay on him, he became angry and stated that if the firm published the text he would leave it.

Painfully aware that Frost's objection was an ultimatum and that the firm could not afford to lose its leading author, Thornton—by then president of the company—abjectly submitted. Madison, distressed that the action not only yielded to spitefulness but also did violence to Henry Holt's acknowledged ethical firmness and independence, managed to sell the plates to a friendly executive at Harper & Brothers slightly below cost. He also kept the outraged Zabel from suing the firm for breach of contract by absorbing the permission fees amounting to several hundred dollars. The deplorable incident was never again mentioned by either side—Frost did boast about it to Professor Thompson—but Madison felt that the Holt firm had lost something precious as a consequence.

Frost's regard for the Holt management was not enhanced by this experience. Nor was it strengthened when his friend G. R. Elliott wrote him in February 1938: "Are you going to publish your next book through Holt's? Don't. Holt's?/ They're Dolts/ In need of jolts." In reply Frost raised the question whether his criticism of the firm might not be based on a rejection of a manuscript. "I'll tell you this about them," he added, "their literary department is pretty nearly on the rocks. I have my doubts of their future."

About that time he learned that Herbert Bristol, a director and son of the chairman, intent on replacing Thornton as president, was urging a reduction in Frost's monthly payments. To help Thornton, whom he liked, he wrote him:

> Make any adjustment for your comfort. I have had a feeling that my monthly check might be an embarrassment. . . . The three thousand a year was a promise of extra effort on your part to stretch the sales. I don't want it to be too much of a strain for friendship. It is necessary for me to be friends with my publishers above all things. You may name $150 a month as a compromise between your fears of Mr. Herbert Bristol and your anxiety for me. Hadn't you better go the whole length for him, whatever that is. All I ask for the present is what the books can earn and your assurance you will do your best for them.
>
> You understand me. I am saying use me in any way to strengthen your position.

When the sop of reducing the monthly payments to $150 did not save Thornton's position, and he had to leave the firm, Frost was again alienated. Once more he was seriously considering going to another publisher and was entertaining several offers. He favored Harcourt, but hesitated to make the break until he could obtain Holt's release of his published books. While in this state of indecision, he heard in November from T. J. Wilson, the college manager who was temporarily acting as Holt's emissary to him, that Blue Ribbon Books was offering an advance of $4,000 on an inexpensive edition of *Complete Poems* and advised acceptance. A fortnight later E. N. Bristol, head of the firm, wrote Frost to assure him that, although the trade department was losing $30,000 that year, it would be continued under a new manager. He added equivocally: "I didn't know what passed between you and Mr. Thornton when your monthly stipend was reduced from $250. Your royalty earnings by and large seemed to justify the larger sum, and we are of course ready to continue it until you would call for a change." He concluded with the main purport of the letter—that Wilson was to visit him to arrange future terms to his entire satisfaction.

Frost was not easily reconciled. To Untermeyer he wrote: "What's eating me at the moment is how to compose a tactful letter to Edward Bristol to get a friendly release from Henry Holt & Co. I wish I could talk with you about it." Before he had time to write the letter, however, he received one from Wilson indicating how far Holt was ready to go to keep him:

> If you will give us all your future books, whether in verse or prose, for publication by us, we will pay you a royalty of twenty percent of the published price on all copies sold. We will also pay you henceforth a royalty of twenty percent of the published price on all copies sold of those books by you which we published prior to the present date, December 12, 1938. Furthermore, we will pay you, during the remainder of your lifetime, the sum of $300 monthly, until you consider such a payment an unfair burden to us. These monthly payments shall not be considered returnable to us under any circumstances.

Flattered by these unusually generous terms and pleased with the news of the employment of William Sloane, an able young editor and writer, as manager of the trade department, Frost decided to remain with Holt. He soon developed a close relationship with Sloane, whose classical knowledge and literary flair greatly appealed to him, and quickly cooperated with him in bringing out an updated edition of *Collected Poems*. When the attractively printed volume was ready in February 1939, he received from Sloane the following telegram: "No satisfaction could be keener than that with which we publish today your *Collected Poems. Exegisti monumentum perrenius aere* (you have erected a monument more lasting than bronze)." Greatly exhilarated by this show of enthusiasm, Frost wrote Untermeyer: "I got a telegram partly in Latin from Holt's yesterday saying it was their pride to let me know that my latest book was that day on the market. The Latin gave me a stir that I never expected to have again in this world from publication." And to Sloane he wrote:

> May I say through you to the firm that I have a great sense of being published? The telegram, particularly the Latin of it, gave me a thrill I had never expected to have again from being published. The book itself is here and in noble form. I see your taste and judgment in the text of both the fold-ins of the jacket. I am happy to be in your hands.

Sloane's energetic promotion caused the 1,200 copies of the limited edition to be increased by an additional 350. The regular edition also sold in large numbers.

In July 1939 Frost read Sloane's *The Edge of Running Water* and wrote him: "I shall look up to you now as a publisher who knows writing from having written, and respect your judgment accordingly." In the same letter he stated: "I made it a resolve to be chary of my poets with my publisher, if only for the reason that poets as a rule butter no parsnips. Your friendship and mine will surely stand the strain of our disagreeing a little about one poet.''

When Sloane learned the following year that a remark of his had irritated Frost, he hastened to write to Kathleen Morrison, Frost's secretary:

> The house owes him a debt of gratitude for his loyalty, and I should be sorry if anything I said or did conveyed any other impression. Frankly, my feeling is that a man who has worked so well and importantly for so long as Robert has is entitled to be accepted on whatever terms are most welcome to himself, and I would hate to have any remark of mine upset him in any way.

In 1940 Sloane asked Frost to help the firm celebrate its seventy-fifth anniversary by letting him publish his new poems as well as a volume of prose. Frost's response was warm and cooperative: "Tell me right back in your next letter what's the latest you can wait for the prose book. I, of course, want to do all I can to celebrate your (I was going to say our) seventy-fifth anniversary.... And don't worry about me too much.. But thanks for caring.''

(Sloane was concerned about Frost's well-being from their very first meeting, for the poet had undergone traumatic experiences in the illness and death of his wife and the illness of his children. Of Elinor he had written to Untermeyer, in sharp contrast to his earlier statement: "She has been the unspoken half of everything I ever wrote.... I have had almost too much of her suffering in this world.'' And when she died in March 1938, he went through a long black period before he regained his equilibrium: "I've been crazy for the last six months. I haven't known what I was doing.'')

Sloane was delighted with Frost's promise, telling him: "It is practically too good to be true, and you are a veritable life-saver. God bless you.... Last Friday the directors were most emphatic in asking me whether I was sure that I had done everything for you which you would like. They all feel, as I do, that anything in our power is not too much.''

His promises notwithstanding, Frost did not have either volume ready for the anniversary. When he did prepare the poems, the Japanese attack on Pearl Harbor and the American commitment to all-out war raised the question whether a book of poems could be published successfully in a time of such deep stress. Sloane, however, strongly favored publication, and *A Witness Tree* was issued early in 1942. That June, having heard from Sloane of its success, Frost replied: "Really ten thousand in less than two months beats everything.... You were right about publishing this spring and we are glad you stuck to it—war or no war.'' And when the volume gained Frost his fourth Pulitzer Prize, Sloane intensified his rightful pride with the following comment (not knowing then that the judges had favored another book but were overruled by the trustees):

> This is the first opportunity I have had to write you a real note about the Pulitzer Prize. You can imagine how we all feel about it here and how glad for you we are. It seems to me that the outcome could not have been happier; you and we did nothing to try to win the prize, but retired (so to speak) from the active lists. However, the book was so infinitely the best of the year that even the Pulitzer Prize judges

could find no competitor—and that is that. Four times in a single lifetime is a tremendous honor, it seems to me.

In 1943 Holt published *Come In and Other Poems*, edited with comments by Louis Untermeyer. Aimed largely at the classroom, the volume sold steadily and was included in Editions for the Armed Forces in 1944 and as a Pocket Book in 1946; in 1951 it was supplanted by the enlarged *The Road Not Taken*. Holt also brought out two Frost plays—*A Masque of Reason* in 1945 and *A Masque of Mercy* in 1947. Of the first, Sloane wrote to Mrs. Morrison: "It is loaded with dynamite from beginning to end and I don't think that Robert has ever been more incisive, brilliant and triumphantly wayward." Sloane further endeared himself to Frost by having Holt present him with the duChene bust of himself. "The great surprise," Frost wrote to a friend, "was the Holt gift to me of the Araldo du Chene bust I so long wanted someone who could afford it to buy in out of neglect."

Frost underwent another wrench in his relationship with the Holt firm when Sloane left because of a change in its financial control. Although he once more missed the comfort and confidence which he had come to expect from his publisher, and which Sloane had given him in full measure, he now felt himself too committed to heed the siren allures of rival publishers. Fortunately for him, Alfred C. Edwards, who had recently joined the company as financial manager and who had neither editorial experience nor literary pretensions, offered the septuagenerian poet the admiration and advice which he now needed more than publishing guidance. Edwards's simple sincerity appealed to him, and before long they developed a warm reciprocal relationship.

Denver Lindley had replaced Sloane as editor, but he failed to give Frost the adulation and devoted attention he had come to expect. In November 1946, shortly after the publication of *The Steeple Bush*, Mrs. Morrison had to write Lindley: "If your letter had not come this morning I should have called you up. Mr. Frost has been slowly disintegrating up there at Hanover perfectly sure that none of the firm like his poems." Only then did Lindley write a highly laudatory letter.

Two years later Frost had to urge Glenn Gosling, acting editor after Lindley had left, to make new plates for the 1949 edition of *Complete Poems*:

> You would be striking a fateful blow for me by so doing. I mean my reputation would be furthered, I'm sure, by such a mark of your belief in me. I have some repute, I suspect. I'm in no position to tell you how much. . . . Many may be against me for good or bad reasons, often party-political. But there is evidence some are for me. Of these latter it would encourage me to have my publishers show themselves the foremost. Am I asking too much?

Edwards, apprised of Frost's request, arranged for the book to be handsomely reset and printed, and Frost expressed his warm appreciation: "It was great having that long pre-publication ride with you toward our better and better acquaintance. . . . Friends are bobbing up in every mail and calling from hundreds of miles off on the telephone to compliment me on the send off I have had from my publishers." Four months later he again wrote: "Of course [Mrs. Morrison] and I are glad we are going to stay with you for advice, consultation, and everything now that we have become such friends." Morrison also assured Edwards: "You have become RF's friend. I can't tell you how much that means to him. He hasn't had one since Sloane broke out of Holt, and he's felt a bit forlorn. Now apparently you have set it right."

Complete Poems, 1949 was awarded the gold medal given every three years by Limited Editions Club to a work "which is judged most nearly to attain the stature of a classic." Just before Christmas of that year Edwards informed Frost: "Mr. Rigg [the new president] and I want to tell you how much it has meant to us to be able to publish your *Complete Poems, 1949* and how delighted we are at the really wonderful reception it has had." Mrs. Morrison responded: "Many thanks for the wonderful year. It has been the best in the history of Robert's publishing."

Frost's royalties were sizable all through the 1940s, and in 1950 they exceeded $10,000. In that year Sen. Robert Taft had the United States Senate pass a resolution honoring Frost on his seventy-fifth birthday: "Resolved, that the Senate of the United States extend him felicitations of the Nation which he has served so well."

Time deepened the intimacy between Frost and Edwards. The latter devoted himself to the old poet's interests—personal, financial, and literary—both because he liked the man and because it preened his ego to associate with a prominent poet and his literary friends. And Frost, although remarkably youthful for a man in his late seventies, really needed that kind of solicitous attention. In gratitude he made out a new will in 1951 in which Edwards replaced Sloane as "executor and trustee under this latest will." Thus Edwards became his "banker" and confidential adviser; and as demands on the aged poet's time and energy increased, Edwards did his best to protect him from unimportant or gratuitous tasks. They saw each other often, and Edwards went out of his way to accompany Frost on trips in order to ease his discomforts of travel.

Frost did not publish a new book of poems for fifteen years—until *In the Clearing* appeared in 1962. In the interim he "talked" his poems on the lecture platform, accepted numerous honorary degrees from leading universities, and in general performed well as the nationally honored poet and sage. When Stanley Burnshaw, a poet in his own right, joined the firm in 1958, he assumed the editorial functions in connection with Frost's writings.

The climax of Frost's career as a poet and public figure came with his designation as Honored Poet at John F. Kennedy's Presidential Inauguration. *In the Clearing*, published the following year, at once became a best seller. The poet's eighty-eighth birthday was celebrated in Washington by ceremonies at the Library of Congress, at the White House, and at a formal dinner attended by the most prominent persons in the capital as well as by many literary notables. Secretary of the Interior Stewart L. Udall and Edwards were co-hosts, and Chief Justice Warren, Adlai Stevenson, Justice Frankfurter, and Robert Penn Warren paid homage to Frost. His response was warm, witty, and wise. Nor did he forget to praise his publisher: "I have had perfect publisher relations since 1915. I have never asked for anything from them. I have never sent an accountant into the office to see whether they were cheating me, and I have grown richer and richer and they have grown richer and richer."

In its 1963 annual report, soon after Frost's death, the Holt management commented on its long and intimate relationship with him, and concluded: "As his sole publisher for nearly a half century, our company could not have had more distinction. Robert Frost's work will live through the ages. We shall never cease to be proud and grateful to be his publisher."

In 1964 the documentary film, *Robert Frost: A Lover's Quarrel with the World*, produced in cooperation with the Holt firm, won an Academy Award.

12.

Mark Twain
as
Author~Publisher

Money motivated Samuel Clemens's career as a writer; Mark Twain's genius as humorist and storyteller was impressed into Clemens's service—however much it overflowed into the realm of literature. And it did, so much so, that Mark Twain's business letters seemed to have been dictated by Clemens, having little of Mark Twain's vivacity and play and revealing almost nothing of the humanity and spirit that enlivened William James's business letters.

Writing came easily to young Sam Clemens. At the age of sixteen, already setting type, he had two anecdotes published in the *Saturday Evening Post* in far-off Philadelphia. He did not expect payment and received none, for at the time mere publication was to him compensation enough. Over the following few years he piloted boats on the Mississippi, dabbled in mining in the Far West, and gradually drifted into journalism in that part of the country.

From the first his writing on newspapers gave evidence of his quick sense of humor and verbal felicity. When chance brought him in contact with Artemus Ward and other popular humorists, he soon emulated their banter and salty wit with a literary flair that made him stand out among his fellow journalists.

As his popularity grew, and his articles were copied and quoted all along the Pacific Coast, he realized the personal disadvantage of anonymity. With a *nom de plume* being the fashion of the time, he hit upon the name of "Mark Twain"—having learned that the pilot who had used it for his own writing had recently died; the term was a pilot's call signifying two fathoms, or twelve feet deep, and indicated deep water. With his editor's permission he first used it on February 3, 1863, in a political report from Carson City, Nevada. In a short time Clemens came to be known by his pseudonym rather than by his actual name.

In 1865 Mark Twain wrote the story, "Jim Smiley and His Frog," for a volume edited by Artemus Ward. He did not, however, send it in time to be included. Somewhat later, urged by his friends, he collected a number of his published pieces, including "Frog," and sent the material to G. W. Carleton, who had published the Ward book. Carleton rejected the manuscript, and years later he told Mark Twain: "My chief claim to immortality is the distinction of having declined your first book." Soon after, however, Charles Henry Webb published the collection. While it was well received, Mark Twain's reward was more in prestige than in royalties. Nor did he expect anything more, considering himself primarily a journalist and lecturer. In a letter to his family he stated: "I published it simply to advertise myself, and not with the hope of making anything out of it."

Toying with the notion of a trip around the world, the expense to be paid by his "letters" to newspapers, he was strongly attracted by the announcement of the *Quaker City* Holy Land Excursion. What appealed to him particularly was the information that Henry Ward Beecher, Gen. William Sherman, and other men of prominence were to be members of the party. Eager to join the group, he proposed to the editor of *Alta California* that the newspaper send him as reporter of the excursion. To his great joy the management of the newspaper agreed to have him serve as its "Special Correspondent." "Your only instructions," he was told, "are that you will continue to write at such times and from such places as you deem proper, and in the same style that heretofore secured you the favor of the readers of the *Alta California*." Neither Beecher nor Sherman was on board, but he found congenial and stimulating company among the passengers; and his letters from various ports, descriptive history graced with buoyant humor, brash banter, and lively prose, were reprinted in various other newspapers.

On his return in November 1867 Mark Twain received offers of employment from the *Tribune* and the *Herald* in New York, from the *Tribune* in Chicago, as well as proposals for articles from several magazine editors. The New York *Tribune*, commenting on the printed letters, declared: "We are not aware whether Mr. Twain intends giving us a book on his pilgrimage, but we do know that a book written from his peculiar standpoint, giving an account of the characters and events on board ship and of the scenes which the pilgrims witnessed, would command an almost unprecedented sale."

Elisha Bliss, Jr., director of the American Publishing Company of Hartford, read the comment and immediately wrote to Mark Twain proposing that he rework his letters into a book. To excite Mark Twain's interest, he boasted that the firm had sold 100,000 copies of a book by A. D. Richardson. Although the firm was organized as a subscription house only two years before, he stated: "We are perhaps the oldest subscription house in the country, and have never failed to give a book an *immense* circulation. . . . If you have any thought of writing a book, or could be induced to do so, we shall be pleased to see you, and will do so."

Mark Twain still considered himself a journalist rather than a man of letters. But the temptation to earn a good sum of extra money by compiling material he had already written and printed induced him to respond favorably. He mentioned his readiness to delete from and add to the *Alta* letters and even write new ones, if needed. Bliss was enthusiastic. He offered him $10,000 for the book's copyright or a 5 percent royalty, and advised him to take the royalty arrangement. Attractive as $10,000 in cash looked to him, Mark Twain took Bliss's advice and later stated it was "the best business judgment I ever displayed." To his family he wrote:

> The great American Publishing Company kept on trying to bargain with me for a book till I thought I would cut the matter short by coming up for a *talk*. . . . My percentage is to be a fourth more than they have ever paid any author except Greeley. . . . These publishers get off the most tremendous editions of their books you can imagine.

For several decades after the Civil War, when many veterans, crippled or otherwise disestablished, became available as agents, subscription publishing of standard works was a highly aggressive form of merchandising. The books were prepared by prominent or popular authors, who extended them to around 600 pages inclusive of illustrations. Usually manufactured cheaply and priced relatively high—the actual price varying with the quality of the binding—the books were sold by canvassers, sometimes numbering in the thousands, who went from door to door in quest of subscribers. Subscription publishers long maintained that while one in twenty potential purchasers of a book will go to a bookstore—of which there were few, and almost none in smaller towns—one in six will yield to the urging of an agent. It should be stated that few subscribers were normally book-readers and that most of them seldom actually read through the books they bought. Many of the books merely decorated the parlor table. The lead taken by the American Publishing Company was due to Bliss's shrewd business sense and his concentration on only two books a year during the early period of his directorship.

Soon after Mark Twain began to edit the *Alta* letters, he learned that the newspaper's management, tempted by their popularity, was about to copyright them for publication as a book. He immediately protested, and when his letter was ignored he borrowed an advance of money from Bliss and hastened to San Francisco in order to have it out with "those *Alta* thieves face to face." Confronted in person, the *Alta* editors agreed to give up the project; Mark Twain did accept their proviso to acknowledge in the preface that they had "waived their rights" to the letters.

Mark Twain remained in San Francisco to complete the book. He revised the *Alta* letters radically, stating later: "I used several of them—ten or twelve perhaps. I wrote the rest of *The Innocents Abroad* in sixty days, and I could have added a fortnight's labor with the pen and gotten along without the letters altogether." This was somewhat of an exaggeration, as the second half of the book was largely *Alta* material.

When some of the directors of the American Publishing Company, men of conventional piety, learned of the content of the book, they considered it in part irreverent if not blasphemous, and urged cancellation of the contract. Bliss, however, certain of the book's potential popularity, threatened to publish the book on his own if they persisted in urging rejection. Faced with the loss of dividends, they yielded, insisting only that the title be changed from *The New Pilgrims' Progress* to *The Innocents Abroad*.

The manuscript completed, Mark Twain lectured widely under James Redpath's management, receiving one hundred dollars a lecture. This delayed his proofreading on the book. When it ultimately appeared in 1869, it sold 67,000 copies in its first year. Mark Twain was jubilant. In January 1870 he wrote to Bliss: "Yes, I *am* satisfied with the way you are running the book. . . . I never wander into any corner of the country but I find that an agent has been there before me, and many of that community have read the book. . . . I'll back you against any publisher in America, Bliss—or anywhere."

On the *Quaker City* Mark Twain became friends with young Charles Langdon and learned about his sister Olivia, a photograph of whom enraptured him. On their return Charles arranged for Mark Twain to visit his family in Elmira, where the elder Langdon was a wealthy coal dealer and leading citizen. Mark Twain fell wholeheartedly in love with Olivia at their first meeting and began to woo her with an ardor and adoration that before long ended successfully. The engagement took place in February 1869 and the wedding a year later.

The extraordinary popularity of *The Innocents Abroad* established Mark Twain as a nationally prominent writer. Magazine editors and book publishers made him attractive offers. When Bliss chided him for considering the proposals of rival publishers, Mark Twain replied: "I would merely have asked you to climb along up *as near that figure as you could and make money*, but I wouldn't have asked any more. . . . I have never had the slightest idea of publishing with anybody else but you."

Indeed, he still continued to think of himself as primarily a journalist, and his ambition was to become part owner of a newspaper. When he learned of the opportunity to buy a third interest in the Buffalo *Express*, he was ready to undertake a lecture tour—to him an unpleasant chore—to earn the needed money. Jarvis Langdon, Olivia's father, rendered that plan unnecessary by offering him the required amount. The deal was consummated in August 1869, and Mark Twain assumed his position as editor. He worked hard to increase the newspaper's prestige and circulation, but after months of futile effort and a growing realization that Buffalo was not a congenial place for his beloved Livy, he decided to sell his share in the newspaper at a considerable loss and move to Hartford, the home of Elisha Bliss and his new and dear friend Joseph Twitchell.

Circumstances thus turned Mark Twain to book writing. Soon after the successful publication of *Innocents* Bliss began to prod him for another book. At first, still hoping to make the *Express* a profitable enterprise, he would not commit himself. He assured Bliss he could have any book he wrote, when he had the time to do it, "as long as you deal in a fair, open, and honorable way with *me*." Not satisfied with mere promises, Bliss continued to tempt him, assuring him that a book by him on the Far West was bound to sell even better than the *Innocents*. To increase the inducement he offered Mark Twain half of the profits on the new book, which he explained would be the equivalent of 7½ percent royalties on the sale of 100,000 copies—a number he expected the book to reach. By this time Mark Twain realized he was unable to do as well as he had expected on the *Express* and accepted Bliss's offer.

In fairness to Bliss it should be pointed out that it was he who had stimulated Mark Twain to write his early books; that he had suggested the subject for *Roughing It*, and had given him a contract with a royalty half again as large as the one on his first book. Years later, however, yielding to hindsight and assuming he should have received the highest return from the outset, Mark Twain expressed his resentment at the presumed advantage Bliss had taken of him. That this was far from fact was admitted by his laudatory biographer Albert Bigelow Paine:

> The figures remain, however, to show that Bliss dealt fairly. Seven and a half per cent of a subscription book did represent half profits up to 100,000 copies when the contract was drawn; but it required ten years to sell that quantity, and in that time conditions had changed. Bliss could hardly foresee that things would be so, and as he was dead when the book touched the 100,000 mark, he could not explain or readjust matters, whatever might have been his inclination.

Indeed, when the contract was arranged in 1870, Mark Twain was boastful of its advantageous terms and wrote to his brother Orion: "I suppose I am to get the biggest copyright this time ever paid on a subscription book in this country." And the continued popularity of *The Innocents Abroad* at home and in Europe greatly enhanced his admiration of Bliss's achievement. In one of his letters to him at that time he declared, "You are running it in staving, tiptop, first-class style."

The writing of the new book, now that it became his main occupation, was at first slow and irregular, without his usual intensity. The loss of $10,000 on the *Express* continued to rankle; Livy's illness deeply distressed him; and the move to Hartford took a lot of his time. When he had written a good part of the book and felt discouraged by the result, he asked his old editorial friend Joe Goodman, whose critical judgment he valued, to read the material. The latter's enthusiastic approval was balm to his ego and he invited Goodman to stay with him while he wrote the remainder. And in a moment of boastfulness he wrote Bliss:

> When I get it done I want to see the man who will begin to read it and not finish it. If it falls short of the *Innocents* in any respect I shall lose my guess. Nothing grieves me now, nothing troubles me, nothing bothers me or gets my attention. I don't think of anything but the book, and I don't have an hour's unhappiness about anything and don't care two cents whether school keeps or not. It will be a bully book.

And it was. Bliss's agents were in the meantime canvassing subscriptions successfully—the title having been changed from *The Innocents at Home* to *Roughing It*. As a result the sale reached 46,122 three months after publication—not 62,000 as Mark Twain told his friend William Dean Howells—and 62,376 during the first year. Mark Twain had expected an even larger sale and thought that the poor quality of the paper and engravings was largely responsible for this shortcoming. Yet during 1872 he received large enough royalties from his two volumes to be convinced that he would do better at his books than as a journalist.

That year, entertaining Charles Dudley Warner and his wife, Mark Twain directed the conversation toward a discussion of current novels. Both men agreed that most fiction was worthless, whereupon their wives challenged them to write a worthy novel. The men agreed to try and began to write *The Gilded Age*. Although novels were usually not sold by subscription, Bliss wanted to keep Mark Twain as his author and agreed to bring it out and give each of the collaborators 5 percent royalty. Mark Twain was highly pleased, since he considered subscription a more effective selling device than sales in a bookstore. He was eager to have his friend Tom Nast, the political cartoonist, illustrate the novel, but Bliss considered him too expensive and unsuited as well. *The Gilded Age*, published in 1873, was very favorably received and sold 50,325 in its first year. Mark Twain, again expecting an even larger sale, was disappointed.

The notable success of *Roughing It* stimulated Mark Twain to search his memory for other autobiographical material as subject matter for his next book. Creative writing came most easily to him when in his studio on the Quarry Farm, Langdon's summer home. While there in 1872, he began to write *The Adventures of Tom Sawyer*. Looking deeply into his boyhood life exhilarated by pleasurable reminiscence, he wrote as many as fifty pages, or around 5,000 words, a day. As he later stated, he was "wrapped up in it, and dead to everything else." Indeed, he was writing the story of Tom because he enjoyed it and not because of the money he expected to make out of it. Once away from the farm, however, when the Sam Clemens part of his personality was dominant, other matters thrust themselves upon his attention and his "inspiration tank" became fairly empty. It was long before it filled up again, and he did not finish the story to his satisfaction until 1875.

Once the manuscript was ready, he became anxious to see the book published, mainly in order that it might add substantially to his income. His need of money had become greater than ever. His household expenses had increased tremendously, and royalties on his early books had naturally declined. In July 1875 he wrote to Howells: "You see I take a vile, mercenary view of things—but then my household expenses are something almost ghastly."

To his chagrin Bliss seemed in no hurry to begin the campaign for subscriptions or to send the manuscript to press. He had in recent years expanded his publishing program and could no longer devote himself fully to any one book. Mark Twain complained caustically about this presumed neglect: "I think the present extended business is a considerable detriment to my pocket. I think we publish books so fast that canvassers are likely merely to skim the cream of a district and then 'lay' for the next book." Mark Twain was here speaking in the role of both author and member of the firm's board, as he had in 1873 invested $5,000 in the company and was named a director. Bliss rejected this criticism and refused to expedite publication. What concerned him as publisher were the poor condition of the economy, the comparative brevity of the story for subscription purposes, and the assurance of copyright in England—matters which Mark Twain tended to overlook.

Early in 1876 Mark Twain sent a copy of the story to Howells for critical comment and told him about his trouble with Bliss:

I went down to see how much of a delay there was going to be, and found that the man had not even put a canvasser on. . . . But of course the main fact was that no canvassing had been done—because a subscription harvest is *before* publication (not *after*, when people have discovered how bad one's book is).

Howells assured Mark Twain that he had written a masterpiece, and reviewed it in the *Atlantic* seven months before it was finally published in December. For all the praise from reviewers, the book sold only 23,638 copies in its first year.

Deeply disappointed, Mark Twain began thinking of a change of publishers. This was not easily made. Contractual clauses favored the firm; this annoyed him, but he knew it tied his hands. Hamlin Hill, who had made a detailed study of the Twain-Bliss relationship, commented on this point:

> He was convinced that the American Publishing Company, which he could rightly claim he had elevated to its position at the top of the subscription publishing industry, was ungrateful. He had bought $5000 of stock in the company and was a member of the board of directors from 1873 to 1881; he had received a 10 percent dividend in 1873, but from then until he sold out his shares in 1881, Bliss never declared another. . . . There was in Mark Twain's mind a strong suspicion that Bliss was not marketing his books as they should be sold, and there was still the smoldering doubt that Orion had kindled about the royalty on *Roughing It* coming far short of the half profits Twain believed he deserved.

Mark Twain had for some time been courted by James Osgood, the new head of the eminent firm of Ticknor & Fields. In 1872 he asked Mark Twain for a book of sketches, an effort which Bliss quickly scotched. Three years later Bliss again stopped an Osgood proposal by increasing Mark Twain's royalties to 10 percent on *Sketches Old and New* after the sale of 50,000 copies; in fact this was an empty gesture, as the book sold only 27,000 copies in its first year and Mark Twain thereafter agreed to a cancellation of the extra royalty to enable Bliss to issue a dollar edition.

When Bliss's son Frank started his own publishing firm, Mark Twain promised him *A Tramp Abroad*; however, as soon as the older Bliss learned of this arrangement he asserted his contractual right to the book and got it, for he knew how to keep Mark Twain under control. As Hill has pointed out, "Elisha Bliss never surrendered to Mark Twain, always stood his ground, fulminated, attacked, threatened, cajoled, and intimidated the humorist in a fashion that would probably have been as foreign to Frank as it was to Webster." Subsequently Mark Twain compensated Frank for the loss of this book by giving him *The Tragedy of Pudd'nhead Wilson* and *Following the Equator*.

Mark Twain took a long time to write *A Tramp Abroad*—which he did while living in Europe to gather his material—largely because he had to extend its length to subscription requirements, and did not complete it until early in 1880. With economic conditions improved, and with adequate time for canvassing, the book sold 62,000 copies in its first year. With his share of half the profits amounting to $32,000, Mark Twain became confirmed in his suspicion that he had been underpaid on his previous books, and figured that this amounted to $62,000. But before he was able to confront Bliss with this claim, he learned of his sudden death. To his brother Orion he wrote at the time:

> If Bliss were alive I would stay with the concern and get it all back; for on each new book I would require a portion of that back pay; but as it is (*this in the very strict confidence*) I shall probably go to a new publisher 6 or 8 months hence, for I am afraid Frank, with his poor health, will lack push and drive.

It should be stressed that Mark Twain had reached this conclusion ex post facto, without taking into account that conditions had altered over the years. This was made clear by Paine:

> Bliss was not a philanthropist. He was in fact a shrewd, capable publisher, who made as good a contract as he could; yet he was square in his dealings, and the contract which Clemens held most bitterly against him—that of *Roughing It*—had been made in good faith, and in accordance with the conditions of that period. In most of the later contracts Clemens himself had named his royalties, and it was not in human nature—*business* human nature—for Bliss to encourage the size of these percentages.

All the while, of course, Osgood was very much in evidence, and Mark Twain liked the imaginative, socially pleasing, if financially incompetent publisher. At the time of Bliss's death Mark Twain had completed *The Prince and the Pauper*, which he had enjoyed writing, and was in the midst of *The Adventures of Huckleberry Finn*, which he considered the inferior of the two in merit. His original idea, influenced by subscription length requirements, was to issue the two stories in a single volume; but Livy wisely insisted on separate publication, and Mark Twain yielded to her in this as in other matters concerning his writing. To his sister he wrote on this point: "People who fix up agreements with me without first finding out what Livy's plans are take their fate into their own hands." He gave Osgood the completed story on a quasi-partnership basis without realizing that Osgood was inexperienced in the practices of subscription publishing. By bringing out the book in a style unfamiliar to previous subscribers of Mark Twain's books and spending too much money on illustrations and manufacture, Osgood failed to attain a sale—and a profit—which Mark Twain had come to expect.

Mark Twain nonetheless remained loyal to Osgood, and readily accepted his proposal to do a book on the Mississippi—especially when the debonair publisher agreed to accompany him on the trip to the river and on a steamboat to New Orleans. Osgood also agreed to the arrangement whereby Mark Twain paid for the cost of publication and he was to receive 7½ percent of sales for marketing the book—which in fact made Mark Twain his own publisher.

Mark Twain found the writing difficult and complained to Howells that it was becoming an "apparently interminable book." He persisted, however, until he finished it. Osgood again spent too much money on production, and Mark Twain at one time declared, "That book cost me fifty thousand dollars to make.

Bliss could have built a whole library for that sum. But Osgood was a lovely fellow." Nevertheless, he was disappointed with the sale of the book.

For all his fondness for Osgood, Mark Twain in 1884 decided to start his own publishing firm in the belief that this would enable him to receive the entire profit from his books. In this venture he was following the impulse of the inveterate speculator, which had made him an "easy mark" for any scheme that held high, if ephemeral promise. Robert E. Spiller has well stated: "His dream of becoming a millionaire by a stroke of fortune never forsook him; lingering in his blood, the bonanza fever made him a lifelong victim of gold bricks, quick-profit schemes, and dazzling inventions." His most disastrous speculation was connected with James W. Paige's invention of a typesetting machine. This began with a small investment in 1880 and ended with a loss of $190,000 and financial insolvency fifteen years later.

He had no difficulty in persuading Charles L. Webster, husband of a niece, who had already been involved in Mark Twain's luckless investment in the kaolatype process of engraving, to organize a subscription publishing firm in his own name. Webster, according to Paine, "was a busy, industrious young man, tirelessly energetic, and with a good deal of confidence." Mark Twain financed the enterprise and guided Webster on the basis of his experience with Bliss and Osgood. His first book under the firm's imprint, *The Adventures of Huckleberry Finn*, was launched with professional competence and reached a sale of 50,000 copies. When the Concord, Massachusetts library rejected the book as "trash and suitable for the slums," Mark Twain gleefully assured Webster that "That will sell 25,000 copies for us sure." This additional sale did not materialize, but Mark Twain was highly gratified with the result and began looking for other books for the firm to publish.

His great acquisition proved to be Gen. Ulysses Grant's *Memoirs*. As early as 1881 Mark Twain had urged the general to write his war reminiscences, but at that time the old warrior was not interested. Three years later, suffering financial disaster amounting to $800,000 in the failure of his firm, Grant and Ward, Grant responded more favorably to the idea of earning money from his writing. As soon as Mark Twain learned of this, he immediately called on his friend to ask for the book. Told that The Century Company, which was to serialize the chapters, had already made an offer for the book rights, Mark Twain proposed better terms and urged that the work be published by subscription.

> General, I am publishing my own book, and by the time yours is ready it is quite possible that I shall have the best-equipped subscription establishment in the country. If you will place your book with my firm—and I feel that I have at least an equal right in the consideration—I will pay you twenty per cent of the list price, or, if you prefer, I will give you seventy per cent of the net returns and I will pay all office expenses out of my own thirty per cent.

At Mark Twain's advice, Grant accepted the 20 percent royalty. News of this arrangement became headline news, and editors indicated that the author-publisher combination "was of unprecedented importance." Although Grant began to suffer from a cancer of the tongue soon after he started writing, he persisted in his effort to complete the second volume—doing so until a few days before his death. In the meantime Webster had engaged subscription agencies with hundreds of canvassers and drove them energetically in obtaining subscriptions, especially from the thousands of soldiers who had served under the general, so that by the time the volumes were ready the agents had signed up more than 100,000 subscriptions. Shortly before Grant died in July 1885, Mark Twain informed him that his royalties had already reached $150,000. Indeed, when the first royalty payment was made to Mrs. Grant the following February, the check was for $200,000—the largest amount ever paid an author up to that time. The total sale reached 300,000 copies and the royalties came to $450,000.

Another book for which Mark Twain had high hopes was *The Life of Pope Leo XIII*, written with the Pope's blessing by Bernard O'Reilly. He sent Webster to Rome to obtain the Pope's formal signature, and Mark Twain assumed that most Catholics would buy the book. It was published simultaneously in six languages and highly publicized. But the sale fell far short of expectations. Mark Twain and Webster learned to their sorrow that relatively few Catholics felt that a reading of the Pope's life was necessary for their salvation.

Over the ensuing few years the firm published a number of other books, none with notable success and some at an actual loss. A bookkeeper's embezzlement of $30,000 added to Webster's financial difficulties. By the end of 1887 it was necessary for him to borrow money in order to bring out three promising books: *A Library of Humor*, General Sheridan's *Memoirs*, and *The Library of American Literature* in ten volumes. Although these projects proved fairly profitable, the company as a whole was not prospering. Moreover, Webster was overworked, suffered from acute neuralgia, and had to leave the firm—he died not long after. He was replaced by his assistant Fred J. Hall, who did his utmost to keep the business afloat in the face of increasingly unfavorable conditions. Mark Twain's *A Connecticut Yankee in King Arthur's Court*, his first book in five years and "a heart-cry against human injustice," did as well as his earlier books but could not save the firm from its financial encumbrances.

With the oncoming of economic depression in 1891, Mark Twain was financially in dire straits. Royalties from his books no longer sufficed for his household needs, and the demands for additional money from Paige seemed unending. Although the Webster firm remained solvent, it was in grave need of additional capital. As Fred Hall at that time reported to Mark Twain, "In prosperous times we might regard our stock and copyrights as assets sufficient, with money owing to us, to square up quite even, but I suppose we may not hope for such luck in the present condition of things."

Paige accompanied his optimistic reports with requests for additional money. Having become a "remorseless Frankenstein monster," the machine, notwithstanding Paige's repeated assurance that he "was about finished," was draining Twain's money and mind; for the lure of millions was a dream he could not let go; yet the very thought of it began putting him in a "fevered delirium."

Using the last of his capital to keep Paige in funds, Mark Twain, sojourning in Europe, began to ask Hall to sell what he could of the Webster assets to avoid further financial impairment. At one point, seeing himself as he really was, he admitted to him: "I am terribly tired of business. I am by nature and disposition unfit for it, and I want to get out of it. . . . Get me out of business!" On another occasion, soon after, he informed Hall: "What I am mainly hoping for is to save my book royalties. If they come into danger I hope you will cable me so that I can come over and try to save them, for if they go I am a beggar." And again: "Do your best for me, for I do not sleep these nights, for visions of the poor-house." His one tangible contribution to the firm was the manuscript of *Tom Sawyer Abroad*, which Hall brought out shortly before the company was declared insolvent.

With his financial resources at their lowest ebb, Mark Twain, having returned from Europe in the hope of salvaging what he could, was befriended by Henry H. Rogers, an astute partner of the Standard Oil Company. Rogers had long been an admirer of Mark Twain's writings, and the two men found each other highly congenial. Eager to help his new friend, Rogers persuaded his son-in-law, W. E. Benjamin, a subscription publisher, to buy *The Library of American Literature* for $50,000 in order that Hall might pay urgent bills. Rogers also agreed to take control of Mark Twain's financial affairs, telling him: "It rests me to experiment with the affairs of a friend when I am tired of my own. Let me work at the puzzle a little." Mark Twain gratefully accepted this assistance, feeling that with a financial titan like Rogers as his pilot he should be able to weather any storm. Justin Kaplan has characterized Rogers as having "distinguished himself for daring, rapacity, intrigue, and a total lack of business scruple"; paradoxically, he was also a superb friend.

Conditions continued to worsen. On April 14, 1894, the Mount Morris Bank insisted on payment of $10,000 from the Webster company. Thereupon Rogers advised Mark Twain that his only way out was to let the "assignment" take its course. This was done on the 18th. At a meeting of creditors Rogers represented Mark Twain. The assignee found that "liabilities exceeded assets by $98,191, and that Mr. Clemens is individually liable for the debts of the firm, as well as other partners." When the creditors proposed to deprive Mark Twain of his available possessions, Rogers told them that since Mrs. Clemens was the chief creditor—to the amount of $60,000—he insisted on assigning all royalties to her until she was paid; also that the Hartford home was hers and could not be considered part of the assets. After some discussion it was "agreed that Clemens should pay fifty cents on the dollar, when the assets were finally realized upon, and receive a quittance." Mark Twain readily accepted full responsibility and stated he would go on a worldwide lecture tour to help pay his debts:

> The law recognizes no monopoly on a man's brains, and a merchant who has given up all he has may take advantage of the rules of insolvency and start free again for himself; but I am not a business man, and honor is a harder master than the law. It cannot compromise for less than a hundred cents on the dollar, and its debts never outlaw.

In the meantime Rogers, having investigated the likely prospects of the Paige machine, advised Mark Twain to give it up as hopeless. Mark Twain's response was: "Well, whatever I get out of the wreckage will be due to good luck—the good luck of getting you into the scheme—for, but for that, there wouldn't be any wreckage; it would be total loss." And soon after: "You are the best friend ever a man had, and the surest."

Intent on paying his debts, Mark Twain wrote Henry Harper from Vancouver, as he was about to sail for his lectures in Australia:

> I wish to be appearing in print periodically during my trip around the world; for I shall return and make a wide lecture tour in America next year, and all the advertising I can get will help that enterprise. I can't expect to pay off the Webster debts in a single lecturing bout, but I think I can come pretty near if my name is kept alive while I'm away on this long journey. I know my name is alive at present, or I wouldn't be filling these opera houses in the dead summer time.

Nearly three years later, at the end of December 1897, when he had repaid all his debts, he told Rogers: "Land we are glad to see these debts diminishing. For the first time in my life I am getting more pleasure out of paying money than pulling it in."

While Mark Twain was abroad, Rogers had arranged with the American Publishing Company and the Webster assignee for the release of Mark Twain's contracts with them, in order that he might negotiate with Harper & Brothers to take over all of Mark Twain's writings. Since *Following the Equator*, which Mark Twain soon had ready, was a large elaborate travel book which seemed best suited for the subscription market, Rogers let Frank Bliss publish it as a subscription book, and the sale of nearly 40,000 copies helped pay Mark Twain's debts; nor did he object to having Bliss issue Mark Twain's complete works in a uniform edition for the same market.

Even earlier *The Personal Recollections of Joan of Arc*, which Mark Twain wrote with deep admiration for the Maid and which was without his usual humor, Harper first serialized in its monthly magazine prior to issuing the book. Although its reception was slow at first—Mark Twain's readers missed the expected banter—it achieved increasing popularity over the years.

Rogers's arrangement with Harper in 1895 stipulated that Mark Twain was to give the firm all his future books, beginning with *Joan*, and that it was to pay him "upon works of which we should make the plates ourselves, a royalty of 15 per cent. on the retail price of all copies sold up to five thousand copies, and 20 per cent. on the retail price of all copies sold thereafter." On those books for which Mark Twain provided the plates he was to receive an additional 5 percent royalty. This contract was renegotiated in October 1903, giving the firm the inventory and rights in Mark Twain's works from the American Publishing Company, thus making Harper his exclusive publisher; in return it guaranteed Mark Twain a minimum royalty of $25,000 a year for five years. With his older books showing great appeal, Mark Twain rightly estimated that his actual royalties should come to twice that amount. This came about in 1907 when George Harvey, head of Harper, informed him: "Major Leigh handed me a report of the year's sales just as I was leaving. It shows your royalty returns this year to be very close to fifty thousand dollars. I don't believe there is another such return." Indeed, fifty years later, with much of his writing in the public domain, his estate continued to receive as much as $20,000 annually.

During the final decade of his life Mark Twain enjoyed the pleasures of affluence. He was glad to be relieved of the business end of publishing, and he no longer worried about not receiving his full share of the profits from his books. His reliance on Rogers, and hence on the Harper firm, was complete. And Harper executives delighted in paying court and being of service to him. Frank N. Doubleday, during his brief control of the firm, went to considerable trouble to locate a suitable house for him in New York when he was ready to return from his stay abroad. Harvey, who succeeded Doubleday, paid homage to him in person and at resplendent dinners in his honor. Much as Sam Clemens enjoyed this esteem of his peers and the friendship of men of wealth, Mark Twain had periods of pessimistic reflection, which he expressed in such writings as *The Mysterious Stranger*, all unpublished during his lifetime.

Those years had their unavoidable heartaches. He never ceased grieving over the death of his eldest daughter. Later the long invalidism ending in the death of his much-beloved Livy became a consuming grief, so that he wrote to Howells: "If I could only see a dog that I knew in the old times and could put my arms around his neck and tell him all, everything, and ease my heart." Here spoke the true Mark Twain, and his own death came in 1910 at the age of seventy-five.

13.

Dreiser's Troubles with Publishers

No other major American writer had such unfortunate experiences with publishers as Theodore Dreiser. His entire life in a sense, was charged with the pain of frustration: suffering from anguished poverty in childhood, subjected to the quirks of a troubled personality, he deliberatedly paid the price for depicting prematurely the sham aspects of conventional morality.

Born into a large German-American family in Indiana, he spent his early years in the depth of penury. His bigotedly religious father failed as a provider, and felt thwarted at his inability to instill his own children with his strict morality; his mother, peasant-like and illiterate, yet with an understanding heart and overflowing love, held the family together by accepting the waywardness of her children with sympathetic forgiveness. His older brothers and sisters, pretty much on their own, early fought for a foothold in society, resorting to whatever means they had. Young Theodore, keenly sensitive to his family's wretched poverty, found release from the slings of family shame and social ostracism in the bosom of maternal love. A memory that permanently seared his consciousness was the necessity of going barefoot into cold December and seeing the gaping hole in his mother's shoe. Although he loved being in school, he made few friends among his classmates and always hurried away from them to avoid hearing the taunting gossip about his wayward sisters.

An avid reader while in school, he entered adolescence working at menial and degrading jobs in Chicago. Virtually alone in the midwestern metropolis, he felt socially isolated, at times physically ill, without hope of ever freeing himself from the withering barrenness of his humdrum work. While in this state of depression he was one day sought out by Mildred Fielding, his former teacher who had advanced to a principalship in a Chicago school. She had perceived his sensitive response to books and his intellectual aspirations while in her classroom and felt moved to help him to a life more suited to his cultural inclinations. At her urging he accepted her offer to finance his schooling at Indiana University. The year he spent on the campus broadened his thinking more by contact with certain students than by courses he had taken. The death of his mother in 1890 left him at the age of nineteen lonelier and more depressed than before, feeling unprotected and rootless. He was grateful to Miss Fielding, and maintained contact with her to the end of her life, but he lacked the ease of mind for further academic study.

Returning to Chicago, he took the first jobs open to him. He drove a laundry wagon; he became a collector for an installment house. Temporary employment on a newspaper made him eager to become a reporter, and the political convention in 1892 gave him the opportunity he sought. John Maxwell, a copyreader, generally taught him how to report news. Impressed by Dreiser's ability to describe what he saw clearly and incisively, he told him that he was "cut out to be a writer . . . not just an ordinary newspaper man." The city editor likewise favored the solemn youth and recommended him for a better post on a St. Louis newspaper. There he associated with co-workers who were either dreamers or cynics. For several years thereafter he worked on newspapers in cities on his way to New York. A frustrating experience on the *World*, where he was paid for "space" given to his reports, caused him to persuade the partners of his older brother Paul Dresser, the successful song writer, to let him edit a new monthly, *Ev'ry Month*, with a view to promoting the sale of their songs. He was paid little at first, but the magazine did well and his salary was increased. A quarrel with his brother caused him to leave, and he began to make his living as a free-lance writer for periodicals.

While in St. Louis, as a youth of twenty, he met Sara White, later known as Jug, and was strongly attracted to her. Two years his senior and a school teacher, she appeared to him as the loveliest girl he had ever met. She reciprocated his affection and soon talked of marriage, which he feared as a form of bondage. When he left St. Louis, the two corresponded regularly, and in his loneliness he thought of her as the girl of his dreams and finally agreed to marry her. She came to Washington in December 1898, and, after six years of longing and reluctance, their marriage there soon seemed to him as "the pale flame of duty."

While in Toledo in search of work on a newspaper, Dreiser had met Arthur Henry and the two became fast friends. Henry, like many journalists, talked about writing a novel and encouraged Dreiser to write fiction. Early in 1899, after giving up his job and making his home in a large house in Maumee, near Toledo, he persuaded Dreiser to join him in order that both might devote themselves to writing. At Henry's persistent urging, Dreiser wrote a short story. Its acceptance by *Ainslee's Magazine* and a check for seventy-five dollars encouraged him to write several more stories. He had little confidence in being able to write a novel, and after he did start one he dropped it twice; but each time Henry kept after him to continue by praising what he had already written, so that he at last finished it. Calling it *Sister Carrie* at the outset, he soon changed the title to *The Flesh and the Spirit*—only to change it back on completing the manuscript.

Sister Carrie was based on the life of his sister Emma, and Hurstwood was the man with whom she had eloped—although Dreiser put a good deal of himself in the man's later experiences. He wrote about them without conventional restraints in the manner of Balzac and Hardy, with deep compassion for the suffering of the poor and the thwarted—an aspect in life new in American fiction—and with a tolerance for amoral behavior that was frightening to the upholders of the prevalent conventions. He saw no reason for making Carrie suffer for her moral misbehavior; he made Hurstwood steal money not deliberately but only when the door of the safe had closed accidentally while the money was in his hands. When the writing was completed after four months of concentrated effort, Henry and others edited it with a view to pruning the excess verbiage, but all praised its realistic treatment and truthful evocation of human life.

Having previously sold articles to Henry Alden Mills, editor of *Harper's Magazine*, Dreiser sent him the manuscript for consideration by the Harper firm. In the letter of rejection he was told that although it was "a superior piece of reportorial realism," the writing was of uneven merit. He next submitted the novel to Doubleday, Page & Company, assuming that as the publisher of Frank Norris's *McTeague* the firm might be more sympathetic to his book. Frank N. Doubleday received the manuscript, but as he was about to leave for Europe, he asked Frank Norris, now his editor, to read it. Norris reacted enthusiastically and informed Dreiser that he had recommended it highly to his superiors: "I said, and it gives me pleasure to repeat it, that it was the best novel I had read in M.S. since I had been reading for the firm, and that it pleased me as well as any novel I have read in *any* form, published or otherwise." Adding that Henry Lanier was reading the manuscript and that Walter Hines Page would read it next, he continued: "The three of us will have a powwow on it and come to a decision. You may rest assured I shall do all in my power to see that the decision is for publication." And early in June, Page invited Dreiser to the office, where both he and Lanier assured him the book would be well promoted. They suggested a few minor emendations, which Dreiser made before leaving with Jug for a visit to her parents in Missouri.

On his return from Europe, learning of the favor with which his partners regarded *Sister Carrie*, Doubleday took a set of galleys to read over the weekend. Both he and his wife reacted strongly against the novel, considering it "an immoral book." On returning to the office the following Monday, he insisted on stopping its publication. Thereupon Page wrote to Dreiser on July 19:

> The feeling has grown upon us that, excellent as your workmanship is, the choice of your characters has been unfortunate. . . To be frank, we prefer not to publish the book, and we should like to be released from my agreement with you. If you have suffered any injury, we stand ready, of course, to make amends. . . . If you were to ask my advice, I should without hesitation say that *Sister Carrie* is not the best kind of book for a young author to make his first book.

Shocked and dismayed, Dreiser consulted with Henry and was told to insist on publication. In replying to Page he told him that his friends and relatives were expecting to see the book soon, and the firm's refusal to publish it would not only embarrass him but "will work me material injury," inasmuch as it would lessen his value as a writer for magazines. As he continued to brood over this unexpected rejection, he envisioned himself in a bottomless pit: repudiated as a novelist and hurt as a free-lance writer. He felt that the world had callously turned against him and that he had to fight for his very life.

Page in another letter tried to reason with him: "After fuller consideration we became very doubtful of two points—first the financial return from the novel; and second, the desirability, for your own good as well as ours, of publishing it, on account of your choice of material." Dreiser, still in Missouri, saw through Page's reasoning and considered it mere guile. By return mail he informed Page: "I have concluded to publish it as originally planned. . . . I would leave this matter until my return to New York if it were not that my opinion as here given is conclusive and that fall publication if consummated as planned, demands immediate action."

When he called on Doubleday on his return east in August, the publisher told him bluntly that the novel was immoral in its treatment; that no library would buy it and neither would any church person. Dreiser stubbornly insisted that the book be published according to the contract. Thereupon Doubleday, having been advised by his lawyer that it would be simpler to print a small edition and bury it than to go through a lawsuit, told Dreiser: "All right. You stand on your legal rights and we'll stand on ours. . . . I see that a man of your stamp will have trouble with any publisher you deal with and it will please me if you never set foot in this office again."

An edition of 1,008 copies of *Sister Carrie* was printed and published on November 8, 1900. It was neither advertised nor publicized, although Doubleday permitted Norris to send out review copies to newspapers and magazines. As was to be expected, the reviews were mostly brief and critical. A total of 456 copies were sold, yielding Dreiser $68.40 in royalties. As W. A. Swanberg, his biographer, pointed out:

> Not a critic in the nation realized that this was a novel so transcendent in its realism and its humanity that it stood alone, that its imperfections deserved forgiveness, that it called for a new standard in criticism and a fight for recognition. No such recognition was possible in 1900 over a heroine who not only sinned but spoke ungrammatically.

If very few Americans perceived the literary power of *Sister Carrie*—Marion Reedy was one of them—a number of Englishmen found it impressive. William Heinemann, the astute publisher to whom Norris sent a copy, liked it well enough to add it to his Dollar Library of American Novels—Henry reducing the first 200 pages to 80 in order to fit it into the Series. On the sale of his first printing of the novel, Heinemann wrote Doubleday: "I look upon Mr. Dreiser as an author of exceptional merit. . . . I congratulate you heartily in having discovered him. You should make a great fuss of him. How about his next and future work?" It is not known how much Doubleday appreciated the unintended irony of these remarks, but he did forward the letter to Dreiser without comment. Years later, in his privately printed *Indiscrete Recollections* and in his posthumous *Memoirs of a Publisher*, Doubleday wrote not a word about either Dreiser or *Sister Carrie*.

The failure of his book rankled until he felt completely crushed. At first he sought to place the novel with another publisher; his failure to do so deepened his depression. Only F. J. Taylor & Company, a small, obscure firm was interested enough to buy the plates and unsold copies, primarily to encourage Dreiser to complete *Jennie Gerhardt*, which he had begun to write on finishing his first novel.

For a time Dreiser did make a valiant effort to write. When Taylor asked him to make certain changes in *Sister Carrie*, Dreiser put him off by telling him on November 25, 1901, that he was concentrating on the new work: "Just now I['m] straining every nerve—bending every energy to give this new theme its unity, simplicity of progression and force. All my mind is colored by this problem. Barring unforseen difficulties or disturbances nothing will take me from it until I finish the story on time."

The acid of failure, however, continued to ravage his ego. Jug's possessiveness also irritated him to the point of wishing to be free of her. Feeling as he did, he found himself blocked in his writing. R. B. Jewett, Taylor's editor, was warmly sympathetic and sought to lift his spirit, pleading with him to "open the door . . . and sweep out the rubbish of distrust. . . . I know that when the book is finished it will be good." But Dreiser's depression was too deep to be overcome by an effort of will. He told Jewett that he was unable to go on and was very sorry not to be able to repay Taylor's weekly advance of fifteen dollars. Jewett's assurance to the contrary, he did worry about everything. Finally he made Jug return to her parents and he himself moved into a cheap room to stretch his small savings to the utmost.

For nearly two years thereafter he shunned relatives and friends, making feeble efforts to obtain work and, failing again and again, sank more and more into a depression that drained his mind and spirit of the urge to live. On February 27, 1903, he told Ripley Hitchcock, a friendly editor, that he was "still in the dumps in regard to *Sister Carrie*. . . . In fact I seem to be just emerging from a long siege of bad weather and am only now looking to my sails again." In fact, however, he was losing his hold of himself, becoming physically debilitated from actual deprivation. He was living in a 6-by-8-foot room costing $1.25 a week, and he came to a point when he had no money for the rent. Yet he would not let even his brother Paul know where he lived. Later he stated: "I tasted every misery which want can compel." He lost thirty pounds in the process. Thinking of suicide, he one day went to a nearby wharf with that in mind. There a drunken Scotsman passed him, gayly singing. He told Dreiser: "Ah, we're feeling verra low today, but we'll be better by and by." A canal boatman offered him a ride to Towanda saying: "I thought you might be running away from your wife." The bitter humor of the situation quickened his mind; he perceived the incongruity of his position and the urge to live reasserted itself.

Having previously heard that the New York Central Railroad favored writers in need of work, Dreiser applied for a job, but his debilitated condition made him unable to undertake physical labor. A chance meeting with Paul brought him relief. Paul readily saw his condition and had him go to William Muldoon's gymnasium for physical rehabilitation. After six weeks of a strict and strenuous regimen Dreiser felt strong enough to accept the railroad job and worked as a manual laborer for six months.

Pretty much his previous self again, he took a temporary job as assistant feature editor on the New York *Daily News*. His next position was to edit dime novels for Street & Smith and then *Smith's Magazine*. Jug returned to him and provided him with the physical comforts. The Taylor advance remaining on his mind, he paid it with his first savings. Now eager to succeed as a magazine editor, he persevered in his work with positive aggressiveness, stating: "This is the biggest, newest and most interesting country in the world, and to produce a big, new and interesting magazine we must reflect American manners and customs, thought and feeling." Having doubled the circulation of *Smith's Magazine* by April 1906, he accepted the editorship of the more prestigious *Broadway Magazine*. Following the conventional pattern despite the cultural changes brought about by the "muckraking" journalists, which made Upton Sinclair's *The Jungle* a bestseller, he kept the magazine "sweet and refreshing and clean," a policy which furthered his financial and social advancement.

If he behaved outwardly as the conventionally successful editor, he did not for a moment forget his grievous experience as a novelist. Still brooding over it through his years of depression and despair, he had come to believe that Mrs. Doubleday was chiefly responsible for the suppression of *Sister Carrie*, and enlarged upon it at every opportunity. With his improved outlook on life, however, he renewed his effort to republish the novel. Writing to Edna Kenton, a friendly literary critic in Chicago, on May 6, 1905, he told her: "*Sister Carrie* is still in the doldrums but the general situation is a little better. . . . I have made a number of sincere friends through it and besides, at least I own the plates. I am prepared to offer some good publisher very advantageous terms if only I can find one courageous enough to bring it out."

In 1907 Flora M. Holly, his agent, arranged with B. W. Dodge & Company, a small firm interested in contemporary writing, to publish *Sister Carrie*. On March 19 Dreiser conveyed this news to Marion Reedy: "I know you will be interested to hear that *Sister Carrie* has at last secured a publisher. . . . By the way, the book during the past seven years that it has been in my hands has been offered to every first class publishing house in New York, barring none, and then turned down."

Dreiser had bought the plates from Taylor for $550, and Dodge used them to bring out the new edition. Dreiser had also invested $5,000 in the Dodge firm and became its secretary as well as its editor. He went to considerable trouble to promote the book, obtaining favorable comments from prominent writers and making what use he could of favorable reviews. By September the novel had sold 4,617 copies. In 1908 Grosset & Dunlap issued a cheaper edition and sold 5,248 copies that year. The book was also published in Canada.

In June 1907 Dreiser was engaged as chief editor of the magazines published by the Butterick Publishing Company with a salary of $5,000 a year. *The Delineator* was his special interest, and he made it the advocate of the dignity of womanhood, of virtue and morality, and of the traditional conventions—thereby increasing its circulation, and in time having his salary doubled. Simultaneously he was actively, if informally, seeking books for the Dodge firm and articles for *The Bohemian*, of which he was part owner for the four months of its existence.

His relations with Jug had in the meantime deteriorated and she decided to leave him, hoping that he would miss her and ask her to return. Early in 1910, however, Dreiser became infatuated with a girl of seventeen whose mother was employed in his office. When he refused to leave the girl alone, the mother carried out the threat to disclose the affair to his employers. With *The Delineator* preaching the common virtues to its feminine readers, the publishers feared the damage of a scandal and in October they dismissed Dreiser from his position. About the same time the Dodge firm had become financially insolvent and Dreiser lost his investment of $5,000. Thus he was suddenly deprived of his prestigious and lucrative position and part of his savings, and was compelled to strike out anew. This time he was not discouraged, having retained some of the self-confidence he had gained as a highly successful editor. Indeed, he felt a kind of release from his conventional position and decided to resume the completion of his second novel.

Jennie Gerhardt was also based to a large extent on the life of another of his sisters, and once more he sought to portray American life as he knew it rather than as it was usually depicted. As before, he wrote with concentrated emotion and without regard to the niceties of diction or style. As Swanberg commented in this connection, "His writing mirrored the man—a lack of taste combined with nervousness, insecurity and his actual fear of time."

Adhering firmly to the basic content of the novel, Dreiser appreciated critical reactions from persons he respected. Once *Jennie* was finished, he had a number of people read it. James Huneker told him: "Again I say a big book, eloquent in its humanity, *too big*, too many repetitions (you ride certain words to death, such as *big*) and the best fiction I have read since Frank Norris." H. L. Mencken was even more favorable: "I must go to Hardy and Conrad to find its like. . . . You have written a novel that no other American of the time would have written." Yielding to critical consensus, he changed the ending by having Lester Kane marry for social position despite his love for Jennie and then confess it to Jennie on his death bed.

Dreiser was still insecure of himself as a novelist. Writing to Mencken on February 24, 1911, the day he finished *Jennie*, he declared: "I expect to try out this book game for about four or five books after which unless I am enjoying a good income from them I will quit." When Macmillan rejected the manuscript, he sent it to Harper & Brothers. Ripley Hitchcock, then at Harper, accepted the book on April 6, but told Dreiser the manuscript was too long and insisted on cuts and revisions that cost Dreiser $600 in outside editorial charges. Reduced to 425 printed pages, *Jennie Gerhardt* was published on October 19, both in this country and in England. The more important reviews were mostly favorable. Although 5,000 copies were sold in the first month, Dreiser was disappointed. To

F. A. Duneke, a Harper executive, he wrote on February 12, 1912: "You know I'm really astonished at the small sale of J. G. I have an amazing stack of notices which still continue to come—which proves I suppose that there is absolutely nothing in newspaper talk." It was hard for him to realize that a book of his could not possibly achieve the popularity of current best sellers.

For the past months he had been writing *The "Genius"* (the quotation marks he added later) and had been making good progress. But Harper editors were more interested in *The Financier*, on which he was also working, and he agreed to concentrate on the latter novel. As he planned it to be the first of a trilogy— treating fictionally the life of Charles T. Yerkes, the financial magnate who specialized in the control of street railways—he felt the need of following Yerkes's activities in Europe. When he told this to Grant Richards, the English publisher who admired his books, the latter worked out a plan that would enable Dreiser to make the trip and do the desired research. At Richards's urging The Century Company agreed to advance Dreiser $1,000 for three articles on Europe for its magazine and the proposed book. Harper also advanced him an additional $500 on *Jennie* and $2,000 on *The Financier*. With this money for expenses Dreiser sailed for Europe on November 22, and with Richards's help he saw what he wished to see and met the people who interested him. In the interim he abused Richards's hospitality and favors, and the two parted on a sour note.

Jennie Gerhardt sold 12,712 copies during the first six months. Harper also issued a new edition of *Sister Carrie*, much to Dreiser's gratification. When the manuscript of *The Financier* reached Harper, the editors found it much too long for one volume and considered issuing it in three parts. But Dreiser was ready to cut it along the lines suggested by Mencken, and on October 8, 1912, he told him: "I am taking out considerable material, the speeches of course and other financial stuff. . . . Harper's have been very nice in letting me do this as the plates were cast." These corrections, incidentally, cost Dreiser $720.90, but he did not object. When the book appeared, the reviews were mixed, but the sale reached 11,628 by the end of 1913. In November of that year The Century Company published *A Traveler at Forty*, giving his impressions of Europe.

For more than a year, until early in 1914, he concentrated on the writing of *The Titan*, the second volume in the Yerkes trilogy, for which Harper had given him an advance of $2,000. The completed manuscript was set into type and 8,500 sets of sheets were ready for the bindery when Harper executives suddenly decided not to publish the book. On March 6 Dreiser informed Mencken: "Harper's . . . have decided not to publish. Reasons—the realism is too hard and uncompromising and their policy cannot stand it. Doran is considering it at present." Although neither Elias nor Swanberg, Dreiser's biographers, mention J. P. Morgan as the likely reason for the Harper action, the House of Harper had long been heavily indebted to the banker and in his virtual control. With the book being severely critical of American banking and business practices, Harper executives must have thought it best not to risk Morgan's displeasure.

The manuscript was rejected by Doran, Mitchell Kennerley, Century, Dodd, Mead—the latter firm telling Dreiser that if the book was "too strong for Harper's it would surely be too rich" for them. The English firm of John Lane, which had established an American branch under the directorship of J. J. Jones, then agreed to publish the novel and gave Dreiser an advance of $1,000 and a royalty of 20 percent. Published without delay, it sold 8,016 copies by the end of the year—not enough to repay the advances of $3,000. To earn money for his living expenses, Dreiser did much miscellaneous writing for magazines. He also arranged for a final separation from his wife in February 1915.

The "Genius" was Dreiser's next book to reach completion. To his surprise, Harper expressed interest in it. On March 31, 1914, he informed Mencken:

> Harper's have asked me to permit them to publish *The "Genius."* This sounds wild but it is true and they have backed it by an offer of aid. They feel they have made a mistake. Neither will they part with the published volumes now in their possession—at least not yet—the same people who think me unfit for publication.

Jefferson Jones of John Lane, however, expressed strong interest in the book, considered it Dreiser's best novel, and offered him an advance of $1,500, which Dreiser accepted. The novel being found too long and prolix, a Lane editor cut it heavily and Floye Dell also edited it to the same end. Published in October, the book was reviewed less favorably than the previous books and sold 6,577 copies by the end of the year. Dreiser, disappointed, suspected Lane of falsifying actual sales and asked friends in several cities to check bookstore sales. His other novels had, of course, continued to sell, and by the end of 1916 *Jennie* had sold 29,000 copies, *The Financier* nearly 24,000 copies, and *Sister Carrie* over 4,000 copies.

In July 1916, nearly a year after publication, a minister in Cincinnati found the *The "Genius"* filled with "obscenity and blasphemy" and called it to the attention of John S. Sumner, head of the New York Society for the Suppression of Vice. An attentive reading caused Sumner to appear at the Lane office and tell Jones to stop selling the novel or answer criminal charges—having shown him what he considered seventeen "profane" and seventy-five "lewd" passages. Jones complied without protest. Dreiser's reaction was quick and furious. "To me," he wrote in *The New Republic*, "this interference by the Vice Society with serious letters is the worst and most corrupting form of oppression conceivable to the human mind, plumbing as it does the depths of ignorance and intolerance and checking initiative and inspiration at its source." Determined to fight this censorship, and angry at Jones for yielding to Sumner without resistance, he wrote of him to Mencken on November 4:

> My estimate of him is now so low that I can scarcely bring myself to talk to the man anymore. He has broken his word in every matter concerning which we had specific agreement. . . . He's a bag of mush and I want to quit. I really think the man has no real publishing acumen and at the first real chance I am going to leave.

With Mencken in charge of the protest, members of the Authors League of America and others defended the book, although not a few of the 500 protestants disliked both the book and the author. Dreiser also brought a friendly suit against the Lane Company for stopping the sale of the novel, but no action resulted. The net effect of this opposition to Sumner was nil, and the book remained supressed until 1923, when Boni & Liveright brought out a new edition.

Writing to Mencken in February 2, 1919, Dreiser indicated why the novel was being kept out of the bookstores:

> As for *The "Genius"*—I had it all arranged some time ago for Boni to pay Jones $2500 and make me a 5-year contract—and then he jumped the price to $5000 after refusing to answer even telephone calls for weeks!. . . Personally, at this stage I have concluded that literature is a beggar's game—but if you are born a thief—a thief you are and jails must be made the best of.

In July 1917 Horace Liveright, the flamboyant and venturesome founder of the new publishing house of Boni & Liveright, approached Dreiser with the proposal that he become his publisher. He assured him of his admiration for his writing and of his disdain for censors. Not too favorably impressed with the flashy Liveright, Dreiser warily gave him permission to reissue *Sister Carrie* to test his enterprise. Soon after, having difficulty in placing his shorter pieces with magazines and getting his plays produced, he gradually agreed to let Liveright publish several of his new books: *Free and Other Stories* (1918), *Twelve Men* (1919), *The Hand of the Potter* (1919), *Hey-Rub-a-Dub-Dub* (1919), *Newspaper Days* (1922), and *The Color of a Great City* (1923). None of these books sold well enough to satisfy Dreiser, and he again suspected the veracity of the sales figures.

In 1919 Dreiser met Helen Richardson, a distant cousin and an attractive actress, and became enamored of her—more deeply than of various other women he had been associating with previously—and began to live with her without seriously seeking a divorce from Jug. For the ensuing three years they made their home in California.

Liveright meanwhile was making an earnest effort to publicize Dreiser's books as he published them, aware of their limited marketability. His main objective was to get Dreiser to complete *The Bulwark*, a novel he had worked on sporadically. Aware of Dreiser's distrust of him, Liveright wrote him on February 6, 1920: "If you would have a little more confidence in me you would save your soul a lot of bitterness and make it much more fun for me to continue to put my best efforts (poor as I know they are) into your books." When informed by Dreiser that *The Bulwark* was near completion, Liveright exclaimed: "Hurrah! You have put new life into me. When you say that you will do your very best to give me the Bulwark before Christmas, I feel that the trick is turned."

Dreiser nevertheless continued to distrust him, feeling that his chief interest was money rather than books. On August 27, 1920, he told Mencken: "Quietly and under cover I am negotiating a return to Harper & Brothers. All my books published by Liveright are published on a *5-year lease*, so I need only assign the leases to Harper's or any other firm. I have the feeling that Liveright cannot sell books for me." When the Harper negotiations fell through, he approached Scribner and Century in his desire to place his books with what he considered a good and aggressive house.

His distrust of Liveright flared up when he learned that *Sister Carrie* was being sold in a New York department store at the remainder price of ninety-eight cents—thereby depriving him of royalties—presumably unaware that this was a common procedure with books for which the regular market had declined. On October 25 he wrote Mencken: "I own *Sister Carrie*—plates and rights. The same are leased to B & L for royalty. It was specifically understood that the book was to be sold at $2.00. If I can establish this as a fact I will have a heart to heart talk with Liveright. I doubt if he is straight with me."

Meanwhile Liveright learned about Dreiser's secret dealings with other publishers and confronted him with his grievance: "I have published everything you brought to me without any sort of qualifications; even 'The Hand of the Potter.'. . . Your last few letters to me show me that you have no feeling of regard or loyalty for me personally, so our affairs must be regarded in the strict light of business proceedings."

Liveright was further disturbed to learn that Dreiser had again put *The Bulwark* aside. Nor was he appeased when Dreiser informed him in December 1920 that he had begun a new novel, "which I hope to have done by spring." In fact, however, he was then concocting articles for immediate financial gain. Yet Liveright, ever the optimist, expressed his delight: "If I can't sell twenty thousand copies of your next novel I am willing to quit the publishing game."

Liveright had also heard of an autobiographical work, later published as *Newspaper Days*, and asked Dreiser about it. Now reconciled to remain with Liveright, Dreiser in a lengthy reply, asked for an advance of $2,000 on this manuscript and a long-run financial arrangement:

> The thing that troubles me is how to keep an even keel with you for I am not anxious to go bouncing around from publisher to publisher, and yet I am not at all sure that you will see your way to doing what seems to me a very reasonable thing for me to expect from any regular publisher of mine, that is financial support so long as I am really doing honest work and making an honest effort to make money for him and for myself.

Dreiser's opinion of publishers, in the face of rejection after rejection, was of course exceedingly low. To his lawyer, A. C. Hume, he stated on March 20, 1922:

> No American publisher unless it is Harper appears to me to have the faintest conception of the wisdom of taking a man who has a possible future and helping him to build himself up in any way which will make him and them some money in the future or themselves money once he is gone. They have no faith in anyone, really. They live from day to day and from hand to mouth. I can get twenty-seven different American publishers to "take a chance" on some trashy third-rate work.

Refusing, however, to give up his search for a publisher other than Liveright, he communicated with Dodd, Mead, which had taken over the American branch of John Lane. Their conservative position disappointed him, as he explained to Mencken on March 22, 1922:

> The Dodd people are not publishers of liberal books. They approach me about [as] a Baptist snouts a pervert. I am to alter my books. I am to let them pick and choose.

They will see whether I can do anything worthy of them. They do not want "The 'Genius' " unless it is properly pruned around the vitals.

This additional experience again reconciled him to remain with Liveright, and in another letter to Mencken he admitted: "As for Liveright he is certainly a poor fish but a port in storm. He has rendered me one service and another and I am not ungrateful." Late in 1922 he came to a permanent arrangement with him. Liveright bought the plates and stock of the Dreiser books in the control of other publishers, agreed to publish an unexpurgated edition of *The "Genius"*, pay Dreiser an annual stipend of $4,000 against royalties, publish *A Gallery of Women* in 1923, a novel or *The Color of a Great City* in the spring of 1924, volume two of his autobiography that fall, two volumes of stories in 1925, and the third volume of the autobiography in 1926. Liveright thus gambled $25,000 on Dreiser's ability to perform on schedule.

The relationship remained stormy. Dreiser continued to distrust Liveright and accused him of not being square with him. The policy of the latter was to answer angry or insulting letters with mild flattery. In one letter he stated: "Let me reiterate what I have frequently said to you: That I am heart and soul for your work; that we now have a big investment in it, and that from now on you will see a very much greater concerted campaign for the sale of all your work." This he did when he published *Newspaper Days* in 1922, spending $2,000 on advertising, yet when the book sold fewer than 3,000 copies, Dreiser suspected him of falsifying the records. *The Color of a Great City* likewise sold only 2,274 copies by the year's end. *The "Genius"*, however, sold 12,301 copies during the same period, but even that good showing failed to satisfy Dreiser.

All this time Dreiser was struggling with the composition of *An American Tragedy* and failed to meet the deadlines he had promised. "For some reason," he confessed, "this book is harder than any I ever wrote. I might as well be chipping it out of solid rock." Self-conscious about his broken promises to publishers, he admitted to Mencken on November 14, 1924: "All my literary life I have worked on *advanced* royalties. If I hadn't been able to trick the moral publishers out of the immoral money—and to the prejudices of such writers . . . whose books sell—I wouldn't have been able to work at all."

When he finally finished the manuscript, it had nearly a million words. His women editors—admirers of his whom he paid for the work—claimed to have reduced the narrative by half. Liveright's editors trimmed another 50,000 words, although some of the deletions were later restored. Dreiser also did considerable revising in the proofs. It was published in two volumes at five dollars in the middle of December 1925—presumably too late for Christmas gift buying—and Liveright gave a party to celebrate the event. The first reviews were highly laudatory, and sales during the two remaining weeks of the year came to 13,914 copies; a total of 50,000 copies were sold within a year. For the first time in a quarter century of effort Dreiser achieved nationwide popularity.

Liveright, now also a theatrical producer, arranged for the dramatization of the novel by Patrick Kearney, which was highly successful and had a long run. He also approached cinema studios for the movie rights, telling Dreiser he might receive as much as $35,000 if the play was a hit. Dreiser, however, continued to distrust his business dealings and was determined to pay him only a nominal percentage of the amount he would receive. When Liveright arranged for the two of them to close the deal for the movie rights at a lunch with Jesse Lasky and Walter Wanger, Dreiser told him he would ask $100,000 and that he would not give him more than 10 percent. When Liveright tried to exact a higher percentage of the $90,000 finally agreed upon, maintaining that Dreiser had agreed "to take care of him," the latter was so angered that he threw a cup of coffee in his face. And in a letter to Liveright soon after he stated: "I consider that I have been most outrageously insulted and sharply dealt with into the bargain. Neither commercially or socially have I ever lied to you. On the contrary I have been of immense commercial and literary aid to you and you know that." He demanded a written apology—and received it.

Liveright continued to advertise Dreiser's books lavishly, with the result that in 1926 *Sister Carrie* sold 3,412 copies and *The "Genius"* 8,087 copies. When Harper made overtures to Dreiser that year, he used this interest to extract more favorable commitments from Liveright: 20 percent royalties, another $10,000 of advertising on *An American Tragedy*, and a one-volume cheaper edition of it. Liveright even made him a director of the firm.

Dreiser had suddenly become affluent, with an income of $200,000 in 1926 and about half that much the following year. Wishing to enjoy his new wealth, he rented a duplex apartment for $3,500 a year, bought expensive gowns for Helen, agreed to pay Jug $200 a month, and gave frequent lavish parties. He also bought a tract of land near Mount Kisco and built a costly summer home on it.

He continued to bully Liveright by threatening to leave him, encouraged bids from other publishers, and asked his agent if he could get him a contract that would pay him $25,000 annually for ten years and half of that amount for the following ten years. No publisher was of course interested. He had in the meantime invested his surplus cash in stocks, losing about half of it later. By that time Liveright had lost control of his company and had gone to Hollywood to make his way as an agent for Paramount.

Always inclined to favor the poor and oppressed, Dreiser had in the 1920s become involved in reform and radical movements, and gave his name and time to various organizations to the end of his life. In 1927 he accepted an invitation to attend the tenth anniversary of the Russian Revolution as a guest of the Soviet government. While there he visited various parts of the country with the aim of writing a book about it. When it was published, he was accused of plagiarism by Dorothy Thompson, who had also published a book of her interpretation of what she saw and heard. Both had in fact made use of material provided them by Anna Louise Strong, but when Sinclair Lewis publicly accused Dreiser of using his wife's material, the angered Dreiser slapped his face for slandering him.

In 1929 the Liveright firm published *A Gallery of Women*, and its sale that year reached 13,653 copies. Two years later *Dawn*, the first volume of Dreiser's autobiography, sold only 5,992 copies on publication. As before, Dreiser was dissatisfied with the sale of these books. He expected *Tragic America*, a loose and uneven discussion of his interest in reform, published in 1932, to sell 100,000 copies but only 4,562 copies were actually sold. With his need of money intensified by his losses in the stock market, the shrunken sales of his books worried him, fearing that he might be put in the precarious financial position that had embittered his early years as an author.

When the Liveright firm went into receivership, he remained for more than a year without a publisher. The reorganized Liveright company held 13,000 copies of his twenty-two books as well as their plates. He offered to buy the books at twenty-five cents a copy and to pay $2,000 for the plates, but Arthur Pell, who controlled the firm, demanded a dollar a copy and $12,000 for the plates. Dreiser sued but lost, and was ordered to pay a total of $12,789.

Long habitually distrustful of Jewish publishers, he failed to interest any of the non-Jewish firms. In need of a publisher, he yielded to the flattering offer made by Simon & Schuster: an advance of $5,000 and the reissuance of all his books. To celebrate the acquisition of their new author, the firm gave a large party in Dreiser's Mount Kisco home, inviting some 300 guests.

The union was not a happy one. Friction arose almost at the outset in connection with the enlarged new edition of *Moods*, the volume of poems which Liveright had previously published. Interested primarily in Dreiser's new novel, Simon & Schuster felt that an exceedingly long volume of middling verse would be a wrong start for their new author. Yet the mere suggestion of reducing the length of the book angered Dreiser, and he threatened to take the book to another publisher. To R. L. Simon he wrote on February 5, 1935:

> It is my feeling that an author and his publisher should be in fair intellectual as well as critical accord. In this instance the failure to approve of the contents of either the Liveright volume as it stood or this revised version as presented by me, suggests a critical gap which cannot well be overcome.... Decidedly you can understand that I am not interested in either a forced or half-hearted or anything less than a wholehearted endorsement of any volume I propose to publish.

Simon & Schuster placated him by publishing *Moods* as he wanted it.

Still primarily interested in his next novel, M. Lincoln Schuster inquired about its progress. In reply Dreiser ambiguously implied that he was working on *The Stoic* "full time every day," when in fact he was preoccupied with his projected scientific volume, *Formulae Called Man*, which was to hold his interest for over a decade and which he never finished. On January 5, 1936, Schuster again prodded him gently about the novel, stating: "Again our attitude is not one of unseemly impatience, but genuinely profound interest and an effort to plan our important publications intelligently, with the necessary advance work. We rise, therefore, to inquire whether you wish to tell us anything new about the progress of the novel." Forgetting that he was already long overdue on his promise to deliver the completed manuscript, Dreiser replied blandly: "I cannot give it to you for Spring publication. Will it make so much difference if presently I give you a really important book and follow it later with *The Stoic*?" He of course had his scientific book in mind.

With the passing of time Schuster became more pressing. "Dick Simon and I would like ever so much to see you and arrange a session at your convenience." Annoyed by this pressure, Dreiser turned upon them for not bringing his earlier books into print. And when he moved to California he did not even give them his address. In the hope of being taken over by another publisher, he approached Scribner and Viking, but they were not interested. All this time he was so preoccupied with his scientific speculations that he found himself blocked in doing any writing on the novel.

By 1939 he owed Simon & Schuster $10,114.39 in advances and other charges. Failing to find another publisher, he came to believe that Arthur Pell and Leon Shimkin of Simon & Schuster were conspiring to keep his books out of print. To his agent W. C. Lengel he wrote in May 1939: "It may be nothing more than a suspicion but I have had the feeling all along that the dreadful deal I got on my left over Liveright books . . . was arranged between Pell and themselves, through Mr. Shimkin, and that all along he has been a cause as well as a party to their attitude toward me." And when Shimkin asked him about the novel, he replied on December 21, 1939, that Simon & Schuster were never really his publishers, since they had only a "tentative and provisional memorandum of Proposal" with him. He also accused the firm of "dumping" the Liveright books.

> But, as you know, they never did reprint from any of them, but instead, in addition to selling all my bound copies to old book dealers and so avoiding either advertising them or paying me the 15% royalty on the same to which I was entitled, they pocketed the money and in addition turned over the plates to Doubleday & Doran of *Jennie Gerhardt*, *The "Genius"*, *An American Tragedy*, and *The Financier* to reprint and turn over to them [Simon & Schuster] all royalties received by them in order to further reduce my indebtedness to them.

By 1940 Dreiser was a confused, disturbed, and troubled man. Strongly pacifistic, gingerly fraternizing with Communists, he jumped at the chance of being paid $5,000 for writing a small anti-war book for Veritas Press, an obscure little firm operated by a European refugee. By the time the manuscript was ready, patriotic sentiment has become so strong that two printers refused to handle the book. The refugee himself, fearful for his residence status, backed out, and the book was taken over by the radical Modern Age Books. With certain passages toned down, the book made little stir on publication and was suppressed three months later.

Dreiser's financial condition eased when he succeeded in selling the movie rights to *Sister Carrie* for $40,000, and about the same time, being his brother Paul's heir, he received $50,000 for the song, "My Gal Sal." The following year he settled with Simon & Schuster for $8,500 and arranged with Earle Balch of

Putnam's to take him on as author. He announced this transaction to Mencken on April 2, 1942: "After 8 years I managed to get loose from those lice labeled Simon & Schuster and am now in the hands once more of an American publisher." Yet he was unable to make any progress on *The Bulwark*, which he had promised Balch, and was again making the same excuses. In August he stated: "As to *The Bulwark*, all I can say at the moment is that I am working every day on it." (At that very time he was spending eleven days with a new woman friend.)

Tired of waiting, Balch rescinded the arrangement and Dreiser returned the advance. Thereupon he told Mencken on December 4, 1943: "What I am looking for is a publisher who would be willing to take over all my books extant, and publish my next volume, *whatever it is*, and all future volumes, and upon so doing, advertise all my books as a whole." His effort to interest Knopf and Viking failed. They and others had become wary of an author with whom it was hard to get along and who seemed to prefer dubious philosophy to salable fiction. As a consequence he was again without a publisher for nearly two years.

In 1944 The American Academy of Arts and Letters gave Dreiser the Award of Merit Medal and a thousand dollar prize, granted to a distinguished author every fifth year. He accepted it gracefully despite his earlier deprecation of the Academy. Feeling, however, that not enough attention was being paid to him, he declined President Walter Damrosh's invitation to a formal dinner. A month later—his wife Jug dead two years—he arranged to marry Helen after living with her nearly twenty-five years. The ceremony was performed in a small town in Oregon to avoid publicity.

Keenly conscious of his declining vigor, he determined to complete *The Bulwark* and persuaded Marguerite Harris, with whom he had worked before, to come to California and assist him in the writing. This novel had been in gestation since 1912 when Anna Tatum told him the story of her family. He had worked on it sporadically—each time putting it aside, unable to resolve certain aspects of it. Having by now grown old and spiritually mellow, he no longer scorned the emotional leaven of religion. He thus endowed Solon Barnes with the Quaker winsomeness of universal love, so that he emerged in the image of Dreiser's father, only ennobled with an idealism transcending personal shortcomings: "For to know and understand is to love, not hate."

In 1945 Doubleday & Company contracted to publish the novel—the firm thus going full circle in forty-five years. When the manuscript was completed, it needed drastic editing, which was done by Louise Campbell, James T. Farrell, and Donald B. Elder, a Doubleday editor. To the latter he wrote on December 22, six days before he died: "I would like to say right here that you have done an excellent job on the final editing. You have been conscientious, sympathetically sensitive and considerate toward my work all the way through. And I am deeply grateful to you."

With the writing of *The Bulwark* done, Dreiser turned to the completion of *The Stoic*, the third volume of Cowperwood's financial activities. Feeling his age both physically and emotionally, and intellectually less rigorous on the shortcomings of human behavior, he no longer stressed Cowperwood's drive for wealth and power and sensual pleasure, dwelling instead on the aesthetics of beauty and on Berenice's immersion in the philosophy of Yoga. He kept writing until the day before he died, and left the manuscript virtually finished.

The Bulwark was published posthumously in 1946, and *The Stoic* was issued a year later. Both novels were received mostly unfavorably but not harshly so, and both sold relatively well. In the early 1950s Mrs. Dreiser arranged with World Publishing Company to republish Dreiser's six major novels as well as his short stories.

14.

The Doubleday~
Kipling Affinity

Unless Frank N. Doubleday's career as publisher is viewed in its entirety his true image will remain elusive. Thus, his bigoted behavior in 1900 gives, in a sense, an unfair impression of him as a person and as a publisher. It must be understood that his reaction to Carrie's amoral life was in keeping with the mores of the time. His shock at the idea that Dreiser permitted a woman to sin and go unpunished was a normal reaction of his conventional morality. As a man of his generation he was not only typically puritanic, but also, in the spirit of free enterprise, ambitious, aggressive, eager to become the most successful book publisher by following the precepts and practices of leading bankers and businessmen of that day. Dealing, however, with men rather than with money, he manifested a loyalty to principle that placed him a cut above the money-men of the 1900s.

This aspect of his character was early evidenced in his behavior toward Upton Sinclair's *The Jungle*, which he published in 1906. When Armour & Company learned that the manuscript was being considered by the Doubleday firm, it canceled its advertising contract with the company's *World's Work*. This attempt to influence editorial policy was strongly resented by Doubleday. Although he had no sympathy for Sinclair's radical views and would most likely have rejected the manuscript, he was so offended by the thought, as he wrote later, "that a Chicago butcher should tell us how to run our editorial department," that he decided to evaluate the book without prejudice.

On first examination the editors assumed that Sinclair's horrible story of the stockyards could not possibly be true. One of the staff went to Chicago to check the data, and "a careful investigation provided proof that the tale was not overwrought and was essentially true." Also in the book's favor was its vivid style. Doubleday therefore felt it his duty to publish the manuscript. As he admitted subsequently, "It was a disagreeable job, a disagreeable atmosphere, and a disagreeable incident which we had to accept to appease our own consciences." On learning that the manuscript had been accepted, the Armour Company threatened to sue for libel and a half million dollars in damages—but it never did.

The Jungle for a time attracted little attention. Exercising his zeal as re-former, Sinclair sent a copy to President Theodore Roosevelt. The latter, a neighbor and friend of Doubleday, was indignant that the book should have been published. When Doubleday explained that he had accepted it as a matter of duty after he had found its contents accurate in essential particulars, Roosevelt sent an investigator from the Agricultural Department to Chicago. Bribed by the Armour people, the man whitewashed the packing firm. When Roosevelt con-fronted Doubleday with the report, the publisher insisted that the inspector was dishonest. Roosevelt then sent a second investigator, and the latter corroborated Sinclair's accusations. Now outraged by the malpractices of the packers, Roose-velt made the report public, causing a tremendous national sensation. There-upon, as Doubleday triumphantly stated, "The sale of the book moved by leaps and bounds."

Doubleday's relation with Rudyard Kipling began in 1895. He was then man-ager of Scribner's subscription department, having risen to this post from office boy. One day he was asked by Edward Bok, another successful employee of the company, if he could get him a complete set of Kipling's books. There was none at the time, but the query stimulated Doubleday to bring out such a set. Since none of the books were published by Scribner, and since they had been brought out by three different firms, Charles Scribner saw no point in making the effort. But Doubleday was not stopped by this rebuff. He wrote to Kipling, who was then living in Brattleboro, Vermont, for an appointment. Receiving a friendly, if noncommittal response, Doubleday gained Scribner's permission to make the trip, which he did on a cold, snowy day in November. Kipling wrote about this visit in *Something of Myself*:

> To "Naulahka" on a wet day, came from Scribner's of New York a large young man called Frank Doubleday, with a proposal, among other things, for a complete edition of my then works. One accepts or refuses things that really matter on per-sonal or illogical grounds. We took to that young man at sight, and he and his wife became our closest friends.

Doubleday told Kipling that if he favored the idea of a complete set of his books to be sold by Scribner to subscribers, he thought the three publishers would permit him to go ahead—provided they were told that Kipling favored the project. Kipling agreed.

On his return to New York, Doubleday first approached George P. Brett, head of The Macmillan Company, which had eight of Kipling's books on its list. Aware that Doubleday had Kipling's approval, Brett agreed to give the restricted permission for a fee of $2,500. Appleton's one Kipling book Doubleday obtained on the strength of the Macmillan permission. The Century Company balked at first, as it had a similar project in view, but the use of Kipling's goodwill as a le-ver in the end gained Doubleday the needed approval, Kipling was delighted with Doubleday's accomplishment, and Scribner soon published the set with "great success."

When Doubleday in 1897 informed Kipling that he had decided to start his own publishing house in partnership with S. S. McClure, the highly successful magazine publisher, the response was:

> So it's McClure, is it? I thirst for further particulars, because I have a lively recollection of a winter day in Vermont when *McClure's Magazine* was just being born: and for eight (or eighteen) consecutive hours that cyclone in a frock-coat whirled round in our little shanty explaining, exhorting, haling and prophesying. He is a great man but he'd kill me in a week with mere surplus of energy.

He cautioned Doubleday against giving up his secure and lucrative position with Scribner, but when his advice was not taken he had enough confidence in Doubleday to give him his new book. A. P. Watt, Kipling's agent, asked for an advance of £500, which Doubleday did not have but managed to borrow. In 1898 he published *The Day's Work* and sold over 100,000 copies—more than any previous book by Kipling had ever sold.

Although Doubleday was only in control of the new and still unimportant book division of the McClure enterprise, he was too ambitious and too able to permit himself to be overshadowed by the other McClure executives. McClure became aware of this in 1899 and told John S. Phillips, his chief associate: "He can't help forcing himself into your place and mine and he can't help trying to make himself not only first but the only one. . . . I really think he will have to choose once and for all whether he will subordinate himself to being one of us or else quit entirely." The truth of this evaluation of Doubleday became evident before the end of that year when he decided to break with McClure and form his own company, with Walter Hines Page as his junior partner.

Early in 1899 Mr. and Mrs. Kipling sailed for a visit to the United States with their three children. On shipboard Kipling and the children caught colds. By the time they reached New York all but one of the children were sick with pneumonia. They were in their hotel rooms when Doubleday visited them on Washington's Birthday. Mrs. Kipling was in despair, unable to care for her ill family by herself. Doubleday immediately assumed charge of the situation, telling her he "would stay with him until he was well, and do the best I could in the errand-boy kind of service that is needed in a sickroom." He secured the services of two eminent physicians as well as the required nurses. When it became necessary to obtain good whiskey, he went to Andrew Carnegie and received from him all that was needed. Kipling's grave illness quickly became front-page news, and reporters crowded into the hotel to learn of his condition and to secure interviews. To keep them away from the sickroom, Doubleday became Kipling's spokesman. He let none see him, and permitted others only in connection with his friend's treatment. For nearly three months he remained at the hotel, neglecting his own family and his business. Later he wrote:

> My job was to take care of the nurses, see that people were fed; provide plenty of whiskey of the finest quality from Mr. Carnegie's cellar; and do whatever was nec-

essary to keep the ball going. One of the most difficult tasks of all was to see the reporters twice a day. . . . I recall that I was so tired that I could not remember my own name. I slept on the floor just outside of the sickroom, and was busy with these various enterprises until I almost passed away. The whole thing is a horror in my mind, and rather hate to think of it; but in the end Mr. Kipling's life was saved, although Josephine [a daughter] died.

When Kipling was convalescing, Doubleday visited him for about an hour daily; and when he was well enough to return to England, Doubleday accompanied him to attend to his comforts.

Kipling was of course immensely grateful for this extraordinary devotion. While still in New York he began to call Doubleday "Effendi"—an acronym of his initials—as a token of friendship. He also gave him the manuscript of *The Light that Failed* as an expression of his gratitude. To the end of their lives their intimacy was close. Doubleday published his later books, paid him the very highest royalty, and promoted each volume most energetically. "We have succeeded," he wrote, "in finding new ways to sell the books, and have kept a steady pressure on every title."

One of the means by which the firm maximized Kipling's income was to bring out authorized editions of his books which had been pirated before the Copyright Act of 1890 and sell them at prices lower than those charged by the pirates. As late as August 4, 1913, Kipling wrote Doubleday:

> I shall be glad if we are able to deal a proper blow to the pirates. I was quite clear in my talk with Charles Scribner on this subject, and told him quite plainly that my great interest at present was pirates, and that pure spite more than anything else had influenced me in my desire for a free hand, so that I might strike at the pirates.

And in *Something of Myself* Kipling referred to it with pleasure: "Frank Doubleday chased the pirates up with cheaper and cheaper editions, so that their thefts became less profitable."

There was a happy affinity between Kipling and Doubleday, a kind of mutual admiration which overlooked minor differences and emphasized similarities of character and world views. And this intimacy extended to members of their families. Thus when Nelson Doubleday at the age of eight read Kipling's story about an elephant in *St. Nicholas Magazine*, he asked "Uncle Rud" to write similar stories about other animals. He then suggested to his father that he publish these tales in a book and give him a penny for each copy sold. Both Kipling and Doubleday humored the boy, and when more than a half million copies of *Just So Stories for Little Children* were sold, Nelson received a total of $5,000 as his share.

The two families saw each other whenever Doubleday came to England on business. Kipling, grateful for large royalties which Doubleday's aggressive merchandising made possible, welcomed him most affectionately. On January 4, 1921, spurred by the season's geniality, he sent Doubleday his New Year's greetings to express his gratitude to the firm:

> I want to send, through you, to every member of your Firm and Staff in every Department, my thanks and acknowledgments, overdue these many years, for the in-

terest, care, thought, time, and trouble they have always taken over every detail connected with my books. I feel, as I have felt throughout, that I have good friends at Garden City in every branch of the shop. I should like them all to know that it touches me, cheers me, and makes me care to go on. And with my thanks, if they will take them, I send each of them individually my best wishes for their good fortune through this year and the years to come. I could put this better if I did it formally, but in matters of feeling, one does not feel formal.

Nearly six years later, in a letter dated September 7, 1926, Kipling told Doubleday of a visit Charles Scribner had paid him, during which he was a subject of their talk. He then took the occasion to express his persistent admiration for the man who published his books so successfully in the United States:

Day before yesterday Charles Scribner and his wife dropped in, and they both talked of you a lot. So I write to express (one doesn't do it half enough) my ancient and undeviating affection of all those many years. Also to "constate" the fact which I don't remember that I've ever done before, that you really *are* a very big man. In a world (yours is rather worse than ours, if possible) full of alien and imported littleness Big Men are darn' rare. I've been sitting back with a pipe and reviewing as much as I know of all you've done and made and caused to be, and set in motion and inspired in your own land and outside of it. . . . It seemed to me somehow that it wasn't merely the methods and manners of publishing, but the whole spirit and outlook of it, that you have revolutionized by your work *first* in the U. S. and then over here. . . . This is one of the things one thinks over but generally (if one is an Englishman) doesn't set down; and now I've got it off my chest I feel more comfortable—and I hope *you* do, old man. Ever with affection.

Nothing occurred between them to lessen this intimacy. Both men suffered from some of the ills of aging, and they comforted each other as best they could. Their views of world events, as well as of matters more immediate to their own lives, coincided in a common understanding. Writing to Doubleday on November 4, 1927, Kipling stated: "I have worked . . . close on thirty-one [years] with you—and never a thing that could be dignified by name of difference."

During the last several years of his life Doubleday suffered from severe physical discomfort, making it necessary for him to keep moving, mostly in a specially built automobile, to lessen the pain. When his end came in January 1934, Kipling was deeply affected. To Nelson, who had informed him of his father's death, he stated:

Yours of the 26th has come in a few days after the cables telling us that the release had come at last. For it *was* a release—and a happy one for him—in that I find nothing to regret. As for the rest, when you're as old as I, you'll realize what it means and marks to lose a life-long friend and almost a brother.

15.

F.N. Doubleday

&

Joseph Conrad

Not until 1914 was Doubleday's connection with Joseph Conrad fully established; and while it became close thereafter, it was never as intimate as with Kipling. Conrad was of course of quite a different background and character from either Kipling or Doubleday, and for years he was not the kind of author whom most publishers seek to cultivate and promote.

Of Polish birth and upbringing, a seaman and sea captain for nearly twenty years, knowing no English until his late teens, Conrad quit the sea when he was nearly forty and settled in London to devote himself to writing fiction. His first book, *Almayer's Folly*, which he had written in large part while still at sea, Edward Garnett liked well enough to recommend favorably to the publisher for whom he was a reader. The book was generally well received by reviewers, but its sale was small. Yet Garnett encouraged him to continue writing, and persuaded the publisher to give him a small advance on his second book, *An Outcast of the Islands* (1896), which also found favor with reviewers but not with the public. H. G. Wells, having reviewed the volume, told Conrad: "You have everything it takes to become a splendid novelist except skill, but that comes with practice."

Although the income from writing was minimal, Conrad, already married in 1896, decided to persist in his writing rather than resume his work on a ship. To a cousin in Poland he wrote in March of that year: "The only means of existence remaining to me is writing . . . and in this respect I have no qualms about my success. I know what I am capable of. It is just a matter of earning money—which is something quite different from literary merit. Well, I am not sure, but my needs are modest." Yet he had difficulty meeting even these modest needs, as the small sale of his books did not encourage publishers to advance him money on new ones. Garnett did what he could to recommend him to publishers of his acquaintance, but with little success. He did manage after a while to arouse the interest of S. S. Pawling of William Heinemann, and the latter's encouraging offer was deeply appreciated by Conrad, as stated in his letter to Garnett of May 11, 1897:

> I had this morning a letter from Pawling so utterly satisfying to me that there can be no question of even thinking about anyone else as long as he wants me. . . . He promises to give £100 for the next book. To obtain £400 for serial rights. And he writes very nicely. I had rather have his promise than another man's cash down.

Garnett sent chapters of the new book, *The Nigger of the "Narcissus"*, to W. E. Henley, who was favorably enough impressed with them to print them in *The New Review*. The novel, however, was again only a *succès d'estime*, so that while Conrad's reputation was high in literary circles his books had few readers.

His experience in the United States was even more discouraging. Macmillan took his first book but was not interested in the second. Appleton issued it at a loss. Dodd, Mead published *The Nigger of the "Narcissus"* under the title of *The Children of the Sea*, but this novel too suffered the same public indifference. Scribner tried its luck with *Tales of Unrest*, but again without success. Reflecting on this experience, Conrad felt that the promises of further publication in America were "as inviting as a peep into a brigand's cave and a good deal less reassuring." To keep himself in bread he wrote stories which he managed to place with magazines on both sides of the Atlantic.

When F. N. Doubleday organized his own publishing house in 1898, he went to England in search of manuscripts. In his visit with Heinemann he asked him to suggest a possible future Kipling among the newer writers. The English publisher, impressed with Conrad's literary talent despite the small sale of his books, told him, as Doubleday later recalled it:

> I can tell you of at least one. They call him Joseph Conrad, because he has an impossible Polish name, Josef Theodor Nalecz Korzeniowski, and he is almost starving to death. He has written two or three books which have been entirely unsuccessful, and he can't get enough money to keep body and soul together until he can write some more. He is at present writing a novel called *The Rescue*, but he hasn't enough money to live on until it is finished. If you would like to contribute fifty dollars a month, I will advance an equal amount, and he will be provided with the means to get this job done. I am sure it will pay its way, though I have no great expectation of a large sale.

This was agreed upon between them. After more than a year, however, Conrad found himself unable to complete the narrative. He expressed his deep regret, and sent Doubleday the part he had written. This was read, put away, and forgotten.

Conrad's next two books, *Lord Jim* and *The Inheritors*, were published in the United States by McClure, Phillips & Company. In 1902 Doubleday brought out Conrad's *Youth and Other Stories*. The next collection of his stories, which included "The Typhoon," found no American publisher, although some of the stories were printed in magazines. In 1903 Doubleday took *Romance*, but he let

Harper bring out *Nostromo*, and subsequently *The Mirror of the Sea*. None of these books sold above 2,000 copies.

Some time in 1908 a friend of Doubleday told him that Conrad's *Lord Jim* was a very fine novel. To his surprise he found that he was its publisher—having obtained it when he acquired the McClure-Phillips list. He read it and was impressed enough with its literary merit subsequently to take over the other of his books published in the United States. With all of them having been commercial failures he had no difficulty buying the rights and plates for nominal amounts. Only Harper was in no condition legally to yield any of its copyrights.

Knowing that these books had a minimal appeal, he spent little money to stimulate interest in them. Nor did he make any effort to obtain Conrad's new work, so that Harper published *Under Western Eyes* (1911) and *A Personal Record* (1912). All this time, of course, Conrad wrote despite his dire need and while suffering from frequent severe bouts of the gout and other ailments. Thus after fourteen years of struggle he was unavoidably depressed when he wrote John Galsworthy: "I wish sometimes I had remained at sea, which, had I honestly stuck to it, would no doubt be rolling now over my head." It should be stated that his agent, James Pinker, had for years done his utmost to sell his stories to magazines, to obtain advances from publishers, and to lend him money when needed.

Conrad's lack of popularity notwithstanding, his literary repute rose from year to year, and critics began to include him among the outstanding writers of the day. Pinker, capitalizing on this increasing prominence, managed to sell some of his stories to American magazines, although that was not easy. Editors found them too somber. In 1911, for instance, *Scribner's Magazine* rejected "Freye of the Seven Isles" on the grounds that "its overpowering gloom makes it impossible for serialization." *Century Magazine* reacted similarly. Yet Conrad had deliberately sought to adapt this story to popular taste in the hope of acceptance. As he wrote to Garnett on July 29, 1911: "I've tried to do a magazine-ish thing with some decency. Not a very high purpose; yet it seems I've failed even in that! All this is very comical—if not exactly amusing." For he could not violate his artistic integrity. Writing to Garnett a week later, he decried this editorial demand for fictional pap:

> As to faking a "sunny" ending to my story I would see all the American Magazines and all the American Editors damned in heaps before lifting my pen for that task. I've never been particularly anxious to rub shoulders with the piffle they print with touching consistency from year's end to year's end.

In 1912 Doubleday was in England visiting publishers and authors. Again and again he heard highly favorable references to Conrad and recalled that he had his books on his list. It troubled him to think that so reputable an author—whose *Lord Jim* he remembered having read with pleasure—should continue to have so small a readership. With a gambler's intuition he assumed that sooner or later Conrad's books would break through the current neglect. When he learned that George Doran, who was also in London at the time, had arranged for an

American edition of *Chance*—Pinker thinking Doubleday had lost interest in Conrad—he explained to Doran that he aimed to become Conrad's American publisher and wished he would yield *Chance* to him. Doran did so gracefully, and gave him also *'Twixt Land and Sea*, assuming these books had little chance of popularity. Doubleday thereupon arranged with Pinker to publish Conrad thereafter. Conrad, master of irony, was amused to learn that after being one of his publishers for more than a decade Doubleday at last discovered him.

Alfred A. Knopf was twenty years old when he joined the Doubleday firm as an apprentice in the fall of 1912. When Doubleday returned from England with the manuscript of *Chance*, and the regular editors showed no special interest in it, Knopf asked to read it. He was familiar with *Lord Jim*, which had deeply impressed him while at college, and was eager to see the new book. Later he stated that he "was completely bowled over" by *Chance*. He wrote at once to Galsworthy, whom he had met in England the previous summer, to express his delight with the novel and to tell him he was determined to do all in his power to promote it. He also wrote to Conrad to convey his enthusiasm for the novel. In reply Conrad thanked him for his praise but wrote frankly about his opinion of publishers—unaware that Doubleday had by then acquired his old books:

> But the fact remains that Mr. Doubleday might have had all my books up to date in his hands if he had cared. Other people bought them and I haven't heard that they have been ruined by it. . . . There are two methods in the publishing business. The first is speculative. A work is a venture. Hit or miss. To a certain extent it must be so. But here and there a writer may be taken up as an investment. An investment must be attended to, it must be nursed—if one believes in it. I can't develop much feeling for a publisher who takes me on the "hit or miss" basis. A gamble is not a connection. . . . The question for me is: Has the Doubleday, Page & Co. simply bought two books of mine—or is it to be a connection? If it is the last, then you will find me responsive enough. I appreciate warmly the practical evidence of your good will toward my work.

Conrad here touched on an aspect of publishing that came close to the heart of the industry. Ideally publishers are expected to nurse new authors and do their utmost to build up their readership, so that in time their books become profitable to both author and publisher. In reality most publishers are neither astute nor idealistic—and are particularly shortsighted currently, when editors must show an immediate profit to satisfy their corporate employers. More in the past, and less so recently, a publisher will take a book by a new author on the chance that it will prove profitable while it helps fill a gap in a season's list, as had sometimes happened with Conrad. When it doesn't sell well enough at last to repay the investment, the tendency of most publishers is to drop the author and seek others— a gamble that usually benefits neither party. It is only the exceptional publisher who has the wisdom and the critical insight to pick authors of promise and promote their work for the long-term rewards that often come with persistent effort. One such publisher was Alfred Knopf, and his effort in behalf of Conrad was an earnest of his later career.

In their ensuing correspondence Conrad wrote about his dealings with John Quinn, the wealthy New York lawyer and collector of manuscripts. Knopf called on Quinn and was shown Conrad's letters. "I came to read a most remarkable correspondence, one that seemed to me at the time almost heartbreakingly tragic. Conrad was always hard up, frequently ill,—in a generally sorry state. He would discover manuscripts—or pretend to—and send them to Quinn, who would buy them at whatever price seemed fair to him."

Determined to help Conrad by promoting his new book, Knopf printed private letterheads with his name and home address and sent letters to a fairly large number of prominent writers telling them of Conrad's plight and requesting favorable comments on his work for use in the promotion of his new book. To each he sent an advance copy of *Chance*. Some of the writers suspected trickery, but many responded favorably. It should be stated that despite Knopf's lowly position in the firm, his enthusiastic activity in behalf of Conrad persuaded Doubleday to give him his head. He even permitted him to prepare a pamphlet on Conrad's life and writings which he circulated widely. The result was highly gratifying. For the first time a book by Conrad achieved relative popularity, selling more than 10,000 copies before demand slackened.

Doubleday was of course pleased, delighted that his hunch had been correct, and thereafter promoted Conrad's works, old and new, with vigor and persistence. In his private memoirs he stated, referring to *Chance* as well as to the subsequent volumes:

> This was the beginning of his popularity, and I flatter myself that we took advantage of it and did Conrad a service. . . . It was a great satisfaction to think that we were able to earn for him a very substantial amount of money, I should say something over two hundred thousand dollars, so at least he was no longer under the whip of poverty.

Conrad was gratified at last to be getting this attention, and was pleased in 1913 to refer to Doubleday as his "future publisher." With the passing years their relations became close. In 1914 Doubleday capitalized on the increasing interest in Conrad to issue the Deep Sea Edition of his works to date. A year later the firm promoted *Victory* with notable success. With the war in Europe playing havoc with book publishing in England, Conrad came to depend primarily on his American readership. Yet he felt loyal to his adopted country and to his English publisher, and when Doubleday, in his effort to maximize Conrad's prestige as well as his popularity, proposed to bring out a deluxe edition of his books, Conrad pleaded for delay until after the war in order to enable his English publisher to issue simultaneously a British edition. On July 6, 1916, he wrote Doubleday:

> Here addressing you as friend both to my work and my person I must beg you to delay publication till after the war so as not to upset and indeed destroy my plans for an identical English edition deluxe (also of 370 copies) to which I attach no small importance. It is my great desire to see you and Mr. Heinemann work hand in hand in the production of what will be the monument of my literary life on both sides of the Atlantic. If the English edition fails the monument (to my feeling) will not be complete.

This edition, named Sundial by Conrad, was not published until 1920–1921. By that time, ironically, Doubleday had acquired the Heinemann firm and marketed both editions. The royalties from the American edition came to $12,000, and those from the British edition were nearly as high. In 1923 a lower-priced popular set was brought out under the title of the Concord Edition.

In 1918, having written *The Arrow of Gold*, Conrad took the position that it should not be published before it was serialized in a magazine and so long as the public was engrossed in the problems of peace. To this end he addressed Doubleday on December 21, 1918:

> I put this point of view with some diffidence before a man eminently successful in one of those forms of human activity that deal with mankind in the mass. I may be wrong. I think however that I was right in the objection I raised against the proposal to publish A. of G. in book form in January. First of all it seemed to me that, at the date the proposal reached me, there was not enough time left to make the business and publicity arrangements for a novel by J. C. whose merit is not of that kind that could secure a response without all the help the standing, influence and organization of Doubleday, Page & Co. can give him. I also doubted the advisability of publishing a book at a time when, for the next three months or more, the public mind is bound to be absorbed by the problems of peace and the settling of political questions all over the world. Besides, I felt that in justice to myself and also to your efforts in my behalf, I must see proof sheets; not for material alterations, but for the exact setting of the text.

> You'll pardon this long letter. I don't often overwhelm you with long missives. But you are my publisher, and the care of my reputation and my fortunes in the New World are in your hands, and being very sure of your friendly sentiments I have written to you all that was in my mind.

It is of interest to note that when *The Arrow of Gold* was published late in 1919, it achieved the best-seller list.

Twenty-two years after having put the manuscript of the unfinished *Rescue* aside in 1897 because he did not know how to resolve the end of the story, Conrad found the solution and wrote Doubleday that he could have the book. Doubleday published it in 1920 and commented later: "It was, I think, as good as anything he ever wrote, and when published sold fifty thousand copies, which at that time was an unheard-of sale for Conrad."

The friendship between them had deepened from year to year. Each time Doubleday came to England he visited Conrad and enjoyed his hospitality. When the latter learned that the firm was celebrating its twenty-fifth year of existence, he wrote to Doubleday on August 21, 1921:

> I congratulate you heartily on being able (in the judgment of all competent men) to look back at 25 years of work in your selected calling with the conscientiousness of having done much good in your generation. . . . I am touched by your associating my name with your personal feelings about your own achievement. . . . Believe me my dear Doubleday always yours with most friendly regard.

Some six months later, on February 19, 1922, he informed Doubleday of Pinker's death and how indebted he had been to him for all the help and encouragement he had received from him during the bitter years of public neglect. And he added:

> In any case I feel that my affairs in America need give me no concern since your invariable kindness, forethought and interest expressed so often in word and deed assure me that they are in the hands of a friend. This profound conviction, dear Mr. Doubleday, is a source of comfort to me; for it is not "agreements" but certainly of friendly appreciation in those closely associated with his work that give confidence and support to a writer.

Later that year, having completed *The Rover*, he thanked Doubleday for offering to arrange for its serialization in the United States. When this was done despite some difficulty, he wrote him on February 8, 1923: "I am profoundly touched by the warm interest you took in this affair of mine and your unsparing exertions in straightening it out, hopeless as it looked."

After being Conrad's guest a number of times, Doubleday urged him to visit him in Oyster Bay, New York. A victim of the gout and other maladies, feeling even older than his years, always shying away from exposure to public view, and too impeded by a very strong foreign accent to accept invitations to lecture, Conrad nevertheless felt too grateful to the Doubledays to refuse the warm invitation. He therefore accepted it with the understanding that the visit was to be personal and private, with no public appearances. To Garnett he wrote on March 10, 1923: "That trip is not going to be a lectureship tour but simply a visit to Doubleday at his home in Oyster Bay, for three weeks or so. As I don't suppose that Doubleday intends to keep me shut up in his cellar for all that time I fully expect to be let in for some at least semi-public appearances."

The visit from May 1 to June 2 marked Conrad's greatest personal triumph. At the height of his popularity as a writer, he was besieged with invitations; prominent individuals and organizations expressed their admiration for him and their wish to lionize him. Doubleday, however, respected his guest's wishes for privacy and made every effort to prevent all unnecessary strain on him. He did have him meet several persons in whom Conrad was interested, among them Ignace Paderewski, and he also took him for a trip through part of New England. The one semi-public appearance which he had Conrad make was as a guest in the home of A. C. James, where he read sections of *Victory* to the distinguished guests.

This was Conrad's first visit to the United States, and he enjoyed it enormously. To Mrs. Conrad he wrote on May 19: "I continue to be entertained in a princely fashion by the D's." And when he was ready to return to England, the Doubledays accompanied him to London to assure his every comfort. On June 14, with Conrad safely home, Mrs. Conrad expressed her thanks to the Doubledays by telling them that they had brought her a 'renovated and rejuvenated husband."

Conrad, replying on July 10 to Doubleday's letter regarding the Concord Edition, stated:

> I have followed you day by day in my thoughts across the ocean, and now my spirit is haunting Effendi Hill—though of course you are unable to see it. . . . I have been

much cheered by your good letter and the sight of the Concord Edition advertisement. . . . My belief in the Concord Edition is absolute and indestructible. There is an atmosphere of good luck and good will about it which no other scheme seems to have had in the same degree.

And at the end of another letter on September 23 regarding details connected with the Edition, he added a penned postscript: "I hope I am not making myself a nuisance to you and partners with my comments, questions and suggestions. Don't imagine I am *insisting* on anything. I may propose. The decision rests with the House. But I am too strongly interested to hold my tongue always." He wrote again the following day and ended the business part with further assurances of his appreciation: "Be sure dear Effendi that I am most grateful to you for your labours, and profoundly touched by the friendship that prompts you in the task."

In February 1924, having learned that the firm was considering the publication of an omnibus collection of his short stories, Conrad wrote Doubleday as well as Eric Pinker, his agent, expressing his objection. He pointed out that the stories varied in tone, mood, content, and other ways, so that to put them in one volume would vitiate their effectiveness. He argued against it gently, yet with unanswerable pertinence, and suggested instead a briefer volume in two parts, containing all eight stories dealing with the sea.

A month later, told that an arrangement was being made by Doubleday for a French translation of *The Rover* with a publisher other than Gallimard, he objected strongly:

I can not be a consenting party to anything being done otherwise than through N. R. F. and *that* must be left to me. Gallimard has made up his plan of campaign and got together a body of distinguished translators under the direction of Monsieur Andre Gide, and I cannot accept any translation by anybody outside of that group.

Now in his sixty-seventh year, long in poor health, Conrad suffered increasingly from his difficult ailments and died on August 3, 1924.

16.

Charles Scribner

&

Santayana

An introductory note is in order. Charles Scribner II, like Henry Holt, was one of the aristocrats of book publishing who sought to make the industry a gentleman's profession. Inheriting the flourishing firm at the age of twenty-three upon the sudden death of his older brother Blair, he devoted himself to its enlargement and enhancement with solid energy and business acumen, guided by high ethical principles and genuine respect for literary quality. In the process he was motivated not only by strong convictions but also by the prevailing Victorian prejudices, rejecting manuscripts of merit when they did not conform to his moral or religious standards. On the whole, however, he acted sensitively regarding intricate author-publisher relations, cultivating the loyalty and friendship of the major authors on his list.

After two decades of publishing Charles Scribner was generally accepted as a highly respected leader of the industry, and when in 1903 he declined re-election as president of the American Publishers Association, *Publishers' Weekly* commented: "There are few men of the present publishing generation who have shown more public spirit and self-sacrifice in keeping the publishing trade up to the highest standards and setting an example to others among his fellow craftsmen."

Mr. Scribner's business success was achieved largely with the aid of associates who were among the most capable and sensitive editors in book publishing. Early in his career he began to depend upon the critical judgment and sage advice of W. C. Brownell, Edward L. Burlingame, and Robert Bridges. Brownell was an eminent literary critic, and his advice and suggestions were greatly valued by the authors whose books he edited. Burlingame, and later Bridges, were likewise astute judges of good writing, and as editors of *Scribner's Magazine* as well as book manuscripts they contributed mightily to the growth and prestige of the firm. In later years, especially after World War I, Scribner had the good fortune to benefit from the remarkable editorial insight and critical judgment of Maxwell E. Perkins and John Hall Wheelock.

Thus, no other publishing house had more eminent and satisfied authors, and their relations with Scribner and his editors were, on the whole, exceptionally congenial and close. The following accounts of several of these relationships will discuss their development, personal variations, and genuinely mutual friendships. The first is George Santayana.

In Santayana the House of Scribner had an ideal author: he wrote books of solid merit and literary distinction, and never haggled about royalties, promotion, or advances—being both naturally modest and in possession of an income adequate for his restrained needs. Whenever he completed a manuscript—after the firm had published his first book—he submitted it with the understanding that it would be published; and Scribner acted accordingly as a matter of course. For years the relationship remained impersonal, although mutually courteous; as late as 1914, two years after he had left the United States for good and after nearly twenty years as his author he had not even met Mr. Scribner.

In 1863 Santayana was born in Spain of Spanish parents and remained a Spanish citizen to the end of his long life. His mother's first husband was George Sturgis, a Boston businessman whom she had met and married while he was visiting in the Philippines. Before his untimely death in 1857 she had agreed that their three children would be educated in his native Boston. Ten years later, when her second husband; whom she had married in 1862 after her return to Spain, and for whom her affection had cooled, was unwilling to migrate to the United States, she decided to carry out her vow to her first husband and brought all her children to Boston.

When Santayana came to the United States at the age of five, he knew no English and for some time felt the stings of mockery and ridicule of his American schoolmates. It did not take him long, however, to master the vocabulary of everyday English and speak it with only a slight foreign accent. All through his adolescence he was in the vernacular of the time a "sissy," as he avoided athletics as much as he could and spent a good part of his time reading. When he entered Harvard University, he was interested enough in writing to seek publication in student periodicals. On graduation he went to Europe for further study, but the following year he returned to Harvard to complete his graduate work. The faculty in philosophy was sufficiently impressed with his intellectuality to give him an instructorship, although some of the older professors did not find him congenial.

In the meantime he had began to write verse, and in the early 1890s he had enough poems for a small volume, which was published by a local firm. That was not considered of value to a Harvard teacher; he was made to realize that he was expected to be "creative" in a scholarly sense. As he reminisced toward the end of his life, he soon complied:

> I was a kind of poet, I was alive to architecture and the other arts, I was at home in several languages: "aesthetics" might be regarded as my specialty. Very well: although I didn't have, and haven't now, a clear notion of what "aesthetics" may be, I undertook to give a course in that subject. It would help to define my status.

In time he incorporated the substance of the course into a little book, which he called *The Sense of Beauty*. Local publishers rejected it, and Santayana had given up any expectation of getting it printed, when Prof. Barrett Wendell suggested that he send the manuscript to Scribner, his own publisher. W. C. Brownell was at first doubtful of its marketability, but finally accepted it and gave Santayana a royalty of 10 percent. On November 8, 1898, about a year after publication, Santayana wrote to the firm: "I am glad to see that 'The Sense of Beauty' has continued to have a small sale, and I hope it has paid expenses. The reviews have been flattering, although all somewhat unsatisfactory to me on account of their silence on what I regard as the essence of the book—namely, its philosophical position." In his memoirs he commented more modestly: "I sent it to Scribner's; it was printed and did not prove a financial loss to the publisher, although it had neither a large sale nor a warm reception from the critics. However, it was a book, *a fact*; and it established warm relations between me and Scribner's which have lasted for fifty years."

In November 1899 he sent Scribner the manuscript of *Interpretation of Poetry and Religion*. It was accepted without question, and the royalty was voluntarily increased to 15 percent. Santayana gratefully acknowledged its acceptance and thanked the firm "for the generous terms." A year later he again wrote:

> I don't remember ever seeing a book of verse among your publications, but nevertheless it occurs to me to ask you whether you would care to look at a set of poems of various sorts which I'm getting together. My relations with you in respect to *The Sense of Beauty* and the *Interpretation* have been for me, so entirely satisfactory, that I don't like to take steps toward any further publication without asking you whether you would be inclined to undertake it.

The Scribner firm was so inclined, offered him a royalty of 10 percent on the volume, *The Hermit of Carmel*, and published it in 1901.

The following three years were limited to routine correspondence. Santayana had no manuscript to offer, nor was he prodded to produce one. On May 24, 1904, Santayana, now assuming that the firm would publish his writings, informed Brownell:

> I am sending you a first installment of my *magnum opus* "The Life of Reason." There are four more books, which will follow in a few weeks if you are favorably disposed toward the idea of publishing them. . . . This book is not like my former ones, a mere incidental performance. It particularly represents all I have to say of any consequence, so that I feel a special interest in having it done in a way that shall express its own character and suggest the spirit in which I would have it read.

Uncertain of commercial possibilities and eager to have the book designed to his taste, he offered to insure the firm against loss. Scribner not only accepted the manuscript but offered a royalty of 10 percent and agreed to follow the suggestions regarding format and design. Duly grateful, Santayana cooperated with the editor as best he could. A thousand copies each of the first two volumes were printed, and each sold less than 500 copies during the first year. The remaining three volumes were brought out in due course. All were favorably reviewed, but sold slowly. During the first six years their sales ranged from 1,728 for the first volume to 1,215 for the fifth. Scribner did not complain, and Santayana was pleased, stating on April 4, 1906: "It is naturally most gratifying to me that my long book should receive so much recognition and should have such a respectable company of buyers."

This cordial, if impersonal relationship continued placidly for the ensuing decade and more. Scribner regarded Santayana as a distinguished author whom he was glad to have on his list even though he was relatively unprofitable; Santayana considered Scribner, as his publisher, highly satisfactory in every way. When Scribner learned that Santayana was to deliver a series of lectures at Columbia University, he asked if he could publish them as a book. In reply, on January 18, 1910, Santayana told him regretfully that the lectures were to form part of a series and he was under obligation to let them appear under another imprint.

> I know the disadvantage of having different publishers for different books—it happens to me now in a certain measure—and would gladly not enter into relation with any house but yours, which I have found invariably generous and obliging. But as Professor Schoenfield is to take all negotiations out of my hands, and promises me various advantages connected with publication in a series that will be kept continually before the public, I have agreed to let him have my new book.

In 1912 Santayana resigned from his Harvard professorship and went to live in Europe—having never felt fully at home in Bostonian America. Thereafter he preferred to have his work published in England first and by Scribner subsequently. The latter did not object, since the relatively small sale of these books made it economically advantageous merely to import sheets in 500 or 1,000 lots as he needed them.

The war that began in 1914 perforce kept Santayana in England and away from France and Italy, where he would have preferred to live. His contact with the Scribner firm remained friendly but infrequent. When his *Character and Opinion in the United States* was sent to Scribner in 1920, the latter agreed to pay a royalty of 15 percent on the strength of a greater potential of popularity. On the receipt of news two years later that *Skepticism and Animal Faith* was ready, Scribner expressed his delight: "We can hardly overstate the interest with which we shall look forward to seeing the book and publishing it." Eager to have it copyrighted in the United States, he told Santayana of his plan to print the book: "We suppose you must know, although we have never written you directly in the matter, of the greatly increased interest in all your writings, perhaps especially among younger people who are just now getting into the saddle. It is a very striking and gratifying phenomenon." Santayana, always modest and unassuming, told Scribner by return mail that the English publisher Constable was already setting the book into type; moreover, he had no fear of piracy, indeed welcomed it on so technical a work, which he doubted would have much of a sale. As for increased interest in his books, he was of course pleased:

> I have always lived on the hypothesis that I could not expect to attract much attention, and should be content to please a small circle of kindred spirits. But perhaps

advancing years have made me more human, and able to interest a larger public. Perhaps too the temper of the age has changed in a way which, without moving exactly in my direction, has removed some of the barriers between my way of expressing myself and the prevalent mood.

Again several years passed in routine and infrequent correspondence. In 1927 Santayana befriended young Daniel Cory, who had written a sympathetic and perceptive study of his writings. He soon made him his secretary, literary assistant, and almost an adopted son, generously supporting him to the end of his life. Late in 1928 he consulted with Scribner about the legality of willing the publishing rights in his books to Cory. When the desired advice reached him, he thanked Scribner on January 1, 1929, and intimated that "it is not impossible that I may live to offer you a book, of which there ought to be an American Edition, since it might have a larger sale than any of my books in philosophy." Eighteen days later unaware of the nature of the prospective book but eager to have it, Scribner informed him with his customary restraint:

> I was very glad to receive your letter and to hear that there was probability of your offering us a book that we could both print and publish in America. I do not think I need assure you of our interest and I take it that you prefer not to be bothered by my writing every few months to reassure you. We shall therefore wait patiently until we hear further, and when the book is ready there is every reason to believe that it will be a success.

Santayana was indeed referring to *The Last Puritan*. The novel was then very much on his mind, and he mentioned it frequently in letters to Cory. He was at that time also writing *The Realm of Truth*, and turned from one to the other as his mind permitted. Thus in writing Cory on March 4, 1930, he stated: "*Truth* has rather stuck in the mind, and is abandoned for the *moment*; but *fiction* has been moving. A lovely short chapter—picture of budding friendship—written out in ink, quite original, and I think in the right key." On the same day he wrote Scribner to assure him about the novel: "If my novel The Last Puritan should ever be finished (and I have some hopes it may) I have already told you that I should submit it to you directly, to be published and copyrighted by you in America, while Constable could print it separately if he liked." And at the end of that year he told Cory: "Sometime I think that the novel isn't worth the trouble I am taking with it, except as an entertainment for myself."

When Charles Scribner died in 1930, John Hall Wheelock, a former student and admirer of Santayana, became his devoted editor. That December he cabled him to ask permission to issue an American edition of *The Genteel Tradition at Bay*. Santayana of course agreed.

The novel continuing to occupy his attention, Santayana informed Wheelock on March 19, 1931: "I am now at work revising and extending my so-called 'novel,' but I doubt whether it will be ever finished or quite ready to publish during my life time." On the same day he assured Charles Scribner III, the new head of the firm, that 10 percent royalty was sufficient for *Turns of Thought*: "You know that I don't expect to make money out of my writings: what I earn is welcome, but I abstract that from consideration in arranging my work." What interested him more than royalties was a low price for the book. As for the novel, he added, he really hesitated about its publication. "There are personal reasons for not issuing it during my life-time, not so much on my own account as on account of offense which some good friends of mine may take at it." Yet he felt pleased with what he had written, and on April 10, 1933, he stated to Cory:

> I am beginning to feel encouraged about finishing this endless task. It is not as clever and amusing as I had meant to make it, but it turns out *deeper* and more *consistent* than I had suspected. There is a hidden tragic structure in it which was hardly foreseen but belongs to the essence of the subject, the epoch, and the dissolution of Protestantism.

He was now working on the novel much of the time, enjoying the creative development of character and yet somewhat timid about its possible exposure of Brahmin Boston. On August 26, 1934, he wrote Cory: "The novel is moving fast toward completion: very exciting, this act of capping the climax or putting the lid on the boiling pot." A week later, now finished with the writing and ready for its revision, he again confided to Cory: "I think now there would be no objection to publishing the book at once. I am old enough and far enough not to mind the spitballs that small boys may throw at me."

On May 9, 1935, with Constable having accepted *The Last Puritan*, and having in mind simultaneous publication in both countries, Santayana wrote Wheelock:

> Today I am sending you a copy of the type-written manuscript of *The Last Puritan*. . . . I am far from confident of the reception the book will have; some people may be offended, or may disapprove on principle, but the times described are already somewhat distant, and I don't care very much for the opinion of the public, if a few friends are found—as I am sure they will be—to enjoy the spirit of the thing with me.

Wheelock was enthusiastic about the novel, and so were others in the firm. Santayana was less sanguine. He doubted that the sale would reach 7,500 copies, after which the royalty rose to 15 percent. What pleased him, however, was the low price of $2.50 placed on the book. The manuscript was submitted to the Book-of-the-Month Club and was promptly accepted. Wheelock informed Santayana that the Club would pay $10,000 for a sale of 40,000 copies and that this sum was to be divided between him and the firm. Santayana's reaction was a combination of scepticism and gratification. Writing to his nephew George Sturgis, he played upon the fact that the book was one of twelve that the Club had to choose annually; and that although $5,000 was reason enough "to be congratulated," he wondered about the part he had in it. "But you must remember that the twelve apostles were chosen by Christ himself, and one of them was Judas; and although he got thirty pieces of silver, according to contract, it didn't do his reputation much good with posterity."

So confident had Wheelock become of the novel's popularity, that on October 2 he wrote Santayana: "We feel that this book now has the chance of a wide sale, and we are going to spare no pains to bring it about. We hope that it may mean the beginning of a permanently larger public for your books." And shortly after the novel was published, Charles Scribner wrote Santayana: "No novel published in the twenty odd years that I have been in the business has had such an enthusiastic reception from the press, which has showered it with praise without a dissenting note."

When copies of *The Last Puritan* reached Santayana, he liked the format and type but was repelled by the jacket. On February 1, 1936, he wrote: "It seems to me very ugly. . . . And why has my photo been redrawn so as to make me cross-eyed and ferocious? I know that self-knowledge is often self-deception, but I *feel* not at all as this personage looks." The jacket was changed for the later printings, and when Scribner mailed him his share of the Club payment, he added: "I cannot tell you how pleased and proud we are to cap our association with you of so many years with the publication of this novel, which promises to be a national success." This indeed it became, having sold 149,000 in six months.

Highly pleased with so profitable an item in a time of reduced business caused by the prevailing economic depression, and strongly furthered by Wheelock, the Scribner firm decided to honor Santayana by issuing a deluxe edition of his writings. Wheelock informed him of the plan to bring out the first fourteen volumes at $140 a set, and to add subsequent volumes as they became ready. Modest and unassuming still, the elderly philosopher at first reacted negatively:

> Your plan of publishing a limited edition of my collected works seems to me premature. No doubt my age and the quantity of what I have written justified anyone in crying *Basta*! and drawing a sharp line across the account, ready to sum up the total. Yet in fact the total isn't there yet: there are various things I mean to write not yet written, and various things written not yet published. They may not prove worth writing or worth publishing, but one can't tell beforehand.

Nevertheless he was very pleased with the idea of a limited edition of his writings and suggested that it be called the Triton, after Bernini's fountain in Rome's Piazza Barberini. To Cory he later wrote: "They have avoided all splurge and vulgarity. . . . They have managed the thing to perfection."

Santayana was living in Rome in 1939 at the outbreak of World War II. It did not come unexpectedly to his thinking. As early as April 15, fearful of its inevitability, he wrote Cory: "If there is a war, I could keep my thoughts on distant things by writing my recollections, I mean *Persons and Places*." The following year, eager to assure an income for his protégé, he informed Wheelock that he had made Cory his literary executor; and after Cory's return to the United States, he asked that his American royalties be paid direct to Cory, as he had enough for his needs without them.

When *The Realm of Spirit* was being published in 1940, Wheelock suggested that it be combined with the previous three volumes of *Realms* into one book under the title of *The Realms of Being*. Santayana's reaction was one of gratification:

What can I say except that it gives me great satisfaction, being a sign of much readier and more general recognition than I could have expected! I hope you will go on with the project and find it successful. The royalty of 10 percent you propose is ample; I should be perfectly willing to forego all royalty on this work, if that were necessary.

Meanwhile he was writing his reminiscences, and on December 6 he informed Wheelock: "I have written reams of my autobiography, and haven't yet got to my birth." This news excited his editor's enthusiasm, and he wrote him on February 18, 1941: "It would be difficult to tell you how enthusiastic we are about this book. It will not only be a book of the first importance, but is likely to have, in our opinion, a large distribution. . . . Interest in your work is very great, and it would be a most opportune moment for publication." Five months later, in an effort to spur work on the book, he wrote again:

> To be a publisher is to live in a constant state of uncertainty, more particularly as regards the sale of books in which one most believes. It is seldom that a publisher can feel as certain as we feel about the prospects for this autobiography: that in addition to its importance it will have a large sale. You will recall that I prophesied this for "The Last Puritan," but I make the present prophesy with even greater confidence.

The expansion of the war toward the end of 1941 caused the Italian post office to refuse the transmittal of manuscripts, and Santayana informed Wheelock that the autobiography would have to wait until the war ended. Eager to obtain it without delay, Wheelock asked the American ambassador in Rome, William Phillips, to help him get the manuscript. But American entrance into the war blocked further communication with Santayana. It was known that he had for some time been living in the Irish nursing home of nuns called "The Little Company of Mary," but it was not known if he had the means for his daily needs. In the effort to find some access to him, Wheelock asked the Spanish ambassador in Washington to send a message to Santayana, but this was denied. He also wrote to Prof. Carlton Hayes, the new American ambassador to Spain, but at first that too came to nothing.

Wheelock next asked his friend Padraic Colum to intercede with officials of the Vatican, and at his suggestion a letter was written to Msgr. Joseph McShea of the Apostolic Delegation. That brought results. On October 8, 1942, Ambassador Hayes informed Wheelock: "The manuscript has come to me through the kindness of the Papal Secretary of State, the Cardinal Maglione, and of the Papal Nuncio in Madrid. I have chosen the safest means I have at my disposal for forwarding it to you, and trust that it reaches you in good order." It did. The Scribner staff read it with admiration and excitement. It was submitted to the Book-of-the-Month Club and became a dual selection. The editor of the *Atlantic Monthly* offered $1,000 for three 5,000-word excerpts, and the money went to Cory, who was then in need. At the request of the Club, publication was delayed until January 1944.

Persons and Places, the first of a three-volume autobiography, proved to be as popular as Wheelock had predicted, so that the royalties on it amounted to more than $40,000 three months after publication. George Sturgis, long Santayana's financial adviser, objected to Cory receiving the entire sum. Efforts to communicate with Santayana succeeded after the American army had entered Rome, and his decision was that Cory should receive all royalties until they could be paid directly to him. He reported also that he was well and that the nuns were taking good care of him.

In the interim he had completed the second volume. On November 10, 1944, now able to mail letters to the United States, he asked Wheelock how he could transmit the manuscript to him. Wheelock immediately communicated with army officials, and Sgt. Harry A. Freidenberg, who was an admirer of Santayana's writings, was assigned to call on the philosopher and do what he could for him. Freidenberg went out of his way to be of assistance ot him. He provided him with certain necessities—Santayana had been penniless for some time—and sent the manuscript to Wheelock through army channels.

As soon as the Scribner firm learned of Santayana's financial deprivation, it made arrangements for him to receive $500 a month for the ensuing six months. The old philosopher, very grateful, stated to Myron Taylor, in Rome as the American representative to the Vatican: "It adds to much evidence that I already had of Mr. Wheelock's friendly interest in my comfort and peace of mind."

The second volume of *Persons and Places* was published in March 1945 and sold relatively well. The final volume was by agreement brought out posthumously. Santayana continued to occupy himself with his writing, and among his final works were *The Idea of Christ in the Gospels* (1946) and *Dominations and Powers*, both books of limited appeal but highly regarded by men knowledgeable in these respective fields.

A year before his own death in 1953 Santayana learned of the death of Charles Scribner III. Having never met him, or any of the editors in his half century of friendly relations, he wrote Wheelock:

> What you tell me gives me more reasons for regretting this loss to all of us. I seem to have laid my social as well as philosophical eggs twenty or thirty years, systematically, before they were hatched. Those, like you and Mr. Scribner, who ventured to read and publish my "Sense of Beauty" when I wrote it, never have seen me alive; I vanished into another sphere before I became distinguishable.

17.

Charles Scribner
&
Edith Wharton

If Santayana was, from a publisher's standpoint, an ideal author, Edith Wharton proved to be troublesome and unreliable. Although her earnings from her writing were considerable, her extravagant ways forced her to require greater remuneration than she was receiving, which in time inclined her to give her fiction to the highest bidder—a behavior distressing to a publisher.

Belonging to one of the "best families" in New York, among whom authorship was an activity frowned upon as neither genteel nor socially commendable, Edith Jones was almost exceptional in having from early childhood a strong interest in literary expression. Her parents did not approve of this bent, but they humored her during her adolescence. Her mother even collected her early verses—written in emulation of poets she admired—and had them printed privately in 1878, when Edith was in her sixteenth year. At seventeen she became exposed to the balls and dinners of a society debutante. No rebel, she led the life common to her exclusive set, and at the age of twenty-three married Edward Wharton, a man thirteen years her senior and devoted to the activities of the leisured rich, mainly sports.

Although Mrs. Wharton enjoyed the life of a young society woman, it did not fully satisfy her. For years she had been repressing the urge to write in order to conform to the attitudes and activities of her friends. Having early learned that her handsome husband had no interest in books and writing—that he regarded such indulgences as socially undesirable—she sought to adjust herself to his life of sportsman. And in truth she enjoyed the pleasures and excitement he offered her in New York, Newport, and Europe. In 1888 they had four wonderful months on a Mediterranean cruise, even though it entailed the expenditure of their income for that year.

After four years of marriage, having become acutely conscious of its failure, she found the urge to write irresistible. Having composed some verses, she sent one poem each to *Harper's, Century,* and *Scribner's.* All were accepted, but Edward L. Burlingame's letter was the first to arrive and the most encouraging. Toward the end of her life she wrote:

> As long as I live I shall never forget my sensations when I opened the first of three letters and learned that I was to appear in print.... He not only accepted my verses, but (oh, rapture!) wanted to know what else I had written; and this encouraged me to go to see him, and laid the foundation of a friendship which lasted till his death.

Although this foundation did not prove as solid as she implied, the early years of her association with the Scribner firm was both warm and mutually beneficial. Encouraged by Burlingame, she wrote stories which he readily accepted. After reading "The Fulness of Life" he praised her style and treatment. To which she replied on October 2, 1893: "I don't know how to thank you for what you say of my story, but indeed I shall never forget your unvarying kindness to me ever since my first literary endeavor had the good fortune to fall into your hands."

When Burlingame had published a number of her stories in the magazine, he had the book division suggest their publication in book form. "I need hardly say," she answered him, "how much I am flattered by Messrs. Scribner's proposition to publish my stories in a volume." Still considering herself an amateur author, however, she gave most of her time to her social life and made little progress on the collection of her stories. Yet she became more and more conscious of the technique of writing fiction. As late as March 26, 1904, she told him: "Pray, by the way, have no tenderhearted compunction about criticizing my stories—your criticism is most helpful to me and I always recognize its justice."

For nearly a year illness had kept her from her literary efforts. When she regained her health, she and Ogden Codman, the architect who had remodeled her home, became interested in interior design and decided to put their ideas into book form. When the manuscript was submitted to Macmillan, it was promptly rejected. Wharton then showed it to Burlingame, who forwarded it to W. C. Brownell, editor of the book division. He accepted it largely because he liked her short stories. Highly pleased with the type and design for *The Decoration of Houses*, she wrote Brownell on September 23, 1897: "I wish to thank the firm through you for their courtesy in allowing me so much time for revision of the book. I was anxious to make it as thorough as possible and to present the facts to the best advantage, and trust you will find that my work has to some extent justified the delay." The book was published in a small edition and sold very slowly—1,406 copies by February 1901—but the demand for it persisted for many years.

With the book out of the way, Wharton resumed her work on the collection of stories. On July 4, 1898, she informed Burlingame: "I think I can give you a volume of stories to bring out in the autumn, if you still wish it." A week later she told him she had "never sent any story to anyone but you, so you can of course take your choice for the magazine." Yet she hesitated to include her first stories, and added:

> As to the stories of which you speak so kindly, I regard them as the excesses of youth. They were all written "at the top of my voice," and the Fulness of Life is

one long shriek—I may not write any better, but at least I hope that I write in a lower key, and I fear that the voice of those early tales will drown all the others; it is for that reason that I prefer not to publish them.

Once the content of the collection was agreed upon, she became impatient to see the volume in print. Brownell, however, persuaded her that it was advisable to postpone publication to 1899. He offered her 10 percent royalty, to which she agreed, expressing the hope her book would be actively promoted. The thought of becoming a published author effected a radical change in her life. "The publishing of 'The Greater Inclination,' " she wrote later, "broke the chains which had held me so long in a kind of torpor. For nearly twelve years I had tried to adjust myself to the life I had led since my marriage; but now I was overmastered by the longing to meet people who shared my interests." Eager to see authors and persons of intellect, she began to spend much time abroad and invited those who appealed to her to her new and spacious home in Massachusetts.

Shortly after the volume appeared Wharton informed Brownell that John Lane, the English publisher, had agreed to bring out a British edition providing no royalty on the first 500 copies, but would pay a royalty on all copies sold if the sale reached 2,000 copies. She also complained about inadequate advertising of the Scribner edition: "The book has now been out about six weeks, and I do not think I exaggerate in saying that it has met with an unusually favorable reception for a first volume by a writer virtually unknown." Yet, she continued with the aggrieved tone of an ambitious author, she noted that other publishers advertised their new books much more than Scribner did. "Certainly in these days of energetic and emphatic advertising, Mr. Scribner's methods do not tempt one to offer him one's wares a second time."

Her complaint was basically motivated by an increasing need of money. Although both she and her husband each had, by normal standards, a fairly large income, the ever greater extravagance of her way of life—several homes, a retinue of servants, expensive indulgences, all probably in an effort to offset her disappointment in an incompatible marriage—drained their financial resources to their utmost limits. As she was becoming more and more dedicated to her writing, her success in it raising her level of financial expectation, she sought the greatest monetary return from royalties. Thus as early as September 28, 1899, only a few months after the publication of her volume of stories, she informed Brownell:

I have received a letter from a leading publisher—who had already written me twice on the subject—offering me 15% on any volume I will give him.

I am just finishing a short novel of 30 or 40 thousand words, and I do not wish to enter into any arrangement with another publisher without first asking if you care to consider the publication of a volume of that length and what terms you would make.

Thus tested, and loath to lose a rising author, Scribner met the offer of the rival publisher by offering her 15 percent royalty on *The Touchstone*, her new book, as well as an advance of $500. Brownell also suggested that she might consider collecting her late stories into a second volume. She preferred, however, to work on her next novel, *The Valley of Decision*. Nevertheless, after writing about 40,000 words, she found her "tank" empty and turned to writing short stories. Before long, she put her available stories into a volume which she titled *Crucial Instances*, and asked that it be published without delay. To Brownell she stated on November 16, 1900: "I hope you and Mr. Scribner don't think me terribly vague and vacillating about my work. I had to drop *The Touchstone* twice before I finished it, and nothing seems to freshen me up as a complete change of work." Five days later, her plan accepted, like the woman she was she wrote: "Thank you very much for what you say about my change of plans. You are all so kind that I count in advance on being treated indulgently."

When *The Valley of Decision* was going through the press, she did not hesitate to complain about details not to her liking. Of the title page she said: "Words fail to express how completely I *don't* like it." Nor was she satisfied with her photograph used in the advertising of the book. On February 2, 1902, she admitted to Brownell: "I hate to be photographed, because the results are so trying to my vanity; but I would do anything to obliterate the Creole lady who has been masquerading in the papers under my name for the last year."

The Valley of Decision achieved notable popularity both in this country and in England. When the first American royalties reached Wharton—less the $2,000 advance—she gratefully acknowledged the check. "Many thanks for the cheque of $2191.81, which, even to the 81 cents, is welcome to an author in the last throes of house-building." The next half-yearly royalties came to $7,963.20.

For all her avowed devotion to the Scribner firm, Wharton had no compunctions against agreeing to do a book in Italy for The Century Company, with serialization in *Century Magazine*, when Scribner was unable to serialize the volume as promptly as she wished. With feminine blandness she assured Scribner on October 26, 1904, "that, in spite of everything, I still cling to the past, and that not till hope is lost will I listen to the blandishments of your rivals, and drown my despair in a contract with Harper or Macmillan."

At this juncture she was writing *The House of Mirth* at a leisurely pace, sandwiching it between entertaining and travel. The theme was fashionable New York of her youth—the vulgar rich and the genteel elite she knew intimately. As she declared: "There it was before me in all its flatness and futility, asking to be dealt with as the theme most available to my hand, since I had been steeped in it from infancy." Yet she wrote slowly, carefully, in the morning hours at her disposal.

She was not far along when Burlingame informed her that a serial he had been promised had failed to materialize and asked if she could replace it with her own novel. This meant completing the story within the next four or five months. She responded to the urgency, thereby changing "from a drifting amateur into a professional." As she later reminisced:

> I was put to the severest test to which a novelist can be subjected: my novel was to be exposed to public comment before I had worked it out to its climax. . . . I hesitated for a day, and then accepted, and buckled down to my job; and of all the

friendly turns that Mr. Burlingame ever did for me, his exacting this effort was undoubtedly the most helpful. Not only did it give me what I most lacked,—self-confidence—but it bent me to the discipline of the daily task.

For all her gratitude, she did not hesitate to request the best possible terms from the Scribner firm. After a visit with Charles Scribner on April 4, 1905, during which she intimated her demands, she wrote him the following day to emphasize her position and the inducements offered by other publishers:

> I am always rather diffident about offering my own wares, and after I left you yesterday it occurred to me that I had never even mentioned the fundamental reason for my doing so—namely, the fact that I have received repeated applications for serial novels from Harper's and the Century, and wished to let you know of my probable future work before making any business arrangement.
>
> I trust you disentangled this fact from my vague remarks.

Scribner assured her at once of his eagerness to publish her work, and she graciously promised she would do nothing before letting him know. She then stated she would like $8,000 for the serialization of *The House of Mirth* and an increase in royalty to 20 percent after the sale of 10,000 copies. Scribner agreed, and even gave her an advance of $2,500, although he had never before done so on a serialized novel. Having obtained her terms, she remained unsatisfied. To Brownell she confided: "After the Enormous Sales of "The House of Mirth" which I predict for next November you will see my prices leap up."

When the novel was published, she strongly objected to the "Harperesque method of réclamé" on the jacket. "Do all you can to stop the spread of that pestilent paragraph, and to efface it from the paper cover of future printings. I am sick at the recollection of it." The novel immediately became a best seller, and 80,000 copies were sold within a month. The good news smoothed her ruffled feelings: "It is a very beautiful thought to me that 80,000 people should want to read 'The House of Mirth,' and if the number should ascend to 100,000 I fear my pleasure would exceed the bounds of decency." When this figure was soon reached, she wrote Burlingame: "Well, it's all great fun, and you did it all by accepting 'The Last Guistiani' [her first poem that she had published]."

Writing to her about her next novel, Scribner suggested that the hero of the story should be a strong man. Taking advantage of this opening, she wrote him:

> As for the hero, he is going to be a *very* strong man; so strong that I believe he will break all records. Perhaps in consideration of his strength you will think it not unreasonable to start in with a 20% royalty? If you were to refuse, he is so violent that I don't know whether I can answer for the consequences.

Scribner had no choice but to acquiesce in view of the popularity of her current novel. The two also agreed to permit *The Ladies Home Journal* to print a special edition of 10,000 copies of *The House of Mirth* as a subscription dividend. Commenting on this agreement, which of course benefited her financially, she stated to Brownell on June 14, 1906: "All that House of Scribner does is well done, and I meant to restate this in writing after my monosyllabic assent to the Curtis Publishing Co.'s proposal."

Now writing *The Fruit of the Tree,* she again encountered considerable difficulty, but she found Burlingame's encouraging and stimulating comments on the
parts she sent him very helpful. On August 6, 1906, she told him so:

> You will never know what a slough that note of yours dragged me out of! . . . I had
> been sitting so long in fixed contemplation of Amherst and Berry and Justine, that
> every defect in their anatomy had become salient, and I didn't see how any one
> could ever take an interest in such limp and shapeless creatures! But now that they
> strut and prance before me in the fine feathers of your approval, I begin to think
> them worth something, and my only fear is that they may not continue to behave
> sufficiently well to merit your praise.

The novel was well received, although not with the enthusiasm of *The House
of Mirth,* and its smaller sale, caused in part by the current financial depression,
disappointed Wharton. The following year she sent Scribner the summary of a
new novel, *The Custom of the Country.* His reaction was most encouraging: "A
story from you with such a presentation of contemporary society and such a girl
from the West climbing into it would be sure of its interest and readers. I *could*
not let it go elsewhere—even for the magazine." By then, however, her husband's increasing neurasthenia and other matters took up most of her time and
attention, and she did not finish the novel until three years later. Yet in the interim she managed to complete two brief stories which were quickly acknowledged as masterpieces—*Ethan Frome* and *The Reef.*

Ethan Frome was published in 1911. Reviewers readily perceived its literary
excellence, but despite this favorable publicity the little book sold relatively
slowly. With time, of course, its appeal increased, so that several different editions were brought out and it became the work upon which her reputation
mainly rested. Wharton, however, was at first greatly disappointed. On November 16 she wrote Scribner: "As far as it is possible to judge from reviews and
from the personal letters constantly pouring in, 'Ethan' is having a more immediate and general success than 'The House of Mirth.' " As so many authors in a
similar situation she failed to understand why the book was not selling widely
and attributed this failure to poor distribution, inadequate advertising, and in-
sufficient promotion. In replying to this complaint, Scribner assured her that he
had spent more money in advertising the story than was warranted by its expected sale. And he added:

> As you know the book has been splendidly reviewed both here and in London and
> undoubtedly the more discriminating readers have bought it eagerly but we have
> not secured for it the interest of the large public which supports the best seller.
> Nothing is more difficult to meet than the statement of an author's friends that a
> book is selling tremendously or cannot be had at the best bookstores. Retail clerks
> are very apt to say whatever they think a customer wishes to hear.

The explanation did not satisfy her. Despite her sense of gratitude to Burlingame and Brownell for their sage critical guidance, especially during the early
years of their association, and notwithstanding her loyalty to Charles Scribner,
she concluded that the firm was not aggressive enough in promoting her books.
She was in this frame of mind when the Appleton Company again approached

her with an enticing offer. Tempted, she gave them *The Reef.* Her explanation to Scribner on May 3, 1912, was blandly ingenuous:

> Since I last wrote you I have received from Messrs Appleton a very high offer for a novel. As I was just finishing the short novel I have been working on during the last year, and as the terms they offered are so advantageous, I have decided to give them the tale in question, which they are to publish in September or early October.

> I believe this will be to your advantage as well as mine, as it will perhaps be the means of reaching a somewhat different public and—if the story is a success—will in some sort act as a preparation for "The Custom of the Country."

Nearly a year later, on April 13, 1913, Wharton informed Scribner that a New York magazine had offered her $12,500 for a serial, but she wanted to hear from him before she responded. (It should be stated that about this time her need of additional income had increased owing to her divorce.) Although a quality magazine like *Scribner's*, having a smaller circulation, could not well afford to match the high rates paid to authors by mass-circulation periodicals, Scribner agreed to meet the offer—telling her frankly that "it is a little more than we have ever paid." Later that year, continuing to be troubled by the large sums he was forced to pay, he wrote her in connection with Appleton's advance of $12,500 on *The Reef*: "The advance paid by the Appletons seems to be very large and I question whether the book has yet yielded that much in royalty." Nevertheless, forced to meet competition, he agreed to advance her $10,000 on her next novel in addition to $12,500 for its serialization, adding: "I can't remember that we have ever advanced as much as that on any novel." Replying promptly, she assured him suavely: "The terms you propose are perfectly satisfactory."

Yet when a more remunerative offer was made to her about that time, she forwarded the letter to Scribner, knowing that he could not meet it. His reply to this proposal from the editor of *Cosmopolitan* to pay her $15,000 for a serial was as graceful a yielding as he was capable of:

> I was not surprised, as I knew something of the prices paid by the Hearst magazines and I fully realize that we cannot meet competition from periodicals the sales of which are so enormous. In fact I have decided that it will be better for us not to attempt to do so, as we are only drawn into extravagances which we cannot afford. . . . What effect publication in the *Cosmopolitan* would have upon the book's sale I cannot say but I don't see how we could fail to sell as many as we did of "The Custom of the Country," which in that respect was a disappointment to us both. . . . We didn't want to stand in the way of your getting the highest price for the next serial and the sum we have agreed to pay ($12,500) is all we can possibly do and perhaps a little more than we should have ventured. We should, under the circumstances, be content if you accepted the Hearst offer, letting us have the book.

Much as she would have liked to have the additional $2,500, she reluctantly decided to remain with *Scribner's Magazine*, telling Charles Scribner, "I don't think I could have tolerated the idea of appearing in a Hearst publication."

The outbreak of World War I deeply affected Edith Wharton. An ardent admirer of France, she devoted her tremendous energy to the French cause. She conducted a home for refugee children, and assembled contributions from leading authors and artists for a volume entitled *Book of the Homeless*—the purpose of which was to raise money for this home. Scribner, fully sympathetic, agreed to publish the volume at cost and went to great length to produce a beautiful book. When Mrs. Wharton saw a copy on March 30, 1916, she wrote Scribner: "I must tell you at once how delighted I am with it, and how much I appreciate the amount of trouble you and Mr. Updike must have taken to produce anything so artistically perfect, and so satisfactory in its general arrangement."

Yet for all her amicable relations with the Scribner firm, she gave her next book to Appleton. In part this was caused by mutual misunderstanding. In May 1913 she had informed Scribner that she was wavering between two subjects for her next book. Soon after, she settled on what she called *Literature*, which she described as "rather a full and leisurely chronicle of a young man's life from childhood to his end." Scribner agreed to serialize it in his magazine and to publish the book on terms agreeable to her. After the war had started, her mind became too concentrated on relief work to do much writing on the book, so that she decided to postpone the novel until the end of the fighting, when she would again be in the mood to complete the story.

Not having made the change clear to Scribner, he assumed that *Literature* would still be her next book. When shortly thereafter she offered him *Summer*, a brief fictional narrative, for serialization, he felt that the magazine could not well use both stories so close together and decided to wait for *Literature*. Thereupon she gave the book to Appleton, who arranged for its serialization in *McClure's*. To Scribner she explained: "I took up again a long standing offer of Messrs Appleton, which combined serial publication in one of several magazines with book publication by them; on terms so advantageous that, in view of your refusal, I should not have felt justified in rejecting the opportunity."

Scribner felt aggrieved. Replying a month later, he explained why he could not serialize *Summer* in view of the early completion of *Literature*:

> . . . we were expecting that you might wish us to begin "Literature" at the beginning of 1918; for I do not think you ever wrote that the writing of it was postponed until after the war but only that you felt unable to go on with it under present conditions. We should have been very glad to have bought the serial rights of "Summer" for use elsewhere and thus secured the book but I received the impression that that would not be agreeable to you, as you preferred to know just when the story would be published.

Later that year, after Wharton had visited Morocco and had written about it under war conditions, Scribner agreed to publish four of the articles in the magazine as well as the book on it. The following year, when he asked about her next novel, she took the position that he had rejected two of the stories she had offered in place of *Literature*, "the subject of which it was really impossible to treat, with the world crashing around me." Moreover, since he had never actually offered to arrange for serialization of these novels with another magazine, she had "accepted the offers which had long before been made to me by Appleton's."

Eager not to lose her books further, he asked that she let him have her work thereafter. Referring once more to what was to him a painful misunderstanding, he stated that he "had not the heart to re-read the old letters but you certainly interpreted them to mean something never intended by me." Certainly he saw no reason why he should have lost two books even if he could not serialize them.

> In the initial case of *The Reef* we did not decline it as a serial for we were not asked to consider it, nor was it serialized anywhere. Since then when we have had to decline a serial of yours ourselves, it does not seem to me that we should lose the book, particularly when the serial is accepted by a magazine with no book department. . . . You now write that you will be glad to give us a serial for the Magazine but make no mention of book publication, from which I might infer that unless we can use the serial, you will prefer another publisher. Is not this treating us with less consideration than our previous relations entitle us to expect?

Mrs. Wharton merely explained her actions by telling him that she had been receiving serialization offers of $15,000 from three different magazines and similar offers on books by the Appletons.

> Though my old affection for Scribner makes me always wish to see my name on your list, the last few years have been such a strain on me financially, owing to a great reduction in my income, to the heavy taxes we are all suffering from, and to the unprecedented demands for help on all sides, that I feel I must profit by such offers as these I have mentioned, the more as I write slowly.

When the war ended and she realized that she could not again return to *Literature*, she asked Scribner to be released from the contract. Scribner complied: "I do not want you to feel trammelled in any way by our old agreement, either as to story or price." Two years later, when Appleton failed to arrange serialization for *A Son at the Front*, she told Scribner that he could have both serial and book rights as a replacement for *Literature*. On acceptance of both, despite his resentment that the popular *The Age of Innocence* had gone to Appleton, she wrote him: "The manuscript will be placed at your disposal for the price agreed on for the serial rights, $15,000. With regard to the advance royalties on the book, I do not think you mentioned any sum—but you can let me know later. I assume they will be about as usual."

In January 1922 Scribner learned that *Red Book Magazine* was serializing Wharton's *The Old Maid* and wrote her: "Must I infer that the Appletons had secured book publication? If that is not the case, please give us a chance, and you may name your own terms, for I know you only want what is fair." Her information to him was that she had contracted with the Appleton firm for the book before she had finished *The Age of Innocence*. Some months later Scribner again wrote to inquire about her future work. She ignored the question in her reply. In a postscript to a letter to her on May 5, 1923, he added: "You acknowledge my letter of April 5th but say nothing about any future work. If you are not definitely committed elsewhere, and I do not think you can be, I do wish you would let me have sufficient information to make you some proposal." This time she stated that she was not well enough to make plans, but that in fact she has been "getting higher prices from other magazines."

Coming to New York in July 1923 on a brief visit, she visited Scribner at his office. Shortly afterward he wrote her that he was depressed to learn that her new novel was again going to Appleton, "for I thought that the contract was completed and the future was at least open to us." He added that he had been thinking of issuing a complete limited edition of her writings and that he would want to include all her books, "even when brought out by other publishers." Again ignoring the first part of his letter, Wharton told him that Appleton would grant permission to include her books in the complete set.

About this time Scribner published *A Son at the Front*, a story which Wharton had "written in a white heat of emotion," with a first printing of 50,000 copies. It was enthusiastically reviewed and sold in large numbers. Pleased with this news, she wrote: "I believe my books have a certain staying power which, at any rate, I would far rather think they possess than the qualities requisite at present for a sensational sale."

Although she never again gave a novel to Scribner, she continued to cherish her friendships with the men of the firm. On the occasion of a new book by Brownell in 1924, she wrote him: "Well—it is rather lonely at times on the Raft of the Survivors, but not when I think of you, and of what I owe to you, and what I am still going to learn from you, and how, best of all, you have been my friend and guide for so many, many years." A year later, on learning that Charles Scribner was the recipient of an honorary degree at Princeton, she congratulated him most warmly. And when Brownell died in 1928, she readily agreed to write about him in *Scribner's Magazine*, and to Scribner she wrote: "It was a great shock to me, for he was one of the friends of all my life, and seldom as I saw him his friendship was a constant presence to me."

With Charles Scribner's death in 1930, relations between Wharton and the firm, tenuous for some time, lost much of the sentiment which had enlivened it in the early years. Thus when she asked for permission to let Appleton reprint some stories which had appeared in *Scribner's Magazine*, Arthur Scribner, who had succeeded his late brother as head of the firm, wrote her on December 14, 1931, that this permission to a rival publisher would require "a considerable payment." Taking this occasion to tell her of the status of her books on the firm's list, he added:

> ... not having published for you for so long a time it seems impossible for us to keep up a continued sale of some of the early books. From time to time we have considered a number of plans and have made some definite suggestions which were of value. The limited edition of "Ethan Frome", published several years ago, was a distinct success, and the school edition, in the Modern Student Library, published more recently, has greatly increased the circulation of the book, now yielding you, in connection with the original edition about thirty per cent more royalty than before.... "The House of Mirth" is the one book which in its original form still has a remarkable continued sale.

When Owen Davis successfully dramatized *Ethan Frome* in 1935, Appleton obtained Wharton's permission to publish the play—only for both to learn that the Scribner firm still held the copyright on the original book. Admitting the oversight, Wharton agreed to let Scribner issue the play based upon it. About the same time the two houses arranged for each to bring out a collection of her short stories—one limited to those pertaining to ghosts and the other to those of a more general character. Charles Scribner III, acknowledging his pleasure in this agreement, wrote her: "I cannot tell you how happy I am to be publishing this book for you and to have another volume in prospect. My father would have been delighted as he felt very keenly the unfortunate differences which led to your going to another publisher and often spoke to me about it."

This relationship ended with Wharton's death in 1937. In view of her long protestations that an inadequate income had compelled her to seek maximum returns on her writing and disregard her original loyalty to Scribner, it is of interest to point out that in addition to her relatively large earnings from her writings, she was the beneficiary of income from parental trusts amounting to $700,000 as well as from securities valued at $125,000. Her difficulty was, of course, that she lived like an extravagant society woman, whose indulgences were conspicuously costly, rather than as the gifted author dedicated primarily to her art.

18.

Charles Scribner

&

Galsworthy

John Galsworthy and Charles Scribner II were both of the same upper middle class and of similar cultural backgrounds, so that when they got together as author and publisher the friendship that ensued was an affinity of equals both personally and socially. For two decades their close association remained unaffected by Galsworthy's requests for the highest royalties and cash advances he could command—higher than the cautious Scribner wished to give, but nevertheless gave.

Galsworthy was educated at Harrow and Oxford, took honors in law and received an M.A. Called to the bar, he later admitted that his practice was "exiguous." He began to write in his late twenties, and Turgenev's influence was predominant in his early stories. "In novel writing," he stated, "I have learned more from Turgeneff, Tolstoy and De Maupassant than from any other writers." His friendship with Joseph Conrad, which began early and remained close until Conrad's death, likewise exerted an influence.

From an emotional point of view his outlook on life was undoubtedly affected by the fact that in 1895, at the age of twenty-eight, he had fallen in love with the wife of a cousin and married her ten years later upon her divorce. It was indeed this change in his life that swayed him, with her encouragement, toward dedication to writing. It should also be noted that unlike his Polish friend he did not have to depend upon his writing for a living.

For several years he concentrated his efforts on mastering the craft of fiction. During this time he published numerous stories and two novels. Like most new writers he had his quota of rejections. His first mature work, *The Island Pharisees* (1904) was refused by both Duckworth and Constable. Pawling of Heinemann, to whom he went next, perceived its merits and accepted it for publication with the proviso that Galsworthy submit his next book to him. The new novel, *The Man of Property* (1906), quickly established the author's reputation—being the first volume in the trilogy, *The Forsyte Saga*. Thereafter, Heinemann published all his writings in England.

In the United States the House of Putnam published his books up to 1910. For some time J. B. Pinker, Galsworthy's literary agent, had been dissatisfied with the promotion of his client's work and had made informal overtures to Charles Scribner; but being an exponent of the "courtesy" principle, Scribner declined to take an author away from a fellow publisher.

On February 10, 1910, Pinker again approached Scribner, informing him that Galsworthy had decided to change his American publisher and had authorized him to proceed accordingly: "Mr. Galsworthy dislikes change, and therefore it is in the hope that he will not again have to change his publisher that he has authorized me to come to you." He further intimated that if an agreement were reached to their mutual satisfaction, the Galsworthy books now with Putnam would eventually also go to the Scribner firm.

Galsworthy's reputation having by this time become widespread, Scribner was of course interested in adding him to his list of authors, but he first wanted to make sure that Galsworthy would come to him of his own volition. He therefore replied to Pinker with an ethical firmness no longer observed:

> We are interested in Mr. Galsworthy's work but do not wish to interfere in any way with his relations with the Putnams. If he is determined to leave them, for reasons of his own independent of any offer from us, we should of course be glad to negotiate with him. Under the conditions we are not disposed to make any extraordinary terms but I can let you know what I think would be fair.

The terms he suggested were 15 percent up to 5,000 copies and 20 percent thereafter.

Pinker at once assured him that there was no interference from Putnam, that Galsworthy simply felt that the firm had not done as well with his books as he had expected: "His instructions to me are that while he wishes, naturally, to have fair and reasonable terms, it is more important to secure a publisher sufficiently enthusiastic about his work to push it energetically and therefore he does not want you to take it up unless you do feel keen." Scribner readily assured him that Galsworthy "would be sure of our best efforts, for we think this author's books harmonize well with our other publications."

Shortly after an agreement was reached, Scribner informed Pinker that *The Atlantic Monthly* was interested in serializing Galsworthy's forthcoming novel, and this was arranged. Pinker sent him for publication a collection of stories entitled *A Motley*, and *Justice*, a play. Later in 1910 Edward Burlingame asked Pinker for Galsworthy stories to appear in *Scribner's Magazine*; but the sketches Pinker sent him he would not accept because they were already committed to an English periodical, and Burlingame desired full rights. Galsworthy then sent him a short play, which was gladly printed.

The publication of this and other of Galsworthy's writings, particularly *The Patrician*, which was brought out in March 1911, established cordial relations between author and publisher. Both took it for granted that the terms for each work would be mutually satisfactory. Thus, Scribner informed Pinker on April 21: "I am writing hurriedly and have not looked up the question of terms, being pretty sure that we can agree." Somewhat later he inquired when he might obtain the earlier Galsworthy books from Putnam and was informed that Putnam's rights to them lapsed after seven years. This made it possible for Scribner to buy the plates for *The Country House* in 1914, and those for the other books somewhat later.

Galsworthy wrote much during this period, and Scribner published book after book to their mutual gratification. When Galsworthy came to New York to rehearse a play, Scribner entertained him and his wife, and their friendship became cemented by common affinity. On leaving, Mrs. Galsworthy urged the Scribners to visit them in England.

In August 1914, Pinker told Scribner that Galsworthy expected £1500 for the serialization of his new novel in *Scribner's Magazine*, and the amount was paid. About the same time Galsworthy, having become deeply affected by the brutalization in the fighting at the front, submitted an article on the war for which he asked one hundred pounds. Scribner considered the fee rather high, but agreed. In his first personal letter to Scribner, Galsworthy told him to lower the amount if he thought it excessive, but he planned "to give every penny I get for it (and all I can possibly spare from my other proceeds of my work nowadays) to Relief Funds." In reply Scribner stated that he would pay the full amount but hoped that Galsworthy would publish nothing else on the war before the appearance of the article. This he promised. Galsworthy then asked for an advance payment on the serialization of *The Freelands*, as he wished to give the money to Relief; and when Scribner intimated that he would have to pay interest on the money up to the time payment was due normally, he was told by Galsworthy to deduct the interest from the advance.

When the serialization of the novel began, Robert Bridges, then the editor of *Scribner's Magazine*, objected to a paragraph which he considered in questionable taste for a family magazine. Galsworthy agreed to the deletion, but added: "I regret however that what is probably a real piece of scientific discovery, administered in delicate jam, should have to be withheld from your reading public. And I reserve all rights in my contributions to man's knowledge of his origin."

Throughout the war Galsworthy demanded maximum remuneration in order to contribute as much as he could to Relief Funds. Scribner, sympathetic to the Allies, willingly paid what was asked of him. When he was unable to serialize Galsworthy's latest work in his own monthly, he sought to place it elsewhere. When *Cosmopolitan* offered Pinker £3,000 for the serial rights with the stipulation that it was also to be given the next two novels, both he and Galsworthy consulted with Scribner before agreeing to the arrangement. Scribner knew that he could not afford to pay such high fees, and he did not wish to prevent Galsworthy from getting them. Readily agreeing to limit himself to book rights, he wrote Pinker on October 26, 1915: "You will no doubt understand this as meaning that under the circumstances we can not stand in the way though we should like to have another serial by him within the time named."

When Scribner acquired the plates of Galsworthy's early books and thus had all his works, Galsworthy wrote him on June 2, 1916: "I have been meaning for some weeks now to write, and tell you of my pleasure in seeing that all my books have come under your control. It is a great satisfaction to me. And I sincerely hope that you won't have cause to regret it."

As often happens, authors find book jackets and advertisements of their books personally distasteful. When Galsworthy, inclined to moral primness, saw the wrapper on *Beyond* in August 1917, he wrote Scribner: "Frankly I can't bear the young lady on the cover. If you come to a second edition could you substitute one of the 'Cosmopolitan' illustrations—the type of the cover is so hopelessly sensual and wrong. I'm sorry to be 'persnickety.' " In reply Scribner told him that although he had printed 25,000 copies of the book, the sale was going well and he would be going to press again before long and would change the jacket. He then presented the publisher's position in regard to promotion:

> I am not surprised you don't like the wrap. It presents a pretty little school girl more suitable for a bonbon box than for one of your novels but I don't find the type sensual. We will not continue the cover indefinitely but to drop it immediately would be difficult. It is not easy to know what to do in such matters. The salesmen and the Trade seem to demand something pretty or exciting and I can't be continually checking their enthusiasm. I regard such covers as a concession to the selling force.

With the war ended, Galsworthy arranged to visit the United States. Scribner met him and his wife at the boat and took them to the hotel where he had reserved rooms for them. Finding roses on their arrival, Mrs. Galsworthy wrote Scribner: "The glorious roses are full of more joyous life than we have been feeling around us for years now!" During the visit the two families saw a good deal of one another. Two years later, when the Scribners were in England, they were entertained by the Galsworthys with the warmth of genuine friendship.

The Scribner firm was highly successful in marketing Galsworthy's books. The sale of 35,457 copies of *Saint's Progress* by March 8, 1920, was only a few thousand greater than that of *The Dark Flower*. Yet a month later Galsworthy urged Maxwell Perkins, his editor, to see what could be done to stimulate the sale of *Five Tales*, a volume of short stories:

> I hope you may be able to support the sale of "Five Tales" in some way, because I do feel that that is as good work as I have done—if not better; and that it has not yet reached its proper limit in U.S.A. Here, for instance, it has actually sold more copies than it has with you, though I reckon my novels reach about three times (in America) their English circulation.

Perkins's reply, while explaining that volumes of short stories do not sell well in America, sought to reassure him:

> It seems to us doubtful if such an edition would be adaptable to American conditions but we wish to know all about it, in order to see whether this would be the case. . . . Whether through a fault in our advertising or not, it failed to get proper attention and if Mr. Heinemann's plan or any other that comes up should show us a way to counteracting this, we would be quick to take advantage of it.

Toward the end of the year, while sojourning in California, Galsworthy again complained that his novel, *Awakening*, had not been "travelled" enough; that the Marshall Field book department in Chicago had no copies of it; that very few copies were available in California. "I think the demand is in excess of the sup-ply as far as I can judge, and I am sorry, because Xmas comes once a year! If anything can still be done to lift the sale of the little book and to make it a hardy annual, I shall be glad." Perkins readily admitted that the firm was having some difficulty with California bookstores, but that there must be some error about Marshall Field, and he might be confident the firm was doing whatever was pos-sible to promote his books and would make sure that bookstores were stocked.

That same month Bridges again objected to a sentence in a Galsworthy story for the magazine. Writing to Scribner about it on December 30, 1920, Galswor-thy, less prim than Bridges, acquiesced under protest:

> Perhaps you would ask Mr. Bridges to delete the words "all the unappeased sexual instinct of" from the text, leaving the text "and June ached at its loneliness." I do this in deference to your wish. I am, however (quite apart from Freud's teaching— he is something of a monomaniac) convinced that starved sexual instinct *is* respon-sible for very much emotional vagary in many directions.

In the early 1920s Scribner suggested to Galsworthy that he would like to bring out a limited deluxe edition of his works. Galsworthy was highly pleased and was quite fussy about type, format, paper, illustrations, and binding, but he willingly wrote prefaces to each of the sixteen volumes. This Manaton Edition was sold out within two years. About the same time Galsworthy wanted to know what demand there was for first editions of his books, indicating there was such demand in England, and was told by Perkins that there had been few requests by American collectors.

Shortly thereafter Scribner also proposed a one-volume edition of the three-volume *Forsyte Saga*, with the royalty lowered to 15 percent in order to keep the price down to $2.50. Galsworthy agreed, and asked that the firm arrange with a Canadian publisher to issue his own edition of the omnibus volume "because it is important to me that the book should be *exploited in Canada to the full*." This Scribner did.

During this period Galsworthy was earning large sums of money and, both-ered by the income tax forms he had to fill out, wrote Scribner that it was "a prospect that fills me with terror. Would not a holding in Government, State or Municipal securities, which are exempt from American tax, be better for me in this respect? I would rather have a low rate in interest *free from the above con-tingencies*." Although Scribner told him that he and his banker believed that railroad and public utility stocks were among the safest investments, he deferred to his wishes and bought him government bonds valued at $5,000.

In 1923 Galsworthy gave the serial rights to *The White Monkey* to *Scribner's Magazine* and wrote Scribner: "The pleasure of being in *Scribner's* outweighed commercial lures." For the book rights he received a straight 20 percent royalty and an advance of £1,000. A month after it was published in October 1924, Per-kins informed him: "I've been impatiently waiting for the moment when I could write that the sale of *The White Monkey* had passed the highest point reached by any of your earlier books, and now it has come. Today the number sold is

barely short of 35,000. We have printed 80,000 and we are advertising heavily."
A month later Scribner wrote Galsworthy: "When we gave the order for the last
printing of "The White Monkey," which brought the total to a hundred thousand, I cabled so that you might rejoice with us. I hope you will not feel humiliated in having fallen into the class of best sellers." He also informed him that the
sale of the limited Manaton Edition had exceeded 600 sets.

In 1925 Galsworthy gave Scribner the serial rights to *The Silver Spoon*, although the *Ladies' Home Journal* had offered him considerably more than
Scribner's £2,500. Writing to Scribner about it on August 5, 1925, he stated:

> As you know by now, I decided for Scribner's Magazine after all—the liking for
> that home, the lack of illustrations, and the question of vast circulation in the La-
> dies Home Journal, to say nothing of my feeling that you would like it to go to
> Scribner's—outweighed the extra money. I am very happy that—being a sequel—
> it should go on where The White Monkey left off.

That December Scribner proposed issuing an inexpensive edition of Galsworthy's works. Fully agreeable, and naming it The Grove Edition, the latter suggested that the edition should be

> sold either as a set, or in single volumes; the volumes, therefore, not be numbered.
> Edition to be sold by mail, *and* at book stores. . . . It is essential to my mind that
> people should be able to buy *single* volumes freely, as well as at bookstores. As I
> told you in my former letter I view with disquiet the present practical extinction in
> America of the novels other than "The Forsyte Saga" and its sequels.

Scribner explained that sets of books were not handled in America the way
they were in England, but that he would comply with his wishes. He made clear
to him, however, what the American practice was concerning cheap reprints,
which he did not favor; that subscription editions were usually sold separately by
mail or solicitation by agents; and that single volumes were sold in bookstores.
This procedure pleased Galsworthy: "I should hate the issue of my books in this
cheaper edition to pass away from you into the hands of other houses—such as
Grosset & Dunlap, though I know nothing of them. I want to be kept entirely in
your hands and properly nursed by you."

His popularity remained on the rise. On November 9, 1926, Perkins informed
him that *The Silver Spoon* was selling even better than *The White Monkey*:
"The present figure for 'The Silver Spoon' in the United States is 93,146. The
present figure for 'The White Monkey' is 108,865; but in that 'White Monkey'
figure is included a number of thousands of copies sold in Canada."

For some time mass-circulation magazines had been seeking to obtain serial
rights to Galsworthy's fiction. Finally the editor of the *Ladies' Home Journal* offered Pinker $40,000 for a serial. Yielding to the temptation of this large sum,
Galsworthy wrote Scribner apologetically that "$40,000 was too much to
refuse." Scribner's reply on May 31, 1927, was in character:

It was kind of you to write so frankly about the novel and the magazine. Of course I understand the situation and would not wish you to make such a sacrifice for us. We shall look forward to the book eagerly and take pleasure in thinking that our management of your interests here has helped to increase the market value of your work.

The following September, Galsworthy informed Scribner that as a prominent member of the Society of English Authors he had to agree to let his books be published separately in Canada by a Canadian publisher—much as he dislikes to displease him:

In view of the really big American sales of my last novels, and the comparative small sale in Canada, this is really a matter of but little importance to you, still I can't expect you to like the new departure, though I feel somehow that you will sympathize with my view, and recognize that an American would certainly do the same in a like case.

Scribner did not like to give up this Canadian market, but he accepted the deprivation gracefully. He valued Galsworthy's friendship too much to want to strain it in any way. The fact was that Galsworthy was one of his most profitable authors. When *Swan Song* was published in 1928 and sold around 100,000 copies, both men were gratified. By this time the sale of the Compact Edition of Galsworthy's fiction also yielded him $14,250, and a second printing of it brought him another $13,537.50. Continuing to further the sale of his books, he agreed to a 12 ½ percent royalty on the omnibus volume, *A Modern Comedy*, which had to be priced low in order to achieve a large sale. Yet when Scribner proposed in 1930, with the depression already on, to issue a limited edition of *Soames and the Flag*, Galsworthy had no hesitation in asking for an unusually high royalty: "I think however you should pay me 25% whether you make the price 10 or 15 dollars or even if you make it less. If you don't sell 500 copies things will have slumped indeed."

In May 1930, learning of Scribner's death, he wrote to express his deep sorrow. Soon after, eager for a prolonged visit to the United States, and wishing to earn his expenses while there, he asked Perkins if he could arrange eight lectures for him at £250 a lecture. His plan was to reach New York around Christmas, spend the winter in Arizona, and deliver the lectures during the first fortnight in the spring. "I don't want to carry money out of the country, but I do want to make all our winter expenses."

Perkins had to tell him that conditions were too unfavorable for the proposed high fees. He suggested that the firm would arrange the lectures at $1,000 each, absorb the agent's fees and tax, which would amount to about 20 percent of the remuneration. Galsworthy of course agreed to this arrangement, and the Scribner firm paid $200 a lecture as well as a tax of $401.25. The following April, back in England, Galsworthy expressed his pleasure that the lectures had gone so well and added: "I don't expect I shall ever lecture in America again. The pitcher can go too often to the well."

Late in 1931 he told Perkins that his sequel to *Maid in Waiting* was well along and he hoped that *Scribner's Magazine* would make a special effort to meet the amount offered by other periodicals: "A serial of mine ought now to materially increase the circulation of the magazine, especially if well advertised beforehand." With the Depression hitting popular periodicals very hard, the firm was able to meet the competing price of $5,000. Meanwhile *Maid in Waiting* led the list of best sellers, selling 73,533 copies by May 4, 1932—an excellent showing for the time, as books in general sold only around half of the 1929 figures.

Upon learning that Galsworthy had been awarded the 1932 Nobel Prize, the Scribner firm took advantage of the resulting prestige and publicity to issue his four novels of love into a single volume, thereby augmenting the market for those books.

Galsworthy died on January 31, 1933. The House of Scribner, although now managed by younger executives who had been less close to him, continued to promote his works and to look after Mrs. Galsworthy's interests. In February 1934 it made arrangements for the Book-of-the-Month Club to issue *End of the Chapter* as a premium book for a fee of $5,000; a similar plan was carried out in 1945 for an illustrated edition of *The Forsyte Saga*. It also fully cooperated with H. V. Marrot in 1936 in the preparation of his biography of Galsworthy.

19

Maxwell Perkins

&

F. Scott Fitzgerald

Once F. Scott Fitzgerald's genuine literary talent gained him prominence and popularity, he began gradually to suffer from his uncontrolled indulgence in liquor and luxury. Born in 1896 to relatively poor, middle western parents, he was able through the generosity of a wealthy and pious aunt to attend an Eastern preparatory school and Princeton University. Only a passable student, he did feel a strong urge to write and made his mark in both schools by contributions to their literary publications.

A member of the Princeton Class of 1918 that produced several other prominent writers, and aglow with the romantic excitement of America's entrance into the European war in April 1917, Fitzgerald enlisted in the armed services in his senior year. The recurrent thought of possible death in battle caused him to hasten the completion of a novel. Before leaving for Fort Leavenworth, he gave the manuscript to Dean Christian Gauss with the request that he submit it to Charles Scribner's Sons, a firm closely connected with Princeton. Gauss found the writing immature and talked Fitzgerald out of having him do so.

Driven by ambition to become a writer, however, he devoted his free time while in training to the revision and improvement of the story. Upon its completion, he gave it to Shane Leslie, who was one of his teachers in preparatory school and who had befriended him. Leslie read it with interest, corrected the grammar, spelling, and punctuation, and sent it to his publisher, the Scribner firm. In August 1918 Maxwell Perkins returned the manuscript with a note of encouragement, suggesting that he would be glad to see it again after its revision. Thereupon Fitzgerald rewrote it in part and resubmitted it. In October Perkins rejected the novel—having been outvoted by W. C. Brownell and Edward Burlingame. At Fitzgerald's urging Perkins had two other publishers consider it, but both refused it.

Fitzgerald was then in Camp Sheridan near Montgomery, Alabama. At a dance there he met Zelda Sayre, the eighteen-year-old daughter of a prominent judge. Very attractive, boldly unconventional, bright and animated, she immediately appealed to Fitzgerald, handsome in his officer's uniform from Brooks Brothers. He arranged for an introduction, and soon began to woo her with an ardor and persistence that stimulated her response to him. Though a first lieutenant about to be sent overseas and possibly be killed, he urged her to marry him without delay. While she encouraged his courting, she resisted his yearning for greater intimacy. Overwrought emotionally and ordered north for an overseas assignment, he finally persuaded Zelda to accept his engagement ring—only to quarrel with her soon after. When the Armistice in November obviated his going to Europe and soon after resulted in his release from the army, he did everything in his power to resume his wooing of Zelda, who by that time realized she was indeed in love with him.

On his discharge in February 1919, Fitzgerald went to New York to seek employment. He realized that he needed to earn a lot of money if he were to marry Zelda, but he knew that he could not expect to do so by writing—at least not for some time. To this end he joined an advertising agency and devoted his free time to writing stories. But rejection slips came with discouraging regularity. When *Smart Set* did accept a story, the payment was a mere thirty dollars. Moreover, his salary at the Barron Collier Agency sufficed only for his daily expenses.

All the while his longing for Zelda was intense. He feared that, fluctuating emotionally, she might get tired of waiting and break their engagement. As he later stated: "I was in love with a whirlwind and I must spin a net big enough to catch it." Becoming desperate, he went to Montgomery to urge immediate marriage. This Zelda refused, and returned his engagement ring. Although she loved him deeply, she did not feel that he had enough confidence in himself to be the kind of man she wanted her husband to be; she wanted him to get established first, to earn money for the kind of life she hoped to lead, before they were joined in marriage. Severely shaken, he returned to New York, quit his job, and went on a three-week drunk.

When sober again, he decided to leave for St. Paul and rework his novel, convinced that he could now do so successfully and that it would not only establish him as a writer but bring him adequate royalties to enable him to marry Zelda. After working intensively on the revision for three months he again sent the manuscript to Perkins. On September 16 Perkins wrote him: "I am very glad, personally, to be able to write to you that we are all for publishing your book. . . . The book is so different that it is hard to prophesy how it will sell but we are all for taking a chance and supporting it with vigor."

Fitzgerald was jubilant. After months of dejection and hard work he now exploded with joy and hope. "Of course I was delighted to get your letter," he replied at once, "and I've been in a sort of trance all day; not that I'd doubted you'd take it but at last I have something to show people."

All kinds of plans seethed in his mind, stimulated by the hope that Zelda would now agree to marry him. He urged Perkins to publish the novel immediately, and to further his plea he told him he was already working on a new novel, *The Demon Lover*, as well as some short stories. He also wrote to Zelda, after a silence of four months, informing her of the acceptance of the novel and asking if he might visit her. She was delighted to hear from him and told him so. He visited her in November, and before he left they agreed to marry on the publication of the novel. It should be stated that her agreement to become his wife was motivated not by his expected affluence, as he and his biographer had intimated, which she knew was problematical at best, but by her feeling that he had matured and possessed the confidence she had wanted him to have.

Back in New York, Fitzgerald told Perkins of his various plans, and consulted him about the serialization of his new novel, which would make it possible for him to be independent of the sale of stories. With his patience wearing thin while waiting for the publication of *This Side of Paradise*, he again wrote Perkins that for some days he had tried to tell him how upset he was that his book was not being published as soon as he had hoped, but he held back because he personally had been very good to him. Yet he was very anxious to have the book appear without delay—because of financial, sentimental, and domestic reasons, but chiefly because of the psychological effect it would have on him.

When the novel was published on March 26, 1920, it proved sensationally successful, effectively expressing as it did the loosening of moral and conventional bonds required by Fitzgerald's postwar generation. During the first seven months it sold more than 32,000 copies. This success provided a halo under which Zelda and Scott were married in New York a week after publication. Both were deliriously happy and behaved as if they were deliberately seeking to shock people. At the end of April, strictly separating his zany behavior from his daily writing, he sent Perkins eleven stories for publication in late September under the title of *Flappers & Philosophers*.

Early in 1920, Fitzgerald made Paul Reynolds his agent, and Harold Ober was assigned to handle his work; when Ober opened his own agency, Fitzgerald went with him. He soon sold a story to the *Saturday Evening Post* for $400— whereupon the youthful author celebrated his success by getting drunk. Not long after, Fitzgerald revised two old stories, and the *Post* paid $1,000 for them. He now assumed a certainty of acceptance at ever-increasing prices for his stories— which indeed proved correct—and began to indulge in extravagances as if he wished to compensate for his previous financial stringency. Although he later blamed Zelda for this prodigality, Nancy Milford in *Zelda* has presented evidence that Perkins had unfairly blamed her for it when he stated: "Scott was extravagant, but not like her; money went through her fingers like water; she wanted everything; she kept him writing for the magazines." She indeed was a free spender, but it was Fitzgerald who enjoyed the luxury of lavish spending— the feeling that he could be as free with money as the men of wealth, whom he greatly admired despite his occasional socialistic utterances.

In any event, by the end of 1920 he had spent the $20,000 he had earned and had to begin his practice of borrowing from the Scribner firm and Ober. On December 31, 1920, he wrote Perkins that he was in desperate financial difficulties. The bank had that day refused to lend him money on the security of his stock, and he had been pacing the floor wondering what he could do about it. What particularly aggravated him was that his novel was within two weeks of completion, and he already had bills amounting to $600 in addition to $650 he had borrowed from Reynolds as an advance on a story which he was too upset to write. Having made a half dozen starts in the past two days, he continued, he felt he would go mad if he had to write another story of a debutante—which was what the magazine editor wanted.

He asked for an advance of $1,600 and received it by return mail. From then on, money became a recurrent and at times desperate concern to Fitzgerald despite the fact that his earnings from his writings reached as high as $36,000 a year. The fact was that he no sooner came into money than he found ways of spending it, usually on unessentials. Perkins early became aware of this weakness and was unusually indulgent. On May 2, 1921, he told him: "We shall always be ready to advance, not only amounts equivalent to what your books have already earned, although the payments may not then be due, but amounts which may be considered reasonable estimates of what it may be anticipated they will earn." The next day Fitzgerald and Zelda, who was already pregnant—Scottie was born the following October—left for a pleasure trip to Europe. Late that month Fitzgerald wrote Perkins from Venice that they were having a wonderful time and asked for $1,000 on the strength of his intention "to start a new book in July."

On his return to the United States he wrote Perkins from Montgomery to complain that the firm was not promoting his book actively enough. To the best of his knowledge, he claimed, he had not seen one advertisement of *Paradise*, not one in the *Times* or *Tribune* or the Chicago newspapers within six months after publication. The fact was, he insisted, that what publicity the book received from the beginning it got on its own account. The few advertisements the book had were "small and undistinguished" and were confined almost exclusively to college periodicals and *Scribner's Magazine*. In reply Perkins promised to do a big promotion job on his new book and told him to be free with his criticism.

Fitzgerald was at this time hard at work on his second novel, *The Beautiful and the Damned*, originally titled *The Flight of the Rocket*. When Perkins, after reading the manuscript, asked him to modify a slighting reference to the Old Testament, he strongly demurred, maintaining the legitimacy of his criticism. Whereupon Perkins wrote him on December 12, 1921:

> Don't ever *defer* to my judgment. You won't on any vital point, I know, and I should be ashamed, if it were possible to have made you; for a writer of any account must speak solely for himself. I should hate to play (assuming V.W.B's [Van Wyck Brooks's] position to be sound) the W. D. Howells to your Mark Twain.

> It is not to the *substance* of this passage that I object. . . . The Old Testament ought not to be treated in a way which suggests a failure to realize its tremendous significance in the recent history of man, as if it could simply be puffed away with a breath of contempt, it is so trivial. That is the effect of the passage at present. . . . My point is that you impair the effectiveness of the passage—of the very purpose you use it for—by giving that quality of contempt.

Fitzgerald thereupon accepted the suggestion to substitute "Deity" for "God Almighty."

A little later he sent Perkins a discouraging letter from Reynolds regarding the clarity of his stories. Perkins quickly comforted him: "So far as it concerns your writing, I think it represents a temporary condition. The time ought to come when whatever you write will go through and when its irony and satire will be understood." He continued by praising the satiric quality of *The Beautiful and the Damned*, then in proof, which, he feared, "will not of itself be understood by the great simple-minded public without a little help," but he assured him that the Scribner firm would make every effort to provide this help.

When bound copies of the novel reached Fitzgerald, he praised the description on the jacket but found fault with the drawings. He thought it had struck exactly the right note and gave a moral key for the "stupid" critics to go on; moreover, it also justified the book to the many unperceptive readers who might consider the story immoral. Yet the more he looked at the picture on the jacket the more baffled he was about what the artist had in mind. The girl was drawn rather well, and she did resemble Zelda. The man, however, was no doubt a kind of "debauched edition of me." He assured Perkins that he had shown the drawing to a number of people, and they agreed with him that the man was a caricature of himself. That made him "sore"—because when a book had only one drawing to give the impression of the main character of a novel, it should have been drawn more carefully.

An interesting sidelight on how Charles Scribner reacted to this new kind of author in the 1920s was his comment to Edith Wharton on sending her a copy of Fitzgerald's second novel: "Neither book is much appreciated in that academic circle but the first was almost a 'best seller' and this promises well. He certainly has some literary skill and should do well if he will exercise some restraint. He belongs to the latest flight of American novelists."

The Beautiful and the Damned, having been serialized in *Metropolitan Magazine*, was published in March 1922. Although it met with a mixed reception from reviewers, it sold 43,000 in a little more than two months. In the fall Scribner issued another collection of Fitzgerald's stories, *Tales of the Jazz Age*, which sold 18,000 copies—a very good sale for a volume of stories.

Fitzgerald's large earnings did not cover his expenditures, and he had to borrow from Scribner and Ober. He wrote short stories in an effort to reduce his debts; yet notwithstanding the fact that his stories were by then bringing fees of $1,500 and more, at times he felt desperate. On August 11, 1922, he asked Perkins for an advance of $1,000. Optimistic for the moment about the play he was writing, he told him: "After my play is produced I'll be rich forever and never have to bother you again." The play, however, netted him little, and on November 5, 1923, addressing Perkins for the first time as "Dear Max," he told him: "I'm at the end of my rope—as the immortal phrase goes. I owe the Scribner Company something over $3,500 even after deducting reprint money from the Beautiful and Damned." Yet he asked for another $650, and got it.

In May 1924 the Fitzgeralds went to Europe, ostensibly in the expectation of living more cheaply, but Scott's extravagance continued undiminished. He wrote numerous short stories in order to obtain immediate cash, but his chief effort was work on his new book, for which he had difficulty finding an apt title, but finally settled on *The Great Gatsby*. Despite the high prices he was getting for his stories, he considered writing them an irksome chore; yet for all his eagerness to complete the novel, he failed to make the anticipated progress. In April, while still in the United States, he apologized to Perkins for dissipating his time and energy and for his "ragged" efforts at writing. He made clear to him that although he had every hope of finishing his novel by June, he would not let it go unless it measured up to the very best that was in him—if not a little better than he was capable of. In the current novel, he added, he was doing purely creative work—not the "trashy imaginings" he used in his stories but the sustained imagination envisioning a "sincere yet radiant world." For that reason he was working slowly and carefully, and often felt deep distress at not being able to attain his goal. Yet he expected to achieve a novel superior to his first.

Perkins appreciated his artistic maturity and assured him of his understanding and confidence.

> So far as we are concerned, you are to go ahead at just your own pace, and if you should finish the book when you think you will, you will have performed a considerable feat even in the matter of time, it seems to me. My view of the future is—particularly in the light of your letter—one of very great optimism and confidence.

Once he hit his stride in the writing, Fitzgerald became sanguine about its quality and told Perkins on August 25: "I think my novel is about the best American novel ever written. It is rough stuff in places, runs only to about 50,000 words and I hope you won't shy at it. . . . I've been unhappy but my novel hasn't suffered from it. I am grown at last."

When the finished manuscript reached Perkins, he found it unusually good. On November 14 he wrote Fitzgerald:

> I think the novel is a wonder . . . it has vitality to an extraordinary degree, and *glamour*, and a great deal of underlying thought of unusual quality. It has a kind of mystic atmosphere at times that you infused into parts of "Paradise" and have not since used. It is a marvelous fusion, into a unity of presentation of the extraordinary incongruities of life today. And as for sheer writing, it's astonishing.

And in a letter a week later he continued his unstinted praise. Fitzgerald was of course highly elated by this praise and replied on December 1: "Your wire and your letters made me feel like a million dollars—I'm sorry I could make no better response than a telegram whining for money. But the long siege of the novel winded me a little & I've been slow in starting the stories on which I must live."

Optimistic about the appeal of the novel, he predicted to Perkins that it would sell around 80,000 copies. While in this mood he refused its serialization by *College Humor*, thereby losing $10,000 in remuneration, in order to get it published without delay. When *The Great Gatsby* was issued in April 1925, its reception by reviewers was generally very favorable; but its sale came nowhere near his expectation, reaching a total of 20,000 in the first six months. Perkins did his best to comfort him: "I know fully how this period must try you: it must be very hard to endure, because it is hard enough for me to endure. I like the book so much myself and see so much in it that its recognition and success mean more to me than anything else in sight at the present time."

Fitzgerald's depression was not easily dissipated. In reply he thought that the cause of the book's failure to gain popularity was that it had "no important woman character, and women control the fiction market at present." And he continued gloomily:

> Now I shall write some cheap ones until I've accumulated enough for my next novel. When that is finished and published I'll wait and see. If it will support me with no more interval of trash I'll go on as a novelist. If not I'm going to quit, come home, go to Hollywood and learn the movie business. I can't reduce our scale of living and I can't stand this financial insecurity. Anyhow there is no point in trying to be an artist if you can't do your best. I had my chance back in 1920 to start my life on a sensible scale. I lost it and so I'll have to pay the penalty. Then perhaps at 40 I can start writing again without this constant worry and interruption.

Hoping that the final sale of the novel would at least cover his debt to the firm, and stimulated by the emergence in his mind of a new work, he momentarily broke out of his depression and added: "The happiest thought I have is my new novel—it is something really NEW in form, idea, structure—the model for the age and Joyce and Stein are searching for, that Conrad didn't find." Perkins was warmly sympathetic and wrote him encouragingly while welcoming the stories that made up the volume of *All the Sad Young Men*, to be published that fall.

On receiving a letter from Boni & Liveright in May 1925 asking for his next book, Fitzgerald, sensitive to literary gossip, immediately wrote Perkins that he had answered at once to say that Perkins was one of his closest friends and that his relation with Scribner was so cordial and pleasant that he would not think of changing publishers. Indeed, he thought so highly of the firm and of Perkins that he would gladly sign a contract for his next three books if that were desirable. The idea of leaving the firm had never entered his head.

In the same letter he informed Perkins that Owen Davis had been engaged to dramatize *Gatsby*. The play was relatively successful and netted Fitzgerald around $18,000 in royalties. He also received $3,500 for a story from a movie studio. This additional income enabled him to pay his debts but did not keep him long from the need to borrow again—as his income of around $22,000 annually for the past five years did not cover the expenditures of Zelda and himself.

Once again unable to throw off his feeling of depression, he drank hard between spurts of writing what he assumed was his new novel, but which consisted mostly of "destroying and revision." Yet for a time he made believe he was making good progress. In letter after letter he kept assuring Perkins that the novel was "wonderful" and was nearing completion. Then on December 27, 1925, no longer able to delude himself yet clinging to hope, he wrote him from the depth of "one of my unholy depressions" to say that his book was "wonderful" and would be one of the best American novels, but the end was not near. He then reminded him that he had wanted to die at thirty, and that being now twenty-nine, death was still welcome; that his work was the only thing that made him happy, although he also enjoyed getting a "little tight"—an indulgence for which he was paying a high price in "mental and physical hangovers."

Several weeks later, having been encouraged by a favorable comment from T. S. Eliot, he informed Perkins that the poet had "read *Gatsby* three times & thought it was *the 1st step forward American fiction had taken since Henry James.*" And he added optimistically, "Wait till they see the new novel!"

This sanguine attitude was again expressed on May 8, 1926: "My book is *wonderful.* I don't think I'll be interrupted again. I expect to reach New York about Dec. 10th with the ms. under my arm. I'll ask between $30,000 and $40,000 for the serial rights and I think *Liberty* will want it. So book publication would be late spring 1927 or early fall." After Zelda's appendectomy about a month later he stated: "The novel, in abeyance during Zelda's operation, now goes on apace. This is confidential but *Liberty,* with certain conditions, has offered me $35,000 sight unseen. I hope to have it done in January." Then on August 10, 1927, in a more deflated moment, he confessed: "God, how much I've learned in these two and a half years in Europe. It seems like a decade and I feel pretty old but I wouldn't have missed it, even its most unpleasant and painful aspects." All this time he was making no progress on the novel and had to give it up, drinking hard in fits of depression. He did manage to write stories for the *Saturday Evening Post,* and was paid from $3,000 to $4,000 for each.

At the end of 1927 Zelda, Scottie, and he returned to the United States. He was without money, without a manuscript, and very dejected. To earn ready cash, he accepted an assignment in Hollywood, but the script he wrote for Constance Talmage was rejected, and his remuneration was nominal.

His love for Zelda had by then lost its passionate impetuosity, and on one occasion he slapped her when she called his father an Irish policeman. Later that spring, on their return to Europe, Zelda began to study dancing with intensive concentration. Fitzgerald wrote stories, for which he received high fees, but drank heavily—feeling that Zelda's devotion to dancing was a means of hurting him. Both were unhappy and at cross-purposes. "In his suffering," Arthur Mizener pointed out, "he struck out, blindly and unreasonably, at the people and things that mattered most to him." The following October they were back in New York, their life together unchanged. On his thirty-second birthday he noted: "Ominous. No Real Progress in any way and wrecked myself with dozens of people."

In November Fitzgerald sent Perkins the first two chapters of a newly projected novel—having abandoned his earlier story of matricide. The work that now occupied him, which he first called *The Drunkard's Holiday* but which he subsequently entitled *Tender Is the Night,* gave him considerable trouble, and he made little progress on it. Moreover, illness and liquor combined to keep him depressed and inactive, so that when he decided in March 1929 to return to Europe, he wrote Perkins:

> I'm sneaking away like a thief without leaving the chapters—there's a week's work to straighten them out and in the confusion of influenza and leaving, I haven't been able to do it. I'll do it on the boat and send it from Genoa. A thousand thanks for your patience—just trust me a few months longer, Max—it's been a discouraging

time for me too but I will never forget your kindness and the fact that you've never reproached me.

Writing from Europe on June 29 he told Perkins: "I am working night and day on novel from new angle that I think will solve previous difficulties." And in the following November he informed him: "For the first time since August I see my way clear to a long stretch on the novel, so I'm writing you as I can't bear to do when it's in one of its states of postponement & seems so in the air." Yet in January 1930 he explained that his failure to mention progress on the novel "isn't because it isn't finishing up or that I'm neglecting it—but only that I'm weary of setting dates for it till the moment when it is in the post office box."

That April Zelda suffered a complete mental breakdown and was taken for treatment to the Malmaison Sanitarium in Switzerland. For a time she would not see Fitzgerald, and the Swiss psychiatrist diagnosed her illness as schizophrenia. Terribly upset by this tragic turn in his life, Fitzgerald was unable to write.

Reacting to news of Charles Scribner's death, he told Perkins how much he would miss "his fairness toward things that were of another generation, his general tolerance and simply his being there as the titular head of a great business." In another letter in July he confided that "Zelda is still sick as hell. . . . I was so upset in June when hopes for her recovery were black that I could practically do no work and got behind." When she began to improve after months of treatment, she longed for her husband's love and felt she was not getting it, failing to realize how perturbed he was because the high cost of her illness was greatly increasing his indebtedness. His state of mind was almost desperate when Ober no longer felt able to advance him money on stories he had planned but not written, so that he had to turn to Perkins for additional advances.

Late in 1931, Zelda appearing improved, the Fitzgeralds returned to the United States and paid a visit to Montgomery. The death of her father the following November brought on another breakdown. She was taken to Baltimore for treatment, and Fitzgerald went to Hollywood for an eight-week assignment in the hope of reducing his indebtedness. On January 15, 1932, he reported to Perkins, in a moment of optimism, that for the first time in two and a half years he was expecting to be able to spend five consecutive months on his novel—being at the moment $6,000 ahead. He was planning to rewrite the book, keeping what was good in it, adding 41,000 new words. He urged Perkins to keep this plan secret, not to tell it to Hemingway or anyone else—no matter what they thought of him—for only he was consistent in having faith in him.

While in the Phipps Clinic in Baltimore, Zelda missed Fitzgerald and whiled away her time by writing a novel based to a large extent on their relationship—finishing the first draft in six weeks. On his return from Hollywood Fitzgerald settled in Baltimore in order to be near Zelda. He did what he could to help her, yet he felt that their lives were inextricably mixed with no solution in sight. As before, he sought forgetfulness in drink.

A reading of Zelda's manuscript impressed Fitzgerald favorably despite his resentment against her critical portrayal of the character recognizably based on himself as well as her apparently deliberate competition with his own writing. He sent her manuscript to Perkins, telling him it was "now good, improved in every way," and hoped he would agree with him that it was publishable. Perkins agreed that *Save Me the Waltz* was acceptable, no doubt eager to bolster the morale of both husband and wife. When published, the reception was mixed and its sale small.

Despite his emotional depression, his worry about Zelda and Scottie, and the urgency to keep afloat financially, Fitzgerald persisted in his work on the novel, which he now called *Doctor Diver's Holiday*. Yet more than once he broke down and drank himself sick. On January 19, 1933, he confessed to Perkins that he had been in "New York for three days last week on a terrible bat. I was about to call you up when I completely collapsed and laid in bed for twenty-four hours groaning. Without a doubt the boy is growing too old for such tricks." He added that he now planned to abstain from liquor for the next two months and work on the book. In the writing he, like Zelda, made considerable use of events in their life together, and even quoted from her letters and other of her writings.

By September he had made good progress and wrote Perkins: "The novel has gone ahead faster than I thought." He was confident that he would complete the manuscript by October 25, and a week before that he informed him that he would send the first part of the book in a few days—the part that was being serialized in *Scribner's Magazine* and for the whole of which he was being paid $10,000. Intent on completing the novel, he wrote the last third "entirely on stimulant." Finally, in January 1934, he sent the last of the manuscript to Perkins with the following revealing comment:

> The novel will certainly have succès d'estime but it may be slow in coming—alas, I may again have written a novel for novelists with little chance of its lining anybody's pockets with gold. The thing is perhaps too crowded for story readers to search it through for the story but it can't be helped, there are times when you have to get every edge of your finger nails on paper.

Sensitive of the fact that it took him more than seven years to write the novel, he stated defensively two months later that, after all, he was a "plodder." This he had pointed out to Hemingway some years earlier when, notwithstanding all the logic to the contrary—he was at the time the much more popular of the two —he called himself the tortoise and Hemingway the hare. And that proved to be the case. For, having no facility, everything he had ever achieved he did so through long and persistent effort, while Hemingway, having the touch of genius, was able to bring off his fine books without effort.

Tender Is the Night, considered by Fitzgerald "my Testament of Faith," was published in April 1935. With many reviewers then politically radical, their reception of the apolitical story was quite critical. This naturally depressed Fitzgerald. In October Perkins and his wife visited him in Baltimore in an effort to cheer him up; feeling grateful, he subsequently wrote Perkins: "The mood of terrible depression and despair is not going to become characteristic and I am ashamed and felt yellow about it afterwards. But to deny that such moods come increasingly would be futile."

The novel was, as in the past, to be followed up by another collection of stories. But Fitzgerald was not satisfied with some of the published stories, and he found the rewriting difficult. Yet deeply troubled by "his morass of debt" and still suffering from poor health and much drinking, he rationalized about this delay in a letter on August 24: "It is not going to be a money book in any case and is not going to go very far toward reimbursing the money I still owe you, and so I think in view of everything that my suggestion of waiting until after Christmas is the best." Perkins, of course, agreed, and the volume was published in the spring.

Determined to stabilize his financial status, he wrote to Ober in December: "I am getting accustomed to poverty and bankruptcy (in fact for myself I rather enjoy washing my own clothes and eating 20 cent meals twice a day) after so many years in the flesh pots."

His addiction to liquor was by then affecting his entire life, yet he repeatedly fought it—only to break down again and again. That he perceived clearly what drink did to him he indicated in a letter to Perkins on March 11, 1935:

> It has become increasingly plain to me that the very excellent organization of a long book or the finest perceptions and judgment in time of revision do not go well with liquor. A short story can be written on a bottle, but for a novel you need the mental speed that enables you to keep the whole pattern in your head and ruthlessly sacrifice the sideshows. . . . I would give anything if I hadn't had to write Part III of *Tender Is the Night* entirely on stimulant. If I had one more crack at it cold sober I believe I might have made a great difference.

In a postscript he told him that he had not had a drink for nearly six weeks and was not in the least tempted. He was pleased to say that he felt fine despite the fact that his business affairs and Zelda's condition could not be worse.

In the spring of 1935 he became absorbed by his plan for a medieval novel, which he tentatively called *Phillippe, Count of Darkness*. "I think," he told Perkins, "you could publish it either late in the spring of '36 or early in the fall of the same year. It will run about 90,000 words and will be a novel in every sense with episodes unrecognizable as such." He hoped to publish sections in *Red Book* at a high fee, but when the editor reacted coolly, he sought to adapt the material to *Scribner's Magazine*. Perkins, however, also found the material unsuitable. Thereupon he dropped the project altogether.

That summer, accidents to himself, the placement of Zelda in a sanitarium near Asheville, North Carolina, and his illness from an attack of tuberculosis while in Asheville kept him from doing any writing. He was in this wretched state when Thomas Wolfe, having learned from Perkins about him, wrote to his brother Fred:

> There is a poor, desperate, unhappy man staying at the Grove Park Inn. He is a man of great talent but he is throwing it away on drink and worry over his misfortunes. Perkins thought if Mabel [Wolfe's sister] went to see him and talked to him, it might do some good—to tell him that at the age of forty he is at his prime and has nothing to worry about if he will just take hold again and begin to work.

His mother's death that fall brought him an inheritance of $20,000, but that eased his financial difficulties only temporarily. Perkins suggested that he use this money to take time out for "a major book. Certainly it seems to me that here is your opportunity." But Fitzgerald gloomily explained that in order to pay for Zelda's treatment in a private sanitarium and for Scottie's private school he needed an income of $18,000 a year, and the condition he was in rendered him unable to earn that much. In fact, he continued, the year 1936 was the "least productive and the lowest general year since 1926." His mother's money was merely keeping him afloat for a while.

Ever grateful to Perkins and the Scribner firm, he very early began to recommend promising young writers to Perkins. When an unpublished writer asked him in 1936 how to proceed in his effort to get his novel published, he wrote him: "There is one great publisher in America, and that is Charles Scribner's Sons. . . . There is no question that they are more open to talent than any other publisher because of their resources, first, and because of the tradition of taking a chance on a talent that has not yet got itself an audience."

About the same time he informed Perkins that Simon & Schuster had offered to publish his autobiographical articles—the "Crack-Up" sections in *Esquire*, etc.—and wanted to know if Scribner would be interested in such a volume. Perkins replied at once to assure him of his interest in such a book, but suggested that he make it an integrated volume of reminiscence! "You write non-fiction wonderfully well, your observations are brilliant and acute, and your presentation of real characters like Ring [Lardner] are most admirable. I always wanted you to do such a book as that."

Fitzgerald, however, decided against "the idea of a biographical book," preferring to work on a novel instead—one he had planned to write as soon as time permitted. But his persistent financial plight dogged his days. On October 16 he wrote plaintively to Perkins: "The present plan," as near as I have formulated it, seems to be to go on with this endless Post writing or else go to Hollywood again. Each time I have gone to Hollywood, in spite of the enormous salary, has really set me back financially and artistically."

Nor could he accept the advice to cut expenses drastically. "Such stray ideas," he stated, "as sending my daughter to a public school, putting my wife in a public insane asylum, have been proposed to me by intimate friends, but it would break something in me that would shatter the very delicate pencil end of a point of view." Perkins's response was to send him more money and to bolster his ego by telling him that he was becoming his old self again.

Fitzgerald deeply appreciated this friendly concern. Some weeks later, confessing his need of such encouragment, he told him: "Please write me—you are about the only friend who does not see fit to incorporate a moral lesson, especially since the 'Crack-Up' stuff."

In July 1937 Fitzgerald again went to Hollywood. Two years earlier he had stated: "I hate the place like poison with a sincere hatred." Yet so urgent had become his need of money that, his aversion to it notwithstanding, he readily accepted an offer from Metro-Goldwyn-Mayer of $1,000 a week for six months; this contract was later renewed for a year at $1,250 a week. In yielding to financial urgency he figured this time to budget his "nice salary" with a view to paying his debts and hopefully to acquire "a little security." To this end Harold Ober had prepared a plan which limited his personal expenses and divided the remainder of his salary between the payment of his indebtedness and his savings.

Fitzgerald had by then been "on the wagon since January and in good shape physically." Also, having met and fallen in love with Sheilah Graham, he was in an optimistic mood. Shortly after his arrival he wrote to Perkins: "I am happier than I've been for several years." And in September he told him: "All goes well—no writing at all except on pictures."

This euphoria proved to be temporary. Work on picture scripts was uncongenial to him, and the rude arbitrariness with which his writing was deprecated and distorted soon sickened his inmost self. In late February 1938, ready to explode, he went to New York on a three-day "binge." On his return to Hollywood he wrote Perkins apologetically: "My little binge lasted only three days, and I haven't had a drop since. There was one other in September, likewise three days. Save for that, I haven't had a drop since a year ago last January." He added that in addition to working on a picture he was filling a notebook in preparation for a novel.

As always, Perkins replied in the spirit of encouragement, this time by praise of *The Great Gatsby*, occasioned by a letter from a reader: "What a pleasure it was to publish that! It was as perfect a thing as I ever had any share in publishing—one does not seem to get such satisfactions as that any more." A month later, responding to an idea tentatively broached by Perkins, Fitzgerald wanted to know how tangible was the plan of publishing an omnibus volume that would include his three major novels. Anxious to see something done with his books, he urged Perkins not to forget it. He pointed out that, as he might have to remain in Hollywood another two years, it was not advisable to let his name be forgotten as it had been during the long interim between *Gatsby* and *Tender*, especially as he would not even be writing for the *Saturday Evening Post*.

Perkins had to explain to him that the project he had in mind was the publication of such a volume not by Scribner but as a Modern Library "Giant," and that Random House would be interested in doing it only after "you have written a major work" and thus brought his name again to the attention of readers. Conditions being what they were, Perkins intimated that publication of *Phillippe* might serve this purpose: "This book might do very well indeed, and it will get attention, and somewhat of a special sort, as being a different kind of book by you." Fitzgerald reacted negatively to this suggestion, knowing that he would have to give more time to the completion of the medieval novel than he then had, and when he did get the time he would rather write a modern novel.

The failure of the omnibus project made him feel neglected. More and more unhappy in Hollywood, where he was being treated as a hack rather than as a prominent writer, he had hoped that reprints of his novels and stories would have bolstered his position in the studio. This hope thwarted, he wrote plaintively to Perkins on December 24, 1938, that his reputation was being permitted to lapse—even what remained of it. He stated that some people still remembered him favorably and his name still appeared in *Time* and *The New Yorker*, as well as in other periodicals. Why, then, should it be allowed to disappear while there were double-deckers to such writers as James Farrell and John Steinbeck? To keep his reputation alive he was desperately keen to have his novels republished first, and then his stories. This, he thought, would be a gesture of confidence that would revive his reputation. He admitted that it was very distasteful to him to blow his own horn in this manner, but it was only because he felt so strongly that something of the kind had to be done, if his literary standing was to be saved.

By now no longer able to continue as a script writer—"I think it would be morally destructive to continue here on the factory worker's basis"—nor really wanted any longer by the studios (M-G-M did not renew his contract at the end of 1938), he decided to become a free-lance writer and give his free time to a new novel. But his drunken escapades at Hanover, New Hampshire, where he and young Budd Schulberg were to work on a film script, had not endeared him to Hollywood directors, and he received few assignments thereafter. His work on the novel was repeatedly interrupted by his "old malady."

Perkins, eager to encourage him to write his novel, sought to cheer him up at every opportunity. Early in 1939 he wrote him: "I am mighty glad that you got going on it,—and I won't bother you with inquiries all the time—you know I'm anxious to hear any news whenever you can tell it."

Again in need of financial support, Fitzgerald sought to interest *Collier's* in the serialization of the novel in progress. He sent the editor the finished portion, but he was not sanguine as to acceptance: "Of course," he told Perkins, "if he will back me it will be a life-saver, but I am by no means sure that I will ever be a popular writer again." When the editor wanted to see more of the story before he made his decision, Fitzgerald feared rejection and backed off.

In his chronic need of money he in 1936 had arranged for a life insurance policy that would repay his debts to Scribner and Ober in case of his death. In immediate need of cash in 1939—he had to "hock" his old car for a few dollars—he sent some stories direct to magazines in order to expedite their payments to him on acceptance. Although he stated in each case that Ober was his agent, the latter resented this move on his part. Financially pressed himself, and assuming that Fitzgerald could have obtained "movie work" if he wished, Ober informed him he would no longer advance him any money on unwritten stories. Fitzgerald was hurt and shocked. Ill with a "lung cavity" and a persistent temperature, he felt that his longtime agent and friend had turned against him: "For change you did, Harold, and without warning—the custom of lending up to the probable yield of a next short story obtained between us for a dozen years." Thereafter he would have no dealings with him. In a telegram to Perkins he stated that he was in bed with tuberculosis and added:

Ober has decided not to back me though I paid back every penny and eight thousand dollars in commission. Am going to work Thursday . . . in studio at fifteen hundred dollars. Can you lend me six hundred dollars for one week by wire to Bank America Culver City. Scottie hospital with appendix and am absolutely without funds. Do not ask Ober cooperation.

Perkins sent $1,000 out of his own funds, and advised him not to judge Ober too harshly. Acknowledging the money on December 19, 1939, Fitzgerald continued:

> Your offering to lend me another thousand dollars was the kindest thing I ever heard of. It certainly comes at the most opportune time. The first thing is this month's and last month's rent and I am going to take the liberty of giving my landlady a draft on you for $205.00. for January 2nd. . . . Max, you are so kind. When Harold withdrew from the questionable honor of being my banker, I felt completely numb financially and I suddenly wondered what money was and where it came from. There had always seemed a little more somewhere, and now there wasn't. Anyhow thank you.

When his health permitted, he worked on the novel. Although he was infrequently given a temporary assignment on a picture, he no longer expected much from that source. As he told Perkins in May 1940: "I just couldn't make the grade as a hack—that, like everything else, requires a certain practiced excellence." Nor did he any longer retain the illusion of friendship: "Once I believed in friendship, believed I *could* (if I didn't always) make people happy and it was more fun than aything. Now even that seems like a vaudevillian cheap dream of heaven, a vast minstrel show in which one is perpetual Bones." Perkins's reply was prompt and encouraging:

> Your letter sounds sombre but good. . . . As for your position, it is a mighty high one. I never see an editor or writer, hardly, but they ask about you. It shows what you did, for think of all the writers who were thought to be notable, and whose output has been much larger, who have simply vanished without a trace. But we know the "Gatsby" was a truly great book.

Informed that 25,000 words of the novel were already written, Perkins was delighted. "I am awfully glad you have been able to make all that progress, and it may have magnificent results."

Yet Fitzgerald found the writing more and more difficult. He was too ill and too troubled emotionally to concentrate on it. In November he wrote Zelda "The novel is hard as pulling teeth, but that is because it is in its early character-planting stage. I feel people so less intently than I did once that this is harder. It means welding together hundreds of stray impressions and incidents to form the fabric of entire personalities."

That month he had his first serious heart attack. While recuperating, he thought of how he could further the narrative of the novel. On December 13, he informed Perkins:

> The novel progresses . . . in fact progresses fast. I'm not going to stop now till I finish a first draft which will be sometime after the 15th of January. However, let's pretend it doesn't exist until it's closer to completion.

> This is the first day off I have taken in many months and I just wanted to tell you the book is coming along and that comparatively speaking all is well.

Two weeks later a second heart attack proved fatal.

The incomplete novel, *The Last Tycoon*, was published in 1941 and was well received. Some reviewers stated that it contained some of Fitzgerald's best writing. His autobiographical pieces entitled *The Crack Up* were edited by his close friend Edmund Wilson and issued in 1945. Throughout this period, Zelda remained in a sanitarium and died in a fire that broke out there in March 1948.

20.

Maxwell Perkins

&

Thomas Wolfe

Thomas Wolfe was a striking phenomenon among American authors. He had an insatiable hunger for experience and reacted to everything with extraordinary volubility, writing tens of thousands of words without concern for organization or relevancy. Yet for all its originally chaotic form, much of his writing possessed the exciting beauty of poetry and deep feeling.

He was equally remarkable as a person. His enormous body of six and a half feet was topped by a relatively small head. Possessed of immense energy, he used it extravagantly by writing for many hours on end, mostly at night, eating only at long intervals, and then ravenously. He neglected his appearance and had almost no sense of time, yet he made himself exceptionally likable to many people. Neurasthenic, easily hurt, reacting violently to criticism, he nevertheless manifested the quality of genius.

Born in Asheville, North Carolina, in 1900, he was babied by a very strong-willed mother into an infantile childhood. Nursing him until he was nearly four years old, she kept his hair in curls even longer, until he became too conscious of them in relation to other boys. So attached to her was he during his childhood, that he was never quite free of his devotion to her. This maternal bond later expressed itself in favoring women older than himself. At school he made his teacher, Mrs. Margaret Roberts, the "mother of my spirit who fed me with light," and he confided in her through the years. At the age of twenty-five he fell passionately in love with Mrs. Aline Bernstein, nineteen years his senior, and for five years she was as much his mother as his mistress. He dropped her when Maxwell Perkins became his friend and mentor, satisfying his need for a spiritual father—until toward the end of his short life he, with painful deliberation, drew away from him in an effort to assert his literary maturity.

Wolfe began to write while in high school. During his second year at the University of North Carolina he wrote "Buck Gavin," a one-act play that was performed by students and later included in *Carolina Folk Plays, Second Series* (1923). "I wrote it on a rainy night, when I was seventeen, in three hours." It was the influence of his drama teacher that prompted him to enter Harvard University in order to further his study of playwriting in Prof. George Baker's famous "47 Workshop." Determined to be a great dramatist, he remained under Baker's tutelage for three years.

He had no means of evaluating his own work, yet he was consumed by literary ambition. To his mother he wrote in May 1923: "I believe I am inevitable. I believe nothing can stop me now but insanity, disease, or death. . . . I don't know yet what I'm capable of doing, but, by God, I have genius.

His genius notwithstanding, his plays failed to gain acceptance in New York theaters. In need to earn his living, he took a teaching job in freshman English at New York University. His yearning to become a writer persisted, and in the spring of 1925 he, having saved a little money and ready to live on bare essentials, took time off to go abroad and devote himself to writing. Fully disillusioned with the theater by now, he wrote for writing's sake—at the time, travel impressions. To Mrs. Roberts he wrote from France on March 21, 1925: "I want to write—nothing else—and I have neither the patience nor the time nor the inclination to pull wires with literary agents, and so on. And honestly, I know of no one who would publish my account now; because, as I said, I shall write this once as I please."

In September, on his return voyage to New York, he met Aline Bernstein on the boat. He was then, in the words of Elizabeth Nowell, "still a frustrated, wild, eccentric boy." A mutual attraction between him and Aline Bernstein quickly ripened into passionate love. Before long her unwavering belief in his genius and her financial assistance and moral encouragement stimulated him to begin the book that was to make him famous when it was published. In 1926 he went to England to write. In July he stated to Margaret Roberts that he had begun work on a novel which he thought he would call *The Building of a Wall*, although he was not yet sure; it was only because he was very tall and had a fidelity to walls and to secret places that he was considering that title. What he aimed to do, he continued, was to pour out all the passion of his heart and life into this book—a work that would swarm with human life, peopled by a city, and be in part terrible, brutal, bawdy. The whole would be unified by the story of a powerful creative element seeking to achieve elemental isolation.

His outline of the book was "the length almost of a novel." He wrote assiduously until late December, when he returned to New York. With Aline Bernstein's financial aid and strong encouragement, he continued to devote his time to writing, mostly between 11 o'clock at night and 6 in the morning. Early in June he wrote to Margaret Roberts: "I have poured all my life, my strength, and almost all my time for almost a year into my book, which is now nearing its end. . . . I have learned that writing is hard work, desperate work." Then at the height of his infatuation with Aline Bernstein, he glorified the relationship that July: "There is nothing in my life as important as this: I was a lonely out-cast, and suddenly I became richer, in the one true wealth, than Maecenas."

Having finally finished the novel, which he called in turn *O Lost* and *Alone, Alone*, he prefaced it with a long statement to publishers, informing them: "I have never called this book a novel. To me it is a book such as all men may have in them. It is a book made out of my life, and it represents my vision of life to my twentieth year."

Aline Bernstein submitted a copy to Boni & Liveright. Upon its rejection as too long and discursive, she took it to her friend Melville Cane, a poet and the lawyer for Harcourt, Brace & Company. He examined it but did not think it would interest the firm. She also gave a copy to the critic Ernest Boyd, who showed it to his wife Madeleine, a literary agent. The latter submitted the manuscript to Covici, Friede. That small firm also refused it but was sufficiently impressed by the writing to ask for an option on the author's next book. Madeleine Boyd then asked Maxwell Perkins to consider it. He liked the opening scene, but lost interest in later sections and asked one of his readers to examine the entire manuscript. Struck by the quality of much of the manuscript, the reader made this known to Perkins. "I dropped everything," Perkins wrote later, "and began to read again, and all of us were reading simultaneously, you might say, including John Hall Wheelock, and there never was the slightest disagreement among us as to its importance." He then wrote to Wolfe in Europe:

> I do not know whether it would be possible to work out a plan by which it might be worked into a form publishable by us, but I do know that setting the practical aspects of the matter aside, it is a very remarkable thing, and that no editor could read it without being excited by it, and filled with admiration by many passages in it, and sections of it. . . . What we should like to know, is whether you will be in New York in a fairly near future, when we can see you and discuss the manuscript.

Wolfe found the letter on his return to Vienna from a side trip and replied immediately: "I can't tell you how good your letter made me feel. Your words of praise have filled me with hope, are worth more than their weight in diamonds to me!" He assured Perkins of his full cooperation on the revision of the manuscript and continued: "I want the direct criticism and advice of an older and more critical person. I wonder if at Scribner's I can find someone who is interested enough to talk over the whole huge Monster with me part by part."

On his return to New York, Wolfe immediately arranged a meeting with Perkins. In his anxiety about the acceptance of the manuscript he was ready to discard the parts considered objectionable, and was surprised and delighted when Perkins objected to relatively little specifically. His favorable reception and the approval of an advance of $500 made him feel "drunk with joy." To Madeleine Boyd he wrote: "I am terribly excited about the book. I have seen Mr. Perkins twice, and unless I am quite out of my head, they have decided to take the book. . . . I am full of energy and hope—I know I have a big job ahead, but with this encouragement I can do anything." And a day later, acknowledging recept of the contract, he wrote Perkins that although he was writing him a business letter, he wanted to tell him that he was looking forward with joy and hope to his connection with the Scribner firm. He also wanted him to know that the day he had received his letter became a grand day in his life; that he thought of his relation with Scribner with affection and loyalty and that he hoped this would be the beginning of a long association that the firm would have no cause to regret. He was of course aware that he had a lot to learn, but he expected to go ahead with the writing and knew there would be far better work in the future.

Perkins went over the manuscript with him to indicate general reorganization, the parts in need of revision, passages which might be omitted, and places which required additional material. Soon, however, he realized that Wolfe was unable to cut and revise as he had suggested. By now interested as much in the author as in the manuscript, he took over the process of detailed revision, explaining, cajoling, urging, directing. When he needed to get in touch with Wolfe he wrote him instead of phoning, in order not to waken him, as he soon learned that he would find him asleep most of the day. Thus in March 28, 1929, he wrote: "I want to arrange to go over the manuscript thus far, in order to show cuts I would like to suggest, and to consider others;—and this might take an hour or two. Besides we ought to get on now as rapidly as we possibly can with the book."

Two months later Wolfe explained the work of revision to his sister Mabel by telling her that he was working daily with Perkins, that his heart bled to see big chunks of the manuscript removed from the narrative, but he knew it was "die dog or eat the hatchet." Both he and Perkins, he continued, hated to take so much out of the book, but they realized it was necessary to shorten the novel and make it easier to read; also, as they were giving up some good stuff they were gaining unity. Consequently he greatly admired Perkins's skill and thought him the greatest editor in America and was ready to yield to his judgment.

When the manuscript was finally edited and sent to the printer, Wheelock took charge of seeing it through the press, and he too soon developed a close relationship with Wolfe. In the process Wolfe began to deal with him more informally than with Perkins, for whom he for some time retained greater awe and depended upon him for advice, criticism, and self-confidence. In July Wolfe wrote Wheelock:

> I am far from being melancholy—I am more full of strength and power and hope than I have been in years—I have in me at the present time several books, all of which are full of life and vanity, and rich detail. . . . I feel packed to the lips with rich ore. . . . I want to tear myself open and show my friends all that I think I have. I cannot tell you how moved I was by your letter—by its length, its patience and care; it is a symbol of my entire relation with you and Mr. Perkins. I could not a year ago have thought it possible that such good luck was in store for me—a connection with such men and such a house and editing as painstaking and intelligent as I have had.

Wheelock responded in kind, assuring him that he and Perkins greatly admired his "genius" and that they have "an almost fatherly solicitude for the fortunes of your work in the world." Thanking him for his last letter, Wheelock continued:

> It gives a remarkably vivid impression of your present mood and environment, as well as a sort of panorama of the past, and it is permeated by a certain positive quality which is to me one of the finest elements in your work: its great love of things, discernible even in the midst of bitter satire and ridicule.

Aware that he had no doubt violated the sensibilities of the people he had written about in his novel, Wolfe wrote defensively about it to a college friend, telling him that he had simply written a work of fiction, and as such he had not written it out of thin air but out of the materials of human experience. Yet he had done everything possible to make the outline less harsh; also, Scribner had carefully deleted his good Anglo-Saxon words for the sexual act and other human functions so that he failed to see how anyone would be shocked by it—although he feared it might.

And to another college friend he stated: "Scribners has been magnificent—their best people have worked like dogs on the thing—they believe in me and the book."

The novel, renamed *Look Homeward, Angel,* originally contained around 330,000 words. It was reduced by about a third, and the sections were tightened and knitted together to read as a flowing narrative. Scribner did some good advance publicity, obtaining a sale of 1,600 copies before publication, and another 1,000 copies were sold within three weeks after it was issued. Most reviews were enthusiastic. The English firm of Heinemann bought the British rights and gave Wolfe an advance of one hundred pounds. Because he nevertheless still had to teach to earn his living, he complained to a friend: "During all this palpitating time I've got to teach school as usual and grade Freshman papers. God! The torture of it!"

The publication of the novel caused a furore in Asheville. The narrative being intimately autobiographical and highly revealing of the life and foibles of the people in his milieu, it made a number of persons, including his own kin, become deeply shocked and chagrined when they saw themselves in unflattering portrayal. Mrs. Roberts felt so hurt that she did not write to him for the next six years. The anger of his immediate family was partially allayed by pride in his new-found fame.

Much as this resentment wounded him, he was at the same time more sorely tormented by his increasingly unwanted intimacy with Aline Bernstein. Once the manuscript was accepted and his friendship with Perkins ripened, he began to have qualms about his relationship with her—basically because he no longer needed her admiration and support. He began to see her as an elderly woman and a Jewess—his parochial attitude of the Christian toward the Jew now asserted itself toward her as well as toward his Jewish students. Yet he continued to long for her affection. When the novel was published he gave her both the manuscript and a printed copy—and in the latter he wrote: "This book was written because of her, and is dedicated to her. At a time when my life seemed desolate, and when I had little faith in myself, I met her. She brought me friendship, material and spiritual relief, and love such as I have never had before." He still felt that way when he wrote his mother that if he should die soon his estate should be divided between her and Aline Bernstein: "She is a fine and lovely woman and the best friend I have ever had, and you may depend on her to look after everything with the utmost ability and integrity."

Nevertheless, after nearly five years of passionate intimacy, he had become determined to break with her and rejected all her efforts, at times pitifully frantic, at a reconciliation. This strength, if not callousness, he had gained when Perkins gradually replaced her as his surrogate parent, friend, and confessor.

With *Look Homeward, Angel* launched successfully—even remarkably so for a first novel—Perkins once more assured Wolfe of his confidence in his future writing by offering to underwrite his second book with an advance of $4,500 in installments of $250 monthly—assuming that he should be able to complete the novel in eighteen months. Wolfe's response was one of gratitude and affection:

> You are now mixed with my book in such a way that I can never separate the two of you. . . . My mind has always seen people more clearly than events or things— the name "Scribners" naturally makes a warm flow in my heart, but you are chiefly "Scribners" to me: you had done what I had ceased to believe one person could do for another—you have created liberty and hope for me. . . . You are one of the rocks to which my life is anchored.

The advance enabled Wolfe to give up teaching. Some weeks later, having been awarded a Guggenheim Fellowship of $2,500, he stopped the Scribner advance and did not ask for it again until three years later. He once more went to Europe to write, and in May 1930 he told Perkins how much he missed him and the others at Scribners—all of them having "become a part of my life and habit." He further informed him of the favorable reception *Look Homeward, Angel* was having in England and how much he liked Frere-Reeves of Heinemann.

Then came Frank Swinnerton's damning review. The shock to Wolfe's ego was traumatic. Already suffering from loneliness, aggravated by the break with Bernstein, he considered the condemnation a fatal blow to his life's ambition. Forgetting the previous favorable reviews, he could think only of the "catastrophe" of the English edition. Driven nearly mad, he wrote Wheelock: "I have stopped writing and do not want ever to write again." And on the same day he informed Perkins: "I shall not write any more books. . . . I want to thank you and Scribners very sincerely for your kindness to me, and I shall hope some day to resume and continue a friendship which has meant a great deal to me."

Perkins replied immediately to tell him that "if anyone were ever destined to write, that one is you." He followed this note with a letter elaborating his reasons for encouragement:

> I could not clearly make out why you had come to your decision; and surely you will have to change it;—but certainly there never was a man who had made more of an impression on the best judges with a single book, and at so early an age. Certainly you ought not to be affected by a few unfavorable reviews—even apart from the overwhelming number of extremely and excitedly enthusiastic reviews. . . . There is no doubt of your very great possibilities,—nor for that matter of the great accomplishment of the "Angel." . . . You know it has been said before that one has to pay somehow for everything one has or gets, and I can see that among your penalties are attacks of despair,—as they have been among the penalties great writers have generally had to pay for their talent.

Wheelock also wrote him a long and soothing letter, assuring him that critical reviews are not often valid and need not concern him. "The greatest writers of all periods have been subjected to just this sort of thing but have had the courage and the serenity to come through it and to weigh it for what it was worth, which isn't much."

Even before these letters reached him Wolfe had emerged from his deep depression and cabled Perkins: "Working again. Excuse letter. Writing You." Perkins expressed his delight and suggested a return to the United States. This Wolfe was not yet ready to do, as he was again absorbing the sights of Europe and writing.

In January 1931 he heard from his family that it was hard hit by the Depression and asked Perkins to send his brother Fred $500 and charge the amount to his account. When he learned that this was done, he told Perkins "I'll never forget it." He was then in London, and after describing his plans he asked him to find an apartment for him in New York. Before sailing in February he cabled: "Sailing on Europa Thursday. Need no help now. Can help myself must work six months alone. Best wishes."

Having settled in New York, Wolfe concentrated on his writing. As before, he wrote what came to mind out of the depths of his emotional experience without regard to outline or unity. Periodically he saw Perkins and showed him some of the written pages. More than a year later Perkins wrote Frere-Reeves: "He is turning out a great amount of work anyhow, and good work too. There is the problem though, of getting it all compressed into one unified book."

Wolfe continued to be strongly affected by what he heard about himself. Continuing to write while in this emotional turmoil, he informed Perkins on August 29, 1931, that there was no chance of his completing the manuscript soon. He raved about the "dirty rotten lies" literary gossips have spread about him, and that he was "perfectly content to return to the obscurity in which I passed almost thirty years of my life without great difficulty." Nor did he feel apologetic about not having a finished book for publication. Two years ago, he stated, he was full of hope and confidence, with ideas for "at least a half dozen long books." Now, however, he had "a feeling of strong self-doubt and mistrust—which is not to say that I feel despair. I do not."

Even more than his distress at unfriendly gossip was his deeply troubled inability to free himself from his emotional dependence on Aline Bernstein. As late as November 1931 he felt the urge to unburden himself—to bare his soul in an outpouring of emotional lava—to Perkins, whom he now considered his closest friend and adviser and to whom he had become attached as to a father. He told him that at first he felt like a young fellow who had gotten himself an elegant and fashionable mistress, and was quite pleased with his conquest. Then, without knowing how or why, he found himself desperately in love with her. The thought of her began to dominate his every moment. He wanted to own and devour her and became insanely jealous. After a while, however, his passion for her ceased; yet he continued to love her and could not endure the thought of her loving another. In his effort to get away from her he left New York. And he continued:

I must not die. But I need help—such help as a man may hope to receive from a friend. I turn to you for it now. You know how warmly and gratefully I feel toward Scribners, but you are the only person there I can turn to. . . . Try to help me to get away from this loneliness and to find a place in my own country where I can talk to a few people. . . . If this is a frenzied appeal, understand that it is also a real and earnest one. . . . I am in *terrible trouble*, and I need a friend. This is the first appeal of this sort I have ever made. I do not know what to do, where to turn, but I want to live in my own country, and I want to forget this horrible business entirely. Someday, when we are both, I hope, better and calmer, I trust I can see her again and be her friend.

It was now four years since the publication of *Look Homeward, Angel*, and although Wolfe had in the meantime written hundreds of thousands of words, he had no coherent material for publication—except that some of the extracts were printed as stories. That he was aware of his difficulty he indicated in a letter to a friend in February 1933:

I think I write with the most extreme difficulty: the trouble is not so much a lack of material but an over abundance of it. Condensation and brevity are terribly difficult for me, my manuscripts are hundreds of thousands of words long and almost my whole effort at the present time is to get my book within some reasonable length.

One bit of good fortune came to him that summer when the $5,000 Prize Short Novel Contest conducted by *Scribner's Magazine* was divided between him and another author.

Wolfe's chief problem lay in the autobiographical nature of his writing. His desire to obviate this criticism caused him to flounder in the effort to achieve his desired objectivity. Perkins early perceived that Wolfe did not know how to organize his material, much of which he found very good, and decided to help him to this end. Later he wrote:

I, who thought Tom a man of genius, and loved him too, and could not bear to see him fail, was almost as desperate as he,—so much there was to do—But the truth is that if I did him a real service—and in this I did—it was in keeping him from losing his belief in himself in a crisis by believing in him. What he most needed was comradship and understanding in a long crisis—these things I could give him then.

Once he perceived the basic trouble with Wolfe's material, he had him start where *Angel* had left off. The mammoth manuscript, bearing the general title of *October Fair*, was divided into two parts, and the section dealing with his experiences after his twentieth year became the subject for their discussion, organization, and revision—including drastic cutting of irrelevant material, and considerable filling in of gaps. This process took more than a year of evenings, during which both worked steadily and concentratedly—with Perkins guiding, encouraging, cajoling, praising, and urging. Wolfe described this activity in a letter to his sister Mabel as early as February 1933. Perkins, he told her, had intimated that he had been desperate about him in his effort to figure out what was wrong with him and how to get him out of his difficulty; that if Perkins was desperate, he continued, she could imagine his own state of mind. Yet somehow relief had come to him: he seemed suddenly to have found a way of getting started which met with Perkins's approval, and having made that start his writing continued going with a rush.

Two months later, having gone over about 300,000 words of manuscript which Wolfe had submitted to him, Perkins reported to Charles Scribner:

> There is more to be done to fill in, but the book is almost in existence now. There are many questions about it which will have to be argued out, and much revision and all that, just as was true of "The Angel."—But I really think that this book has half dozen chapters in it that are beyond anything even in "The Angel"; and it may be a distinctly finer book than that.

To Frere-Reeves Perkins wrote that the difficulty with Wolfe was his inability to control his material: "He takes up an episode which is to be part of the book, and a small part, and by the time he is through with it, it is big enough to make a volume by itself." Yet he did his best to keep Wolfe from going too far afield— for which the latter was grateful, as he was with Wheelock's praise and encouragement. In June he stated to him: "It makes me so happy that I succeeded with you and Max in saying what I wanted to say because there are no other two people in the world whose judgment and good opinion mean as much to me as yours."

Learning in August that the German edition of *Angel* had been very favorably received, Wolfe asked Perkins why Scribner was not taking advantage of these reviews to promote the book. "I see no reason at all to be ashamed of the fact that my book got fine reviews in Germany and Austria, and I do not see why that is not publicity which could be honorably and creditably used." With Hitler's Germany unpopular in the United States, Scribner only sent out a literary notice to periodicals.

As late as December 1933 Perkins was still examining the huge pile of manuscript, separating the sections reserved for later publication and giving some organization to the retained parts. At that time Wolfe reminded him that he had often told him that if he would give him something he could put his hands on and see it as a whole he would pitch in and help him get the manuscript into shape. Now, he stated, was his chance. True, a desperate piece of work was ahead for both of them, but if he thought the job was worth doing and urged him to proceed, there was literally nothing he could not do. Yet he urged Perkins to be honest with him and straightforward in his criticism, regardless of how hard it would be for him to take after all the work he had put into it—because that was the only way in the end.

Perkins quickly assured him that he expected "greatly to enjoy it, for I have always enjoyed reading what you have done, and working in connection with it. It is a thing that does not happen to publishers often." The two worked evening after evening throughout 1934. Wolfe's gratitude was lavish. To his agent Paul Reynolds he wrote how delighted he was with Perkins's help, "since I no longer seem to be able to tell what's what myself." And he continued:

God knows what I would do without him. I told him the other day that when this book comes out, he could then assert it was the only book he had ever written. I think he has pulled me right out of the swamp just by main strength and serene determination. I am everlastingly grateful for what he has done. He is a grand man and great editor, and from the bottom of my heart I know that he is hoping far more for my own success and development than for any profit which may come to Scribner's as a result of it.

With the editing and most of the proofreading done, Wolfe went to Europe. He had informed Perkins that he was dedicating the book to him, and was told not to do it unless he really felt the manuscript was not "mutilated." The dedication read:

To

MAXWELL EVARTS PERKINS

a great editor and a brave and honest man, who stuck to the writer of this book through times of bitter hopelessness and doubt and would not let him give in to his own despair, a work to be known as *Of Time and the River* is dedicated with the hope that all of it may be in some way worthy of the loyal devotion and the patient care which a dauntless and unshaken friend has given to each part of it, and without which none of it could have been written.

When Perkins read the dedication after the book was printed, he wrote Wolfe:

I have seen the dedication in your book and, whatever the degree of justice in what it implies, I can think of nothing that could have made me more happy. . . . I think it a most generous and noble utterance. Certainly for one who could say that of me I ought to have done all that it says I did do.

Of Time and the River was published on March 8, 1935. Perkins cabled Wolfe: "Magnificent reviews, somewhat critical in ways expected, full of greatest praise." Wolfe, dizzy with anxiety and drinking hard, cabled back: "You are the best friend I have. I can face blunt fact better than damnable incertitude. Give me the plain straight truth." Perkins again assured him of the great praise and urged: "Enjoy yourself with light heart." The book indeed had a fine reception, selling over 40,000 copies by the end of the year.

Wheelock joined Perkins in assuring him of the book's fine reception: "I do not recall any book during my quarter of a century with the House which has been greeted with such overwhelming admiration, enthusiasm, and excitement." Yet Wolfe could not stop fretting and fuming inwardly because of certain criticisms, and finally wrote Perkins in a letter over fifty pages long that the book was put out too fast and too soon; that another six months would have made it "more whole and perfect," that then it would not have been criticized as "episodic"— "for, by God, in purpose and in spirit, that book was not episodic but a living whole." And he continued:

It is a work of frenzied, desperate, volcanic haste after too much time had slipped away, and no one will know that I was not ready to read proof. I was not through *writing*—the fault is my own. . . . Max, Max, I cannot go on, but I am sick at heart—we should have waited six months longer—the book like Caesar, was from its mother's womb untimely ripped.

After raving about his presumed enemies, which included nearly every prominent reviewer and critic, he concluded: "I tell you, Max, I cannot put in another five years like the last—I must have some peace, security, and good hope—I must be left alone to do my work as I have planned and conceived it, or the game is up. I am tired and ill and desperate, I can't go on like this forever."

Perkins also heard from Mrs. Bernstein. She wanted to send him the manuscript of *Look Homeward, Angel* if he would promise not to give it to Wolfe. "We loved each other," she added, "and I still love him, and since I can no longer work my mind turns back to him. I know I will never talk to him again, nor look into his face, and my wound is as fresh today as the day he found it necessary to turn away from me."

Nor did Wolfe forget her. In a letter he never sent, dated March 2, 1935, he stated that although he had kept away from her for the past five years, he still loved her and was loyal to her. And finding a letter from her on his return from Europe, he replied: "My heart is full of affection and loyalty for you—it had always been: I am devoted to the memory of everything you have ever said to me, of every kind and generous thing you ever did for me."

In April 1935 he had gone to Germany to spend the royalties on the German edition—he could not bring them out of the country—and was received royally by admirers of his book. While there, in an expansive mood, he asked Perkins to go slowly on the book of stories which they had agreed upon for fall publication, as he wished to improve the writing of some upon his return. As for the book still to be published, he expressed his confidence that he could eliminate previous faults. He assured him *October Fair* was going to be a grand book and that he would try to meet the criticism of certain reviewers and show them that he was improving as a writer right along. The book he was living for, he continued, was the one about Pentland, and that was swelling and gathering in him like a thunderstorm—that if there was any chance of his doing good writing before he was forty it would be found in that book.

As things turned out, he did almost nothing for more than a year. On his return from Europe he went to Colorado to lecture before aspiring writers on his method of work, the content of which was later published as *The Story of a Novel*. This little volume tended to intensify a rising resentment against Perkins and the Scribner firm. Eager to have the *Story* priced very low, he agreed to a royalty of 10 percent. When it was priced at $1.50, he called this "a sharp business practice," quarrelled with Perkins, and demanded his regular royalty of 15 percent. Although he apologized for his anger the following day, Perkins increased the royalty but explained that the price was based on costs and not on the lower royalty. Wolfe then asked that the matter be forgotten:

> All the damn contracts in the world don't mean as much to me as your friendship means. . . . But I do want to tell you again just how genuinely and deeply sorry I am for boiling over the way I did the other night. . . . I am now started on another book. I need your friendship and support more than I ever did, so please forget the

worse mistakes I have made in the past and let's see if I can't do something better in the future.

This was only the least of his troubles at the time. Several legal suits greatly perturbed him. The first was that of Madeleine Boyd, who claimed she had not been paid agency commissions on his books. His response was that he had dismissed her as his agent in 1932 when he learned that she had not reported to him the payment made to her by the German publisher. After considerable discussion and aggravation he paid her $500 for relinquishing all claims on his writing after *Angel*. When he learned that she was in need, he gave her an additional $150. The other legal harassments also cost him money and annoyance.

At this juncture he engaged Elizabeth Nowell as his agent. He had met her in Scribner's editorial department some time ago and had confidence in her ability to edit and market his stories. This she in fact did to his entire satisfaction, cutting and editing his writing to make the stories more marketable—reducing one from 15,000 words to half that number. Gradually he also made her his confidante, and she was highly devoted to his interests. Subsequently she edited his letters and wrote his biography.

Perkins was eager to publish a volume of Wolfe's stories in the fall of 1935. Away on his trip west, Wolfe failed to read proofs as scheduled. By September Perkins was irritated enough to write Frere-Reeves: "I am only afraid that he will now want to add other stories to them which have yet to be written, but I will fight hard against this. He seems to feel a certain shame at the idea of turning out a book of reasonable dimensions."

The legal annoyances prevented Wolfe from concentrating on his writing. He was also still smarting from the criticism of certain reviewers that he could only write about himself, and his effort to obviate this impression gave him no peace of mind, so that in effect he felt blocked. Then came Bernard DeVoto's devastating accusation in *The Saturday Review of Literature* that Wolfe could not write a book without the help of "Mr. Perkins and the assembly-line at Scribner's."

The accusation affected Wolfe as traumatically as the Swinnerton review. After brooding over it for days he felt he must leave Scribner in order to prove that he could write a book on his own. While in this state of agitated depression he became painfully aware of his differences with Perkins: he again believed that Perkins had hurried him to let *Of Time and the River* go before it was really finished; that he opposed his liberal views on politics; that he had insisted that nothing must be written about Scribner personnel; that he had criticized his story, "No More Rivers," even after it was revised, with the comment that it "could do no one any harm now—except perhaps Thomas Wolfe."

At this point he stopped visiting the Scribner office and requested that his mail be forwarded. He also wrote a letter to publishers, which he did not mail, informing them of his availability. To his mother he wrote in October 1936: "It was a pretty hard and bitter year, full of disillusioning experiences, and I found out the hard fact that there are people who call themselves your devoted friends who will sell you out for a little cash."

The break with Scribner became to him unavoidable when both he and the firm were sued for libel by a former landlord of his in connection with the story, "No Door." Charles Scribner, averse to the publicity of a trial, wanted to settle the matter out of court; Wolfe, feeling imposed upon by an unscrupulous landlord, opposed a settlement, yielding only most reluctantly. Depressed and distracted, he wrote a long letter to Perkins, which he never mailed, expressing the reasons for his disappointment in him—whom he had trusted so implicitly—and was therefore impelled to renounce him. He was consequently severing a relationship which no longer existed, and renouncing a contract that was never made, and was thus severing himself from him to his own past grief of doubt and his present grief of sorrow, loss, and final understanding. And he ended:

> With infinite regret, my dear Max, with the deepest and most genuine sorrow, with an assurance—if you will generously accept it—of my own friendship for yourself. Faithfully and sincerely yours.

He did mail a letter in November 1936 asking Perkins to state formally that their dealings have been honorable and faithful. He explained the "differences of opinion and belief, the fundamental disagreements . . . which have brought about this unmistakable and grievous severance," and ended by stating that he was still his friend. Perkins promptly wrote the requested letter, and stated that the firm had done nothing unfair to him.

While in New Orleans in January 1937, Wolfe became outraged at Perkins for giving his address to his own lawyer. Almost paranoid in his fear of the law and lawyers, he felt that Perkins was betraying him to his enemies. He telegraphed on January 7: "How dare you give anyone my address?" Two days later he again wired: "What is your offer?" To which Perkins replied by telegram: "If you refer to book we shall make verbally when you return as arrangements will depend on your requirements. Gave no one your address but suggested two possibilities to your lawyer who thought it important for you to communicate."

Wolfe thereupon sent him the "personal letter" which he had written the previous December and which extended to twenty-eight single-spaced, typewritten pages: a volcanic outpouring of his feeling toward him, his various grievances, his fears and resentments; also his gratitude to him for his "profound and sensitive understanding, of utter loyalty and staunch support, at a time when many people had no belief at all in me." He then stressed his ability to write his own books: "As you know, I don't have to have you or any other man alive to help me with my books." Moreover, he asserted, for all his sympathy with his writing, he did tend to hold him back. And he no longer wanted such restraint: "There has never been a time when I've been so determined to write as I please, to say what I intend to say, to publish the books I want to publish, as I am now." Claiming that he was "a righteous man" whom few understood, he insisted on feeling secure with his publisher. "I'm not going to pour my sweat and blood and energy and talent into another book now, only to be told two or three years from now that it would be undesirable to publish it without certain formidable deletions."

This feeling of wanting to have published whatever he wrote without change or deletion, he stated shortly afterward to Sherwood Anderson:

> I feel at times like getting every publisher by the scruff of his neck, forcing his jaws open and cramming the manuscript down his throat. . . . I will be published, if I can: I've got to be—and I will have my own picture of life, my own vision of society, of the world as, thus far, I have been able to live, sweat, feel and think it through.

Perkins replied to the long letter by assuring him of his complete agreement as to the aim and purpose of a writer. "But," he added, "there are limitations of time, of space, and human laws which cannot be treated as if they did not exist." As far as his own previous relationship was concerned, he had given him help only when it was requested; changes in the writing were made only after they had agreed upon them. "You were never overruled."

Additional lawsuits continued to distress Wolfe. When his mother wrote Perkins in March 1937 to inquire about her son, he replied that Wolfe "is working hard and accomplishing much, and while he is troubled by those lawsuits, I think that one of them will soon be settled, and that the other one cannot be very harmful." And in July he wrote Wolfe: "I hope everything is going well with you— that you are really getting a rest, which I do not think you have really had since I first knew you." The following month he again wrote in a friendly vein about personal news. Upon being asked by Fred Wolfe for news of his brother, he wrote: "He has also turned his back on me, and Scribner's, and so I have not seen him at all, though I would very much like to." When Wolfe learned about this letter, he felt that Perkins had impugned their friendship, although neither of them could understand how this trouble arose between them. Yet he did know that the trouble between them had been going on for a long time and that it would be misleading and untruthful for either of them to say that he had no idea what it was about.

He proceeded to tell him that from the first his editorial restrictions "had the total effect of clampening my hope, cooling my enthusiasm, and almost nullifying my creative capacity, to the work that I had projected." Yet at this time, when he was "eating my heart out thinking of the full and tragic consequences of this severance with people with whom I've been associated for eight years . . . the thing that chiefly was worrying you was the tremendous question of whether I am going to 'write about you'."

Wolfe now began to seek another publisher. Robert N. Linscott of Houghton Mifflin seemed to him a likely editor, and he explained his problem to him in connection with the available manuscript material. On being told, however, that the firm disclaimed responsibility for manuscripts, he did not know that the disclaimer was a mere formality and dropped the negotiation. Harper & Brothers, having expressed keen interest, won his confidence when they proposed an advance of $10,000 against a royalty of 15 percent and the assignment of Edward C. Aswell as his editor. Wolfe took to Aswell at once, and soon wrote him: "It has been my fortunate lot always to have as publishers in this country people of the finest ability and the highest integrity. For that reason, I am glad to know that with the New Year I shall be associated with a House like yours."

He also wrote to Charles Scribner that he left the firm without rancor. "I think you are not only the finest publishers, but among the finest people I have ever known. Whatever comes of all this, I know we will be friends, and now that I am committed to a new, and for me, very lonely and formidable course, that knowledge gives me the deepest comfort."

Ready to work on his next book, he began consulting with Aswell frequently and freely, though not with the close intimacy he had felt for Perkins from the beginning. Still restless, however, he decided to take a trip westward, stopping to lecture in a midwestern university, and then continuing to the Pacific Coast. There he readily accepted the invitation of a federal park inspector to visit some nine national parks, covering around 4,500 miles. He then went to Vancouver by boat. Sharing a pint of whiskey with "a poor, shivering wretch," he became sick with the man's influenza. While in a high fever, he traveled to Seattle and remained five days in a hotel before he was taken to a hospital—having contracted pneumonia. He also began to suffer from violent headaches and some irrationality.

Wolfe's sister Mabel, and later his brother Fred were with him. In August Fred informed Perkins about his brother's condition, and the latter at once wrote a long chatty letter of a personal nature and mailed it to Fred for his decision whether or not to let Wolfe read it. When it was shown to him, he disregarded doctor's orders to scrawl a reply:

> I'm sneaking this against orders—but "I've got a hunch"—and I want to write these words to you.
>
> I've made a long voyage and been to a strange country, and I've seen the dark man very close; and I don't think I was too much afraid of him, but so much of mortality still clings to me—I wanted most desperately to live and still do.
>
> Whatever happens—I had this "hunch" and wanted to write you and tell you, no matter what happens or has happened, I shall always think of you and feel about you the way it was that 4th of July day 3 yrs. ago when you met me at the boat, and we went out to the cafe on the river and had a drink and later went on top of the tall building and all the strangeness and the glory and the power of life and of the city below—yours always, Tom

When the doctors at the hospital failed to diagnose the nature of Wolfe's serious illness, the family decided to take him by train to Johns Hopkins Hospital in Baltimore. There brain surgeons operated on him and found that tubercular germs, loosed by pneumonia, had caused "miliary tuberculosis of the brain," which resulted in his death.

Mr. and Mrs. Perkins reached Baltimore too late to see Wolfe alive, but went with the family to Asheville for the burial. Perkins had been named literary executor in Wolfe's will, and he performed the service with complete devotion. When

William Wisdom, a New Orleans insurance broker, who had met Wolfe in that city and became one of his strongest admirers, decided to acquire all materials belonging to Wolfe with a view to presenting them to an interested library, Perkins helped him in every way possible. It was he who persuaded Aline Bernstein to sell Wolfe's letters to her with the understanding that they would be deposited in the Harvard Library; and the $800 which Perkins thought she should be paid by Wisdom was given to the Federation of Jewish Charities "In memory of Thomas Wolfe." In the letter to Perkins she added: "I smile because it will be a retaliation for all the insults to the Jews that Tom hurled at me."

Aswell did his utmost to organize and edit Wolfe's voluminous written material. Out of it he carved *The Web and the Rock*, *You Can't Go Home Again*, and *The Hills Beyond*. "Even so," he stated in 1941, "much of the manuscript still remains unpublished. What is left beyond this book will probably go eventually to some college library." This of course it did, becoming part of the Wolfe materials in the Harvard Library.

21.

B.W. Huebsch

& James Joyce

B. W. Huebsch was in a sense a maverick publisher. He entered book publishing as a printer and was from the outset interested in bringing out works of merit regardless of their marketability—assuming somehow that a good book will pay its way. "I enjoy," he declared, "an author's first book more than publishing those subsequent ones whose results can be calculated." Early a lover of music, politically idealistic, and a follower of Henry George's single-tax economics, this self-educated man with little capital was readily attracted to writers who strove for freshness in art and ideas. It was natural for him to be drawn to those who expounded ideals of reform or radicalism, and he stated: "I was always more likely to succumb to the persuasion of authors who wanted to make the world over than to those who celebrated the world as it is." Consequently he was inclined to accept manuscripts which other publishers rejected—often to his financial loss—thus making available books which American readers might otherwise not have had. This soon became apparent to members of the industry, and most of them held him in the same regard as did Lovatt Dickson, the English publisher, who characterized Huebsch as "kinder than any man need to be. It overflows from the well of his good nature. To be an Idealist, and a philosopher, to be clever and kind, and at the same time to be a good publisher, shows what man is capable of becoming."

If this estimate is generous, it is fully deserved. Huebsch's character was molded and stimulated in its development by the lofty morality of his rabbinical father and tested by the mundane wisdom of his uncle Samuel Huebsch, who had tutored him after his father's early death. Forced to go to work in his teens, he was apprenticed to a lithographer Later his older brother took him into his printing shop which specialized in the production of yearbooks and perpetual calendars. When his brother decided to resume his scholarly pursuits, young Huebsch ran the shop alone. Not interested in business as such, he devoted his free time to lectures, concerts, and book reading. For a year, in 1889, he served as music critic on the New York *Sun*; for many years he played the cello in a private string quartet.

Very early in his career as a publisher he was confronted by the problem of effective book distribution, which for all his effort he failed to attain for the lack of organization and drive. Concurrently he was also challenged by the issue of censorship, very much alive in the early decades of the century. As a founder of the American Civil Liberties Union and an upholder of the First Amendment, he spoke out against the current "Grundy" activities without equivocation. When in 1913 Anthony Comstock of the Vice Society began to harass Mitchell Kennerley for publishing a presumably indecent novel, Huebsch criticized Kennerley's prosecution in a letter to *Publishers' Weekly*:

> Mr Kennerley was prosecuted for publishing and mailing a book in which freedom of expression went no further than in a hundred novels of the past decade. Nobody seriously denied that it possessed both literary merit and social significance. It would have been a simple matter for Mr Kennerley to plead guilty (following precedents in the cases of booksellers) and pay a fine, but to his credit he chose the difficult, hazardous, and expensive alternative of standing trial. His acquittal by a jury is a vindication of free press and a triumph for democracy. Specifically the case concerned Mr. Kennerley alone, but actually he fought for a principle, and thus made every American publisher his debtor.

In 1914 Huebsch was in London seeing publishers about likely books for his list. Grant Richards showed him James Joyce's *The Dubliners*, and Huebsch bought the American rights to it despite his awareness that some of the stories offered serious censorship handicaps—having learned that as early as 1906, when the book was finished, Richards had considered publishing the volume but was intimidated by the fear of censorship. At the time Joyce dismissed the critics of the book's morality in a letter on May 5, 1906:

> I cannot alter what I have written. All these objections of which the printer is now the mouthpiece arose in my mind when I was writing the book, both as to the themes of the stories and their manner of treatment. Had I listened to them I would not have written the book. I have come to the conclusion that I cannot write without offending people. . . . I do not see how the publication of *The Dubliners* as it now stands in manuscript could possibly be considered an outrage on public morality.

Richards, keenly fearful of the strictures of English censorship, had tried to circumvent them by suggesting to Joyce that the needed changes concerned "only words and sentences" and that Joyce knew the English language well enough to get around them. Although Joyce reluctantly changed numerous words, Richards remained fearful of the censor and rejected the manuscript. This understandably cautious, if hardly courageous attitude on the part of British publishers Joyce had to contend with until the 1930s.

The manuscript next went to Elkin Mathews, who had published Joyce's poems, *Chamber Music*, but he too shied away from it for the same reason.

George Roberts of the Dublin firm of Maunsel and Company then accepted the manuscript, printed a thousand copies—but quite suddenly had them burned as if they were the source of a plague.

By 1914 Richards thought that the moral climate had improved sufficiently to enable him to publish *The Dubliners* with a minimum of risk. He printed 1,250 copies in May and sold 499 by the end of the year—including the 120 copies which Joyce had to buy as part of the contract. The sales figure is of interest in that Joyce was to receive no royalty on the sale of the first 500 copies.

On his return to the United States, Huebsch interested H. L. Mencken in accepting two of the stories for *Smart Set*. Without the capital needed for the undertaking, he ordered sheets from Richards as soon as he was able and published the book in 1916. The previous year Joyce had suggested that Huebsch also publish *A Portrait of the Artist As a Young Man* and *Chamber Music*. "I hope," he wrote, "you will see your way to take on one or the other of these books as Mr. Mencken wrote me about your house in the highest terms." At the same time Byrne Hackett of Yale University Press, to whom Harriet Shaw Weaver had written about *A Portrait*, had told her that he had talked to Huebsch, "and I would consider both you and Mr. Joyce fortunate, were you to be able to make arrangements for its publication through Mr Huebsch who has made an enviable name for himself as a highly intelligent and successful young publisher" Huebsch was of course interested in everything Joyce wrote. In communicating with Miss Weaver, who was becoming Joyce's strong admirer and benefactor, and who was publishing *The Egoist* in order to serialize *A Portrait*, he wrote her on June 16, 1916:

> Glad to publish *Portrait*, though I am inclined to believe that such success as it may attain will be artistic rather than popular Nevertheless it will afford a foundation for Mr. Joyce's other works on this side.
>
> I should be willing to print absolutely in accordance with the author's wishes, without deletions. . . . You will see that I am anxious not only for my sake but for Mr. Joyce's, to get all his works so that by concentration of interest and economy of effort, he may be properly introduced on this side.

For *A Portrait* Huebsch used the corrected sections of the novel serialized in *The Egoist*. Meanwhile, no British publisher or printer would take the book; so that when Miss Weaver decided to publish it herself, she could not find a printer willing to risk printing it. She therefore arranged with Huebsch to import 750 sheets of his edition. Thus Huebsch had the honor of publishing the first edition of *A Portrait* in December 1916, a month Joyce preferred; Miss Weaver's edition in England appeared the following February. In 1918 Huebsch also brought out Joyce's *Chamber Music* and *Exiles*, a play which baffled most American reviewers but which was the subject of several perceptive reviews.

In 1918 Ezra Pound arranged with the editors of *The Little Review* to serialize Joyce's *Ulysses*. It printed thirteen of the eighteen chapters before John S. Sumner of the New York Society for the Suppression of Vice brought action against the editors and stopped further serialization of the novel. Although Huebsch had agreed to publish the book when completed, he now realized that it would be confiscated if issued without considerable emendation. Nor was he encouraged to risk it in view of the fact that no English publisher would undertake it. When Joyce asked him about its publication, he replied in July 1920 that he could not do so without first making sure the book would not be stopped on publication.

> It is not that I am less desirous of publishing your book than before nor that I wish to make any changes as my course with "A Portrait of the Artist" proves but if I should have any objection or should raise a point, it is certainly wiser that this be done before rather than after signing the contract.

A year earlier Joyce was in financial difficulties, as he often was during that period, and Huebsch informed him that he was sending him money obtained by Padraic Colum from a generous friend (Scofield Thayer):

> With his fine enthusiasm Colum immediately determined to lay the matter before a wealthy young man, whose soul is not crushed by his money, with the result represented by the enclosed check, the equivalent of $700 which he contributed to be used as you see fit, either for the payment of your deficit, or, if the nature of that obligation is not such as to require that you meet it, for your own use. The idea is that you are to be freed of the difficulties that interfere with your health and work.

In June 1920, still hopeful of publication, Joyce sent Huebsch all but the last part of the *Ulysses* manuscript and wrote: "I hope you will be able to arrange your publication for January next when the English edition is also to come out. . . . The whole book has taken six years." Soon after, of course, he learned that the novel was to be published in neither country.

In 1921 Joyce mentioned the matter of Sylvia Beach, who operated the Shakespeare Bookshop in Paris. An admirer of his work, she undertook to bring it out herself by printing a thousand copies for expected subscribers. She did not at first realize the tremendous task required of an inexperienced bookseller to solicit subscribers and oversee the innumerable details involved in the publication of a book of this length and complexity. She was fortunate in having interested a firm of highly skillful French typesetters in Dijon to take on the job of printing. They struggled daily but in the end successfully with the long manuscript and made publication possible on February 2, 1922. The novel quickly became the most notorious as well as the most celebrated novel of the period. The demand for it increased right along, and Miss Beach strove heroically to supply it with printing after printing, selling copies without French interference and giving Joyce 60 percent of the net profit.

Toward the end of the 1920s a pirated edition of *Ulysses* was being circulated clandestinely in the United States. When Joyce and his friends learned of it, they realized that only an authorized edition of the book would stop the piracy. By that time they were encouraged of this prospect by the fact that federal courts, following more enlightened opinion, put an end to the ban of Boccaccio's *Decameron* and other comparable established works.

The Viking Press, with which Huebsch had become associated in 1925, was naturally interested in the likelihood of the legal publication of *Ulysses*. In 1931 Harold Guinzburg, head of the firm, communicated with Sylvia Beach about an American edition. Miss Beach, having been given world rights to the book by Joyce, and wishing to take advantage of this new interest in the book on the part of regular publishers, asked for terms which Guinzburg considered prohibitive—her original request was a payment of $25,000; later she lowered her demand considerably.

Soon after, Bennett Cerf, president of Random House, approached her, eager to acquire Joyce as an author. Knowing that he could do better by direct contact, he went to Paris to discuss terms with her and Joyce. Obtaining satisfactory conditions, he gave Joyce an advance of $1,500 and agreed to do his utmost to legalize the publication of *Ulysses* in the United States. On his return to New York he ordered a copy to be mailed to him from Paris. Joyce, bitter about his publishing difficulties, was not too sanguine about the outcome and wrote to Cerf on April 2, 1932:

> Publishers and printers alike seemed to agree among themselves, no matter how divergent their point of view on other matters, not to publish anything of mine as I wrote it. No less than twenty-two publishers and printers read the manuscript of *Dubliners* and when at last it was printed some very kind person bought out the entire edition and had it burnt in Dublin—a new and private *auto da fé*.

The copy of *Ulysses* was confiscated by the Post Office customs officials, and Cerf brought suit to have it released. The case came before Judge John M. Woolsey. He spent a good part of the summer reading and pondering the novel, and at the end of the trial he lifted the ban in an opinion that became a milestone in the fight against censorship. In ruling that the novel was basically not obscene and therefore importable—inferentially, publishable—he stated:

> I am quite aware that owing to some of its scenes *Ulysses* is a strong draught to ask some sensitive though normal persons to take. But my considered opinion, after long reflection, is that whilst in many places the effect of *Ulysses* on the reader undoubtedly is somewhat emetic nowhere does it tend to be aphrodisiac. *Ulysses* may, therefore, be admitted to the United States.

The decision was appealed, but the circuit court upheld Judge Woolsey's ruling.

Cerf no sooner learned of the favorable decision than he ordered the typesetting started. The unexpurgated novel was published late in January 1934 at the relatively low price of $3.50. The years of spicy gossip about the book and the wide publicity given to it by the trial and Random House gained it exceptional popularity. Within a relatively brief period the sale reached 60,000 copies. Later a Modern Library reprint sold over 100,000 copies. In 1935 the Limited Editions Club brought out a special edition of 1,500 copies with six etchings by Henri Matisse.

The publication of *Ulysses* by Random House did not sever Joyce's friendly relations with Huebsch. They continued to write to each other and Huebsch remained interested in "Work in Progress." When Guinzburg was in Paris about that time he offered to publish the book when it was ready, but Joyce preferred to wait, having given Crosby Gaige permission to issue a special edition of a part of the book. On November 28, 1938, he wrote to his agent Ralph Pinker:

> I had already declined this offer of Mr. Guinsburg's (Fifteen per cent royalties, of which a thousand dollars in advance, on a ten dollar publication), made to me here in July. I am advised that I ought not to undersell in America the privately printed fragment (*Anna Livia Plurabelle*, fifty-eight pages) of the book I am engaged on, is-sued, signed to subscribers at fifteen dollars the copy, by Crosby Gaige of New York. If the Viking Press decide to issue the book at the same figure or a higher fig-ure and renew the same terms, I will sign the copy.

Some time later he agreed to let Viking publish the book, but inserted a clause in the contract, as telling as it is rare, to certify his devotion to Huebsch. This is made clear by Stuart Gilbert, a warm friend of Joyce, in his edition of *Letters of James Joyce* (1957):

> The relations between Joyce and his first publisher in the United States, Mr. B. W. Huebsch, were of the happiest. Though he was disappointed by Mr. Huebsch's refusal (in 1921) to transgress the laws of his country—the time was not yet ripe—by publishing *Ulysses*, unless some alterations were made to bring it into conformity both with law and what was then the consensus of mature public opin-ion, he did not take umbrage and, as I gathered from conversations with him on the subject, came to realize that Mr. Huebsch's determination not to publish *Ulysses* in 1921 not only showed a wise discretion but, in the long run, served its author's in-terests. Proof of this may be found in the agreement he made in 1931 with the Vi-king Press regarding "Work in Progress" (i.e. *Finnegans Wake*). When in London Mr Pinker handed Mr Huebsch the agreement, the latter was amazed to find in it a proviso obviously inserted under express direction of Joyce, who was then in Paris.

> This clause, with its unusual stipulation, is at once a pleasant reminder that the personal relations between an author and his publisher are quite often (despite the "Barabbas" witticism) of the happiest.

The inserted clause read as follows:

> 13. If at any time during the continuance of this agreement Mr. B. W. Huebsch should sever his connection with the said Viking Press and either set up publishing on his own account or acquire interest in another firm of publishers than the Vi-king Press, then the said author shall have the option of transferring the benefits of this contract to such a new firm.

Thus, with the exception of *Ulysses*, Joyce's books were published by Huebsch and later The Viking Press in the United States. In 1936 Joyce offered Huebsch *Pomes Pennyeach*, of which he had given him a personal copy five years earlier. This little volume was published simultaneously by Faber & Faber in England and The Viking Press in America. The following year Viking brought out Joyce's *Collected Poems*.

Finnegans Wake was completed after eighteen years of effort. The work was considered too esoteric to arouse the guardians of public morals. Its publication did not go through smoothly, however, largely because of technical difficulties—its obscure language causing numerous typesetting irregularities. Thus in March 1939, irritated by British publishing delays, Joyce wrote to Mary M. Colum:

> So far it has been a hopeless bungle. As for the date every week we hear something different. The book, printed and bound, has been lying on my table for the past two months but the sheets for Mr Huebsch's limited edition have not yet left England.

The book was published in both countries in May 1939. The limited edition was priced in England at £5.5 and at $25 in the United States; the price of the trade edition was 25s and $5.00, respectively. The reception was mixed, but its peculiar merit was not questioned; later several books of explication were issued, as well as an abbreviated edition.

In 1966 Viking reissued Stuart Gilbert's 1957 edition of Joyce's *Letters* as volume one of the three-volume *Letters*—the two additional volumes of more recently collected letters having been edited by Richard Ellmann, Joyce's biographer. Joyce had died in 1941; Huebsch in 1962.

22.

B.W. Huebsch

& D.H. Lawrence

D. H. Lawrence's first American publisher was Duffield & Company, a small firm which brought out *The White Peacock* in 1911. Two years later Mitchell Kennerley, a nonconformist of fine literary judgment but questionable financial dealings, published *Sons and Lovers*. In announcing the novel to prospective readers he stated: "I do not ask you to buy it but I do tell you that *Sons and Lovers* by D. H. Lawrence is one of the great novels of the age." He promoted it energetically and sold a good many copies. Somewhat later he expressed strong interest in Lawrence's play, *The Widowing of Mr. Holroyd*, and was given the manuscript for publication.

In 1914 Lawrence, needing money, asked Kennerley for his royalties—having received none as yet. He was sent two checks totaling thirty-five pounds. Both proved worthless, and Lawrence could get no satisfaction from Kennerley subsequently. Having previously sent him the manuscript of *The Rainbow*, he became anxious for its return. In December he wrote from Italy to Amy Lowell, whom he had met recently:

> Is Kennerley indeed such a swine? As for what he owes me—he does not send it, even if it is only ten pounds. I haven't kept proper accounts with him, because Duckworth made the agreement and all that. I will write to them. I will also write to Pinker to see what he can do. I must get the novel out of Kennerley's hands that he has in MS.

The following year George Doran, having arranged for the publication of *The Rainbow* while in England, asked Huebsch if he cared to take over the contract, as his English partners Hodder & Stoughton objected to his doing it. Huebsch readily obliged, as he thought well of Lawrence. He did not know that some time previously an English magistrate had suppressed the novel, which Methuen had published, ordering the destruction of all copies. Told in June that Huebsch was publishing the book in the United States, Lawrence wrote Pinker: "As for Huebsch, if you think it is a good and wise proceeding for him to publish the book in America, then let him publish it. But please tell him all that has happened here.'' By the time Pinker wrote to Huebsch he already had the novel in type. Resolved to proceed as best he could, he wrote Lawrence that the American censor's vigilant activity made formal publication of the book an indiscreet and hazardous undertaking, but that he was hoping to find a way of making it available to interested readers without giving the censor a chance to get at it.

In order to avoid exposing *The Rainbow* to John S. Sumner's censorship Huebsch printed a thousand copies but did not formally publish or promote it. His salesmen told booksellers of the book's availability and thus soon sold out the edition. Meanwhile Lawrence had become eager to learn what was happening to the novel and wrote Pinker in November: "I am glad to hear about *The Rainbow* in America, and very anxious to see the book, to see if they have done anything to it. I shall hate it if they have mutilated it.'' Two days later, the American edition having reached him, he told Pinker: "The omissions from the American *Rainbow* are not very many . . . yet they make me sad and angry.'' Huebsch was not aware of Lawrence's anger at his minor emendations; he felt that by doing so and by his informal marketing of the book he was avoiding its suppression. In 1922, with conditions for its regular publication improved, he wrote Lawrence in self-justification: "I think, and so do my friends here, that in view of the original notoriety my handling of the book has been effective in that there has been no threat of suppression. This leaves the way open to the production of new editions without interference.'' At that time, indeed, he was able to bring out the regular edition without hindrance.

Lawrence, however, was not appreciative of this circumspection on Huebsch's part, especially as he did not realize that the novel was being unobtrusively put into the hands of interested readers. On June 1, 1919, he wrote to his friend S. S. Koteliansky:

> *The Rainbow* was printed by a Jewish publisher called Huebsch, in New York.
> Then the suppression came on, and he dared not bring it out. It still lies, no doubt,
> on Huebsch's hands. I had one copy—a paltry-looking black book, rather like a
> text book, with several pages of the English edition omitted in it.

In fact, the omissions were few and were later reinstated in a new printing. Nevertheless, he encouraged Huebsch to publish his other books. In 1919 he asked him how *Look, We Have Come Through, The Prussian Officer*, and *Twilight in Italy*—all three on Huebsch's list—were selling; also if he had seen the printed essays of *Studies in Classic American Literature*, and added: "I like your list of publications. I hope we shall meet before long." In August of that year he sent him the manuscript of *New Poems* with a new preface and promised to mail the manuscript of the critical essays on American literature the following month. And at the end of September he wrote him:

> I understand that the smut hunters want to raise a howl over you—*canaille!* . . . I
> swear people are no longer people over there with you—sort of stalking emotional
> demons. You no doubt are a Jew—capable of the eternal detachment of judg-
> ment—connoisseurs of the universe, the Jews—even connoisseurs of human life—
> dealers in fine arts and treasures—dealers—you might just tell me what you *really*
> think of the U. S.

Huebsch wisely ignored his remarks regarding Jews or the United States. At the end of September Lawrence wrote again:

> I have finished the *Classic American* essays—end up with an essay on Whitman. The essay on Whitman you many find it politic not to publish—if so leave it out altogether—don't alter it. The rest is unexceptionable. These essays are the result of five years of persistent work. . . . Schaff says you're the only "white" publisher in America.

The misunderstanding regarding *Women in Love*—which is really a sequel to *The Rainbow* and should have gone to Huebsch as a matter of course—was due to Pinker's laxity in letting the manuscript lie in his office for about two years without submission to anyone. It is quite possible that he took Lawrence's remarks about it seriously when he wrote him on November 25, 1916, on sending him the manuscript: "It is a terrible and horrible and wonderful novel. You will hate it and nobody will publish it. But there, these things are beyond us." With the war on during that time, Huebsch had not visited England and therefore had not learned of the manuscript's availability.

In the meantime Lawrence had assumed that Huebsch had seen the manuscript and had decided not to publish it. In 1917, pessimistic about the likelihood of its publication, Lawrence had written to Waldo Frank: "I don't know if Huebsch has got the MS. yet. I don't think anybody will publish this, either." Two years later, in a letter to Huebsch, he mentioned the manuscript more or less incidentally: "I sent the novel *Women in Love*—sort of sequel to *The Rainbow*—to some other New York people who asked to see it—presumed you were not keen on it—you must have seen the MS.—Pinker had it for two years." And in a postscript he stated: "I think I shan't let Pinker make any more agreements—anyway I'll tell you first."

Huebsch immediately cabled that he had never seen the manuscript and wanted it. Lawrence then informed him that Thomas Seltzer had it, having expressed strong interest in the novel. He added: "I am waiting to hear of the MS. of *Women in Love*, which I ordered back to me. Secker wants to print it at once—would you like sheets from him?—When *Women in Love* is really published, I shall have another novel ready—not before—a more possibly popular one." He wrote again on January 16, 1920, as if wishing to dispel the confusion and uncertainty of his publishing transactions:

> I am writing again to Scott & Seltzer about *Women in Love*. Your cablegrams came in Picinisco today. About a month ago Seltzer sent me £50 on account of royalties for the novel. This I accepted conditionally. I write him today, asking him if he will release the MS. to me again, and telling him I wish to return his £50. We must wait for his answer. I can't act without his acquiescence.
>
> Anyhow, I want to get everything on a straightforward basis now. I am breaking my agreement with Pinker—he is willing. I want to act now for myself. And I must be clear and sure about everything. I don't like this half-friendly, in-the-air sort of business. It leaves me irritated and dependent. I don't want charity or kindness or

anything of that sort: at least I don't want it mixed up with business. Let us make a start now, at precise dealing with one another.

With the manuscript in the hands of a rival publisher, the letter only irritated Huebsch and his prompt reply expressed his displeasure. Whereupon Lawrence wrote more agreeably on January 29:

> It is just as well you are angry—I have been so angry, something has happened to me. Pinker, publishers, everybody—even you, previously—treated me with much vagueness and evasiveness, as if I were an amiable imbecile, and left me to contrive to live on sixpence—*no, basta!*
>
> *Abbastanza.* One could eat one's old shoes, while Pinkers and publishers were complaisant and vague. That's why I've done with Pinker: Whatever mess I make in the future, I'll make myself, not through an agent.
>
> Simply, it never occurred to me that Pinker could have had that MS. for almost two years all the while assuring me that he was doing everything possible, without even mentioning it to you. It just didn't occur to me. I thought you'd seen it and turned it down months and months before. Then Seltzer, having heard of it from a friend, wrote and cabled, and I sent him the only final MS.: he was decent, and I more or less agreed with him. If I'd thought Pinker hadn't shown you the MS.—he had three copies—wouldn't I have sent it to you a year ago? Of course I would. There is nothing I believe in more than sticking to one publisher.

Although he wrote to Seltzer for the return of the manuscript, telling him he would refund the advance and pay for expenses incurred on the manuscript, he did not protest when the publisher informed him that he had already sent the manuscript to the printer and that he would do his utmost toward the success of the book. On March 24 Lawrence told Huebsch: "Last week I had Seltzer's letter—he says they have sent *Women in Love* to print, and that he won't think of relinquishing it—so there we are. I've signed his little agreement—you'll think I did it all on purpose: but I didn't. Now I can't help it." Huebsch's reaction was in keeping with his general attitude toward his authors: "I don't blame you for your course concerning your American publishing arrangements, I simply think your judgment is bad."

It should be pointed out that Huebsch was at this time so preoccupied with the pressing problems of *The Freeman*, a well-edited liberal weekly of which he was the intellectually devoted publisher, that he had less time than before for his book publishing enterprise. He therefore did not exert himself to retain Lawrence as an author. Their relations remained cordial, however. In 1920 Lawrence wrote him for help to place his shorter writings in American magazines. He also kept receiving royalties from the books on the Huebsch list, and this served to reinforce their friendly contact.

Lawrence's relations with subsequent American publishers were less durable than those with Huebsch. Scott & Setzer published *Women in Love* in 1920, limiting the edition "for subscribers only" to avoid the hazards of current censorship. Two years later, with the "Grundy" atmosphere considerably cleared, they brought out the regular edition. Seltzer—Scott soon left the firm—and his wife Adele expressed their strong admiration for Lawrence at every opportunity, Seltzer acclaiming him as "the greatest living writer." When Lawrence came to the United States, the Seltzers had him as their houseguest; later they visited him in New Mexico. During the early 1920s they brought out several of his books and promoted them energetically, if not very successfully.

From the first, however, the Seltzer company was on an infirm financial foundation, having started with very modest capitalization. Its troubles with censorship, and its expenditures and efforts fighting it in the courts, gradually brought it to the brink of bankruptcy. In 1925, therefore, Seltzer was forced to sell his list of books to Albert and Charles Boni.

When Lawrence learned of Seltzer's difficulties, he instructed his American agent in January 1925 to give his next book to Alfred A. Knopf. "As for Seltzer," he added, "if only he'd have been open and simple with me, I'd have borne with him through anything. But a furtive little flea who hides his hand from me, as if I were going to fleece him—whether fleas have hands or fleece—why—*basta!*" The following April he informed a friend: "I got a new publisher over here: Knopf—a Jew again—but *rich* and enterprising—seems very nice. Seltzer is staggering, staggering."

Seltzer, still eager to remain in publishing, was loath to lose Lawrence as an author. When he learned that Lawrence's agent was arranging the publication of his new book with Knopf, he telegraphed his protest to Lawrence. The latter, no longer eager to stick to one publisher, as he had stated earlier, was willing to be published by both Knopf and Seltzer. On February 15, 1925, he wrote his agent regarding Seltzer's protest:

> I replied that "St. Maur" was offered to Knopf, but I didn't see why, in the future, we couldn't offer another novel to Seltzer, if all goes well and I mean that. I don't quite believe it is good for me to be monopolized by one publisher in each country. I think two publishers stimulate the sales much better than one.

Seltzer continued his appeal to remain his publisher and assured him he would try to pay his overdue royalties if he did. Sensing a threat, Lawrence minced no words in his reply on November 13, 1926:

> You say you will pay me the arrears if I come back, but not if I don't: which is a sort of threat. And you know why I left you because you left *me* quite in the dark. . . .
>
> I'm awfully sorry things went to pieces. Blame me, if you like, for leaving you. But blame yourself, now as ever, for not knowing how to be simple, and open with me.
>
> And I do hope you will get rich one day—honestly I do.

Lawrence's relations with Knopf were not long to remain as genial as they had begun. Although the firm published his last several books successfully, the two men did not always see eye to eye. The break came in 1929, when Knopf decided against publishing Lawrence's *Collected Poems*. In a letter to John Cournos on July 28, Lawrence made this evident:

No, I haven't got away from Alfred A. yet, but I want to, and shall as soon as I can clear my contract. He refused to take up *Collected Poems* so I've done with him. But am afraid just for the sake of being nasty he'd figure me at more than $150, so I'll go a bit slow and get cheaper.

Lawrence died in 1930.

Huebsch had done little active book publishing in the early 1920s. When *The Freeman*, however, became too great a financial burden, he was forced to stop its publication. Soon after, in 1925, he joined the young partners of the newly founded Viking Press. His interest in Lawrence remained strong, and when he learned that the relationship with Knopf had ceased, Viking arranged with Lawrence's literary executor to take over a number of the books published by Lawrence before and during the 1920s, including *Sons and Lovers* and *Women in Love*. In addition the Viking firm brought out *Apocalypse* (1931), *Etruscan Places* (1932), *Last Poems* (1933), *Phoenix: Posthumous Papers* (1936), *The Portable D. H. Lawrence* (1947), *Selected Literary Criticism* (1956), *Complete Letters* (1962), *Complete Poems* (1964), *Complete Plays* (1966), *Phoenix II* (1968), and *John Thomas and Lady Jane* (1972), an unpublished version of *Lady Chatterley's Lover.*

23.

B.W. Huebsch

&

Sherwood Anderson

Sherwood Anderson was in his forties when he first began to publish his writings. Like so many Americans in the fluid atmosphere at the turn of the century, he had done many things—from a common laborer to the operator of a factory, soldiering in the Spanish-American War, and writing advertising copy. For years, however, he had felt the urge to write creatively, to give expression to his artistic being—his brothers were painters—and did what he could with his pen in his free time. As the father of several children for whom he felt strongly responsible, he could not give up his lucrative employment in the advertising agency; yet was irresistibly tempted to give up his bourgeois existence for the risky but heady life of the creative writer.

He disdained to write commercially acceptable fiction sought by the popular magazines. The stories and books he did write, however, which he considered honest and incisive, failed to find a market. In 1916 Theodore Dreiser, with whom he had become friends and whose work he greatly admired, recommended him highly to his publisher Jefferson Jones, who headed the American branch of John Lane & Company. Jones obliged Dreiser by accepting Anderson's *Windy McPherson's Son* and published it later that year. Francis Hackett's very favorable review in *The New Republic* gave Anderson a measure of prominence among the newer writers and critics, but the book had a small sale.

Jones also published *Marching Men* (1917) and *Mid-American Chants* (1918). These books were also noted with approval by young reviewers, but their appeal to readers remained nominal. Consequently, when Anderson submitted a volume of short stories, Jones was requested by the firm's London office to turn it down. Anderson was not surprised, as he felt that *Mid-American Chants* had made him "the most abused man in the country" among the conservative part of the populace. He had "a hunch" that Jones had "lost his nerve," but did not blame him for the rejection.

He submitted the manuscript to other publishers, but all reacted negatively. He was then advised by friends to send it to B. W. Huebsch, who was well known for his sympathetic regard for new writing. On August 23, 1918, he addressed Huebsch: "So many of the fellows I know have spoken to me of you that I would like to come and call on you." Years later Howard Wolf of the Cleveland *News* wrote that this collection of stories "was rejected all around the publishing industry, until finally it landed with the unbusinesslike one-man firm of B. W. Huebsch. Mr. Huebsch brought it out, not because he expected a sale but because he liked it. He supplied the title, too, *Winesburg, Ohio*." The volume was generally praised for its fresh literary content and sold surprisingly well for a collection of short stories—around 5,000 copies in two years—and subsequently assumed an almost classic dignity. It was reprinted in several editions, and as a Compass paperback it long sold around 50,000 copies annually.

Anderson was of course elated by the book's acceptance. On December 3, 1918, he wrote Huebsch: "I am glad you like Winesburg. From the first I have had a hunch that you are the man I want to publish my stuff. It is so delightful to have a publisher you can have as a friend also. I hope the stuff goes. I shall try to put something real into it." And a few days later he told him: "I can't tell you how glad I am that you are to be my publisher. It makes me feel right."

The following June, with the book published and favorably reviewed, Anderson informed Huebsch:

> Burton Rascoe told me yesterday that Winesburg was a best-seller in Chicago this week. My God, suppose you and I should make some money. Ruin is staring me in the face. However, the book may be dead in a few weeks and we'll be saved. . . . Do you suppose you could buy the plates of Windy McPherson's Son and Marching Men at a low price? I might go in with you on such a deal.

In September, still working in the advertising agency, he complained to Huebsch that his job was hindering his progress on the novel to which he was devoting his free time. "Business has rather got on my nerves. I keep wondering why the devil I should have to spend so large a part of my life in writing fool advertisement in order to live." Some time after that he did leave the agency and accepted the precarious existence of the creative writer.

When *Poor White*, the novel in question, was finished and published in 1920, Anderson wrote Huebsch: "Is the book going to sell? I hope it will not get out of print at Christmas time as Winesburg did." And in December, unsure of the book's appeal and dependent on it for his livelihood, he told Huebsch: "For your sake Ben as much as my own I do hope Poor White sells. I want to see you come out with a whole skin anyway."

In March 1921 Anderson sent Huebsch the manuscript of the volume of stories entitled *The Triumph of the Egg*. "I should like to have the book set up right away," he stated, "so I may have proofs by May 1st. And please have several copies pulled. I do hope Ben you are going to like the book. I believe myself it has in it some of the best writing I've ever done."

Anderson's first difference with Huebsch arose in connection with the Modern Library edition of *Winesburg, Ohio*. In June 1921 Huebsch informed Anderson that he had taken over his Lane books and had also arranged for Modern Library to issue *Winesburg*. In October Anderson complained that people are unable to obtain copies of *Winesburg* and that *Triumph of the Egg* was late in being published. The following month he noticed in his royalty account that Huebsch had paid him only half of the amount received from Modern Library. Unaware that this was in accord with his contract and the custom of the industry, he protested the deduction as unfair. He stated that the cheaper edition had not hurt the sale of the regular edition, and that other writers whom he questioned had agreed with him that a publisher was not justified in taking half the income from a reprint. "As I have said," he added, "I did not intend to say anything about this matter, but having blurted it out before these other men, I cannot in fairness remain silent toward you in the matter. You may, when I see you, be able to convince me, but it will take a lot of convincing."

Huebsch at once explained to him that two leading publishers and the Authors League agreed on the fairness of sharing royalties on a reprint edition. Yet sensitive to the implication in question, he continued:

> I do not want to take up here the justice of what seems to be a general practice, but I am ready to talk it over with you, with a view to modifying our contract, if it seems mutually fair to do so. I do not want to take advantage of merely technical rights. But I do ask, and most earnestly, that you attempt to disabuse the minds of those who carried away a wrong impression of my methods, because you know how easily a man's reputation can get a black eye.

Anderson's response was that "this coming out into the open has a distinct flavor of vulgarity." He ended by thanking Huebsch "for the fine way it seems to me you are doing your end of the job." He was indeed expressing his appreciation at having received $898.46 in royalties during 1921.

Two months later he wrote Huebsch at some length regarding his new novel:

> The book—if the gods let me pull it off—will be a pretty long one and I shall defy the gods to tell whether it is a novel or a new way of handling and intermingling long short stories.

> The title will be "Many Marriages." Now here is the difficulty. This book goes further and is infinitely more bold and daring than anything I've ever done. I'm afraid it can only be printed in a special limited edition as the George Moore and Lawrence's "Women in Love" have been done here.

> What think you? Is there enough of a public now so that we could charge something strong enough to come out on such a book?

> It's a damn shame to make those who will support such a book to pay individually for the prudish laws, but what other way is there out.

Having recently objected to the license taken in *Ulysses*, and being opposed on principle to the commercialization of books written to titillate, Huebsch made clear to Anderson that the "subscription graft" of current limited editions had been worked to death. And he continued:

> To issue a book in that manner is to stamp it as pornography. This new feature in bookselling has resulted in the creation of a class known as book-leggers. They sell

books with a wink and a leer. If the book happens to be a work of art they handle it with slimy fingers. For you to bring out a book in that manner means to limit its reading to one or two thousand persons interested mainly in the collector's value, or the obscenity value, and to withhold it from real audience, ninety-eight per cent of which consists of people who can afford to pay only the normal market price of books.

My advice to you is to walk the straight path with your head high. I do not think that anything you may say will cause your book to be pinched unless, of course, you want to invite the lightning by using unnecessarily bald terminology. With regard to the use of words, though I do not advocate compromising with the vice societies, I believe that in most instances a work of literary art can be presented without employing a style of vocabulary offensive to the great many people who have not yet abandoned the Victorian tradition.

I have not covered the case, by any means, but I have said enough to indicate my attitude, and I hope you will ponder it. I want you to write for the great public, and not for the furtive-eyed erotomaniac.

Anderson needed no further dissuasion, fully appreciative of the sound advice. Telling Huebsch that he left the handling of the book to him, he added:

I think you are dead right and a very charming and sensible kind of publisher for one Sherwood Anderson to have.

Re *Many Marriages*. If it comes off—the gods grant that it may—it will be the biggest, most sustained and moving thing I've done.

As to the method of publishing—I'll forget it and trust to your good judgment.

I think the new prose is going to be unlike any I've written. I am struggling to get . . . something intensely suggestive of modern life. Will I achieve this? The gods know.

Many Marriages was published in 1923 and had a mixed reception. It was in no danger of censorship, but it was without much popular appeal. Subconsciously Anderson felt that the fault was largely Huebsch's, that he had not promoted it aggressively enough.

That April he had nearly ready another collection of stories, *Horses and Men*. In writing about it to Huebsch, he described its content with unrestrained enthusiasm: "You will be interested to know that I am at work on the short story book and I believe it will be a dandy. It will contain several stories that have never been published among them some of the best shorter things I have done." When he submitted the completed manuscript he urged Huebsch to publish it without delay, as he was eager to begin work on a new book and could not do so until he had read the proofs. On its publication that November, he wrote:

The new book came yesterday and, first of all let me tell you what a beautiful job I think you have made of it. I do not know that your making the book with such complete good taste has anything to do with sales but surely you must know what it means to the writer of the book.

Anderson was then in Reno getting a divorce. He urged Huebsch to take good care of his health, and asserted: "What I should do without you I don't know."

Constantly in dire need ever since he had given up his advertising work, Anderson worried about the small sale of his books in view of his growing reputation. It became obvious to him that his meager royalties were due largely to Huebsch's inability to market his books aggressively enough. He began to believe what rival publishers were telling him—that Huebsch was "a nice fellow but not a pusher." Yet he was too fond of him to act. This feeling he expressed in a letter to his friend Roger Sergel on December 18, 1923:

> As for Huebsch, one of the most sincere, lovable men I have ever known, God bless him. Behind the door I would whisper to you that I do not think too much of his artistic perception. He's a queer kind, has ideas, etc. . . . and all the time you grow more and more to love and respect him and to realize you would rather have him as your publisher selling 5,000 than some of the damn smart young men of the publishing world "putting you over" to the tune of 25,000.

It was Anderson's hope that the book he was writing, *A Story Teller's Story*, had a very good chance of achieving popularity. When it was finished he sent it to *Harper's Magazine* for possible serialization, but it was refused. In submitting it to Huebsch, he stated:

> I have never had the same feeling about any book of mine. What I really feel about this book is that if you will go behind it it will sell as no other of mine has ever sold. . . . My point is that I have a feeling that this book is my best chance yet to get somewhere toward making a living and you may now be assured of this—I have never felt right from the beginning about a book of mine being the property of someone other than yourself and am not going to get into such a position again.

This avowal of loyalty notwithstanding, he soon felt driven by necessity to harken to the lures of rival publishers. Huebsch sensed this feeling on Anderson's part and wrote him: "I am planning an energetic season, and expect to push "A Story Teller's Story" so as to make you feel that you have made no mistake in resisting the blandishments of my fellow publishers who are trying to seduce you from me." Yet Anderson's resistance was rapidly wearing away as he thought of the possibly larger income from another publisher, and he decided to withdraw the manuscript. After telling Huebsch the reason for his request, he continued:

> It's rather like cutting off a leg but will I'm afraid have to be done. I can support neither myself or my children as things are going. . . .
>
> I will of course not make any definite arrangement with anyone until I have heard from you but I cannot see how I can do anything else but accept starvation, going back to advertising writing or something like this.

When Huebsch informed him that he had already sent the manuscript to the printer, Anderson felt a sense of relief. To Alfred Stieglitz he admitted: "In a way I was glad. The truth is that Huebsch at any rate is not vulgar, and as a man I admire him." The book was published in October 1924, and Anderson wrote

Huebsch with "lots of love": "Will take it as a special favor if you will continue to keep me in touch with the book's sales progress. I am in none too good shape financially and the matter is of great importance to me." When he saw the advertisement of the book in the New York *Times* he told Huebsch it was "surely a wonder. If the book doesn't succeed wonderfully it won't be your fault." In the same letter, however, he stated that his new novel was ready and a copy was "going to Liveright. I will also send you a copy." This bad news notwithstanding, Huebsch exerted himself to promote *A Story Teller's Story*, and honored Anderson with a luncheon for eighty literary people who were in a position to help the popularity of the book.

The fact was that Anderson, for all his regard for Huebsch, was by this time convinced that he must go to a more aggressive publisher if he were not to return to writing advertising copy. Liveright's tempting offer of financial relief was too attractive to refuse. On November 22, in reply to Liveright's telegram, he wrote from New Orleans of his difficulty in making the change:

> I started to do it last year. I felt like a dog. I wanted to do it and at the same time didn't want to. . . . While Ben never sold my books much, he has been very, very fine with me in other ways. There never has been.any lack of moral support. He published me and gave me his support when no one else much wanted me.

Nevertheless, he accepted Liveright's generous offer of a hundred dollars a week for five years in return for anything he wrote during that period—the total deducted from royalties. At the time it seemed to Anderson an ideal solution of his life as a writer. Yet for several months he found it very difficult to tell Huebsch of his decision. Finally he wrote him on April 15, 1925:

> I was very distressed about the whole situation when I was in New York and more discouraged when I got home and found what a strain this constant worry about finances had been on me. . . .

> The time had come when I could not see my way through so I wrote a letter to Horace Liveright, saying I was open to a proposition if he wanted to make me one. As he has taken a trip south he came to New Orleans and talked the situation over with me. Mr. Liveright made me a proposition so fair that I could not turn it down. . . .

> The whole matter has given me sleepless nights but it is over and done now. . . .

> Ben, I might write volumes to you in this matter but you know what I personally feel toward you and about what my situation has been.

Huebsch's reply was in character:

> I assure you I have no resentment and that somehow I feel that whatever course permits you to do your best work most freely is the right one to pursue. Having said so much I must add, in order that you may not think that I take your separation lightly, that from a purely selfish point of view, your determination to go with another publisher is the last thing that I should have cared to have happen.

Three months later he informed Anderson that he was merging his firm with the newly founded Viking Press. This, he pointed out "means greater efficiency than before and a release for me to devote myself to that part of the work in which I can function most effectively. The direct effect on your books will be greater vigor in promoting their sale."

Liveright's gamble paid off sooner than he had hoped. *Dark Laughter*, which Anderson gave him in 1925, quickly became a best seller, reaching a sale of nearly 100,000 copies. It was the only one of Anderson's books to attain such popularity, as the other of his books published by Liveright sold only moderately. Moreover, as the weekly stipends from Liveright's office kept coming to him, Anderson began to feel more and more uneasy about them and after a while requested that they be stopped. To Ralph Church he explained his action on September 24, 1927:

> I was afraid of the proposal, but was driven into it by necessity. They have been very nice, but the situation has always been on my nerves. I cannot get over the idea of being at work for them as an employee. When a day or week comes that I do not write satisfactorily, I am beside myself.

> Well, you see, I want what writing I do to be incidental, part of my life, not a profession. I am seeking a profession outside of that.

This he soon did by editing a country newspaper in Marion, Virginia, where he had made his home. While there he became interested in the lives of cotton-mill workers in the South, and he sought to write about this aspect of American life from the inside.

When Liveright lost control of his publishing house in the financial crash of 1929, Anderson was not pleased with his successor and made arrangements to have his books published by Charles Scribner's Sons. But the depression was on and the firm did not do as well with his books as he had hoped. Toward the end of the 1930s, when he was writing his *Memoirs*, he was expecting wide popularity for it. Writing to Maxwell E. Perkins about it, he intimated that it would need more vigorous promotion than his previous books had received:

> I haven't really blamed you, Max. I just figured your real interest was in other men.

> It may take a long time, a year or two, to get down all I want to put down in this book on which I am now at work, I have had pretty damn good offers on it. I think I can make it an important book that can be sold by a house that is willing to back it.

He completed the manuscript in the time he had hoped he would, but died shortly before it was published by Scribner in 1942. And its sale was only moderate.

Anderson's friendship with Huebsch remained warm, if not close. He on more than one occasion stated his regret that he had not known of Huebsch becoming a partner in The Viking Press. "As I have more than once told Mr. Huebsch," he wrote Marshall Best, Viking's general manager, "had I known of the prospective reorganization of Mr. Huebsch's publishing business, I never would have left him.''

Over the years he wrote to both Huebsch and Best asking for permission to reprint some of his stories, and even haggled about the division of fees for them. And as late as 1940, he reviewed his association with the Huebsch firm, why he left it, how well Liveright had dealt with him, and asked for the return of the publishing rights to *Horses and Men* and *The Triumph of the Egg*. It is of interest to note, however, that Viking continues to publish his most famous book, the one Huebsch had entitled *Winesburg, Ohio*.

24.

Pascal Covici

&

John Steinbeck

Pascal Covici belonged to the Chicago group of writers and bookmen who made American literary history in the early decades of the century. No creative writer himself, he operated a bookstore in the 1920s and published a small number of *avant garde* books. His shop, like that of Ben Abramson's, was a gathering place for those who wrote and liked books of an unconventional character.

In 1928 he went to New York to join Donald Friede in starting a new publishing house. Friede, the younger of the two and with more capital, had left a vice-presidency at Boni & Liveright to join the partnership, and the two were equally interested in the new and the novel in books. Because of their disinterest in conventional writing, they became hospitable to books which established publishers tended to shy away from.

Their first successful novel was Radclyffe Hall's *The Well of Loneliness* (1928). This novel had been rejected by Harper & Brothers, but Alfred A. Knopf had agreed to publish it. The book was already in printed sheets ready to be bound when news came from England that it had been banned as immoral. This put Knopf in a quandary. Unwilling to lose his investment in the novel, he was nevertheless loath to risk his fine reputation by exposing himself to attack by John S. Sumner of the Vice Society. When Covici learned of Knopf's predicament, he made him an offer for the available sheets which was advantageous to himself and acceptable to Knopf.

To strengthen his position against likely censorship, Covici obtained an introduction to the novel by the eminent sexologist Havelock Ellis and placed what was then a high price of five dollars a copy. In January 1929, shortly after the book was published, Sumner seized the available copies and a magistrate declared the book obscene and ordered a trial. Covici fought the case to the limit of his resources, insisting that the story was a discerning and sensitive study of feminism. When the court finally declared the book publishable, he felt vindicated. Taking full advantage of the wide publicity of the trial, he managed to sell the book in large numbers—disposing of 100,000 by September 1930. Subsequently he issued a two-dollar edition, which also sold widely.

The economic depression of the 1930s was proving ruinous to the newer publishers with small backlists and little capital. Covici was of course affected, and struggled heroically for nearly eight years to keep the firm in being—publishing few but highly meritorious books. By 1938 he was at the end of his resources and too much in debt to avoid insolvency. To his credit, however, was John Steinbeck, an author he had nursed into popularity and with whom he had developed a solid friendship.

In 1934, while in Chicago on a selling trip, Covici was attracted to Steinbeck's *The Pastures of Heaven* on a remainder table in Ben Abramson's bookstore. He bought it for ten cents and read it on the way to New York. Impressed by its style and treatment, he soon learned that Steinbeck had published two other novels and that all had been commercial failures. Nevertheless he communicated with Steinbeck's agent and was informed that a fourth book was going the rounds of publishers and had already been rejected by several. Covici asked to see it, found it to his liking, and accepted it for publication. When he began to sell it, he found considerable resistance among booksellers. But he persisted in assuring them that this novel had greater appeal than Steinbeck's previous ones. His enthusiasm for it in time overcame their initial reluctance to order it. When *Tortilla Flat* was published, it sold over 4,000 copies, nearly twice as many as Steinbeck's previous books—thus giving Steinbeck much-needed, if modest, royalties as well as a small profit to the firm.

With time Covici's faith in Steinbeck's writing deepened. A personal meeting in California confirmed his belief in its ultimate popularity. Not long after, while away from the office on a selling trip, the manuscript of *In Dubious Battle* (1936) arrived. With Friede having by then left the firm to open an agency in Hollywood, one of the editors read it routinely. On his return, Covici inquired about the manuscript and was told by the editor, a political leftist, that he had rejected it because it contained a very confused treatment of Communism. Chagrined, Covici immediately telephoned the agent for the return of the manuscript, only to be told it was with another publisher. Covici then sent a night letter to Steinbeck to explain what had happened and to ask that he wire the agent for the return of the manuscript. This Steinbeck did, and Covici published the novel to their mutual profit.

Covici's enthusiasm for Steinbeck's fiction came to fruition with the publication of *Of Mice and Men* in 1937. A selection of the Book-of-the-Month Club, the novel sold around 150,000 copies. Successfully dramatized, the play furthered Steinbeck's popularity as well as his prosperity. In the fall of the year Covici issued *The Red Pony*, which was widely read.

All this time, aware of Steinbeck's tendency to depression, Covici wrote him strongly encouraging letters and telegrams in an effort to bolster his fluctuating self-confidence. Steinbeck deeply appreciated these warm and reassuring missives. Thus, notwithstanding his awareness in 1938 of Covici's financial difficulties, he wrote him: "Your wire only confirms the old opinion that I have the best publisher in the world."

This loyalty soon asserted itself when it became necessary for Covici to dissolve the firm and to sell its list. Several publishers were eager to acquire Steinbeck as an author, but he insisted that Covici remain his editor and that he would go to the publisher who agreed to this arrangement. Harold K. Guinzburg eagerly assented, and Covici thus became an editorial associate of The Viking Press.

Covici realized, of course, that the permanence of his position at least for a time depended on the popularity of Steinbeck's fiction. In his letters to him, however, he kept encouraging him to follow his own intuition, to obey his artistic impulses, and to listen to none but his own inner voice. The first book Viking published, *Long Valley*, did only moderately well, yet Covici persisted in his encouragement and critical guidance. In return Steinbeck assured him: "I am very, very proud to have you for my publisher."

All Viking editors were bullish on Steinbeck's next novel, *The Grapes of Wrath*, and a first printing of 50,000 copies was ordered. The novel, dealing with the most unfortunate victims of the current economic depression, was widely and enthusiastically reviewed, and soon became acclaimed as "the epic of the contemporary dispossessed," so that within a year the book's sale reached 430,000 copies. It was voted the "Booksellers' favorite novel of 1939" and was awarded the Pulitzer Prize in 1940.

The intimacy between Covici and Steinbeck grew warmer and stronger with every communication. In July 1941, for instance, Covici wrote him affectionately: "In my little life, which is about three-quarters done, you are my rarest experience. Take that with all its implications, cynically as well if you want to." Two months later, learning of an incident in which Steinbeck had refused to be lured by money to write commercially, he told him: "I am filled with pride that you will not write for publication which does not compellingly drive you to it."

Steinbeck's new book, *The Moon is Down* (1942), had an advance sale of 65,000 copies and sold an additional 100,000 subsequently. *Cannery Row*'s advance was 90,000 copies, with an equally large sale after publication. For some time reviewers had been treating Steinbeck as a major novelist, and Viking promoted his reputation at every opportunity. Late in 1945, wishing to bolster Steinbeck's temporarily drooping self-confidence, he wrote him: "Well, you didn't get the Nobel Prize this year, but I am willing to make a bet that you will in the next three years. It is inevitable." Although he did not guess the year, he was certainly right about the inevitability. Two years later Steinbeck's new book, *The Wayward Bus*, was again highly popular, having been selected by the Book-of-the-Month Club with a distribution of a half million copies and reaching an advance sale of 100,000 copies.

In 1949 Steinbeck confided to Covici that he wanted to build up a reserve for his family before writing his next novel. Aware of his then depressed condition,

Covici sought to bolster his morale by reminding him that he had written *The Grapes of Wrath* with a much smaller reserve and yet suffered no financial depletion: "What you need to my way of thinking is peace of mind and a great urge to do your novel. It is a terribly important piece of work, you know it and you feel it, but you are side-tracking it, pushing it away from you." Four months later, in response to a less pessimistic note, he wrote him: "The one great gleam in your letter is your telling me that something is really jelling in your mind and you mean to tackle it soon. That to me is most exciting—your creative self coming back." Steinbeck needed this confidence and encouragement all the more because he was experiencing marital anguish and had become fully dependent on Covici for emotional guidance and comfort.

Early in 1951 Steinbeck was ready to begin the novel that had been gestating in his imagination over the past two years. His association with Covici was by then so close that he felt impelled to include him in the actual process of writing. What he did was to begin each morning's stint by addressing Covici, as a sort of alter ego, on the separate left-hand page of a large pad supplied to him by Covici, penciling freely what came to his mind as a means of "warming up" for writing the novel on the right-hand page. Three weeks after this was started, on February 22, 1951, he wrote self-consciously: "I am not going to have much time to visit with you. Has it struck you that this is a crazy kind of thing? Writing you what amounts to a letter which you won't even see in under a year. It's fun in a way too."

These "letters" were in a sense outpourings; Steinbeck jotted down whatever came to his mind as he sat down at his writing table: trivialities, cliches, current incidents, momentary reactions, the minutiae of his most personal activities, but also sensitive and incisive feelings and ideas as well as discussions of the content of his novel as he was developing it. Still somewhat self-conscious about this daily procedure, he noted on March 21:

> You must think I waste an awful lot of time on these notes to you but actually it is a warming-up period. It is the time of drawing thoughts together and I don't resent it one bit. I apparently have to dawdle a certain amount before I go to work. Also if I keep dawdling in this form I never leave my story. If I wrote my dawdles some other way I would be thinking all over the map.

As he finished a week's writing—Monday to Friday—he would give the pages to Covici for a reading and typing. They were returned to him—always with words of encouragement. Early in April, reacting to Covici's chance remark about the hoped-for sale of the book, Steinbeck wrote on the tenth:

> You said this morning you had to sell X thousands of copies. I am sure, after all our years together, you will not ask me to make one single change for the sake of sales except in terms of clarity. I am not writing for money, any more now than I ever did. If money comes that is fine, but [if] I knew right now that this book would not sell a thousand copies, I would still write it. I want you to remember that, Pat. I have not changed in that respect even a little bit.

Much as he respected and appreciated Covici's comments on the weekly portions of the writing, he began to feel that the criticism of a work in progress could not necessarily be too helpful; that it tended to disturb the trend of his thinking concerning the development of the story. On April 16, after one of the weekly sessions with Covici, he jotted down:

> I want to ask and even beg one thing of you—that we do not discuss the book any more when you come over. No matter how delicately we go about it, it confuses me and throws me off the story.... Once it is done you may tear it to shreds if you wish and I won't object and I'll go along with you.

The next day, apprehensive of Covici being hurt on seeing what he had written, he admitted that his fears were "silly."

Steinbeck's hobby had long been carpentry and cabinetmaking. Having decided in May to give the manuscript to Covici at Christmas as a token of his deep appreciation, he began working on a mahogany box in which to put it. On May 7 he noted: "I guess I should start work on your present. It is going to take a very long time to do. And I hope it is going to be beautiful and that you will like it." In time he carved the wood to his satisfaction, lined the inside of the box with heavy green felt, and on the face of the removable cover he carved the words EAST OF EDEN and the Hebrew word תמשל meaning "may you govern"—a phrase that plays a key part in the novel. The box and its contents were delivered to Covici at Christmas.

As the story progressed, Steinbeck used the "letters" to discuss the development of his characters—their individual traits, their variegated background and individualized behavior as he perceived them in his imagination with all the attributes of living people—most of them, in fact, being based on persons he knew well as a boy or from hearsay. One of them for all her evil traits, intrigued him and he dwelled on her for days in his communications to Covici. Thus on May 31 he wrote:

> I think you will find that Cathy as Kate fascinates people though. People are always interested in evil even when they pretend their interest is clinical. And they will mull Kate over. They will forget I said she was bad. And they will hate her because while she is a monster, she is a little piece of the monster in all of us. It won't be because she is foreign that people will be interested but because she is not. That is not cynicism either.

Five days later, after another session with Covici, he wrote:

> I was interested last Friday in your sense of shock over the end of the Kate story. I had the same sense of shock writing it. I think you were shocked that I could think such things and so I was also. But the fact seems to be that I can think almost anything. But I believe what the sheriff says—that anybody is a murderer if you find the key to his trigger finger.

In June Steinbeck and his family went to Nantucket for the summer. His writing, however, continued without a break, using his late afternoons for companionship with his wife and boys as well as the chores only he could do about the house. His wife continued to read in the evening the pages he had written during the day—and her favorable reaction of course encouraged him. Every Friday afternoon he airmailed the week's portion to Covici and usually accompanied it with requests for pencils—he worked with sixty at a time and replaced them as soon as they got somewhat short—paper, definitions of given words. Occasionally he felt self-conscious about putting Covici to this trouble, and on June 22 he wrote: "Tell me, have you ever been this closely associated with a book before? While it was being written, I mean. I don't think you have but perhaps." Two weeks later, asking for a copy of Bartlett's *Quotations*, he again asked. "And do all these requests and commissions bother you? You have only to say and I will stop it. Don't let me impose on you. I don't mean to but maybe I go too far. I do depend on you so much." Whereupon Covici urged him to continue asking for whatever he needed: "You seem to forget that what you are asking me is nothing compared to the riches of mind you are giving me."

On July 9, during one of his depressed periods, he wrote: "I have the fear that comes with starting and the usual lack of self-confidence." It was this lack, indeed, that had caused him to resort to the bolstering effect of the *Journal of a Novel*, published in 1969 after Steinbeck's death. As the writing of the novel progressed, he began to ask Covici about his reactions to what he had already written, especially for his opinion of the more prominent characters. He also wondered what the general reception of the novel would be and how clearly he had presented his characters. In his "letters" he let his thoughts roam freely, and in his correspondence with Covici he used him as a kind of guinea pig on the assumption that if he liked the story it was most likely well written.

At the beginning of August Covici visited him for a week. Steinbeck continued his routine of working all morning, often until two o'clock in the afternoon, and then spent time with his friend. When the latter, naturally eager for the completion of the novel, remarked jocularly about the possibility of speeding up the writing, Steinbeck reacted negatively in his notes:

> The other day you made a joke—I hope it was a joke—about increasing my word rate. That isn't even a joke. It is a destructive suggestion and not even to be joked about. A book, as you know, is a very delicate thing. If it is pressured, it will show that pressure. So—no more increases. . . . I need time and lots of it.

As Steinbeck was beginning to see the end of the first draft he began to feel more and more uneasy about its quality. On August 24 he noted: "Suddenly I feel lonely in a curious kind of way. I guess I'm afraid. That always comes near the end of a book—the fear that you have not accomplished what you have started to do. That is as natural as breathing." He became impatient to finish the writing, and yet he feared finishing it. On October 31, the last day recorded in the *Journal of a Novel*, he stated: "The days stretch on and on. I think finally I can see the end but I am afraid to say it any more."

When the novel was published in 1952, it had the following dedication:

To Pascal Covici

The dedication is to you with all admiration and affection that have been distilled from our singularly blessed association of many years. This book is inscribed to you because you have been part of its birth and growth.

Disappointed that *East of Eden* was not taken by one of the major book clubs, Covici wrote Steinbeck:

> Do you remember when I argued that the book clubs were bound to be limited by the prejudices of so many readers? When the readers tell you what to write and publish, you can't have very good books. Maybe that is our trouble now. Writing for readers instead of ourselves.

Nevertheless Viking ordered a first printing of 110,000 copies and had to reprint later. For one month it reached first place on the best-seller list.

For all his periods of uncertainty, Steinbeck was a productive writer. During the ensuing decade he completed *Sweet Thursday* (1954), *The Short Reign of Pippin IV* (1957), *Once There Was a War* (1958), and *The Winter of Our Discontent* (1961). These books were written with the consultation and encouragement of Covici. Their continued extraordinary closeness emerged in clear focus in their correspondence. So dependent had Steinbeck become on Covici's letters when abroad, that he dreaded coming to a new place and not finding a letter, but in each place he found one awaiting him. And in each missive Covici fed him the admiration that buoyed his spirits. Thus, in November 1954 he told him: "I am perfectly willing to stick my neck out and say there isn't an American writer today who has the depth and breadth of humanity that you have in your books. I hope I don't have to convince you of your importance in American letters." Steinbeck's typical reaction was: "I do not think all the things in my books are good but all things in my books are me." And as a birthday greeting in 1958 Covici wrote: "That you were born and in some small way I have been of use to you in bringing your books to light means a great deal to me, possibly infinitely more than you may ever realize."

Later that year, when Steinbeck was under emotional tension and relatively unproductive, Covici sought to cheer him by writing: "My worry was you. I felt you were under a terrific nervous strain because you were not sufficiently moved to write.... You are entitled to sit back and let things soak in.... One of these days you will feel the stir of new buds and the urge and flood to create, and the thing will come." Steinbeck was pleased to reply: "Strange how periodically my life force goes into hibernation very like death and then it stirs very drowsily to life and one day the words begin to rush out and every other consideration dissipates like mist. I am very fortunate in many ways." And in 1960 when he was receiving various suggestions from friends and critics, Covici sought again to bolster his self-confidence: "The point I want to make is that you examine all revisions suggested, you should make none unless they convince you. You cannot afford to make somebody else's mistakes. In the last analysis you have to follow your own creative instincts."

Two years later Steinbeck was awarded the Nobel Prize for Literature. Covici felt that the encouragement and helpfulness he had extended to him for thirty years were amply rewarded. Earlier that year Steinbeck's *Travels with Charley* had been a selection of the Book-of-the-Month Club, and news of the award brought the book to the top of the best-seller list.

For all his honors and success, Steinbeck remained loyal and affectionate to his longtime friend and publisher. On learning of Covici's death on October 14, 1964, he stated:

> Pat Covici was much more than my friend. He was my editor. Only a writer can understand how a great editor is father, mother, teacher, personal devil and personal god. For 30 years Pat was my collaborator and my conscience. He demanded of me more than I had and thereby caused me to be more than I should have been without him.

25.

Sinclair Lewis

&

His Publishers

Sinclair Lewis, endowed with latent literary gifts, began his career with serious handicaps. Early in adolescence he became acutely self-conscious of his asymmetrical and acned face. Equally damaging to his sensitive ego was his father's browbeating—the cold and caustic comments which served to intensify his sense of insecurity. Yet he was also fully aware of his agile mind. On January 3, 1903, at the age of seventeen, he noted in his diary: "I am 17. Tall, ugly, thin, red-haired, but not, methinks, especially stupid."

Lewis's father, a callous and calculating country doctor in rural Minnesota, was, in the words of Lewis's biographer Mark Schorer, "rather cold, rigid, parsimonious, almost compulsively methodical, absolutely without self-questioning." His righteous puritanic position, strictly enforced, early antagonized his young son; unable to resist, the youth deeply suffered this domination.

Sent at seventeen to the academy of Oberlin College to prepare himself for acceptance at Yale University, young Lewis was sufficiently influenced by its religious atmosphere to consider becoming a missionary. In March 1903 he recorded in his diary: "For some time my resolve for missionary service has been re-forming (that is, forming again) so that I am as much inclined to foreign missionary service as I was last fall."

Entering Yale in the fall of 1903, he made few friends. He roomed alone and often felt lonely. Again and again he recorded taking walks by himself: "Walk solus." He was by this time writing verse and became the first freshman in his class to publish a poem in the Yale *Literary Magazine.* He also worked on the college newspaper.

In his first year he took his courses seriously and did well in them. The following year, however, he tended to dawdle and waste time, so that his grades suffered accordingly. But his literary activity increased markedly, and that year he published five stories and ten poems. In June 1905 he wrote an article about an act of plagiarism in a currently popular novel, which *The Critic* accepted and paid him twenty dollars for it. Here he appeared for the first time as Sinclair

Lewis—having changed it from Harry S. Lewis, which his close friends continued to call him.

This success furthered his tendency to nonconformance as a student and confirmed his belief in himself as a writer. Time did not, however, allay his loneliness nor his yearning for acceptance and admiration. Dissatisfied with his
courses and the college atmosphere, he left Yale in his senior year to serve in a
menial capacity at Upton Sinclair's Helicon Hall in New Jersey. No longer imbued with religion, he was ripe for conversion to socialism—and a pseudo-social-
ist philosophy never left him—but several months later he had enough of the socialist colony and soon after published his experience in the New York *Sun*. As
Schorer summed up this period:

> When Harry Lewis left Yale his was still a scattered self, as, really, it was always to
> remain. The complacent gentility that characterized the intellectual life of Yale in
> the early years of this century could not, on the one hand, assimilate him, and, on
> the other hand, it gave him no target for rebellion. . . . The undirected dissidence of
> Harry S. Lewis remained largely the frenetic expression of his personal uneasiness,
> his psychic restlessness.

After several journalistic as well as other activities, he went to Carmel, California, in 1909 to serve as secretary to two women writers, whom he had known
at Helicon Hall, a job he accepted because it would give him time to do his own
writing. Somewhat earlier he had sold a story to *Red Book* for seventy-five dollars, but most of other efforts met rejections. After six months he resigned his job
and went to San Francisco, where he worked first on the *Evening Bulletin* and
then for the Associated Press. At this time plots for stories came to his mind with
rapid frequency, and he sold a number of them to Jack London, getting in turn
seventy dollars for fourteen plots and fifty-two dollars for nine. He also sold plots
to other writers.

Although his writing continued to be rejected by magazine editors, he was determined to succeed: "And by God," he asserted in his diary, "I'm going to go on
working toward the end of getting to be a really great writer, even if gray hairs
find me still plugging along." And to his father he wrote: "I'm a born writer,
and nothing in this broad work-a-day world but a writer. So I'm born; and I've
been getting a good bit of experience. It's about time for the clock to strike."

On the basis of this self-generated confidence, he asked his father to lend him
money to live on modestly while waiting for his stories to find acceptance—he
was figuring on five months and was ready to pay 7 percent interest on the
loan—but all he received was a discouraging refusal: "I am not going to put my
self short to make you a loan for I want a lot of it for fun this fall and my many
years of hard work entitles me to that."

In need of earning his livelihood, and back in New York, Lewis obtained work
with Frederick A. Stokes Company, doing manuscript reading and publicity. After two years with the firm, he left to work for nearly a year as assistant editor of
Adventure. In August 1913 he was employed by Publishers Newspaper Syndi-
cate at sixty dollars a week, but the following year he joined George H. Doran &
Company as editor and advertising manager. All this time he associated with

young writers and journalists—those who lived in Greenwich Village and hoped for literary prominence. He also sought intimacy with girls of his acquaintance, but his unsuccessful efforts to rid himself of acne rendered him luckless in his amatory pursuits, until he met Grace Hagger whom he married in 1914.

In 1912 he was ready to write a novel. The first draft of *Our Mr. Wrenn* was considered amateurish by his friends who read it. W. E. Woodward told him: "You're not cut out for a writer, and that's all there is to it. It's just not your game, and if I were you, I'd forget all about it." Lewis put the manuscript away—only to return to it somewhat later and rewrite it completely. Macmillan, Century, and Holt declined it, but Harper accepted it on May 6, 1913. When *Our Mr. Wrenn* was published the following spring, reviewers liked its lifelike characters and whimsical humor, as well as its combination of romance and realism. The sale, however, was relatively modest even for a first novel. Undeterred, he wrote *The Trail of the Hawk*, later to be considered by him a prophetic intimation of the early career of Charles Lindbergh, and which was largely an autobiographical adventure story in which the power of phantasy transformed factual events. Reviewers considered the book an advance over the first novel—one calling Lewis "the foremost member of the younger group of American novelists"—but for all their praise the book failed to appeal to the general reader. His short stories, however, found a welcome reception in the *Saturday Evening Post* and other popular magazines. This encouraged him to give up his job in 1916 and devote all his time to writing.

The two published novels had established Lewis as a serious realistic novelist with satirical overtones. Eager to further his literary position, he stated about his third novel: "I'm making *The Job*, my next novel, just as big as I can, and may not get it finished till the end of the summer, simply shan't think of the element of time, for first of all I want it to be as big, as real, as sincere as I possibly can." Published by Harper in 1917, it was praised widely as a work of realistic fiction, although some reviewers were not too comfortable with its realistic emphasis. The public again remained fairly indifferent.

During the years with Doran, Lewis frequently lunched with other book editors, among them Alfred Harcourt, manager of the trade department of Henry Holt & Company. In their frequent talks about publishing, Lewis complained that the Harper firm was not promoting his books vigorously enough, whereupon Harcourt proposed that he give his next book to Holt. He was particularly interested in having Lewis write a novel dealing with life in a typical small town. Lewis was interested but was not sure he could "wriggle out" of giving his current manuscript, entitled *The Innocents*, to Harper in fulfilment of his contract. He did say that if his editor should leave Harper, which was likely, "then it's Harcourt ho! and let's see if we can't give this damn province a real realistic novelist, Gawd and Alfred Harcourt assisting that poor boob Sinclair Lewis."

Not long after, Lewis visited Harcourt in his office, closed the door, and said: "Alf, I am going to write that small-town novel which you have been pestering me about. I've got a title for it—'Main Street,' and don't you mention it to a single person. When it is done, you've got to publish it.'' Shortly thereafter, in May 1918, he wrote Joseph Hergesheimer: ''And now, today, I start the novel, *Main Street*, and go on with it, breaking off now and then for short stories.''

The writing proved more difficult than he had anticipated, and for a time he floundered in an effort to mold his material to his own satisfaction. Harcourt urged him to write as he wished regardless of the outcome, assuring him that he would thus produce a work of literary merit. Thus encouraged, he soon hit his stride. On September 10 he wrote to Ellen Ayers, Harcourt's secretary: ''The novel, the great and only presumably-to-be-issued novel, is going strong. I've written eighty thousand words. Looks as though it would be about 130,000 in all. But that probably will be considerably cut.''

About that time Lewis took a long automobile trip west in order to describe it in a serial for the *Saturday Evening Post*. About 30,000 words in length, it read well enough for Harcourt to suggest that Lewis expand it for book publication. By now a facile writer, Lewis readily agreed, adding another 25,000 words. In March 1919 he signed the contract for *Free Air*, at which time Harcourt told him: ''And I hope, before the year is over—MAIN STREET!''

Several weeks later, after a disagreement with Henry Holt over a book by Bertrand Russell, Harcourt resigned from the firm. Other publishers were ready to employ him, but he was thinking of starting his own publishing company. Having written to Lewis in Minnesota about his changed status, he received a telegram requesting that he meet him at Grand Central Station that Sunday morning. Harcourt came from his home in Mount Vernon to meet the train. Lewis told him he had driven 125 miles to catch the train because he wanted to talk to him about his next step:

> What I came to say is, ''Don't be such a damn fool as ever again to go to work for someone else. Start your own business.'' I'm going to write important books. You can publish these. I've got a little money saved up—you can have some of that. Now let's go to your house and start making plans.

The firm of Harcourt, Brace & Howe was incorporated on July 29, 1919, with Donald Brace, who had left Holt, where he was in charge of book production, and Prof. Will Howe of Indiana University as partners. They were encouraged by a number of Holt authors, with whom Harcourt had become close, agreeing to give their forthcoming books to the new firm. Some even invested money in the company.

Lewis and Harcourt discussed by letter the problem of how best to cancel the contract with Holt for *Free Air* as well as the informal commitment for *Main Street*. Harcourt advised Lewis to ask Holt for release from the contract: ''Set yourself down, and with all the skill you can muster, write to Henry Holt & Company (our correspondence is in their files) explaining if you wish, how you came there because of personal relations with me, and ask them to let you have the *Free Air* contract back. I think you will get it all right.'' Before the letter reached him, however, Lewis wrote suavely to Roland Holt, the gentle and gentlemanly oldest son of the firm's founder:

Despite my long and hearty respect for the Company and my personal liking for you and others, yet after all Harcourt has always been the man in the firm whom I have best known and with whom I've done business, as book reviewer and fellow publisher and author, and while I don't know what his plans are, I want to be loyal to him and stick by him.

I understand that one of the fundamental principles of the Company has been to hold authors by their own desire rather than by the semi-compulsion of contracts, so I put this directly to you, and hope that you will see it in the decidedly friendly light in which I see it.

Roland Holt graciously returned the contract.

In the meantime the editor of the *Saturday Evening Post*, having read the supplementary part of *Free Air*, wanted to serialize that also. As this meant additional income to Lewis, but also some delay in the publication of the book, Lewis wrote Harcourt: "I hope to God this works out all right. I think I've given enough previous proof of my interest in your success so you may be sure that, while craftily grabbing off this money, I also devote a whole lot of thought and worry to you, and hope and pray that I haven't been either inconsiderate or foolish in this." Of the money he was getting for the serial, he invested $2,000 in the firm.

Free Air was published in October 1919. Harcourt had made a printing of 8,000 copies—"enough to see how the cat is going to jump." Promoted energetically, the book sold more than Lewis's previous books, and Harcourt suggested a reduction in royalty to enable him to spend more money on promotion—to which Lewis readily agreed, as he did in connection with the advertising of his later novels.

During this time Lewis was working intensively on *Main Street*. "My hope," he wrote Harcourt on February 20, 1920, "is that you're going to have that for your big book for next fall, and possibly as a big seller for some seasons thereafter. I believe that it will be the real beginning of my writing." He managed to deliver the completed manuscript on July 20. Harcourt read it at once, reacted enthusiastically, and suggested relatively minor emendation, which Lewis accepted in large measure. Both were sanguine about its popular success, but neither expected a sale in excess of 20,000 copies. Harcourt planned a vigorous campaign of promotion, with hundreds of copies sent to reviewers and men of literary prominence, and with heavy periodical and newspaper advertising—part of the cost of which he expected to regain from the reduction in royalty during the active period of promotion. Both men were, of course, astounded by the sensational reaction of reviewers and readers; indeed, the novel's reception became the most exciting publishing event in the previous two decades. James P. Hart wrote in *The Popular Book:*

Published in 1920, *Main Street* became the most popular book of the year in which Harding was inaugurated, bringing to all the Main Streets of the nation Lewis's view of the "village virus": the smug, intolerant, unimaginatively standardized belief that whatever the town banker does not know and sanction is heresy, not only worthless to know but wicked to consider.

The book sold more than 180,000 copies in six months; totaled more than 400,000 in hard covers, and around a million in reprints. It was sold to the movies for $40,000. Lewis was of course very grateful to Harcourt, and in thanking him for submitting a copy to the Pulitzer Prize Committee—a copy of *Free Air* had previously been submitted at his urging—he added: "I don't see how a publisher could possibly get behind a book more actively and more intelligently than H B & H have behind MSt."

As Harcourt had confidently expected, the three men on the Pulitzer novel jury voted unanimously for *Main Street*—only to be overruled by the Columbia trustees in favor of Edith Wharton's *The Age of Innocence*. The indignant jury made its rejected recommendation public, and Lewis was chagrined.

By now in top form as a writer and aware of the advantage to his next novel if it appeared fairly soon after the current one, Lewis lost no time in his work on it. To Harcourt he stated:

> I think the title of the next realistic not-to-be-serialized nov. by Mr. Sinclair Lewis, which will be the story of the Tired Business Man, of the man in the Pullman smoker, of our American ruler, of the man playing golf at the country club at Minneapolis, Omaha, Atlanta, Rochester, will be the name of the central character, and that name, and title, will be (I think) PUMPHREY. How does that strike you?

Not long after that, the name pleased neither him nor Harcourt, and he changed it to Alexander Fitch. Then he hit upon what he considered exactly the right name: George F. Babbitt, with the initial standing for Follansbee to avoid confusion with and libel suits from real people with that name. He was soon well along in the writing and sanguine about the novel's prospects. Predicting a sale of 100,000 copies, he assured Harcourt of his willingness to keep his royalty down to 10 percent while the book was being advertised heavily. Harcourt, on his part, exhilarated by the extraordinary success of *Main Street*, volunteered sage advice for which Lewis was duly grateful:

> I suppose you realize the change that has come over your position as a novelist because of the success this book has had and is going to have. . . . I should think that with an author whose fortune seems sometimes to depend a good deal on the whim of the public, the jealousies that grow up are apt to be even more acute. You have now made a great success, and it is going to be a good deal bigger, and so very early in the game when there is no particular reason for saying it as far as you are concerned, I am giving you this little lead out of my own experience with a warning to watch your step in your letters, and perhaps most of all, watch from whom you accept any favors.

Eager to concentrate on the new novel and to free himself from the need to write popular stories for magazines, Lewis asked Harcourt for an advance for his living expenses. Thereupon Harcourt proposed a monthly payment of $500—certain that the royalties would more than cover that amount. And as the sale of *Main Street* continued to spiral upward, this advance was doubled.

Before writing the first draft of *Babbitt*, Lewis prepared an elaborately detailed outline. As his wife Grace wrote Harcourt: "Hal has made the most astonishingly complete series of maps of Zenith, so that the city, the suburbs, the state are as clear as clear in Hal's mind. We had such fun making the plans of and furnishing Babbitt's house." When the manuscript seemed well along, Harcourt suggested that Lewis come to New York and bring the written part for examination:

> You come home about April, let me read what is done on *Babbitt* over a week-end; then you and I take my car and drive to Atlantic City or somewhere, just talking all over loosely as we drive. When we get where we are going, stay a week or two and say all we have to say, lay our heads for advs. and for all sorts of things, and get our heads all around it all—and incidentally have a damned good time.

Concentrating on the completion of *Babbitt*, Lewis could not keep from thinking of ways and means to further his prestige and popularity. The "steal" of the Pulitzer Prize for *Main Street* continued to rankle, so that he became condemnatory of literary conservatism and rejected the offer of membership in the National Institute of Arts and Letters—an act applauded by Harcourt. He daydreamed of winning the Nobel Prize and thus expose the smug traditionalists among the established writers. With this in mind he suggested that Harcourt apply for the "Nobel Prize on *MST.* or a later novel." He also advised him to get someone to write a brief biography of himself for promotion purposes. This Harcourt did, and the pamphlet was written by Stuart P. Sherman.

Babbitt was published on September 14, 1922. Having done an energetic job of promotion, and having in hand advance copies of highly laudatory reviews, Harcourt wrote Lewis the day before publication.

> It's lining up just right. You'll have [reviewers] all flopping to get right side up first by next Monday. There has been just enough silence, delay, knocks, soft answers, and enthusiasm to catch the press part just right. Right-O! Stay home, take it easy, and keep quiet.

> 200,000 before Christmas, Son! It's a damn good book. Nuf sed.

George Jean Nathan well expressed the consensus of reviewers when he termed *Babbitt* as "one of the sharpest, most biting satirical and best written novels ever written by an American." The reception in England was equally favorable. In both countries a few critics maintained negatively that the novel was only a successful self-portrayal; that Lewis was not enough above Babbitt to give an intimation of the more human side of his personality; that Babbitt's tragedy was in having made his life a matter of mileage and not of destination. Controversy only accelerated general interest in the book, which in time sold more than a quarter of a million copies in the regular edition and nearly two million in reprints.

Eager to capitalize on his current popularity, Lewis wished to see his early novels republished and offered to rewrite them. Harcourt assured him it would be better for the novels to appear as reprint editions and for him to devote his time to a new book. Lewis was agreeable. He had for some time been interested in a novel about a hero of labor, which he called *Neighbor*, and had spent time with Eugene V. Debs, the veteran socialist labor leader, with the thought of making him the ideal protagonist. But for all his reading and ruminating on the subject—and he never quite abandoned the hope of writing such a book—his thoughts failed to jell for the narrative. What he wanted was a worker who had the personality and power to become a labor leader and electrify the labor movement, but such a hero never gripped his imagination. As he wrote on August 29, 1922, "I am melancholy—I feel rather lost. I don't believe I shall be able to do the *Neighbor* novel—that is, to do it right.

While in Chicago late in 1922, Lewis met Dr. Morris Fishbein and Paul De Kruif. After several conversations with them his interest in writing on the theme of medical research became crystallized. The son of a country doctor and long concerned with the idea of medical dedication, he knew nevertheless that he could not tackle the subject without technical assistance. The more he talked with De Kruif the better he liked him and the more certain he became of his ability to provide him with the details of medical research with the accuracy and realism which he needed. He was therefore delighted when De Kruif agreed to assist him on the project. The arrangement was for De Kruif to receive advances on 25 percent of the royalties. To Harcourt, Lewis stated: "Yuh I AM thinking about the next novel—a lot, it's ripening slowly but I hope it'll be the real big thing when it belooms." On January 10, 1923, while on the way to Barbados with De Kruif, he wrote Brace: "Paul and I find we can work together perfectly. Each day I have greater respect for his totally unusual and fine though fiery brain." And a month later to Harcourt: "It gives me joy to inform you that De Kruif is perfection. He has not only an astonishing grasp of scientific detail; he has a philosophy behind it, and the imagination of the fiction writer. He sees, synthesizes, characters."

Harcourt responded with encouraging enthusiasm. The more he learned about the nature of the narrative, the better he liked it. As early as February 1923 he wrote Lewis:

> I think you said once that your distinguishing personal characteristic is a hatred of bunk. I think that is true, though at the same time you understand it and don't hate the persons but only their bunk performances. The hero of this new book is perhaps the only hero you picked so far that feels as you do, and that ought to warm up the book a good deal.

For nearly two months Lewis and De Kruif cruised the Atlantic and Caribbean waters in the vicinity of Central America, gathering material for the book in various laboratories. Lewis educated himself in the details and general nature of bacteriology and epidemiology. "It's extraordinary," he informed Harcourt, "how well De Kruif and I work together; we've been together practically twenty-four hours a day now for a month and a half, and never a row, never a disagreement—except some extremely interesting ones on an abstract theme." From the Caribbean area the two went to England to visit laboratories there. Then De Kruif departed, and Lewis began to write the first draft. Always tempted to be on the move, he traveled to France and Italy—working on the book but also enjoying the changes of scene.

While thus out of reach in October 1923, he failed to receive letters and cables from Harcourt who wanted to know if he would accept $50,000 for the serialization of the novel in *The Designer*. Pressed for an answer, Harcourt decided in the affirmative—having written earlier: "if I am forced to a decision before I can hear from you, I will accept the offer." Later he told him: "I hope by all that's holy that you approve. Unless you're entirely satisfied to have me settle things like that for you, don't again go out of reach of cablegrams for so long. At any rate this is the highest bona fide price for magazine serialization that I've ever heard of." He also informed him that while the postponement of book publication would affect sales, it would not do so seriously.

Lewis replied a week later: "I'm thoroughly grateful to you for your thought and work on this, and I understand how much against *your* interests, as publisher, it was." He insisted, however, that although he'd cut the manuscript for the magazine editor, "I will not change the thing into a sunny sweet tale—nor will I permit him to. DOES HE UNDERSTAND THAT?"

As before, the title of the new novel gave him some difficulty. He began by calling it *The Barbarian*. As the writing proceeded, he began thinking of other titles, at one time sending nine to Harcourt for his consideration. But he finally narrowed it down to *Arrowsmith*. By the time he returned to the United States in May 1924 he had completed both versions of the manuscript. On the title page he included a lengthy note of acknowledgment to De Kruif. When he expressed surprise that he had not heard from the latter for some time—De Kruif had become estranged from him—Harcourt informed him: "There is one thing you can be dead sure of—he has been most expertly and completely helpful in the advance publicity work on *Arrowsmith*." What Lewis failed to perceive during his association with De Kruif was the latter's disillusionment with him toward the end of their collaboration. This De Kruif made explicit in a letter to Elmer Davis on October 28, 1928: ". . . he's looking down in the dirt, and I'm looking at the stars that show over the tips of the balsam-firs in the latitude fortynine—so we're too far apart for friendly council."

The novel was published on March 5, 1925, with an advance sale of 51,750 copies; a limited autographed edition of 500 copies had appeared earlier. The reception was highly favorable, and on the day of publication Harcourt told Lewis: "Arrowsmith is going over with a bang. There are reviews everywhere—ads everywhere." For ten weeks a full-page advertisement appeared in *Publishers' Weekly*. Harcourt had Harrison Smith, a firm editor and friend of Lewis, write another biographical pamphlet on Lewis, which was widely distributed. Highly pleased with everything done about the book, Lewis asked Harcourt: "Any thoughts of pulling wires for Martin [Arrowsmith] for Nobel Prize?" Harcourt had several persons of prominence make the recommendation to the Swedish committee.

Despite his extraordinary literary success, Lewis was driven by an inner restlessness caused by a combination of insecurity and a soaring ambition. More and more he behaved as if governed by a frenzy of repressed melancholy. He seemed constantly on the move, partly in order to obtain material for his next book, but equally as much out of dissatisfaction with himself and those close to him. It also resulted in excessive drinking, as if he sought to sink his mind into alcoholic excesses. By this time he was beginning to break up his marriage with Grace, leaving her temporarily in August 1925 because of her "extraordinary bullying." Yet he kept writing to her, and generously supported her and their son.

During this period he wrote *Mantrap* as a serial, and Harcourt published it in book form. Reviewers found it an inferior work of fiction, but assumed that Lewis had written it in a light vein and were gentle in their comments. Its sale was moderate, but the movie rights brought Lewis $50,000.

When he learned that *Arrowsmith* might be awarded the Pulitzer Prize, he informed Harcourt that he would reject it because it had not been given to *Main Street* or *Babbitt.*

> I hope they do award me the Pultizer prize on *Arrowsmith*—but you know, don't you, that ever since the *Main Street burglary*, I have planned that if they ever did award it to me, I would refuse it, with a polite but firm letter which I shall let the press have, and which ought to make it impossible for any one ever to accept the novel prize (not the play or history prize) thereafter without acknowledging themselves as willing to sell out.

When he did receive notice of the prize, he wrote his letter of refusal and sent it to Harcourt for comment, admitting that in a sense his act was "an asinine, fantastic, useless, expensive gesture, refusing this prize. But . . . I can do not other." The letter to the trustees, with the approval of Harcourt, stated at the end: "I invite other writers to consider the fact that by accepting the prizes and approval of these vague institutions, we are admitting their authority, publicly confirming them as the final judges of literary excellence, and I inquire whether any prize is worth that subservience." Harcourt's comment on the letter was: "You have done a perfect job and I am proud of you." A few commentators challenged Lewis as a publicity seeker, but most men of the pen respected his judgment. Lewis was satisfied with the reaction and asked Harcourt to pay De Kruif $250—which would have been his share of the prize.

In 1926 he was at the peak of prominence. The London *Mercury* declared: "His name is probably better known abroad than that of almost any other transatlantic writer. In a sense one might say that he overshadows almost all of his contemporaries." Yet at that very time Lewis felt rather deprecatory of himself as a writer: "I've already done my best work, and of that *Babbitt* will probably be rated my best book—though my own favorite will always be *Arrowsmith*." Some of the staff in the Harcourt firm, influenced by his frenetic behavior, began to assume that "Red is finished," for he was then not only breaking up his marriage but drinking to such excess that Harcourt had to take him to a private sanitarium for persons no longer able to control their consumption of liquor. He had great resilience, however, and after a week of treatment he seemed well and energetic.

In preparation for his next book he attended church services, read widely on religion, visited ministers of various denominations, lived with the Reverend W. L. Stidger for a fortnight in Kansas City, and remained in the city for more than two months with a view to experiencing the religious life of a typical midwestern community. As with *Arrowsmith*, he soon found an able research assistant in the Reverend L. M. Birkhead, and with his aid and encouragement he was not long in saturating his mind with the qualities and shortcomings of religious practices in the United States. He even preached in churches, and with a passion that was much appreciated by the parishioners. At one time he said, "I must stop this! I *could* have been a preacher."

With the research finished, he wrote *Elmer Gantry* with his usual concentration and zeal. The hypocrisy and cant of organized religion had aroused his indignation—"the book I wrote is what I saw"—and he dwelt on it with acidulous coldness. When the manuscript was ready, both Harcourt and Brace were enthusiastic over it. After suggesting that he tone down certain passages, Harcourt told him: "Although you may suspect it, you don't know what a great novel you have written." The preliminary publicity was very effective, and the advance sale came to 100,000 copies. The Book-of-the-Month Club adoption added another 40,000 copies to its early distribution. Suppression of the book in Boston accelerated interest in it in the rest of the nation. Some ministers condemned the novel, denouncing it as "slime," "venomous," "filthy." But most reviewers praised it highly, and the public bought it in greater numbers than it did *Babbitt*.

Now definitely separated from Grace and more restless than ever, Lewis sought diversion in Europe. On July 8, 1927, while in Berlin but planning to return to the United States, he met Dorothy Thompson, who had just been divorced from Josef Bard. She invited him to her birthday party, and that very evening he proposed marriage to her. Attracted to him yet held back by a sense of caution, she allowed him to court her with his characteristic intensiveness. In the meantime he had arranged with Grace to go to Reno for a divorce. Pursuing his ardent courtship, he persuaded Dorothy to join him in a walking tour in England. On their return to Berlin, Dorothy prepared to go to Moscow to attend the tenth anniversary of the Revolution. Lewis soon followed her there.

All this time he was preparing material for his next novel. In the interim, however, he wrote a 15,000-word monologue for *The American Mercury* entitled "The Man Who Knew Coolidge." It was a satiric portrayal of an absurd bore, and Lewis enjoyed writing it. "I love this sort of drool—and it'll be my swan song to Babbittism." Telling H. L. Mencken that he had decided to make a book of this "complete obscene imbecility," he informed Harcourt that he was adding sufficient additional monologues to make a book. The latter tried to stop him, urging him not to "force the new material to 50,000 words if it doesn't come naturally." Lewis, however, was not to be dissuaded and maintained that the book would sell 200,000 copies. When published in April 1928, many reviewers found the volume "dismal," and the sale was comparatively very small.

Meanwhile he was working on his long-planned novel, which he first called *Exile* but finally changed to *Dodsworth*. His courtship of Dorothy served to limit his drinking, so that his general health improved. To W. E. Woodward he wrote on January 12, 1928: "I have really managed the miraculous come-back which, a year ago, I didn't think I could possibly achieve. I feel better, more peaceful, more like working than I have for three or four years." Shortly thereafter he and Dorothy went to Italy for a holiday visit. When Grace was granted a divorce in April, Dorothy agreed to marry him. They went to England for the ceremony and then spent most of the summer on the road in the English countryside. In August they returned to the United States and were Harcourt's houseguests for a while. Soon after that they bought a farm house in Vermont and rented an apartment in New York.

After reading the first draft of *Dodsworth*, Harcourt began to publicize the book as the best Lewis had yet written. By December 5, when the final draft was finished, Lewis was physically exhausted and went with Dorothy to Florida for a rest. In February 1929, with his eagerness to be awarded the Nobel Prize rekindled by the expected success of his new book, Lewis wrote to Harcourt: "*Dodsworth* ought to go to my Swede publisher as early as possible." Late that year he confessed to Gardner Jackson that winning the Nobel Prize was his great hope in life.

Dodsworth was published in the spring of 1929. In view of the failure of the *Coolidge* book, the advance sale of 50,000 copies augured well for the popularity of this major novel. In the character of Dodsworth, Lewis portrayed the counterpart of Carol Kennicott; in Fran Dodsworth, modeled after Grace, he depicted his own restlessness and rootlessness. Reviewers liked the book, and the sale reached 85,000 copies by July. Having spent $6,000 on its promotion shortly after publication, Harcourt planned a similar expenditure in the fall—keeping Lewis's royalty at 10 percent during this period.

Lewis was also wishing that all his books were receiving additional promotion. Having spent large sums of money on remodeling his Vermont house, he felt poor. And when Jonathan Cape informed him in May that he was planning to reissue his novels in a five-shilling edition, he brought that to Harcourt's attention:

> Jonathan writes me that he is thinking of getting out a five shilling collected edition of my books. It seems to me that we ought, with the Bacon illustrated *Babbitt* as a beginning, to think of something of the same sort. I believe we could get more out of (at least) *Main Street*, *Babbitt* and *Arrowsmith*, than we are now, just having them to be buried among the Zane Grey books in the G & D collections. Let's talk it over.

Harcourt's response was mildly agreeable:

> I am digging out just what Grosset & Dunlap have been doing with the old books. I have some ideas of my own about a scheme for handling all cheap editions, which I

think will ripen in the course of the year, and which, if it does ripen, will interest you almost as much as it does us. I'll save that to talk about when we meet.

The two discussed the matter during the next several months. In August, Harcourt wondered if it would not be better to wait until sales improved. Lewis was agreeable, but suggested that Dorothy obtain prefaces from prominent persons and have the books appear in more costly library editions. "After months of thinking," he wrote, "it seems to me more important to make this a really fine edition—say $3.00 or $3.50 a volume, or even more—rather than a five shilling edition like Jonathan's. The cheap edition can, however, come later, if this goes over."

Harcourt, on his part, doubted the practicality of an expensive edition:

We can't see a library set of your books now—that is, at $3.00 or $3.50 a volume. . . . About what we call for the sake of definition the $1.25 set to be printed on good thinner paper and bound nicely, looking a good deal like the Cape edition but with introductions, we are ready to do that whenever you are ready.

Lewis agreed to the compromise and urged quick action. While in Vermont that summer he received a letter from a young Harcourt editor about an article on him by Paul Morand. Lewis asked that the article be translated and offered to *The Saturday Review of Literature*. After he had done so, the editor informed him that "nobody had fallen for it." This brash phrase, plus being addressed as "Red" by someone he hardly knew, outraged Lewis. On the impulse he tried to reach Harcourt by telephone to express his annoyance, and when he failed to find him anywhere his anger was intensified by the recollection that Harcourt had done nothing on the collected edition. Tempted to break with him at once, he was persuaded to wait until he had a new novel ready. Yet his resentment against the firm's treatment of him continued to rankle. For the less confident he became of his literary powers, the more demanding was his puffed egotism, so that he needed confirmation of his greatness more and more.

He was in this state of agitation when news reached him early in November 1930 that he had been awarded the Nobel Prize for Literature. Somewhat earlier Harcourt had heard that the award was to go to an American writer—to Dreiser or Lewis—but he had kept the information from Lewis for fear that he might spoil his chances by some impulsive statement. Now that the news was official, Harcourt and others flocked to congratulate him.

Lewis and Dorothy went to Stockholm to receive the award. Lewis's speech of acceptance, critical of conventional established writers and favorable to the newer and less orthodox ones—Thomas Wolfe in particular—had a mixed reception in the United States. Some critics even questioned the committee's judgment.

Harcourt was of course enthusiastic, and cabled: "Warmest congratulations. Splendid speech." Lewis was not mollified. He wanted Harcourt to express this enthusiasm concretely in an extraordinary act of promotion that would acclaim Lewis as the first American novelist to be awarded the Nobel Prize, thus furthering the sale of his books. When little evidence of such promotion reached him, he felt that Harcourt had let him down.

In addition to his own grievances he now recalled Dorothy's attack against Harcourt's financial practices. Having examined his royalty statement of May 1930, she was outraged to find that the firm had long been taking unfair advantage of Lewis's financial laxity, especially in connection with foreign editions of his books. "Hal," she wrote him, "what Harcourt and his agents have been taking out of your foreign books and serial rights and still are, is scandalous." Hardheaded journalist that she was, she saw no reason for Harcourt appropriating a third of his foreign royalties; for taking 10 percent of movie fees when Lewis's agent Ann Watkins was already charging him that. What angered her especially was to note that on some foreign rights Harcourt deducted a third in addition to 10 percent for Lewis's later agent, Curtis Brown, and another 10 percent to a foreign agent. Her position shared by established writers whom she had consulted, she wrote Lewis:

> I don't see where Harcourt on these deals is contributing anything at all. It seems to me 20% to two agents ought to be sufficient to place your work. Why in hell you should have to pay 33-1/3% commission on German serial rights of Mantrap is more than I can see.
>
> But when we come to Dodsworth that I get maddest because I thought you had changed all of this with Dodsworth. On the English rights Harcourt is only taking 10%. But I don't understand the French & the Czechoslovakian editions. On the French & C-S editions of Dodsworth you are paying 20% commission (to whom not indicated) plus a 25% commission to Harcourt—in all 45% of your total royalties, low anyway, *in* commissions! . . . Babbitt, Arrowsmith, and Dodsworth are likely to go on selling abroad indefinitely—and will Harcourt always and eternally, take 1/3 of your royalties.

After brooding over the matter for several weeks, he wrote Harcourt from London on January 21, 1931:

> I have the impression, and the impression is backed up by too many facts to be merely fanciful, that the firm of Harcourt, Brace & Co., and you personally, feel that they have just about done their duty by Sinclair Lewis. And I feel that I have just about done my duty by Harcourt, Brace & Co. I am sure that you have for some time known how I feel. My outburst to you at lunch at my flat last spring was a sign of it. If I hadn't felt so tied to the firm, by the fact that we all began our careers together, I would have been more definite then, though also, probably, more polite. . . . To put it brutally, I feel that the firm has let me down, let my books down, in regard to the prize award. It seems to me that you failed to revive the sale of my books as you might have and that, aside from this commercial aspect, you let me down as an author by not getting over to the people of the United States the way in which the rest of the world greeted the award.

Harcourt, strangely, and perhaps not so strangely, made no effort at a reconciliation. On February 3 he returned the unfulfilled contracts and wrote:

> I know you have some idea of how sorry I am that events have taken this turn. You and we have been so closely associated in our youth and growth that I wish we

might have gone the rest of the way together. If I've lost an author, you haven't lost either a friend or a devoted reader.

When it became known that Lewis had broken with the Harcourt firm, several publishers sought to sign him up. Dorothy, from Germany, wrote to him in London to caution him against making an undesirable publishing arrangement:

> Hal—you can't go to Hearst. Not for a million ... if you do it, it will be a terrific disappointment to your real friends. Your novel will be a study of American Idealism and the people who really love you and appreciate your work—Ben [Huebsch] and Lewis Gannett and FPA [Adams]—will simply receive the book under the worst possible impression.... Several people here who've had experience with American publishing say "don't go to Viking—swell people but no sales organization." I think we ought to do a little investigation at home. Anyway, I know you won't close, until we're both home.

One of the publishers who was tempted to approach Lewis was Alfred A. Knopf. Before doing so, he consulted with H. L. Mencken: "I don't honestly believe that a publisher would have any difficulty with Red over finances. But to have him camp on your doorstep and talk endlessly would, of course, be quite another matter." Mencken, who knew Lewis well, responded: "I suggest offering him a reasonable advance, *payable when he completes the manuscript.* If you don't make that condition he may never complete it at all."

Before Knopf had decided what to do, Nelson Doubleday had gone to London to see Lewis and offered him terms and conditions agreeable to him. The contract was signed later in Garden City. Among the terms contained in it was an advance of $25,000 on Lewis's next novel and an agreement to spend a similar amount on its promotion. A royalty of 15 percent was to be paid on the sale of the first 60,000 copies, and an increased royalty thereafter. Lewis was in good spirits on the occasion and told Doubleday: "I like you. You're so God-damned commercial." His editor became Harry Maule, with whom he remained when he left Doubleday to join Random House.

Once the excitement of the Nobel Award wore off and the change of publishers was arranged to his satisfaction, Lewis again felt the gnawing restlessness that led him to excessive drinking. His inflated yet unstable ego was deeply troubled by Dorothy's spirited career. She was widely in demand as a lecturer on current affairs, her friends were legion and among world leaders, and her obiter dicta on international politics were highly respected. Thus, not only did her prominence overshadow his, but her activities carried her away from him much of the time. Yearning for her presence, depressed, he tended to drink to allay his loneliness.

Shortly after their return from Europe in March 1931, Lewis attended a dinner given in honor of the Russian writer Boris Pilnyak. Theodore Dreiser was also there. He and Dorothy had both published books resulting from their visit to Russia, and each had accused the other of plagiarism by having used verbatim material given to both, as stated earlier, by Anna Louise Strong when they were in Moscow. When Lewis was invited to speak, he rose and said: "I do not care to speak in the presence of a man who has stolen three thousand words from my wife's book, and before two sage critics who have lamented the action of the Nobel prize committee in selecting me as America's representative writer." At the end of the dinner Dreiser asked him to step into a side room and repeat the accusation. Lewis did, and Dreiser slapped him. It is of interest to note that Lewis did not let this personal assault keep him from praising Dreiser as a writer in a lecture he delivered in Washington soon after. And in 1944 he strove zealously, and successfully, in behalf of Dreiser being awarded the gold medal for literature by the Academy of Arts and Letters.

All this time Lewis was working on *Ann Vickers* and completed the writing in August 1931. It was serialized in *Red Book*, and Doubleday published it the following January. Lewis cooperated with the sales staff on its promotion. A novel feature was the printing of a first edition of 2,350 copies, with the idea of giving one copy to booksellers with every order for 25 copies of the trade edition. Aided by many favorable reviews, the novel sold 133,849 copies—being for a time the leading best seller. The book was also issued simultaneously in thirteen languages and sixteen countries.

Lewis's restlessness increased at the awareness that his marriage to Dorothy was a failure. He admired her prestigious position as a journalist; but much as he continued to love her he could not reconcile himself to her greater popularity. Unable to cope with this problem, he drank and traveled to Europe and back, feeling lonely and depressed. From Portofino, where Dorothy was at the time, she wrote him that his excessive drinking was becoming too difficult to put up with:

> It seemed to me that our life together was falling into exactly the pattern of your life with Grace: that it would move in the same direction and to the same dénoument, and that nothing I could do would help you stop it.... I really tried hard not to love you, I confess it. I have been too hurt in my life, Hal, to dare even to think of being hurt in the same way again. Only it wouldn't be the same way now, but much, much worse.

In New York, Lewis was at work on a novel dealing with hotels. He had the assistance of young Louis Florey, and made meticulously detailed notes about the places and persons he was to treat in the narrative. He took a trip to the West Coast, then went to his farm in Vermont, where he worked on the book, *Work of Art*, and waited for Dorothy's arrival from Europe. He had stopped drinking hard liquor and was making good progress on the writing. When the novel was finished, the Doubleday firm promoted it vigorously, but reviewers found it lacking in distinction—a "fantasy of the perfect Rotarian"—and its sale ceased after 50,000 copies.

The relative failure of the novel in a year when Hervey Allen's *Anthony Adverse* achieved exceptional popularity, intensified Lewis's troubled restlessness. As Schorer pointed out: "His problems were no doubt multiple, but chief among them was his need for adulation that cost him nothing in responsibility." His drinking again increased; his quarrels with Dorothy sent him in a rage which made him feel guilty as soon as he cooled off. Dorothy, unwilling to break with him, yet distressed by his "pathological drinking," told him: "I suffer intensely from it as every one about you does, because when you are drunk you act exactly like an insane person. . . . What I blame you for is that you show no disposition to want to be cured, as I believe you could be if you wanted to."

Although a decade earlier he had rejected membership in the National Institute of Arts and Letters, he now readily accepted it, and two years later he was elected to the Academy. In 1935 his ego was bolstered by the successful dramatization of *Dodsworth*, but soon suffered from the relative failure of *Selected Short Stories*.

When he learned that some German booksellers refused to handle his books because his name appeared in an anti-Nazi periodical, he decided to stop publishing his books in Germany. His German publisher, in sympathy with his stand, cabled: "I will inform the German book trade of [your decision] in order to let them see that there are still men among writers."

The incident stimulated him to devote his next book to the subject of fascism in the United States. With dedicated concentration he worked on this novel, entitled *It Can't Happen Here*, seven days a week, finishing the manuscript in August 1935. In the political treatment of fascism he was greatly influenced by Dorothy's preoccupation with it. The book was published in October and quickly succeeded as a *cause célèbre*. Reviewers were affected more by its political "shock" than by its literary merit. Doubleday promoted it energetically, and in time it sold 320,000 copies. The novel was dramatized by Lewis and a collaborator and was produced by the Federal Theater in eighteen cities.

Despite Dorothy's unwillingness to break with Lewis, time only worsened their relationship. His diatribes against her when drunk she was able to endure only by concentrating on her work—and this angered him the more. In this state of frustration, he sought diversion in acting in *It Can't Happen Here* and in *Angela is Twenty-two*, which he wrote at that time. While in the theater, he met Rosemary Marcella Powers, a stagestruck girl of eighteen. She attracted him at once—being pretty, naïve, uncritical, ready to adore him, and a person whom he could love without threatening his freedom of movement. She let him take charge of her career and was willingly his mistress. For nearly a year he helped her get parts in plays and enjoyed their intimacy. Then he left her, drank heavily—at one time having to be put into a straitjacket until he sobered—but soon after returned to her.

In the summer of 1939 he finished *Prodigal Parents* by a rigorous effort of will, temporarily giving up drinking after breaking a rib from a fall while in delirium tremens. When the novel was published, a number of reviewers considered it "shockingly bad" yet Doubleday's vigorous promotion resulted in the sale of around 100,000 copies. His next book, *Bethel Merriday*, which he wrote soon after, was the least successful of his novels since *Free Air*, selling around 33,000 copies, plus another 50,000 from a book club adoption and reprints. Significantly, the book was reviewed by second-string critics, as if it was the work of a novelist of minor importance.

In 1941, when Harry Maule left Doubleday to join Random House, Lewis no longer felt at home with the firm. In September he wrote Nelson Doubleday: "You have not the slightest interest in me, nor in my novels as anything more than items on your sales list. All this past year I have felt as though I had no publisher at all." He thereupon severed relations with the company and arranged for Random House to publish his future work.

Continuing to drink heavily, increasingly restless, he began to insist on a divorce from Dorothy. When she tried to delay the final rupture, he told her that they hadn't been living together for the past four and a half years and that he wanted to be free of her. "You say that your highest desire was that 'our marriage should be productive—creative.' Well, to my powers of creation it has been disastrous. That is why I want it broken, before it is too tragically late." Thereupon she instituted proceedings and was granted a divorce on January 2, 1942.

In the meantime Lewis began working on *Gideon Planish*, a satirical treatment of charlatans. He had become very sensitive to the sound of his prose and had his new editor, the discerning and sympathetic Saxe Commins, read the manuscript aloud to him to make sure of the verbal authenticity. When Random House published the novel in April 1943, reviewers reacted negatively and some pointed out that the vocabulary was dated. "The blame," one stated, "may lie with a world that has moved faster than Mr. Lewis." Yet Random House gave it vigorous promotion and managed to sell around 50,000 copies.

In the grip of a hectic restlessness, Lewis rented a large apartment in New York, spent $10,000 furnishing it, and used it for large parties and numerous houseguests. In May 1944 he went to Minnesota to obtain material for his new novel, *Cass Timberlane*, and remained there till late August. He completed the manuscript that fall and spent many hours going over it editorially with Commins. In the story Cass Timberlane behaves somewhat like Lewis—an older man making love to a young girl—but the narrative had inherent popularity. It was serialized in *Cosmopolitan* and was a selection of the Book-of-the-Month Club—the two arrangements yielding him fees amounting to $125,000. In addition Lewis received an advance of a quarter of a million dollars for the movie rights from M-G-M, as well as considerable amounts for foreign rights. In all editions the sale exceeded a million copies. All this did not allay his unhappiness, and Schorer epitomized it: "In February he was sixty years old and often in despair of himself, sunk in fits of melancholy that even a birthday dinner *à deux* with Miss Powers at the Chambord could not very long dispel."

Settling in 1946 on a farm near Williamstown, Massachusetts, he began to write *Kingsblood Royal*. He finished the first draft in five weeks and spent the remainder of the summer revising it. Then for a week Commins and he edited it before it was sent to the printer. As was his habit, he had made a thorough study of Negro and interracial relations, talking to many blacks and reading widely in the literature. The main character, a respected young banker, makes it known that he has a small fraction of Negro blood and is treated shabbily by the community as a consequence. Reviewers were sympathetic but indicated that the story was sociological rather than a work of creative fiction. The controversy aroused by them helped Random House in its promotion, and the jacket copy proclaimed it to be "a blazing story with a theme that will jolt the nation." The Literary Guild, then near the height of its popularity, distributed nearly three-quarters of a million copies; the regular edition sold upward of 115,000 copies; and reprints helped to make the total upward of 1,500,000 copies. *Ebony*, the Negro periodical, gave it an award for having done most to advance interracial understanding in 1947.

Lewis was by now artistically spent. Although he persisted in his writing, it was largely to maintain the illusion of his literary distinction and not because he needed to express an inner artistic urge. He returned to his labor novel, on which he had in the past done much planning and research, but was unable to come to grips with it and turned his attention to life in Minnesota of the 1840s. He labored zealously on this book, producing a plan that extended to 110,000 words. When he finished the manuscript, named *The God-Seeker*, he and Commins spent five days editing it. For all this effort, however, the novel was feeble both technically and as a work of fiction. As Schorer indicated: "He had probably never worked so hard, certainly never to such little point." Reviewers were either lukewarm or severely critical, and its sale was relatively small.

While in Italy, Lewis received a letter from Jonathan Cape in which the English publisher was critical of *The God-Seeker*. Deeply irritated—Cape had disliked the previous novel as well—Lewis responded in anger: "When you wrote me about *Kingsblood Royal*, I didn't say anything, I just said to myself, 'That's only Jonathan.' But now you have gone too far, and I wouldn't let you have this novel if you wanted it." And to Frere-Reeves of Heinemann he wrote of Cape's "condescending jocularity . . . regarding my new book . . . *God-Seeker* may be the best book I have ever written. It is certainly the most serious."

Yet he inwardly knew better, and resorted to intensive drinking in an effort to quiet this nagging awareness. On his return to his farm in Massachusetts he became ill with penumonia; and although he recovered fairly soon, it was in a sense the beginning of the end.

Sometime earlier, while still in Italy, he decided to write a novel about an American girl in Europe and her relations with expatriate Americans. When Harry Maule visited him, the two discussed the projected book and agreed upon a contract. The serial rights were sold to *Cosmopolitan*. On completing the manuscript of *Over the Body of Lucy Jade*, he was told by the editor of the magazine that it was unacceptable. Both Maule and Bennett Cerf found it lacking in merit, but their suggested modifications were angrily rejected by Lewis. He denounced Random House, grew very depressed, and drank himself into delirium tremens. On recovery he dropped the manuscript and arranged with his brother Claude for a tour of Italy. By that time he was suffering from polyneuritis, which settled in his legs. His face looked ravaged, and his hands shook with palsy.

This physical debility notwithstanding, he began writing *World So Wide.* In January 1950 he wrote his English publisher that it would "deal with the Anglo-American colony here, especially with an American who is lured from the sensible security of money-making into the sick-sweet perils of scholarship." What he actually did was to use some of the material from *Lucy Jade* to produce a somewhat improved version of the rejected manuscript. It is of interest to note that in it his characters talked very much like those in his early novels. When it was serialized in *Woman's Home Companion* and published posthumousiy, it read like a parodied version of *Babbitt* and *Dodsworth.*

Lewis had his first heart attack in 1950. Later in the year, while in Zurich, he suffered two more attacks five days apart. On recovery he returned to Rome, and there he died on January 10, 1951.

26.

Harper & Brothers
&
Edna St.Vincent Millay

Edna St. Vincent Millay's early poems, and particularly the "Fig" verses which included the "candle" quatrain, made her, in the words of her first biographer, Elizabeth Atkins, "the unrivaled embodiment of sex appeal, the It-girl of the hour, the Miss America of 1920." Vincent Sheean, a close friend, was more discerning in commenting on the effect of the evocative quatrain:

> These lines were caught up and quoted, or more usually misquoted, by every jejune hedonist of the rebellious era, every girl or boy who wanted to experiment with the recently discovered benefits of alcohol, sexual experience, or simply late hours, and wild talk. . . . And the immediate, inevitable consequence was that Edna herself became symbol, legend, almost standard-bearer, for a social upheaval which was in reality outside her interest.

Edna St. Vincent Millay was born in Rockland, Maine, on February 22, 1892, and grew up in nearby Camden. Her mother added "St. Vincent" to the name of her first-born because her brother was at the time a patient in St. Vincent Hospital; and for much of her life she was called "Vincent" by her close friends.

A precocious child, she began composing verses in her fifth year. Although a tomboy, she also read Shakespeare with sensual delight in her eighth year. For years she read *St. Nicholas Magazine* and was a member of its League. Her first poem appeared in the magazine in October 1906; three more poems were printed the following year, and one of them was awarded a prize of five dollars. She continued to publish verses in the periodical until she became too old for membership in the League on reaching her sixteenth birthday.

Her parents were divorced when she was nine because her mother refused to suffer the consequences of her husband's uncontrolled gambling. A person of strong will and considerable ability, Mrs. Millay managed to support and educate her three daughters, who remained on good terms with their father. And when he became severely ill years later, Edna went to his bedside to care for him.

Edna St. Vincent Millay was eighteen when she began writing "Renascence." Some time later, Mrs. Millay saw the announcement of a poetry contest with $1,000 in prizes and publication of the best poems in book form. Proud of her daughter's poetic gift, she urged her to submit "Renascence" to the contest. Around 10,000 poems were submitted, but the editor of the volume, Ferdinand Earle, was so impressed with Edna's poem that he wrote to tell her so and intimated that it would be awarded first prize of $500. In the end, however, he was outvoted by the two other judges.

The volume, *The Lyric Year*, was published by Mitchell Kennerley in 1912, marking the year as "the dawn of the poetic renaissance" in the United States; a statement attested by the establishment of the magazine *Poetry*. Soon after the book's appearance a number of readers maintained that "Renascence" should have received first prize because it was the finest poem in the volume. Arthur Davison Ficke and Witter Bynner, youthful Harvard classmates and intimate friends, whose poems were also included in the volume, were so strongly impressed by the poem's freshness and originality that they wrote the editor that it "really lights up the whole book. . . . Are you at liberty to name the author? The little item about her in the back of the book is a marvel of humor. No sweet young thing of twenty ever ended a poem precisely where this one ends: it takes a brawny male of forty-five to do that."

When the letter was forwarded to Millay, she replied: "I simply will not be a 'brawny male.' Not that I have an aversion to brawny males; *au contraire, au contraire.* But I cling to my femininity." This started a correspondence and lifelong friendship with both. When Ficke asked her if "she got it from a book?", she replied sharply: "I never get anything from a book. I see things with my own eyes, just as if they were the first eyes that ever saw, and then I set about to tell, as best I can, just what I see."

Somewhat earlier she had read the poem before a group of summer guests at a local hotel in Camden. Caroline Dow, of the New York YWCA, was so moved by the poem that she offered to help Millay with the money to defray the expenses of a Vassar education. In January 1913 Millay went to New York to take preliminary courses at Barnard College. In the city she met other poets and was befriended by Mitchell Kennerley, who offered to publish a volume of her verses. This she discreetly postponed, and to her family she wrote on April 18, 1913: "Mr. Kennerley wants me to let him publish a volume of my stuff but I don't believe that's a very wise thing." She did, however, let him publish some of her poems in *The Forum*, which he edited. When he sent her a check for twenty-five dollars for two poems—the only money she ever received from him—she sent it on to her mother.

Entering Vassar in the fall of 1913, she was soon behaving with a freedom and unconventionality that perturbed, and at times outraged, some of the staid members of the faculty. More than once in trouble, she managed to extricate herself and complete her education, and make a reputation as a poet and actress.

When Kennerley persuaded her to let him publish her first volume, *Renascence and Other Poems*, he promised to give her an advance of $500. Although he took her to expensive restaurants, he ignored her requests for the advance, and later did not even answer her demands for the payment of royalty. Nevertheless she was gratified by the highly favorable reception of the book.

On graduation from Vassar, Millay sought work as an actress, but all she could get were brief engagements in little theaters. She did, however, publish a poem in every issue of *Ainslee's Magazine* during 1919 as well as a number of prose pieces under the name of Nancy Boyd. Affected by the strong anti-war atmosphere in her Greenwich Village environment, she wrote the pacifist play, *Aria da Capo*, which was produced by the Provincetown Players in December 1919. Its high merit was later commented on in *The Provincetown*: "The play's beauty, its subtle mingling of satire and lyricism, and the excellence of the production marked it immediately as the best presentation of the year." Subsequently it was also produced in colleges and little theaters over the country. In 1920 *Reedy's Mirror* published the play as well as a number of her sonnets, thus greatly enhancing her reputation. And in May of that year she was awarded a prize of one hundred dollars by *Poetry* for one of her poems.

Millay's vibrant personality and delicate beauty appealed to many young men of her acquaintance. Witter Bynner, Floyd Dell, John Peale Bishop, and Edmund Wilson were among those who courted her. She liked them all, but Ficke attracted her deeply. Twice she told him so in letters—which he never answered despite his affection for her, feeling overpowered by her personality; he remained close to her all his life, but he married another. Millay accepted this relationship as best she could, though she told him they "would never escape from each other." In 1945, when she learned that he was dying of cancer, she wrote him that she would have given him her love, but she had done that long ago; in the same letter she admitted having denied that she had written a love sonnet to him because she did not want him to know "how terribly, how sickeningly in love" with him she had been at the time.

For a time after World War I Edmund Wilson was assistant editor of *Vanity Fair*, and at his urging Millay became a frequent contributor of poems as well as prose pieces, "Distressing Dialogues," under the signature of Nancy Boyd. In 1921 Wilson arranged for her to go to Europe as the magazine's foreign correspondent—her two monthly articles paying her expenses. To her mother she wrote that she was accepting the assignment because she wanted to travel.

From the first, editorial tinkering with her writing infuriated her. When she suspected that Frank Crowingshield, editor of *Vanity Fair*, was making changes in her material under her name, she wrote Wilson that she did not want a single word altered: "Don't let Crownie do anything to anything that's signed by my own name—as for Nancy, that's a little different."

While in Paris she wrote *The Lamp and the Bell*, a play Elizabethan in form, which was produced at Vassar in June 1921. She also accepted an advance of $500 from Boni & Liveright for a novel, *Hardigut*, which she never actually completed, but which gave her the means to provide her mother with a longed-for trip to Europe. As late as November 1922 she still fully intended to write the novel, and stated to Liveright: "The book will be amusing, satiric, ugly, beautiful, poetic, and an unmistakable allegory." Ill health, however, finally caused her to abandon the project.

Renascence being a notable success, Kennerly urged Millay to prepare another volume of poems. Despite her annoyance with his postponement of royalties, she gave him the manuscript for *Second April*. By then, however, he was in financial involvements that led to his insolvency, and he kept postponing publication. Meanwhile she let Frank Shay in 1920 bring out a paperback chapbook, *Salvo*, containing some of her poems under the title of "Figs from Thistles." One of the poems included the "candle" quatrain.

Kennerley's delaying tactics continued to irritate her. To Bynner she complained on October 29, 1920:

> My book isn't out yet. It's dreadful. I write Mitchell all the time, and he won't answer my letters; and every time I call up the office they tell me he is out, and I know darn well he is so near the telephone all the time that I can hear his breathing. I had no communication from him whatsoever since last May. Isn't it frightful?

Kennerley managed to publish *Second April* in 1921, and the volume was applauded by most reviewers. On September 14 Millay wrote to her mother from Europe:

> Mitchell Kennerley, or his secretary, has sent me a great sheaf of clippings, reviews of *Second April*, exceedingly good. They have received the book very well, much to my astonishment. It is not so good as it should have been, actually. But I am glad, as long as I myself am not taken in, that it is selling, and pleasing, and that I shall not be in disfavor at the time of the appearance of my next book, which is going to be darn good.

In another letter to her mother she explained why "The Ballad of the Harp-Weaver" was the only poem she had written since coming to Europe:

> That was just what I wanted, you know, not to write a word of poetry for a year. When it begins to get a little *easy*, or when one begins to write in certain forms almost from habit, it is time to stop for a while, I think, & almost forget that one is a poet—become a prose writer, for instance—and then let it all come back to one later, fresh, and possibly in a newer form.

In April 1922 Frank Shay brought out "The Ballad of the Harp-Weaver" in pamphlet form. In the same year an expanded edition of "A Few Figs" plus eight additional sonnets were included in *American Miscellany of Poetry*. This brought her the Pulitzer Prize for Poetry in 1923—the first woman to receive that award.

With Kennerley's firm in bankruptcy, Edna St. Vincent Millay was delighted with the offer of Harper & Brothers to publish new editions of her printed verse as well as a volume of new poems as soon as she had one ready. She was then still quite ill with intestinal trouble developed during her sojourn in Europe, but she exerted herself to complete a group of poems. These and others were published in 1923 under the title of *The Harp-Weaver and Other Poems*, much to her enhanced reputation.

She was thirty-one years old when she married Eugen Boissevain, who was, ironically, introduced to her by Ficke, whom she had not ceased to love. The morning after the wedding she entered the hospital for major surgery which, while successful, left her very weak for some time. During this period of convalescence she let Ficke read the proofs of the new book.

Boissevain was of Dutch birth and education. He became an importer when he decided to settle in New York. A big-bodied man, twelve years older than Edna, previously married, and natually jovial and easy-going, he proved admirably suited to the mercurial and agonizingly self-critical poet. He at once dedicated himself to her person and work, soon abandoning his business career in order to give all his time to her affairs. As Vincent Sheean stated: "He served and guarded Edna like a priest of a temple. He cooked, washed dishes, kept house, was gardener and chauffeur, business manager, banker, engineer, and everything else, besides lover and husband and the best friend she ever had." In 1925 the two bought a farm near Austerlitz, New York, which they named Steepletop. Edna thought it "one of the loveliest places in the world" and made it her home to the end of her life.

In 1924 she published *Distressing Dialogues*, the prose pieces she had previously printed in magazines under the Nancy Boyd pseudonym, with a preface signed with her own name.

Early in 1926 she agreed to write the libretto for the opera, *The King's Henchman*, for which Deems Taylor was commissioned by the Metropolitan Opera Company to compose the music. It was as a result of his experience in this collaboration that Taylor later stated: "She was ruthlessly self-critical, and would agonize for days over a simple, imperfect line." The opera, produced the following year, proved a success, and the libretto itself went through nineteen printings.

With this assignment out of the way, Edna Millay began to concentrate on the completion of the poems for *The Buck in the Snow*. With her popularity steadily increasing, Harper's planned to issue a limited edition as well as a trade edition. Learning that Crosby Gaige had asked her for an arrangement to issue limited editions of her books, Eugene Saxton, her Harper editor, wrote Boissevain, who was handling most of her correspondence:

> Since the time Miss Millay came to Harper's, our constant effort has been to establish the entire body of her works with the book trade in the unique position it deserves. And the success of the books has been so remarkable that we hope nothing will be done to weaken our position as her authorized publishers.

Millay agreed that this arrangement was best and decided that she no longer needed an agent. "Therefore any future contracts between you and me should be referred to me directly." And in another letter, refusing an advance, Boissevain told Saxton: "I am delighted to be put in a position that I can crow over Harper & Brothers. So often we have been delinquent on our side."

When the question of royalty on the new book came up, Eugene Saxton told Miss Millay that while the firm was pleased to give her 20 percent on the limited edition, he could offer her only 15 percent on the trade edition. "20%" he pointed out, "allows only a narrow margin and we think it would entail a serious loss to both of us if we did not have margin enough to do the various things that are necessary to stimulate the interest of the bookseller and the public." He did propose an increase to 20 percent after the sale of 25,000 copies. Agreeing to this arrangement, Boissevain wrote: "It is awfully decent of you to suggest an increase of royalty after the first 25,000."

Several months later, furthering the feeling of friendliness between them, Saxton wrote:

> I want to talk over with you a new project we are discussing of a limited edition of all your volumes, hand set on some beautiful face and printed on large paper. This is a project in which we should want to enlist the services of an expert like Bruce Rogers and the books would be a fine example of book making. The volumes might come out one at a time over the period of a year.

Millay and Boissevain were of course delighted. Two weeks later, intent on cementing this relationship, Saxton wrote again for assurance to enable the firm become "a hundred percent effective in building up a great property for you." This assurance, he suggested, should be given in the form of contracts for several books "or by a general agreement that we are to publish all your books in the future upon definite terms." He concluded his letter by asserting: "There are no books on the Harper list that are published with more pride than yours." Boissevain replied for his wife:

> She hates contracts. The way things are now she would stay with Harper's contract or no contract. Still if you would like it she is perfectly willing to sign a contract for the next two books. . . . I can assure you that she would not be likely to leave your publishing house, as she fully realizes the advantage of having one publisher and the disadvantages of changing.

Almost fanatically concerned about the perfection of her poems, Millay could not bear to let anyone see verses not yet in finished form. When the Harper firm was preparing the promotion material for the forthcoming *The Buck in the Snow*, Saxton asked for several poems to be used in a dummy for the salesmen. Her reaction was one of consternation. As Boissevain reported it: "You have thrown Miss Millay in a panic. . . . Why, my good Sir, the new poems are not yet written! At best they are half written, or two thirds written, or even seven eighths written." And he suggested that the firm use the poems already printed in magazines.

When the book was published in September 1928, its serious tone disappointed some of her early admirers, but the popularity of this book was extraordinary—40,000 copies were sold in three months! And the limited edition was quickly oversubscribed.

The following July, highly gratified by Millay's wide readership, Saxton sought to consolidate their relationship still further:

As I said to you in our talk a year ago, we want to have your advice and approval of whatever we do with your books, past and future. . . . And since you know that we genuinely want to do what you want done, you can be sure that we shall not take amiss any suggestions or criticisms you want to make. We are tremendously proud of your books and we want all details in connection with them to be on the basis of friend to friend.

This relationship was indeed strengthened from year to year, despite occasional outbursts of temper. Saxton tried hard to please her, and she generally appreciated the firm's efforts to maximize her income from royalties. For she tended, or was forced, to spend money with a freedom not always justified by her income. Thus, although her royalties in 1929 were $25,194.60, and her additional earnings from magazines and public readings were considerable, she was short of money that year. When she was in Paris that April she cabled: "Cable please fifteen hundred dollars . . . am stranded." Two years later she wrote Saxton: "Can Harper's advance me three thousand on my royalties—I'm broke again, of course; I don't know how it happens, but there we are." And in February 1933 she asked for an advance of $500: "I need it like the very deuce—as usual." Again in February 1935 she cabled from Cuba: "I'm broke please send five hundred airmail care American Council Habana Cuba."

Edna St. Vincent Millay's *Fatal Interview*, published in May 1931, was a series of fifty-two sonnets about a perturbed yet fervid love affair; its sincerity and universality were readily appreciated, and its musical quality heightened the emotional experience. The volume was highly praised, and although it appeared in the depth of economic depression it in time sold over 55,000 copies.

Always very much concerned about the appearance of her books, she had definite ideas for the format of the play, *The Princess Marries the Page.* Reacting to the illustrations suggested by the firm's production department, she wrote Saxton:

Woodblocks won't do at all. The play is too slight to be printed so seriously. What I really want—and if it is too expensive just now to bring it out this way, then I would really rather wait, I think, until everybody has more money—what I really want is a big, flat book perhaps 14 by 10 with many colored illustrations, pictures of the Princess, the Page, etc. . . . I want the book to be a Christmas gift book and as gaudy as a Christmas tree.

Acknowledging the receipt of the manuscript of *Wine from these Grapes* on July 20, 1934, Saxton wrote:

I delayed this letter for a day or two until I had an opportunity to go over the book, and it is difficult to tell you how deeply the poems have moved me, particularly the sonnet sequence which I have now seen for the first time in rounded form. I do indeed congratulate you.

The final section of the book, entitled "Epitaph for the Race of Man," particularly impressed critics with its boldness of imagination and beauty of form. Some years later Max Eastman expressed a widely held opinion of this group of poems: "Brief as it is, it is the only poem in the language since Milton that can be compared in mental boldness with Dante and Lucretius."

Published in November, the volume sold 37,784 copies during the first three months; together with the continued sale of her other books, her royalties for the period were relatively large. Aware of her financial condition and of her need for periodic encouragement, Saxton again wrote to assure her of the firm's desire, so far as her books were concerned, "to get the greatest return over the longest period, with the maximum of enthusiasm and a format worthy of the text. Our interests are one in this." As evidence of the firm's good will, he informed her that thereafter her royalties were to rise to 20 percent after the first 5,000 copies.

In 1935 George Dillon, a scholarly poet Millay admired, asked her to write an introduction to his projected translation of Baudelaire's *Les Fleurs du Mal.* Agreeing to do so, she soon found herself so interested in the problems of translation that before long she became his collaborator. She even went to France in order to familiarize herself with Baudelaire's birthplace. Because she was the more prominent of the two, Dillon, who had expected The Viking Press to publish the volume, yielded to the Harper claim of publishing all of Millay's writings.

Once the translation was finished, Millay concerned herself with the proper format of the book. When the sample pages were submitted to her, she approved of the typeface and the appearance of the facing pages but objected to what she considered the overcrowded page. Urging a reduction of the number of stanzas on each page, she claimed that otherwise the pages "won't look handsome at all, except of course to pure artists like Mr. Rushmore, who are interested only in making up a thrillingly beautiful page, and don't give a darn whether or not anybody is ever going to read the words in it."

Although Arthur Rushmore, a type expert and head of the production department, did his best to meet her wishes, problems arose in the proofreading which annoyed her. On December 25, 1935, she wrote Dillon:

> It is obvious that Harper & Bros. are trying to kill us, so that they'll never have to have anything to do with either of us again. You will have noticed that when they give us a week's extension they give the printers a fortnight. . . . I'm perfectly furious with them.

Two weeks later she complained to Saxton about the firm's niggardliness with sets of proofs as well as with the time given for proofreading:

> It all comes down to this: you have your troubles; I have mine. I expect you to hold me to as close a schedule as possible. This only is important, so far as I am concerned: refrain from treating me as if I were either a child or a mental defective; I have ceased to be the one, and I was never the other. Tell me what you expect of me, what you hold me to; but refrain from swathing your honest angular stipulation and exactions in disingenuous cotton-wool.

When the book was ready, however, she telegraphed him: "Am entranced with book. It is beautiful. Everybody who sees it says but of course this is a special edition."

With the Baudelaire book out of the way, the Boissevains went to an island in Florida for a rest and for Millay to gather rare shells. They checked in at the Palms Hotel and immediately went to the beach. Some minutes later the hotel was in flames as a result of a defective flue. The Boissevain baggage was completely destroyed—including the only copy of her manuscript of new poems. Boissevain wrote Cass Canfield in May: "The whole Ms. was burned. She is now hard at work trying to recapture the contents.—Thank God, she has an exceptionally good memory and will know most of them by heart." In reply, Saxton was of course deeply sympathetic yet practical: "If by great good luck a new manuscript can be plucked from Miss Millay's memory and you are satisfied of that now, by all means telegraph me as the news will be of the greatest importance for the sales conference in which we are buried the whole of next week." He was of course too optimistic, as the book was not published for another year.

That the effort to restore the poems was not as easy as it seemed at first, Millay indicated the following October in reporting on her progress: "Fortunately, I have a very good memory, and have been able to recall all those that were completed; but with those on which I was still at work I've been having an exhausting and nerve-wrecking time."

What greatly aggravated matters was her accidental fall from a station wagon while turning a sharp curve, which injured several of her nerves and required considerable and repeated surgery and treatment. Thereafter, the high hospital and doctor bills kept her constantly in financial need. In asking Harper's for advances of money she was of course ready to pay the going interest, but Saxton rejected the very notion of interest. In a letter on June 10, 1936, he stated to Boissevain:

> As to your generous suggestion about the drawing of a note bearing interest, we have decided against that, not because we don't appreciate your feeling in the matter, but because our relations as publisher and author have always been on the most friendly basis and we are glad to be able to meet Miss Millay's wishes without recourse to bank procedure. The money advanced is really an anticipation of royalties due or to be earned by the books published or to be published.

The fact was that by that time the Millay books had sold around a half million copies—an extraordinary popularity for works of poetry—and the Harper firm had every expectation for the continuance of their wide sale. And her new book of poems, *Conversation at Midnight*, which she had so painfully reconstructed from memory, and which was too dialectic and diffuse to avoid certain prosiness, quickly became a best seller and more than repaid her indebtedness.

Edna St. Vincent Millay continued to suffer from the injuries suffered in the automobile accident, so that she had to spend months in hospitals. Her state of mind was also deeply agitated by the rise and excesses of fascism. Early a pacifist and libertarian, she had given much of her time and effort in the 1920s to free Sacco and Vanzetti, the two anarchists convicted of murder by questionable means. After 1936 the Spanish Civil War caused her much anxiety. And the brutalities in Germany under Hitler aggravated her deeply. When war broke out in Europe in 1939, and the Nazis invaded and conquered Holland, thereby depriving Boissevain of his only source of income, she dedicated herself to the anti-fascist cause.

To make up for her husband's loss of income, she had to, ill as she was, give readings in various places to earn some money. And fearful for the fate of the democracies in Europe, she could not refrain from expressing her anger and anguish in her new volume of poetry, *Make Bright the Arrows*, published in 1940, which had wide appeal but lacked her former poetic quality.

Her devoted friend Arthur Ficke felt that the verses she was writing during the war years were "largely hysterical and vituperative." He advised her not to publish this material, and he did persuade her to omit "at least half dozen of the most blatant and crude" verses. Although she was fully aware of their agitated content and unfinished form, she felt too pressed for time to work on their improvement.

Once the urgency of the war effort had ceased in 1945, she broke down under the years-long strain of writing "acres of bad poetry"—which she hoped would be ploughed under now that fascism was defeated. Again she had to spend months in hospitals. For a long time she felt too ill and depressed to be able to write a line of poetry. In August 1946 she informed Edmund Wilson that she was having a "life-size" nervous breakdown as a consequence of her exertions during the years of war:

> For five years I had been writing almost nothing but propaganda. And I can tell you from my own experience, that there is nothing on this earth which can so much get on the nerves of a good poet, as the writing of bad poetry. Anyway, finally, I cracked up under it. I was in the hospital a long time.

In September 1938 Boissevain complained to Saxton that someone at Harper's had sold marked proofs of *The Buck in the Snow* to a rare book dealer for $400. "As you know," he continued, "Miss Millay often makes remarks on her galley and page proofs which are meant only for her publishers and never were intended to go to the general public." Saxton was regretful, but denied any knowledge of the transaction on the part of anyone in the firm.

In January 1942 Millay was once more distressed to learn that proofs of another of her books, containing a sonnet which she had deleted because she felt it needed further work, and was therefore uncopyrighted, were sold to a collector. Complaining to Saxton about it, she wrote:

> Now it has happened again. This is the third time, I believe. . . . Since I do not wish such poems of mine as I consider unready for publication or any material in the form of marginal notes along the edges of the proofs directed to the reader, to the setter of type or to the publisher (all of them being, as I pointed out to you in the instance of the first unpleasantness in this line, personal notes, and not intended for

the eye of any one not connected with the production of my books) I should be obliged if you would let me know at once what you intend to do about this.

Saxton again assured her that he could trace the proofs to no one in the firm, and that all he could do was to write to the printer to exercise the utmost caution with proofs and to return all marked sets to the company.

Persistent illness and consequently high medical expenses kept Millay in financial need during the last decade of her life. Although her royalties in 1939 amounted to over $16,000, the sale of her books kept unavoidably declining and she produced no new books to offset the lessening of her income. Thus in 1940 her expenditures exceeded her royalties, and Saxton arranged for an advance of $10,500 to be paid in monthly installments. He did intimate that unless she was able to produce a new volume, or a new edition of her older work, her royalties would not even out the $1,000 monthly payments being made to her.

Her need persisted, however, and she was forced to issue a cry for help in a letter she wrote Saxton on March 10, 1941, in which for all her effort to begin on a facetious note she admitted that "the matter is really far from funny":

> I am writing this very long letter because I could not bear to write simply asking Harper's once more to advance me money on royalties and asking you to do your best to help me get it; I wanted to tell you not only the fact but also the nature of my predicament, for I felt sure you would understand it,—you who also have been in several kinds of distress at once, with the mental and spiritual kinds of pain twisting and tightening the knots of the physical.

On June 15, 1942, with the money advanced to her spent and her health still very poor, she wrote Saxton again, asking for $600 monthly payments for the coming year:

> I am in a bad corner and hope that Harper's will be able to help me once more. . . . That will give me a year to get my strength back, enabling me to write again and give readings, etc. When, every five years or so, I tour the country giving readings from my poems . . . I make quite a lot of money. I expect to be in good financial shape then; for the coming year I must have help, and must ask Harper's to grubstake me once more. And it is urgent.

Her physical health did not improve as she had hoped; what writing she did was devoted to the war effort, and she was in no condition to give readings. Consequently she was again in need of financial assistance in 1943. When Saxton died in June of that year, she was not only distressed by the loss of a friend but disturbed by the break of her intimate contact with the Harper firm. In July she wrote to Saxton's assistant, Amy Flashner: "There seems to be nobody at Harper's to whom I can go now with my troubles, now that Gene is gone." She told her how kind he had been to her "with his white face and sad, unhappy eyes— happy only when we were quoting Latin poetry to each other." Now she could not write or think about him without crying, and she needed him now: "If I don't get some money I can't go on writing, can't go on doing anything. . . . The point is I'm stone-broke. Can Harper's help me, Miss Flashner?"

Cass Canfield, who replaced Saxton as her editor, saw to it that she should receive the financial assistance she needed. The following year, after some figuring, he told Boissevain that the firm was renewing the arrangement to advance his wife $500 monthly for the coming year, and added:

> As I pointed out to you, it is doubtful whether the current earnings on old books would justify payments of more than approximately $250 a month, but I have no doubt that in due course we can work out some new project with Miss Millay which will change the picture.

These monthly payments, reduced to $250 when Millay would not agree to proposed new combinations of her published work, were granted from year to year. When this was done by Canfield voluntarily in 1949, she acknowledged the favor with pathetic appreciation:

> I was astonished by your letter and deeply touched, I would never again have written asking for this loan—for it had become truly a loan: it could no longer be regarded as an advance on royalties, since no book by me, in so far as you could properly expect, after so long a silence, would ever be forthcoming. You must have known, after my letter last year, that I would never ask for it again.

> I accept, however, with gratitude your offer which I now truly may consider again an advance on royalties.

She went on to tell him that after seven months of hard work she had only a few poems "finished to my satisfaction."

Canfield acknowledged her letter and assured her that the continuing sale of her books "makes these payments possible without your being in debt to us. In other words, we are merely providing you with an accommodation and should not be given credit for doing you any special favor."

After having written "bad" poetry during the war years, Millay found herself unable to write at all for a long time afterward. Continued serious illness, nervous exhaustion, and emotional depression seemed to silence her poetic voice, which in previous years had sung so freely and exuberantly. Her self-imposed high artistic standard, which in the past had kept her finished lines pure and lyrical, now rejected the verses with which she sought to express her anguished spirit. This meticulousness about the accuracy of observation and lyrical quality in her poetry caused her to resent any criticism with which she did not agree.

An instance of this occurred on December 11, 1945, when Canfield informed her that a scholarly friend had brought to his attention that in one of her sonnets the name Aeolus should have been Ixion, and asked what she would like to do about it. Indignant that her classical knowledge was being questioned, she telegraphed: "Under no circumstances at any time ever subject my poetry to the mayhem which you now contemplate, namely, that of altering, on the advice of a brash and spurious scholar, one word in one of my poems." Not satisfied with this firm stricture, she followed it up with a long letter a week later, in which she stated her professed belief in the inviolability of her poetry: that a publisher may not "alter one word in one of my poems"; that any change in them must be made by her alone; and she continued:

> Only I, who know what I mean to say, and how I want to say it, am competent to deal with such matters. . . . The faults as well as the virtues of this poetry, are my own; and no other person could possibly lay hands upon any poem of mine in order to correct some real or imaginary error without harming the poem more seriously than any faulty execution of my own could possibly have done.

Canfield's reaction was agreeable submission:

> I offer my unconditional surrender. My forces are spent and I have no arms left to lay down. Your eloquent and interesting letter places in proper perspective the artist in relation to the individual with a mind so literal that meaning escapes it. . . . I think I need not tell you that this House intends to preserve your poetry as it is; to do otherwise would make us as guilty as an art dealer who tampered with an El Greco painting.

Aware of her great need of money for medical expenses and sympathizing with her inability to produce new volumes of poetry, he sought to stimulate sales by suggesting different combinations of her published work. Appreciative of his helpful attitude and recognizing the legitimacy of his commercial schemes in her behalf, she was nevertheless too self-critical to acquiesce in them unless they seemed to her fully justified. Thus, she approved of a collected volume of her sonnets, which brought her much-needed income. Yet when he proposed in October 1947 a one-volume collection of her plays, she rejected it as artistically unacceptable:

> I am afraid I must disappoint you here, although I hate most dreadfully to do so. The fact is, I have too much pride and too much faith in myself as a dramatist, to permit the publication in one volume of seven dramatic works of mine, of which only three—*Two Slatterns and a King, The Princess and the Page*, and *Aria da Capo*—are good plays, and only one of these, *Aria da Capo*, of any significance.

Moreover, still hoping to produce a new book of good lyrics, she thought it would be inadvisable for her as well as for the firm to have it preceded "by a book of bad plays." To further the company's expectation of the new volume, she continued:

> I am writing. I have not many new poems finished, but those that I have are good. The effect of writing so much propaganda during the war—from the point of view of poetry, sloppy, garrulous, unintegrated—is to make me more careful and critical of my work even than formerly I was, so that now I write more slowly than ever. But there will be a book.

When Canfield and others at Harper's continued to suggest combinations of her work that might produce good sales, she in May 1948 asked them to "stop nagging" her. She apologetically admitted that it was "perfectly natural and understandable" for them to think of schemes "for making people buy more of my books:

But on the other hand, it is a fact, that you harass me so, you run me so ragged, with your one proposition after another, propositions which, more often than not, I feel unhappily obliged to turn down, that you destroy all my serenity of mind. . . . If you really want a book from me, why not stop worrying me for a while, and give me a chance to write it? . . .

Trusting, however, in closing, that for one more year it may be said of me by Harper & Brothers, that although I reject their proposals, I welcome their advances.

Previous proposals she had rejected because she did not think them worthy of her name; the one made by Arthur Rushmore she considered insulting. In May 1948 he had suggested that she prepare an edition of her poems to be entitled *The Love Poems of Edna St. Vincent Millay.* Regarding it as an invasion of her privacy, she told him that, being a reticent person, she "consistently and in all circumstances refuses to make in print any statement whatever regarding any poem whatever." As to his assertion that she would be acquiring new readers with this volume, she stated: "The indubitable fact that, even as I was winning my new readers, I should be losing entirely the good esteem of the more sensitive and by me the most valued, of the readers I already have, does not seem to have occurred to you."

Canfield sought to calm her: "We won't be bothering you in coming months with either bright ideas for collections or whatnot, but I keep hoping that in due course we will have the opportunity of publishing a new Millay book."

She continued to work on new poems as her health permitted. Her emotional overflow, once so quick and pure and powerful, seemed slack and slender, so that she sometimes struggled with a line for days before molding it to her satisfaction. Yet she persisted day after day to the limit of her feeble strength. When not in a hospital for treatment, she clung to the seclusion of Steepletop.

In the summer of 1949 Eugen Boissevain, who had been attending to her needs and who cherished her with complete devotion, developed a cancerous growth, underwent surgery, and died on August 30. Edna Millay had to be hospitalized for months afterward, but when she felt somewhat better she insisted on returning to the isolation of Steepletop. She saw no one except a friendly neighbor who brought her necessary provisions and did some of the chores about the house. It was in a letter written to Canfield at that time that her old friend William Rose Benét remarked: "Trouble with V. [Vincent] is—she has too long been the dream maiden in the glass case on the mountain top."

In August 1950, having written a poem for Thanksgiving and feeling as if her poetic flow was quickening, she declared: "It is wonderful to be writing again!" Two months later, on the way to the stairs leading to her library, she suddenly slumped to the floor and died. Her neighbor found her several hours later.

The finished poems were collected and published in 1954 in a volume entitled *Mine Is the Harvest.*

27.

The Macmillan Co.

&

Margaret Mitchell

Gone With the Wind was a rare phemomenon in the book world: a first novel of merit that attracted more readers than any work of fiction in the history of publishing. Its author, Margaret Mitchell, was born in Atlanta on November 8, 1900. Ever since her pudgy little hand could hold a pencil, she spent much time writing for the love of putting words together; none of her writing during her childhood showed any marked literary talent, but that did not lessen her enjoyment of the activity.

On graduation from high school, she went to Smith College. Late in her freshman year her mother died, and she returned to Atlanta in June to keep house for her father and brother. Never having lost her interest in writing, she soon became a reporter and feature writer for *Atlanta Journal Sunday Magazine*. As part of her assignment she wrote a series of biographical sketches of Georgia military and political leaders active during the Civil War period. Long interested in Southern history, which she had heard from the elders around her since childhood, and proud of the Confederate effort, she eagerly delved into local records for the facts she used in her newspaper stories.

On July 4, 1925, she married John R. Marsh, who was a newspaperman before he joined the Georgia Power Company, and the following year she left her job on the newspaper. Soon after, recovering from a broken ankle, she began to write more or less at random on her favorite subject: the South during the Civil War era. To heighten interest in the narrative, she decided to give it fictional form; writing for her own pleasure, she wrote the end of the story first. As a trained journalist, however, she soon devoted much time to research in order to give her account of the Confederacy the stamp of authenticity. Having no thought of publication, she made no attempt to give her material literary finish. After working at it fairly regularly for three years, she returned to it only sporadically, primarily to satisfy an inner artistic urge.

As her interest in the narrative became more definite, she sought not only to give the material the flesh of fiction but also to depict the South as she knew it best: not of white columns and slavocracy, but as she perceived it in the Atlanta area, which was not yet wealthy enough to indulge in pseudoclassic architecture and the leisure activities of the master class. This she made clear in a letter to a friend on October 15, 1937: some people, she stated, insisted that the Old South was largely white columns. Yet the section of Georgia in which she lived had been rather crude in part. No doubt another generation of cotton money might have given it many white columns, but in fact that money went into land and slaves. It was this circumstance that made her write about it, as previous writers had written about white columns but had not touched this aspect of the South.

Of a sociable nature, highly likable, and having numerous friends, Margaret Mitchell made no effort to keep from them the information that she was at work on a novel. One of these friends was Lois Cole, who was employed in the Atlanta office of The Macmillan Company. Some time later she was transferred to the firm's New York office. When Harold S. Latham, editor-in-chief and vice-president, decided in 1935 to visit some Southern cities in search of publishable manuscripts—a pioneering move on his part, as New York publishers had hitherto tended to ignore that region of the country—Miss Cole told him to be sure to see Margaret Mitchell.

Harold Latham was a gentle, perceptive, but generally traditional book editor. As head of the large trade department, he made annual trips to England, and backed by the mother-firm in London—no longer in full control of the American firm, but still very influential—he managed to obtain a relatively large share of British solid books. In the 1930s he became keenly interested in the literary ferment in various parts of the South. Although he disliked the seamy and abnormal aspects of Southern life stressed in current fiction, he was impressed by the literary merit of certain of the Southern writers. He therefore decided to visit a number of Southern cities in order to meet local writers in the hope of uncovering likely manuscripts. His prominent position in the largest publishing house and the novelty of having a Northern editor go to the South in search of authors assured him of a welcome wherever he went. The firm's agents and the local press publicized his trip.

When he reached Atlanta, he was not long in being told by several book people that Margaret Mitchell was one of the persons he should see. This he did at a luncheon arranged in his honor by the editor of *Atlanta Journal Sunday Magazine*. At his first opportunity he questioned Mitchell about her writing. She seemed startled, hesitated, and said: "No, I have nothing." Latham did not press her. The following afternoon he saw her again at a literary tea given for him by a local department store.

"How about that novel of yours today?" he began. "Has it become more of a reality now than you permitted it to be yesterday?"

"There is no novel," was her reply. Undeterred, he told her that he was puzzled by her denial, since her local friends and Lois Cole had urged him to discuss her novel with her. Whereupon she asked him to stop asking her about it, as she had no manuscript, and instead invited him for a drive to see Stone Mountain.

On the way he asked her to let him be the first editor to see any manuscript she might write. This she promised to do.

That evening the telephone rang in Latham's hotel room and he heard Margaret Mitchell asking him to meet her in the lobby. There he saw her sitting on a divan, "and beside her was the largest manuscript I think I had ever seen, it towered above her shoulders." She rose, said, "Take the darn thing before I change my mind," and fled.

Latham was leaving for New Orleans the following morning. Normally he would have asked the Atlanta manager to ship the manuscript to the New York office for a first reading. This time he was too curious to part with it. He bought a large suitcase to put it in and started to read it on the train. He found no opening chapter, and many of the pages showed the wear and tear of a decade's handling. Yet he became engrossed in the throbbing life and excitement of the narrative and realized he had come upon the unfinished draft of an important novel.

When he reached his hotel in New Orleans, he was given a telegram stating, "Send it back. I've changed my mind." This he did not do. Instead he wrote her how impressed he was with the material. Now persuaded that a Northern editor was interested in her story of the War Between the States, she wrote him on April 16, 1935, how pleased she was with his favorable reaction to her manuscript. Indeed, if she had not been impressed with his "honest face," she would have assumed he was merely joking. The fact was that she was oppressed by the knowledge of what good writing really is, as she had read manuscripts for years while on the *Journal*. And she always felt that she lacked that something which other authors had—a passionate belief in the quality of their work. It was for this reason that she was so pleased to have him think well of her writing.

She then pointed out the faults in the manuscript: the lack of an opening chapter, unsatisfactory drafts of some of the chapters, missing interstitial material, lags of interest in the narrative, and incomplete background information. She assumed that these faults made it difficult for a reader to get the full impact of the story, but she was nevertheless agreeable to let him consider the manuscript for publication.

She wanted him to decide about taking the manuscript back with him to New York or return it to her for revision. As things were, she could not do anything on it before June, since her aching back would not be sufficiently recovered before then.

When the manuscript was not returned by July, she wrote Latham to ask for it with a prescient irony that foretold the cause of her tragic death fourteen years later. For she considered herself one of those clumsy people who are always meeting with some accident: always being run over by drunken drivers, sat on by horses, or struck by bottles tossed playfully by a friend. Now, however, she told him that she was well enough to work on the book and did not wish to tempt Providence by delay. For it seemed that her writing must be done between one accident or another, and she was whole at the moment.

Latham apologized for the delay, expressed continued enthusiasm, and asked for a little more time because a very good outside reader was going over it. Two days later he telegraphed acceptance of the manuscript and offered a contract stipulating an advance of $500, 10 percent royalty on the first 10,000 copies sold, and 15 percent thereafter. Mitchell wired acceptance and then stated in a letter that the telegram had given her a real thrill—one which she never had expected to have. For actually, she had written the book mostly to please her husband and herself as well as to keep herself occupied while lame. Even when he took the manuscript with him and wrote her those encouraging letters, she had never really expected it would be accepted.

In his reply on July 22, Latham included the highly favorable comments of the outside reader along with the manuscript. He again expressed his great pleasure to have her as an author, and cautioned her against the tendency of inexperienced writers to revise too drastically.

> Please do not think for one moment of ripping it all to pieces and doing it over. All that you should do, as the reader suggests, is to bridge the existing gaps with a few lines, fill out a scene or two, and catch up a few loose ends. I think it will be a serious mistake if you attempt to do too much.

Ten days later she wrote to thank him for everything. "How nice you've been to me! Nice is a too inadequate word. I wish I could do something equally nice for you. Perhaps finishing up the book in a hurry and doing something about my slovenly rhetoric would help show my appreciation."

She did what she could to improve the writing. She also changed the heroine's name from Pansy, popular during the Civil War years, to Scarlett. The title gave her some trouble, but she settled for *Gone With the Wind*, a phrase from Ernest Dawson's *Cynara*, which she later realized was more apt than she at first thought. By devoting nearly all of her time to the revision, she was able to send most of the final draft on December 19, and the last of it on January 28, 1936.

A word count of the manuscript was found to make 1,024 compact pages. An estimate of the cost of manufacture, promotion, and royalty on the basis of a printing of 10,000 copies indicated that the firm would lose four cents a copy even if priced at $3.00—a high price for a novel in 1936. Latham therefore explained this situation and suggested that the royalty remain at 10 percent on subsequent printings. Miss Mitchell readily agreed.

The Macmillan firm lost no time in its campaign to promote the novel. When galleys were pulled, sets were sent to the Book-of-the-Month Club, with letters and telephone calls seeking to interest the judges. Simultaneously it spread the news in book circles that it had a new best seller. When William Allen White, one of the Club's influential judges, reacted enthusiastically, his colleagues adopted the novel for distribution in July. The firm took advantage of this good news in its publicity, and booksellers soon began to double and redouble their orders, responding to the interest of their customers.

The windfall of the adoption changed Macmillan's original cost estimate and raised its sales prospects, so that it decided to increase Mitchell's royalty to 15 percent after the sale of 25,000 copies—with the proviso that the royalty should revert to 10 percent in any year in which the book's sale was fewer than 5,000 copies. Lois Cole informed her of this change in the contract, stating:

We want you to be happy in your publishing relationship with us, and we want you to feel that we are doing everything we can to see that you share in the antici-pated returns. You were very gracious and helpful in agreeing to reduce your roy-alty at the time that it seemed imperative. We now are making the same gesture to you.

Mitchell's response was a telegram expressing grateful enthusiasm, with three cheers for Macmillan and thanks to everyone in the firm, and stated that more good news would wreck her nervous system.

When *Gone With the Wind* was published on June 30, 1936, the response of reviewers and readers was overwhelming. The novel, indeed, possessed story-telling elements that appealed to an extraordinarily wide readership. In its favor, also, was its appearance at a time when people were eager to forget their eco-nomic worries and personal troubles in a book that took them to a different era and dealt with the life of fascinating characters. The Macmillan firm, having early become persuaded of its potential popularity, made every effort to kindle interest in it among booksellers. Thus, on June 19, it sent out the following news note: "*Gone with the Wind*, the forthcoming novel of the South in the middle sixties and seventies, by Margaret Mitchell, of Atlanta, is having a record-break-ing sale. Already—two weeks before publication—it has piled up the largest ad-vance sale of any book in many years." On publication it announced the fifth printing; and two weeks later it stated that the sixth printing made a total of 140,000 copies in print. And to cope with the avalanche of orders, new printings were ordered until the total in December reached a million copies.

Macmillan saw to it that review copies of the novel reached every newspaper and magazine expressing interest in it. It was helped tremendously by front-page glowing reviews in various periodicals. The one in the New York *Times* "Book Review" was written by its editor, J. Donald Adams, and he stated ecstatically: "This is beyond doubt one of the most remarkable first novels produced by an American writer. It is also one of the best." Hundreds of other reviews were equally laudatory. Shortly after her death in 1949 an article in the *Saturday Review of Literature* stated more perceptibly:

It has something, or everything, that the public wants, a magnificently told dra-matic narrative and a love story so imperatively moving that Rhett Butler and Scar-lett O'Hara had become the lineal descendants of all great fictional lovers of the past, and the fall of Atlanta in our Civil War became one with the siege of Troy.

Another typical judgment was expressed by James D. Hart in *The Popular Book*:

Scarlett O'Hara and Rhett Butler, the two strong figures, and Melanie Hamilton and Ashley Wilkes, the two weak ones, were products of external charactization rather than psychological motivation, yet they gave the appearance of reality in manner and dialogue, seeming to be shaped by inner stresses and social forces rather than by prefabricated temperaments. The discussion of character, therefore, was as great as that of action, making a dual appeal. Readers, when they come by the millions, are less tutored and less demanding than those who read much fiction, and to them it seemed that Miss Mitchell's characters were as accurately portrayed as her authentic Atlanta topography.

Honors came to Mitchell along with wide acclaim. It was practically a foregone conclusion that her novel would be awarded the Pulitzer Prize—and it was. The American Booksellers Association chose it as the most distinguished novel published in 1936. Two Southern societies presented her with gold medals, and colleges gave her honorary degrees. In the meantime sales of the book kept increasing from month to month, breaking all records.

The unexpected tremendous popularity of *Gone With the Wind* made life difficult for Margaret Mitchell. She began receiving letters by the score; most of them merely expressed enthusiasm and gratitude, but a number asked questions about the sources of the story and the origin of the characters. A conscientious person, she had to give much of her time to their mere acknowledgement. To reviewers she felt bound to write at greater length. To one prominent Southern journalist she stated on July, 8, 1936, how much she appreciated the statement in his review that her characters were not taken from real life—which they weren't she assured him. She reminded him that she was, after all, a product of the Jazz Age: having short hair, wearing short skirts, and being the kind of hardboiled woman who, preachers said, would go to hell or be hanged before she was thirty. Consequently she felt embarrassed to be considered the incarnate spirit of the Old South.

To another correspondent a month later she wrote: "You ask me about my next book. I hope you will understand when I say I hope I never write another book." This response she also made to Latham when he gently prodded her from time to time. As late as December 1947, when he once again inquired about her writing plans, she wrote him to say that he was very kind to want her to write another book. As she had told him long ago, he would be the first to be told on the day she began to write again. And in fact, there were many books she would like to write. But all would require time for uninterrupted work. It seems, however, that a Merciful Providence had long ago decided that she should spend her time in the sickroom rather that at the typewriter. She had reference to the fact that for the past half dozen years she had first to nurse her invalid father until his death in 1944, and then devote her time and attention to her husband after his heart attack had greatly limited his normal activity.

From the first she was also plagued by crank claims of distortion and plagiarism. Some of these flimsy assertions were obviously made for the purpose of obtaining a nuisance settlement. Usually this is done by both author and publisher to avoid the cost and trouble and notoriety of a court trial. Mitchell, however, insisted on making no such settlement, and went to considerable expense to expose the absurdity of these claims. In each instance the Macmillan firm fully cooperated with her. One of the silliest of these accusations was made by the author of a work on the Ku Klux Klan. He claimed that his rights were invaded because *Gone With the Wind* was bound in the same Confederate gray as his book.

Mitchell initiated a suit herself against a Dutch publisher who had assumed that her novel was without the protection of international copyright and therefore in the European public domain. Macmillan, however, had complied with the provisions of the Bern Convention on Copyright, and the publisher was forced to make an accounting of his edition—which did not repay the cost of litigation but did strengthen the protection of copyright for all authors.

In addition to her large correspondence and numerous requests for public appearances, she had to contend with scores of persons who sought to make her personal acquaintance. She complained of this to Latham in response to his request for an item of publicity on the book, telling him that she was really desperately anxious to keep out of the limelight. For she had discovered that any personal item about her in the newspapers brought hundreds of tourists to her door, so that she often had to flee from home, and she hated to do that.

Margaret Mitchell and Harold Latham early became close friends. She was attracted to his "honest face," and warmly appreciated his continued efforts in her behalf. Their exchange of letters concerning matters that required discussion or affirmation soon became a deepening expression of genuine mutual affection. Latham looked after her interests with personal concern, and kept her fully informed of the various editions of her book which the firm was bringing out to make the most of the available markets for it: one as low as sixty-nine cents in connection with the popular movie, and another issued in two sumptuous volumes at the then high price of $7.50. He also reported all arrangements for the numerous foreign translations—twenty-five in all—although she had an agent handling her rights. She in turn sent him copies of each translation as it appeared for his library shelf. Latham did all this to lessen the burden these transactions entailed, and he also helped her avoid most of the numerous requests for meetings, personal appearances, and articles for publication.

Margaret Mitchell fully appreciated his exertions in her behalf and made it evident on frequent occasions. She invited him to visit her in Atlanta at every opportunity, and several times she and her husband came to New York to see him. The last time they did so, they invited him to dine with them in their Waldorf suite—she avoided appearances in public whenever possible. That afternoon Latham had ordered an orchid to be delivered to her, but it was not brought up before he himself arrived, somewhat to his embarrassment, until he saw how delighted she was to receive it. As he recalled the evening some years later:

> The three of us had a quiet and rewarding evening recalling amusing or serious happenings in the eventful years that had passed since our first meeting. It was in some respects a kind of summation of our association, though none of us could know that it was to be, in very fact, the last of such happy reviews.

On August 11, 1949, the Marshes decided to see a movie, *A Canterbury Tale.* Mitchell drove the car to the theater and parked it nearby. As they were crossing the street, with no traffic in sight, a car suddenly came toward them at high speed—the "drunken autoist" she had feared—and before she could get back to the sidewalk she was struck down and fatally injured. Five days later she died.

Gone With the Wind continued to sell in large numbers in every part of the world. In 1950 the American sales alone exceeded 50,000 copies, more than any other book on Macmillan's list. In 1961 the firm celebrated the 25th anniversary of the book's publication by issuing an attractive pamphlet—fuller than any of the previous ones—on the history of the novel during the two and a half decades, and stated that its sale had by then reached 5½ million copies in English and 4 million in translations. These figures have increased by 2 million since then.

28.

Clifford Irving
and
Current Publishing

In the latter half of the nineteenth century the leading American publishers, as already indicated, sought to give their business the aura of a gentleman's profession; their failure to do so may be ascribed as much to the increasing dominance of commercialization as to the fallibility of human aspiration. After 1900, and especially after World War II, publishing became more and more a purely business enterprise. This was effected to a large extent by two major factors: the rise of the literary agent and the pervasive control of corporate ownership.

The first influential literary agent was A. P. Watt, who began functioning in England in the early 1880s. In an interview published in *The Bookman* in 1892 he stated that he had started his agency because he assumed "authors might be glad to be relieved of what Mr. Besant has called 'the intolerable trouble of haggling and bargaining,' and one author recommending my services to another . . . I gradually came to occupy the position I now hold."

In his effort to get for his author-clients the maximum income from their writings—and thus for himself as well—Watt naturally antagonized certain publishers. What they resented even more than the lessening of their profits was the disruption of their close relations with authors, as Watt and later agents insisted on representing their authors in arranging for the publication of their books. The resentment of such publishers as Henry Holt and Charles Scribner in America was openly stated; William Heinemann in England also expressed annoyance in strong terms. Refusing to deal with Watt in 1893, he declared: "This is an age of the middleman. He is generally a parasite. He always flourishes. I have been forced to give him some attention lately in my particular business. In it he calls himself the literary agent." Nine years later, still unwilling to deal with agents, he claimed there was an advantage to authors in being in personal communication with their publishers. He maintained that agents "foster in authors the greed for an immediate money return"; that the publisher was discouraged "from taking up new authors, if they are, as soon as he has borne the first risk and launched them, to be put up to public auction."

Not all authors resorted to engaging an agent, as they preferred to deal directly with their publisher. One of them, Angela Thirkell, gave in *Pomfret Towers* an acidulous definition of the literary agent: "Someone whom you pay to make bad blood between yourself and your publisher." Most authors in England, however, were pleased to let Watt and others represent them. Walter Besant claimed that Watt had tripled his income, even after he had deducted 10 percent for his services.

In time publishers, fearful of losing prominent authors, came to accept the literary agent as an unavoidable fact of life. Some even employed him to sell their books to magazines and to American publishers. Thus for twenty-five years Watt remained an important influence in British publishing—accepted by publishers despite his insistence on obtaining the highest royalties and largest advances for his authors.

Watt's success stimulated the establishment of other agents. His first major competitor in England became J. B. Pinker. Although D. H. Lawrence called him a "little parvenu snob of a procurer of books," Pinker developed a large and, on the whole, satisfied clientele. He was very helpful to young authors whose work he liked, and often provided them with financial assistance as well as guidance in their relations with publishers. One of these authors, as previously stated, was Joseph Conrad, who told John Quinn, the collector, that his books "owe their existence to Mr. Pinker as much as to me." And when Pinker died suddenly in 1922, Conrad wrote: "I have suffered a most painful loss in my old friend J. B. Pinker. . . . Our friendship lasted for 22 years." Another prominent author, Arnold Bennett, who unlike Conrad was commercially astute, relied on Pinker to get him the best terms. "There is *no* other really good agent in England," he remarked. "The difference between a good and a bad agent might mean a difference of thousands [of pounds] a year to me."

Curtis Brown and Paul R. Reynolds were the first Americans to attain notable success as literary agents, both having been as active in England as in the United States. They and others gained approval of the Authors League of America, founded in 1912, which stated in a pamphlet: "The writer, owing to his temperament, his lack of business training, and his frequent isolation from other members of his profession, is especially unfitted to drive a good bargain with those who buy his manuscripts." This attitude on the part of most authors gave publishers no choice but to deal with their agents. In time, moreover, publishers discovered that the agent could serve them as well as authors, particularly in the sale of books to England and other countries, and some came to depend upon them for new authors of potential popularity.

Most professional authors expect agents not only to get the best terms for their writings but also to help them in various other ways. Some turn to them for practical ideas for books, for the publisher who could best market their work, for the editor in a publishing house who was likely to work well with them. Certain authors, however, become so friendly with a publisher and so much at home with his firm that they cease having an agent or refuse better terms from rival publishers obtained for them by their agents. A notable instance was Bess Streeter Aldrich's refusal to leave Appleton although Doubleday had offered her agent an advance of $20,000 and a considerable increase in royalties.

It should also be pointed out that some authors develop friendships with agents as intimate as those with publishers. In such cases the tendency is for the agent to replace the publisher as friend and guide and critic. This is particularly true of popular writers whose loyalty to publishers is incidental and whose prime interest is in getting the highest income from their writing. An exception might be cited in the case of F. Scott Fitzgerald, who was as close to his agent Harold Ober—up to the last year of his life—as he was to his editor Maxwell E. Perkins.

In recent years agents have intensified competitive bidding for potentially popular books. Previously certain publishers refused to participate in such bidding, stating, as did Henry Holt, that they would evaluate a manuscript on its merits and without regard to the bids of other publishers. This no longer holds, as changes in management and ownership have virtually eliminated such dignified refusals.

The quest of publishers for popular authors has enabled agents to make bidding general. Ambitious, enterprising editors now court agents in order to gain their friendship and first news of likely manuscripts. In most such instances, however, not friendship but the highest terms are the decisive factor. In 1944, for instance, Paul Reynolds, Jr. sold Mussolini's ghosted memoirs to the esteemed House of Scribner for an advance of $42,000; with the end of the war interest in the Italian dictator declined drastically, and the firm suffered a loss of about $25,000. When the prestigious firm of Houghton Mifflin refused to bid more than $35,000 for Dean Acheson's memoirs, his agent managed to obtain an advance of $200,000 from the equally reputable company of W. W. Norton, which succeeded in getting its money back from the sale of the book.

Agents have sought to control secondary rights as well as movie rights in order to obtain for their authors—and incidentally for themselves—the highest possible prices. Publishers have, of course, fought against this control, but not always successfully in cases where the agent has the upper hand. When Samuel Shellabarger's *Captain from Castile* achieved wide popularity, Paramount Pictures offered $30,000 for the movie rights. Reynolds believed he could get more; but Shellabarger, in need of money, instructed him to accept the offer. Before doing so, however, Reynolds telephoned Fox that Paramount had made a good offer for the rights but if Fox were interested it could have the rights for $100,000. The offer was made and both Shellabarger and Reynolds were the gainers.

The auction scramble for popular books has greatly increased the advances paid for them. Paul Gitler managed to obtain the highest-known guarantee against royalties when he arranged for a four-book deal—three novels and a biography—between Irving Wallace and Bantam Books, the amount being $2,300,000. Bantam sold the hard-cover rights to Simon & Schuster. "Mr. Gitler," the New York *Times* stated, "is an expert at wielding the new power that authors' representatives have acquired within the publishing industry." And in February 1973 Scott Meredith obtained from Little, Brown an advance totaling a million dollars for the new novel, yet to be written, by Norman Mailer—the highest advance for a single work of fiction.

Meredith, one of the more successful of the agents, favors this method of auctioning off manuscripts as the fairest arrangement for both author and publisher. He maintains that if an author submits his manuscript to one publisher at a time, he might have to wait a year or more "to gather together an accurate picture of the market value of his work." The auction price, on the whole, is obtained fairly quickly; and while the amount might be higher than under the older arrangement, it "is equally fair to both sides, allowing an agent to offer a hot property in a way which enables him to get an appropriately hot price for it, and at the same time allows *any* interested publisher a crack at getting the property for himself." The reference to a manuscript as a "property" and to the advance as a "hot price" indicates the extent to which commercialization now dominates the publishing industry.

The auction bidding and the high advances on popular books would not of course have been possible if book publishing had remained in the control of "gentlemen publishers." Early in the present century, however, these proud men began to give way to the commercially oriented younger publishers who were more interested in profits and expansion than in quality and taste. Frank N. Doubleday, for instance, manifested a flair for marketing disdained by his gentlemanly peers. And two decades later the "non-books" popularized by such firms as Simon & Schuster not only overshadowed their quality books but stimulated authors and agents to concoct ideas for books that catered to ephemeral popular interests. And the more general attention they could arouse for these projects, the higher were the terms for their publication.

This surge toward the acquisition of transitory best sellers on the part of publishers became more widespread after World War II. The industry itself entered a period of change. Elderly owners of certain long-established houses, wishing to protect their heirs from what seemed to them excessive inheritance taxes and aware of the lack of family interest in the business, began to dispose of their assets in the open market. With the book industry booming in the 1940s, especially in the textbook field, Wall Street investors turned an eager eye toward the purchasable firms. R. J. Apple, Jr. wrote at the time in *Saturday Review*: "Wall Street, after decades of treating the publishing industry with indifference, has suddenly decided that it merits the kind of feverish attention the Street devotes to industries it deems to have the potential for rapid, dazzling growth."

Soon the industry became rife with rumors and firm information concerning mergers and "going public." Old and staid companies began to split their stock, to the enrichment of their "inside" stockholders, and sell the "watered" shares to eager investors. For a decade it seemed as if the entire industry was more interested in financial deals than in bringing out good books. Firm after firm either merged with others or came under the control of large investors. Henry Holt & Company absorbed two smaller firms in 1959 and was in turn taken over by CBS in 1967. Random House acquired control of the Knopf firm in 1960, only to be bought by RCA in 1966. The Macmillan Company, in the 1930s the largest publishing house in the country, became a subsidiary of Crowell Collier in 1960. Numerous other mergers and acquisitions left few independent firms in the control of their original owners. All of this of course tended to make the industry almost wholly commercialized. Seldom was the head of a house able to publish a book because of its literary merit; the need to assure stockholders of their expected dividends perforce became his paramount guide.

It was this requirement to show an operating profit, plus the fact that the larger firms had the capital with which to swing big deals, that furthered the scramble for popular books without regard to their intrinsic merit. This brought onto the best-seller list whatever attracted general attention: memoirs of prominent politicians, leading soldiers, and popular figures in various fields of activity; also books titillating eroticism of catering to emotional problems. Sums reaching six figures and more were paid as advances for ghost-written volumes that became piles on remainder tables soon after they appeared. Thus, in not a few instances the sale of books plus the income from secondary rights failed to repay the original advance.

The phenomenal growth of the paperback market likewise had a deleterious effect on the quality of hard-cover books. Since many readers of paperbacks at that time possessed relatively low reading intelligence, the tendency of both book editors and agents was to encourage writers to cater to this mass audience. Nor were a number of those authors less mercenary than their publishers. Encouraged by agents, they demanded a greater share of the income from secondary rights, rejecting the long-established arrangement of the publishing firm sharing this income equally with the author.

A case in point is Philip Roth. For years the paperback editions of his fiction had sold in the millions, and Random House deducted half of the royalty as its share. In 1972 he told the firm that he wanted the entire income from the paperback edition of his new book. This Random House would not do, although it became agreeable to lessening its share; for it not only could not afford to yield this lucrative income entirely but it also feared to establish a precedent for its other popular authors. The result was a parting of a long-established relationship, and Roth went to Holt, Rinehart & Winston, which had no popular novelists and was eager enough to obtain one to acquiesce in Roth's terms. It paid him a large advance on the hard-cover rights for two books which it did not fully recover. Fortunately for the firm, Roth's third book showed promise of a profit.

The hoax perpetrated by Clifford Irving illustrates the possibility for debasement of current publishing—an incident conceivable only because of a concatenation of singular circumstances. In the days when publishing was a personal enterprise of modest dimensions, when the individual owner was interested in the quality of his books, and when the reading public was relatively small and discriminating, an undertaking of the kind proposed by Irving would have been too bizarre for serious consideration. For a gigantic firm like McGraw-Hill, however, or for perhaps a dozen other large publishing houses today, a project requiring nearly a million dollars was in fact highly desirable. The main factor the executives considered essential was its commercial validity, and of that they were soon satisfied.

It should be stated at the outset that the behavior of McGraw-Hill executives in this matter was upright and understandable. Irving's proposal had its unique aspects. Howard R. Hughes was one of the world's richest men, extremely eccentric, leading a life at once singularly strange and intriguingly mysterious, so that the publicity his behavior had guaranteed made him a glamorous world figure. Indeed, from the point of view of the publisher he had everything in his favor: great financial and personal achievement, a tantalizing sex life, deliberate furtiveness—and all of it inexplicable. With his associates having hitherto successfully suppressed the publication of material about him, a biography written with his cooperation was likely to be the most widely read book of the year. The more the McGraw-Hill people thought about it the more interested they became, envisioning a financial bonanza.

Although they had checked his data carefully, they had no reason to be suspicious of Irving in any way. He had been one of their authors for over ten years, and while his books had thus far sold only modestly, the editors had enough confidence in his future prospects to have arranged a four-book contract with him for which he had received advances totaling $68,000 out of a total of $150,000 to be paid on delivery of material over a four-year period—an unusually large amount for an author of his stature. As the authors of *Hoax* have pointed out: "Irving's $150,000 advance for his next four books seems generous in retrospect, but it was made in inflationary times. If it appears high, this is because Irving's literary reputation was not."

Irving told McGraw-Hill editors that he had sent a copy of *Fake!*, his latest book which dealt with art forgery, to Howard Hughes, who had received it favorably enough to propose a collaboration for his own biography. The editors were greatly surprised by Irving's luck, since they at once saw the book as a best-seller, and it did not occur to them to question the veracity of the information. Irving's statement that Hughes had insisted on complete secrecy until the manuscript was ready for publication merely struck them as another piece of evidence of his eccentricity. Months later, when Richard Suskind, whom Irving had engaged as his researcher, wondered about the naïveté of the McGraw-Hill people, Irving explained it astutely—with an irony that underlined the truth:

> Because they *believe*. First they wanted to believe, and now they have to believe. They want to believe because it's such a coup for them, it's weird and wild, it's Howard Hughes and the Richest Man in the World and they're personally, vicariously, in cahoots with him. . . . I'm their buffer between reality and fantasy. It's a fairy tale, a dream. And the beauty part for them is that they'll make money out of it, too. Corporate profits justifies any form of lunacy. There's been no other hoax like it in modern times.

This perceptive evaluation was of course ex post facto. At the time forty years old, he had up to then achieved little as a person and writer. The son of a comic-strip cartoonist, he had a spotty education, married at the age of twenty, and was divorced from his third wife before he met and married Edith Sommer, an abstract painter recently divorced, in 1967. His first two novels were published by Putnam and had little sale. McGraw-Hill accepted his third novel, *The Valley*, in 1960, and *The Thirty-eighth Floor* soon after, and neither book lifted him out of the low average as a writer. In Ibiza, Spain, where he had made his home since 1953, he had become interested in Elmer de Hory, the art forger, and had obtained his cooperation in writing *Fake!*, which sold somewhat better. Nor did two of his other books—*Spy* and *Battle of Jerusalem*, neither issued by McGraw-Hill—advance his reputation as a writer. As the authors of *Hoax* stated: "Clifford was feeling bored and inactive and old and unfulfilled. He had just celebrated his fortieth birthday and he didn't seem to like the view on the other side of the watershed."

He was in this state of mind when he came upon *Newsweek*'s story of Howard Hughes's flight from Las Vegas to the Bahamas and the excitement it caused in the press. As he read the account he thought of the wild notion of faking a biography of this eccentric millionaire. Having seen earlier reports of his peculiar behavior and his hermit-like existence, he had the hunch that Hughes would not take the trouble to deny or denounce him openly. He also assumed that McGraw-Hill would jump at the opportunity of publishing an authorized biography of Hughes, which would certainly be a best seller. After discussing the idea with his friend Richard Suskind, who was a writer and whom he wanted as researcher, he said: "It's worth a try. They're always looking for best sellers. Hughes would never be able to surface to deny it, or else he wouldn't bother." The two thereupon agreed to proceed.

On January 3, 1971, Irving wrote to Beverly Loo, his editor at McGraw-Hill, about the idea of a Hughes biography. He told her how he had communicated with Hughes and that the millionaire had expressed interest in working with him on a book that would set the record straight so far as his life was concerned. What he wanted to know, he continued with simulated naïveté, was whether the firm would prefer that he proceed with his novel or drop it to work with Hughes on his biography.

Miss Loo cabled him to fly to New York without delay and bring the Hughes correspondence. This Irving did. Having seen a facsimile letter by Hughes in *Newsweek*, he had practiced the script until he thought he had approximated it and wrote the several letters indicating Hughes's interest in the project. In one of them he had him write: "It would not suit me to die without having certain misconceptions cleared up and without having stated the truth about my life. . . . I would be grateful if you would let me know when and how you would wish to undertake the writing of the biography you proposed."

In New York Irving met with several McGraw-Hill executives. On reading the Hughes letters they accepted them as genuine and urged Irving to proceed with the book. As a matter of caution they asked him to consult with the firm's legal department about the agreement he was to make with Hughes. Their confidence in Irving was complete, having previously found him honest and entirely reliable. On February 17 Irving was back in New York and reported that he had two meetings with Hughes and that the latter wanted to know what terms the firm would offer for the book.

In view of the great interest people continued to take in Hughes, so that a biography with his approval was bound to have a large sale, and aware of the tremendous income it would bring from secondary rights, the McGraw-Hill executives agreed to pay a half million dollars as an advance against royalties: $100,000 on the execution of the contract, another $100,000 on the completion of the research, and the final $300,000 on delivery of the completed manuscript. When they specified that they would like an officer of the Hughes corporation sign the contract, Irving, playing on Hughes's penchant for secrecy, quickly pointed out that Hughes had never met Chester Davis, his own lawyer for many years, and would certainly object to anyone signing for him. He offered to go to the Bahamas and have Hughes himself sign the contract. This was entirely agreeable to the executives. Irving thereupon flew to Puerto Rico and returned with Hughes's signature on the contract. On March 21 Harold McGraw, president of the firm's book division, countersigned the contract for "an untitled authorized biography of 'H' (Senor Octavio) with a preface by 'H'." When Irving left the firm's office he was one of the best-paid writers in the United States.

Presumably at Hughes's insistence, the contract stipulated complete secrecy about the project: "The Publisher agrees that it shall undertake no advertising or promotion or sale of the Work prior to 30 days after acceptance by the Publisher of complete and satisfactory manuscript for the Work." This secrecy was also demanded of those who bought the secondary rights. Payments were to be made directly to Hughes. "It's just prudent business practice," one of the firm's officers explained to Irving. "It means you have proof that the right person received the money." The session ended with everyone feeling elated.

At an early opportunity Ralph Graves of *Life* was offered in all secrecy the serial rights to the book. He became as excited about the project as the McGraw-Hill people and suggested $100,000 for the American and Canadian rights. The editor who dealt with him demanded a much larger amount, and the two finally agreed on $250,000 for world and newspaper rights. In the contract Graves hedged by including a proviso that if Hughes reneged, McGraw-Hill "shall refund to *Life* all sums paid to McGraw-Hill pursuant to this agreement." The pledge of secrecy kept *Life* from making the deal known to its staff or from checking on Irving as to his facts.

Irving and Suskind began to search library and periodical files for material on Hughes. They combed the New York library, then Irving obtained permission to examine the Hughes folders in the library of Time, Inc., where he came upon confidential files containing information on Hughes not to be had elsewhere. He and Suskind had similar luck in their search for material in Washington, Houston, Las Vegas, and Los Angeles.

While in California, Irving came upon a singular piece of good fortune. He met Stanley Meyer, an old acquaintance who was a friend of Noah Dietrich, Hughes's one-time close associate. He soon learned that Meyer had a copy of Dietrich's memoirs written for him by James Phelan, a seasoned newspaperman. Dietrich had severed relations with Hughes in 1957, and twelve years later, having become an octogenerian, he was determined to expose his former employer by means of his uninhibited reminiscences. Phelan, having previously written several articles on Hughes, was recommended to him as a collaborator. Not satisfied with Phelan's treatment, however, he was looking for a more polished writer and asked Meyer to help him find one, giving him the manuscript to this end. On meeting Irving, Meyer thought of him as a likely choice and asked him to look over the material with this in view. Irving and Suskind spent the night examining what they soon realized was a treasure trove, and early the next morning they made two photocopies before Irving returned the manuscript to Meyer with the statement that the project did not interest him. Later he stated: "Possession of the Dietrich manuscript gave us a tremendous psychic lift." Although he found little in it that he had not already come upon in various files, it gave him the feel of Hughes's personality, his actual way of doing things, so that it enabled him to give the stamp of authenticity to his own writing. One item of great value was the appendix, which consisted of an actual transcript of a taped talk between Hughes and Frank McCullough, at the time head of the *Time* bureau in Los Angeles.

By late summer Irving and Suskind had completed the faked typed interviews with Hughes and were ready to write the book. So pleased were they with their accomplishment that they decided that the material was worth more than the half million they had contracted for. On August 28 Irving cabled Miss Loo from Pompano Beach, Florida, stating that Hughes, having learned about the serialization in *Life* (part of an organization he despised), had become difficult about money and demanded a million dollars for world rights. The reply was that he and Hughes were under contract and would be held to it. Irving then informed Miss Loo that he had succeeded in persuading Hughes to reduce his demand to $850,000, and added that although he was having a hard time with the eccentric millionaire he did think that the value of the book had increased because it had become an autobiography. When McGraw-Hill continued to insist on sticking to the original terms of the contract, Irving flew to Nassau, presumably to discuss the matter with Hughes; actually he went there to obtain stationery of the Beach Inn on Paradise Island. When he returned to New York he had with him two letters by Hughes. One gave McGraw-Hill permission to publish the book as his autobiography and stated that he "warrants that he has the sole proprietory rights granted to AUTHOR" and that none of the Hughes enterprises had any claim on the book; further, should they bring suit against the publisher, he would bear expenses of the litigation. This warrantee was made, it should be pointed out, to quiet the fears of McGraw-Hill officers that Rosemount Enterprises, which had control of any writings by Hughes, might seek to restrain the publication of the book.

The second letter was addressed to Irving and declared that if McGraw-Hill did not agree to his terms by September 21, he authorized him to offer the manuscript to another publisher. To show that Hughes was serious, Irving had with him a check for $100,000 signed by H. R. Hughes on a Geneva bank. Alarmed by this turn of events and aware that Hughes was both unpredictable and intransigent, yet loath to lose a book of such potentially high profit, McGraw-Hill executives agreed to increase the advance to $750,000. Irving all this time expressed sympathy with them rather than with Hughes and promised to do his utmost to persuade him to accept the new terms. He also let them examine three-quarters of the transcribed tapes, which impressed them as "terrific." On September 12, having informed McGraw-Hill that he had succeeded in persuading Hughes to agree to the increased advance, Irving was given a check for $25,000 to his account and another for $275,000 to Hughes.

With the basic material for the book in hand, McGraw-Hill was soon able to arrange with Dell Publishing Co. to purchase the paperback rights for an advance of $400,000. The Book-of-the-Month Club also agreed to make the volume a monthly selection, paying the unusually high price of $375,000. These amounts together with that from *Life* came to $1,100,000—$450,000 above the advance to Hughes. It was this large boon plus the profit from the sale of the book in hard cover that tended to lessen the vigilance of the McGraw-Hill officers and inclined them to accept Irving at his word. As the authors of *Hoax* have declared: "The prospects of huge profits somewhat reduced the capacity among McGraw-Hill executives for critical analysis. The mere idea of fraud was a nightmare dismissed to the recesses of the mind."

In their defense it should be stated that despite the commercialization of the industry, publishers continued to depend on their authors' gentlemanly virtues of trust, friendship, and loyalty. Irving kept telling them that although Hughes was an extremely eccentric and unpredictable person, he was able to keep him under control. Indeed, the experiences he had presumably with Hughes struck the editors of *Life* as having the material for a good story and arranged to use it as an advertisement for the serial.

On December 1, 1971, McGraw-Hill began to publicize the forthcoming book about "Howard Robard Hughes, billionaire, aviator, movie mogul, real estate magnate, airline boss, gaming *supremo*, litigator, womanizer, and ecologist." The publication date of the volume, entitled *The Autobiography of Howard Hughes, Introduction and Commentary by Clifford Irving*, was set for March 27, 1972.

Carl Byoir & Associates, the firm handling Hughes's public relations, at once denied the existence of any book in which Hughes was involved. The Hughes Tool Company likewise issued a denial. Albert Leventhal, head of the McGraw-Hill department which was to publish the book, rejected these refutations, stating to the New York *Times*: "We have gone to considerable effort to ascertain that this is indeed the Hughes autobiography. And we believe what we say is correct." Donald M. Wilson, vice-president of *Life*, joined him: "Oh, we're absolutely positive. Look, we're dealing with people like McGraw-Hill, and, you know, we're not exactly a movie magazine! This is Time, Inc., and McGraw-Hill talking. We've checked this thing. We have proof."

Chester Davis, Hughes's lawyer, was determined to prevent the publication of what he considered a fraudulent work, and he wrote to Harold McGraw on December 17: "There is no doubt that you have been deceived into thinking you have acquired material which you could publish and that someone is responsible for most serious misrepresentations to you and through you to the public."

McGraw waited six days until he received the report from the holograph expert to whom he had submitted the Hughes letters. Satisfied with the assured authenticity of the letters, he in turn questioned Davis's credentials. "If you represent Mr. Hughes as legal counsel, we must insist on your specific authorization from Mr. Hughes relating to the autobiography."

Their confidence unimpaired, the McGraw-Hill people inserted a two-page advertisement in *Publishers Weekly* of January 3, 1972, to assert the authenticity of the book and to quote a statement by Hughes to this effect—supplied by Irving:

> I believe that more lies have been printed and told about me than about any living man—therefore it was my purpose to write a book which would set the record straight.

> I have lived a full life and, perhaps, what may seem a strange life—even to myself. I refuse to apologize, although I am willing now to explain as best I can. Call this autobiography. Call it my memoirs. Call it what you please. It is the story of my life in my own words.

Thus challenged, the Carl Byoir publicists arranged an interview on January 7 between Hughes and seven journalists who had previous dealings with him and were in a position to recognize his voice and manner of speech. For three hours Hughes talked from his room in Nassau to these reporters in Los Angeles. In the colloquy he said that the business about the book was new to him and the name of Clifford Irving was completely unknown to him. "I don't know him. I have never heard of him until a matter of a few days ago when this thing came to my attention."

When newsmen reproduced part of the conversation for Irving's reaction, he said blandly that Hughes's voice "was a damn good imitation" but declined to give further details of his own meetings with Hughes because of contractual obligations. Five days later Chester Davis filed suit to block the publication of the book as an infringement on Rosemount Enterprises, Inc.

These charges and countercharges became a daily feature on the front pages of most newspapers. The McGraw-Hill and *Life* executives continued to insist on the genuineness of the Hughes letters and signatures in their possession. In response to the suit instituted against his firm, Harold McGraw declared:

> McGraw-Hill's reputation is of primary importance to me, and, as the papers submitted by the plaintiff are full of claims of hoax and fraud, I make this affidavit in order to set the record straight. I believe the book Clifford Irving has produced is precisely what it is represented to be: the story of Howard Hughes in the words of Howard Hughes himself. . . . All of us are completely convinced of Irving's integrity. As we have read the manuscript we were convinced it was an authentic work.

He and his fellow officials gained unforseen support from Frank McCullough, for many years associated with *Time* and the journalist who had long followed Hughes's career and was the last journalist to interview him (in 1958). After he had read the manuscript and questioned Irving, he was convinced of the authenticity of the material—having found in it information known only to Hughes and himself, material Irving had copied from the confidential files of Time, Inc.

In the meantime Government officials had entered the case and soon learned that checks made out to Hughes had been deposited in a Swiss bank by a woman. This news shook somewhat the confidence of McGraw-Hill officials and *Life* editors, and both agreed to postpone publication of the book until doubts were resolved. When Irving was questioned about the identity of the woman, he asserted it must have been one of Hughes's "loyal servants." It soon also became known that the Swiss police were seeking the woman for questioning because she had used a forged passport.

Having persuaded his wife to deposit the Hughes checks in the Swiss bank by giving her name as Helga R. Hughes, Irving realized that she was now in danger of incarceration. Moreover, he began to fear that he had come to the end of his fraudulent venture. On January 24, 1972, he made known that the missing woman depositor was his wife. Events began to crowd each other, and within the following week it became evident to all concerned that Irving was a forger and imposter. *Life* editors quickly canceled its contract with McGraw-Hill, and the deceived firm began to seek the return of the advances.

At the advice of his lawyer, whom he had duped up to then, Irving agreed, and so did Suskind, to go before the grand jury and make a clean breast of the hoax. Harold McGraw, asked his reaction to the situation, admitted: "We found out we were taken and we've had to take our medicine." Leaders of the publishing industry were shocked, if not dismayed. Roger Straus, heading a relatively small, high-quality house, reacted with unwarranted censure: "The avarice and stupidity of McGraw-Hill is not to be believed." Charles Scribner, the solid and dispassionate administrator of an old and esteemed firm, spoke more realistically: "I'm sure it could happen to any publisher."

While there was still uncertainty as to the fraudulence of Irving's manuscript, he appeared brazenly confident in public and readily agreed to be interviewed on Mike Wallace's television program, "60 Minutes." For fifteen minutes he seemed at ease and unhesitating under sharp questioning. Inwardly, however, he felt as if he were sinking into a bottomless pit, falling deeper with each brash lie. After he had watched himself on the screen, he later wrote:

> I stared at myself for fifteen minutes. I had never seen a more nakedly insincere man in my life than the Clifford Irving on the twenty-inch screen. Anyone who knew me, I thought, would see I was lying. There wasn't a single natural gesture. The smile was forced, the laughter brittle, and my hands waved clumsily to emphasize every important point.

A day before McGraw-Hill had planned to publish the book, Irving was indicted in court on conspiracy to defraud, using forged documents, using the mails to defraud, and perjury. Suskind and Edith Irving were indicted at the same time. All three pleaded guilty, and on June 16, 1972, Judge John M. Cannella sentenced Irving to two and a half years imprisonment, Suskind to six months, and Edith Irving to two months. Before being sentenced, Irving stated:

What I have done, you and the court well know, and I know. And the consequences have been a loss of almost everything for me—my reputation, my honor, the financial debt that may last for years, or the rest of my life, and a loss of credibility which is very valuable to me, which I deserve to lose because I lived a year on a lie.

In order to enable one parent to look after the two children, the judge permitted Irving to be with them until after his wife had served her sentence. During this period he wrote the story of the hoax, with a truthfulness and flair that makes one wonder what would have happened if he had written the biography as a work of research rather than perpetrating a hoax. As it was, the paperback he published appeared as an anticlimax and disappointed the publisher. He began serving his term on September 4, 1972, and was pardoned on February 14, 1974.

One cannot help wondering why Irving should have made a mess of his life; why did he expend his remarkable ingenuity and literary skill on a project that was bound to explode in his face? There is no ready answer, but a hint may be found in his own attempt at an explanation:

I had always been a gambler, not at the gaming table but in life. . . . The whole Hughes affair had been a venture into the unknown, a testing of myself, a constant gauntlet of challenge and response. . . . I had never realized I was committing a crime—I had thought of it as a hoax. The money had always been there for restitution . . . but the feeling of guilt was still there.

Source Materials

I came to this book with a backlog of research: the reading I had done on *Book Publishing in America*, which consisted of an examination of the Henry Holt & Company files for nearly a century, copies of *Publishers' Weekly* from 1872 to 1965, the files of other publishers concerning individual authors, and scores of books, memoirs, and articles on the subject of publishing—all of which are listed in the Bibliography of the above-mentioned book.

Specifically, for this volume, I have gone over the correspondence of F. N. Doubleday with Kipling and Conrad, now deposited in the Princeton Library; the B. W. Huebsch correspondence with Joyce, Lawrence, and Anderson, now in the Library of Congress, where I also found a number of letters by Margaret Mitchell; the correspondence of Scribner executives and editors with Santayana, Edith Wharton, Galsworthy, Fitzgerald, and Wolfe, now also in the Princeton Library. These letters, as well as the published letters of other authors, form the basic material used in the treatment of the relationship between writers and their publishers or editors. I have used the titles listed below as additional sources.

Anthony, Katherine. *Louisa May Alcott.* New York, 1938.

Atkins, Elizabeth. *Edna St. Vincent Millay and Her Times.* Chicago, 1936.

Atlanta Historical Bulletin, The, The Margaret Mitchell Memorial Issue, , 1950.

Auchincloss, Louis. *Edith Wharton: A Woman in Her Time.* New York, 1971.

Austin, James C. *Fields of The Atlantic Monthly: Letters to an Editor, 1861–1870.* San Marino, Calif. 1953.

Ballou, Ellen B. *The Building of the House: Houghton-Mifflin's First Half Century.* Boston, 1970.

Bell, Millicent. *Edith Wharton and Henry James: The Story of Their Friendship.* New York, 1965.

Bradsher, Earl L. *Mathew Carey: Editor, Author, and Publisher.* New York, 1912.

Bruccoli, M. J., ed. *As Ever, Scott Fitz.* Philadelphia, 1972.

Burlingame, Roger. *Of the Making of Many Books.* New York, 1946.

Campbell, Louise, ed. *Letters to Louise: Theodore Dreiser's Letters to Louise Campbell.* Philadelphia, 1959.

Canfield, Cass. *Up and Down and Around.* New York, 1971.

Charvat, William. *Literary Publishing in America, 1790–1850.* Philadelphia, 1959.

Charvat, William. "Longfellow's Income from His Writings, 1840–1852." *Papers of the Bibliographical Society of America,* vol. 38, 1944.

Cheney, Ednah D., ed. *Louisa May Alcott: Her Life, Letters, and Journals.* Boston, 1928.

Cory, Daniel. *The Letters of George Santayana.* New York, 1955.

Cory, Daniel. *Santayana, The Later Years.* New York, 1963.

Cowley, Malcolm. *A Second Flowering.* New York, 1973.

Derby, J. C. *Fifty Years Among Authors.* New York, 1884.

DeVoto, Bernard. *Mark Twain at Work.* Cambridge, Mass., 1942.

Doubleday, F. N *Memoirs of a Publisher.* Garden City, N.Y., 1972.

Dreiser, Helen. *My Life with Dreiser.* Cleveland, 1951.

Dudley, Dorothy. *Forgotten Frontiers: Dreiser and the Land of the Free.* New York, 1932.

Elias, R. H., ed. *Letters of Theodore Dreiser,* 3 vols. Philadelphia, 1959.

Ellmann, Richard. *James Joyce.* New York, 1959.

Ellmann, Richard, ed. *Letters of James Joyce,* 3 vols. New York, 1966.

Exman, Eugene. *The House of Harper.* New York, 1967.

Fay, Stephen, Chester, Lewis, and Linklater, Magnus. *Hoax: The Inside Story of the Howard Hughes-Clifford Irving Affair.* New York, 1972.

Ferguson, DeLancy. *Mark Twain, Man and Legend.* Indianapolis, 1943.

Fields, James T. *Biographical Notes and Personal Sketches.* Boston, 1882.

Fields, James T. *Yesterdays with Authors.* Boston, 1886.

Garnett, Edward. *Letters from John Galsworthy.* New York, 1934.

Garnett, Edward. *Letters from Joseph Conrad, 1895–1924.* Indianapolis, 1928.

Gerber, P. L. *Theodore Dreiser.* New York, 1964.

Gilbert, Stuart, ed. *Letters of James Joyce.* New York, 1957.

Gould, Jean. *The Poet and Her Book: The Life and Work of Edna St. Vincent Millay.* New York, 1969.

Harcourt, Alfred. *Some Experiences.* Riverside, Conn., 1951.

Hart, James D. *The Popular Book: A History of America's Literary Taste.* New York, 1950.

Hepburn, James. *The Author's Empty Purse and the Rise of the Literary Agent.* New York, 1968.

Hill, Hamlin. *Mark Twain and Elisha Bliss.* Columbia, Mo., 1964.

Irving, Clifford. *What Really Happened.* New York, 1972.

James, H. M., ed. *Letters of Sherwood Anderson.* Boston, 1953.

Jean-Aubry, Gerard. *The Sea-Dreamer: A Definitive Biography of Joseph Conrad.* Garden City, N.Y. 1957.

Joseph Conrad, A Sketch. Garden City, N.Y. 1924.

Jovanovich, William. *Now, Barabbas.* New York, 1964.

Kaplan, J. *Mister Clemens and Mark Twain.* New York, 1966.

Kaser, David. *Messrs. Carey and Lea of Philadelphia.* Philadelphia, 1951.

Kilgour, R. L. *Estes and Lauriat, A History, 1872–1898.* Ann Arbor, Mich., 1957.

Kilgour, R. L. *Messrs. Roberts Brothers.* Ann Arbor, Mich., 1952.

Kipling, Rudyard. *Letters of Travel, 1892–1913.* Garden City, N.Y., 1920.

Kipling, Rudyard. *Something of Myself.* London, 1937.

Knopf, A. A. "A Footnote to Publishing History," *Atlantic Monthly,* Feb. 1958.

Knopf, A. A. *Joseph Conrad: The Romance of His life and His Books.* Garden City, N.Y. 1914.

Latham, Harold. *My Life in Publishing.* New York, 1965.

Lehmann-Haupt, H. *The Book in America: A History of Making and Selling Books in The United States.* New York, 1939.

Longfellow, Samuel. *The Life of Henry Wadsworth Longfellow.* Boston, 1886.

Lyons, Peter. *Success Story, The Life and Times of S. S. McClure.* New York, 1963.

Macdougall, A. R., ed. *Letters of Edna St. Vincent Millay.* New York, 1952.

Milford, Nancy. *Zelda.* New York, 1970.

Mizener, Arthur. *The Far Side of Paradise.* Boston, 1951.

Moore, Harry, ed. *The Collected Letters of D. H. Lawrence.* New York, 1962.

Nowell, Elizabeth, ed. *The Letters of Thomas Wolfe.* New York, 1956.

Nowell, Elizabeth. *Thomas Wolfe.* Garden City, N.Y. 1960.

Oberholzer, E. P. *The Literary History of Philadelphia.* Philadelphia, 1906.

Oswald, J. C. *Printing in the Americas.* New York, 1968.

Paine, A. B. *Mark Twain: A Biography,* 3 vols. New York, 1912.

Paine, A. B. *Mark Twain: Letters.* New York, 1917.

Perkins, Maxwell E. "Thomas Wolfe," *Harvard Library Bulletin.* Autumn, 1947.

Petrullo, Helen D. "Dorothy Thompson's Role in Sinclair Lewis's Break with Harcourt, Brace," *The Courier* (Syracuse Library), vol. 8, no. 3, 1971.

Putnam, G. H., and J. B. Putnam. *Authors and Publishers.* New York, 1897.

Reynolds, Paul R. *The Middle Man: The Adventures of a Literary Agent.* New York, 1972.

Rutherford, A., ed. *Kipling's Mind and Art: Selected Critical Essays.* Stanford, Calif., 1964.

Santayana, George. *Persons and Places.* New York, 1963.

Schorer, Mark. *Sinclair Lewis: An American Life.* New York, 1961.

Sheean, Vincent, ed. *Dorothy and Red: A Literary Biography.* Boston, 1963.

Sheean, Vincent. *The Indigo Bunting: A Memoir of Edna St. Vincent Millay.* New York, 1951.

Sherwood Anderson's Memoirs. New York, 1942.

Skeel, Emily E., ed. *Mason Locke Weems.* His Works acd Ways, New York, 1929.

Smith, Harrison, ed. *From Main Street to Stockholm, 1919–1930.* New York, 1952.

Steinbeck, John. *Journal of a Novel: The East of Eden Letters.* New York, 1969.

Stewart, J. I. *Rudyard Kipling.* New York, 1966.

Swanberg, W. A. *Dreiser.* New York, 1965.

Terry, John S., ed. *Thomas Wolfe's Letters to His Mother.* New York, 1943.

Thompson, Lawrance. *Robert Frost, The Early Years.* New York, 1966.

Thompson, Lawrance. *Robert Frost, Years of Triumph.* New York, 1970.

Thompson, L., ed. *Selected Letters of Robert Frost.* New York, 1964.

Ticknor, Caroline. *Hawthorne and His Publisher.* Boston, 1913.

Tryon, W. S. *Parnassus Corner: A Life of James T. Fields, Publisher to the Victorians.* Boston, 1963.

Tryon, W. S., and William Charvat. *The Cost Books of Ticknor and Fields.* New York, 1949.

Turnbull, Andrew, ed. *The Letters of F. Scott Fitzgerald.* New York, 1963.

Untermyer, Louis. *The Letters of Robert Frost to Louis Untermyer.* New York, 1963.

Wagenknecht, Edward. *Longfellow.* New York, 1955.
Wecter, Dixon. *Sam Clemens of Hannibal.* Boston, 1952.
Wharton, Edith. *A Backward Glance.* New York, 1933/34.
Wheelock, John Hall, ed. *The Letters of Maxwell E. Perkins.* New York, 1950.

Index